MOTHERS of a NEW WORLD

MOTHERS of a NEW WORLD

MATERNALIST POLITICS AND THE ORIGINS OF WELFARE STATES

EDITED BY SETH KOVEN & SONYA MICHEL

ROUTLEDGE   NEW YORK   LONDON

Published in 1993 by

An imprint of Routledge, Inc.
29 West 35 Street
New York, NY 10001

Published in Great Britain in 1993 by

Routledge
11 New Fetter Lane
London EC4P 4EE

Library of Congress Cataloging-in-Publication Data

Mothers of a new world : maternalist politics and the origins of
  welfare states / edited by Seth Koven and Sonya Michel.
    p. cm.
  Includes bibliographical references and index.
  ISBN 0-415-90313-0 (cloth)—ISBN 0-415-90314-9 (pbk.)
    1. Maternal and infant welfare—Government policy—History.
  2. Motherhood—Government policy—History. 3. Women social
reformers—History. 4. Welfare state—History. 5. Feminism—History.
I. Koven, Seth, 1958– . II. Michel, Sonya, 1942–
HV697.M68 1993
362.83—dc20   92-42493
                                                 CIP

British Library Cataloguing-in-Publication Data also available.

In memory of our mothers,
Harriett Schulberg Koven
and
Frances Smirnoff Michel

Contents

Acknowledgments

This book began in a series of conversations among members of the Study Group on Women in Modern Europe at the Center for European Studies at Harvard University. We were each struggling to uncover and understand the interconnections between the history of women's movements and welfare states, and between recent developments in state theory and feminist scholarship. These conversations in turn led to a series of conferences held at the Center for European Studies in 1986 and 1987. We owe a debt of gratitude to the center for hosting these conferences, in particular to Abby Collins, and to our co-organizers, Frances Gouda, Jane Jenson, and Jennifer Schirmer, whose intellectual and organizational labors helped to make this book possible. The participants at these lively conferences played important roles in shaping our ideas and the volume as a whole. In particular, we would like to thank those scholars who delivered papers or round-table presentations at these conferences but whose work for various reasons could not be included in this volume: Martha Ackelsberg, Polly Beals, Miriam Cohen, Nancy Fraser, Linda Gordon, Michael Hanagan, Claudia Koonz, Daniel Levine, Barbara Nelson, Karen Offen, and Theda Skocpol.

The Center for European Studies, the Committee on States and Social Structures of the Social Science Research Council, and the Goethe Institute of Boston provided generous funding. Much of the editorial work for this volume was conducted while the editors had individually received Spencer Fellowships in the Humanities from the National Academy of Education, which released each of us from teaching obligations. The Department of History at Villanova University generously underwrote our use of Georgi Kilroy's extraordinary skills in computer technology and typing, which saved us on many occasions from the disasters of long-distance collaboration. The Research Board of the University of

Illinois at Urbana-Champaign provided Sonya Michel with research assistance. We are particularly grateful to Father Gallen and the Office of the Vice President of Academic Affairs of Villanova University for granting us a subvention to prepare the index.

Susan Suleiman, Victoria Vandenberg, and Colin Weil offered us expert direction as we searched out a work of art for the cover. The good humor and wisdom of William Koven, Claire Mollard, and Colin and Joshua Weil supported us throughout this project. Most of all, we are grateful to Jeffrey Herf and Nadja Michel-Herf, and Joan, Daniel, and Zoe Koven, who lovingly yielded their natural rights over use of the telephones for many years so that we could kibbitz about gender and welfare states.

We Will be the New Mothers of a New World. . . . The history of the past need not bind us—it is not *our* history! . . . A new historic period is opening before us. A world in which the more normal human type, the woman, shall find full expression. . . . Her natural atmosphere of peaceful industry, of tender, watchful care, of far-seeing affection, now jealously secluded by each man in the home, for his own satisfaction, is to be unloosed, expanded, spread far and wide throughout the world.

Charlotte Perkins Gilman, "The New Mothers of a New World"

Introduction: "Mother Worlds"

Seth Koven and Sonya Michel

Woman is the home maker and her "sphere" extends to the
uttermost ends of the earth. To limit it is to limit all growth,
and to hold not her alone, but her children also in bondage.
The people are her children, and they cry aloud now for her
care.

—I. D. Pearce, "An Awakening Womanhood"[1]

"Mother Worlds" and the Politics of Motherliness

Mary Beard, in the preface to her 1915 study *Woman's Work
in Municipalities,* ironically appropriated and rewrote the founda-
tional myth that men's misfortunes originated in women's trans-
gressions. The time had come, she insisted, not to abandon but
to reinterpret "that age-worn slogan, 'Cherchez la femme,' so long
the final suggestion to those who would do detective work into
the causes of waywardness in men." The modern woman was
"quite near to being the source of all good" in society. A genteel
warrior, she engaged in deadly combat not with "man" but with
the "common enemies of man and woman."[2]

The figure of Eve hovers on the margins of Beard's brief preface—never acknowledged, but unmistakably present in her text.
To so many women of Beard's generation[3] the task of reinventing
Eve, the mother of all humankind, was linked to the project of
authorizing and constructing their identities as women committed to making society in their likeness. Read in this way, Beard's
book suggests that the modern city, beset by the sins of capitalism,
was also the site on which a newly imagined Eve would perform
her redemptive acts as woman, mother, and citizen. Beard concluded that the legacy of women's "social movements" (notice, not

1

"suffrage" or "feminism") demanded a thoroughgoing reevaluation of "women's work in civilization."

This volume is a response, many years later, to Beard's challenge to historians to seek out and trace women's activities. We concur that women's varied social movements fundamentally changed their relationships not only to "civilization" but to each other, to men, to the state, and to society. Like Beard's study, the essays collected here pick up "hitherto disconnected threads"—the overlapping and interlocking histories of the emergence of women's social movements and welfare states—and show that these two developments not only coincided in time, place, and sometimes personnel, but also reinforced and transformed one another in significant and enduring ways.

Women focused on shaping one particular area of state policy: maternal and child welfare. It was in this area, closely linked to the traditional female sphere, that women first claimed new roles for themselves. Using political discourses and strategies that we have called "maternalist," they transformed motherhood from women's primary *private* responsibility into *public* policy. During periods when state welfare structures and bureaucracies were still rudimentary and fluid, female reformers, individually and through organizations, exerted a powerful influence in defining the needs of mothers and children and designing institutions and programs to address them.

Male bureaucrats, politicians, and propagandists often encouraged women in their welfare work. Since the turn of the century, the din of male voices—Catholic, Protestant, and Jewish; liberal, socialist, and conservative—demanding that women take up their sacred duties has ironically obscured women's own initiatives in this area. Modern feminists' subsequent rejection of motherhood and maternalism as incompatible with female emancipation has led some historians to downplay women's influence on the formation of welfare states. This volume offers a reevaluation of the early history of maternalist politics and welfare states.

Maternalist women not only concerned themselves with the welfare and rights of women and children, but also generated searching critiques of state and society. Emilia Kanthack, a midwife and lecturer in infant welfare in St. Pancras, London, observed that "the chain reaches farther and farther back—from baby to mother, from mother to father, from father to existing social conditions swaying the labor market, which in turn result from economic conditions of supply and demand."[4] Some reformers believed that their values should be applied universally to transform the very foundations of the social order. In 1904, the German utopian feminist, Ruth Bré, exalted motherhood as the fundamental life-sustaining social labor and called for root-and-branch restructuring of society on the basis of matriarchal family units.[5]

The American Charlotte Perkins Gilman, writing on the eve of World War I, offered a compelling vision of motherhood that still resonates with limitless possibilities—as well as with a poignant sense of opportunities that, as historians, we know all too well have never been realized. Gilman, whose call for a radical reconstruction of family life led many of her contemporaries to mistake her for an enemy of motherliness, proclaimed the advent of "motherhood as social service instead of man-service." Men, she insisted, "have wasted women's lives like water, and the children of the world have been sacrificed to [their] sins. Now we will have a new world, new-born, new-built, a mother-world as well as a father-world in which we shall not be ashamed or afraid to plant our children."[6]

For a brief moment, women like Gilman the world over dared to imagine what it would be like to enter into their newly born "mother world." While World War I brought with it many short-term gains in maternal and child welfare, the scale and intensity of its human carnage mocked Gilman's dream of military and economic "world peace." However, the fact that most of the women and movements we explore ultimately lacked the political power to refashion the state according to their own vision does not diminish the importance of that vision, their accomplishments, or their legacy. Nor, we hasten to add, should serious engagement with maternalist visions of social welfare be taken for uncritical admiration of them.

Many late-nineteenth- and early-twentieth-century women envisioned a state which not only had the qualities of mothering we associate with welfare, but in which women played active roles as electors, policy makers, bureaucrats, and workers, within and outside the home. Suffrage per se was not a decisive turning point in the history of maternalist politics. Before 1919, women in most Western nations (with the exception of Australia and New Zealand) lacked full citizenship rights, and necessarily operated in the interstices of political structures. Undaunted, women exploited their authority as mothers to expand women's rights in society before and after some gained political enfranchisement.

The cases examined in this volume fall into two separate groups. The bulk of the essays focus on France, Germany, Great Britain, and the United States, where women's political initiatives between 1880 and 1920 influenced social policy during a time of rapid expansion in the state's social-welfare apparatus for women and children. We have also included essays on Australia and Sweden, where broad-scale state development occurred somewhat later, but where the specific interventions made by women offer useful insights into the strengths and limitations of maternalist politics in the other four countries during the preceding decades.

Several distinct patterns characterized the politics of maternal and child welfare in the nations included in the first group. First, the growth of welfare bureaucracies between 1880 and 1920 led to the expansion of caretaking professions dominated by women such as social work, health visiting, and district nursing. As both professionals and volunteers, women entered into new relationships with the state which, in turn, sharpened their political awareness and expanded the rank and file of a wide range of women's movements and movements of women.[7] Professionalism in turn gave rise to new opportunities for women, but at the same time often fomented conflict between a younger generation of women seeking to establish their legitimacy and those working in older networks of voluntary benevolence.

Second, maternalist discourses—often competing—lay at the heart of debates about the social role of women, children, and the family among philanthropists and social workers, legislators and bureaucrats, employers and workers, men and women. The invocation of maternalism by so many different social actors compels us to reevaluate its ambiguous meanings and uses. We apply the term to ideologies and discourses that exalted women's capacity to mother and applied to society as a whole the values they attached to that role: care, nurturance, and morality.[8] Maternalism was the central and defining core of some women's vision of themselves and of politics. However, it was only one piece, albeit a significant one, in the mosaic of social, economic, and political arguments that made up the world views of most of the women examined in this volume and determined their actions. As Seth Koven argues in chapter 2, "[m]aternalist discourses did not exist in an ideological or political vacuum," nor, by itself, did maternalism determine the emergence of the welfare state in Britain or elsewhere. Rather, according to Koven, "[m]aternalism necessarily operated in relation to other discourses—about citizenship, class relations, gender difference, and national identity, to name only a few—and in relation to a wide array of concrete social and political practices." Any number of movements might be labeled "maternalist," but the term "maternalism" does not refer to a specific movement per se. Nor do we use the noun "maternalist" as we might "feminist," to establish the identity of a particular social actor.

The protean character of maternalism, the ease with which it could be harnessed to forge improbable coalitions, is a recurring theme in this volume. So, too, is the subtle shift from a vision of motherhood in the service of women to one serving the needs of paternalists. The same men who applauded women's work on behalf of children were often openly antagonistic to women's aspirations to use their welfare activities to promote their own political and economic rights. They put the interests of children— the nation's future workers and soldiers—before the rights of mothers. Even groups of men ostensibly committed to raising women's status, like the fledgling Labour party in Great Britain and the *Parti ouvrier français* in France,[9] expected women to subordinate their sex-specific demands to the dictates of male-controlled political and economic agendas. The female founders of the Women's Labour League in Great Britain, the subject of Pat Thane's contribution, (chapter 10) initially received little encouragement from their male counterparts, many of whom were anxious to protect their workplace interests not only from the encroachments of capitalists, but from women workers as well. Marilyn Lake and Barbara Hobson demonstrate that similar relations prevailed between women and left-wing parties in Australia and Sweden respectively (chapters 11 and 12).

Susan Pedersen's analysis of the *Union féminine civique et sociale* (UFCS) in France (chapter 7) is perhaps the most striking account of how maternalism, in this case linked to a vision of Catholic womanhood, was deployed by male political actors to undermine even the fairly conservative goals of UFCS women. By the time they recognized the shape their Catholic maternalism had assumed, they were no longer in a position to control its use in policy making. Pedersen's essay intimates that the difficulty in upholding distinctions between a woman-centered maternalism and overt paternalism compelled French feminists to abandon maternalism before their counterparts in the UFCS began to reckon with the consequences of their maternalist strategies.

Maternalism always operated on two levels: it extolled the virtues of domesticity while simultaneously legitimating women's public relationships to politics and the state, to community, workplace, and marketplace. Maternalist ideologies, while evoking traditional images of womanliness, implicitly challenged the boundaries between public and private, women and men, state and civil society.[10] The nature and force of this challenge varied considerably, depending upon the constellation of issues within which it was set. As Sonya Michel's study of child care and mothers' pensions illustrates (chapter 8), maternalism proved a self-limiting and self-defeating discourse for leaders of the American day-nursery movement. Their anxieties over upholding traditional, white, bourgeois concepts of women's familial roles made them ineffective advocates for public funding for child care for wage-earning mothers. By the same token, however, maternalism, fueled the successful campaign for mothers' pensions, which were intended to allow poor women to give up paid employment and remain at home with their children.

Finally, in these industrializing countries middle-class women were usually the first to identify the social-welfare needs of poor and working-class mothers and children[11] and the first to respond to them through a wide array of charitable activities.[12] Seth Koven presents a series of case studies of the founding of juvenile reformatories, schools for invalid children, and school health clinics in Britain (chapter 2). They show how the state relied upon the initiatives of private-sector, largely female organizations and in many instances subsequently took over the funding and management of their welfare programs.[13] Such activities thus constituted an important (but subsequently overlooked) site of public-policy and, ultimately, state formation. Kathryn Sklar's observation (chapter 1) about the American case holds true elsewhere as well, that these maternal- and child-welfare activities often "became an entering wedge for the extension of state responsibility" to other groups, including wage-earning men.

The Swedish and Australian cases diverge in significant ways from the patterns just described. In both countries, which were still largely rural by the end of the nineteenth century, the middle classes were small and weak relative to those of the societies in the first group. Moreover, religious aspects of both national cultures were far less pronounced, particularly in Sweden. Early feminist research on Sweden and Australia suggested that women's movements had little to do with welfare-state development, which appeared to proceed at the behest of national governments (in Australia, there was also considerable activity at the state level).[14] The essays in this volume by Lake and Hobson reveal, however, that here, as elsewhere, maternalist politicians actively sought to shape social policy. Though they mobilized later than women in the other countries, they put forward some of the most radical demands for the welfare of mothers and children made anywhere. In the 1920s, Australian Labor-party women formulated a vision of "maternal citizenship" whereby mothers would earn an independent income from the state for their "nurturant labor" and recognition as citizens in their own right, not by virtue of marriage. A decade later, women in the Swedish Social Democratic party, led by Alva Myrdal, forged crucial links between motherhood and female employment by calling for both married women's right to work and employment protections for mothers. In both cases, maternalist reformers were working within left-wing parties, but this in itself did not guarantee success. The Social Democrats, seeking to consolidate their power in a bid for control of the government, were receptive to the women's initiatives, while the Australian Labor party regarded women's proposals for childhood and motherhood endowment as a direct threat to their campaign for a "family wage."

Male-dominated political establishments were not the only obstacles women reformers faced. Their efforts sometimes set them at odds with the mothers and children they tried to help. Many of the essays collected here focus on the political initiatives of white middle-class women who were free from domestic drudgery and had the educational and financial resources to campaign for social-welfare programs and policies.[15] In the name of friendship and in the interests of the health of the family and the nation, they claimed the right to instruct and regulate the conduct of working-class women. The shared concerns of family brought women of all classes together, but, at the same time, disagreements over control of the workplace and household divided women along the lines of class, race, ethnicity, and religion.[16] Bourgeois reformers often seemed oblivious to the ways in which the economic and social realities of client women's daily lives, as well as their own cultural preferences, undermined the possibility of realizing gender solidarity. For example, at the Berlin meeting of the International Council of Women in 1904, a middle-class British observer wishfully insisted that "the feeling that prevailed was not that of class exclusiveness but that of the solidarity of womanhood"—despite her acknowledgment that few if any working-class women were in attendance.[17]

It is sometimes difficult to disaggregate the many sources of tension among women. In a (relatively) ethnically homogeneous society like Germany, class stood out. Jean Quataert and Christoph Sachße offer differing but complementary accounts of the way that class positioned women with regard to social policy in late-nineteenth-century Germany. Quataert (chapter 4) uncovers a legacy of women's agency at all levels in the development and implementation of social-welfare policy—as female inspectors, middle-class reformers, and working-class clients. The poor female weavers of Oberlausitz she examines initially manipulated gender-biased attitudes about definitions of what constituted "work" and evaded inclusion in mandatory workers' insurance schemes because they could ill afford the financial contributions. At the same time, however, the middle-class female reformers portrayed by Sachße (chapter 3) often fought to expand the scope of protective legislation for laboring women in Germany. But cross-class encounters did not always set women against one another. In the American case, Molly Ladd-Taylor stresses their collaborative and nurturing potential (chapter 9). She found that, despite differences in values, the visiting nurses sent by the U.S. Children's Bureau to assist women on maternal- and child-health matters were welcome advisors and friends to their clients, especially those living in rural isolation.[18]

Race as well as class shaped women's visions of social reform. Eileen Boris's essay (chapter 6) contrasts the strategies and rhetoric of black and white activist women in the United States around the turn of the century. Though both groups invoked the image of the mother, this image carried multiple meanings. For white women, the association with motherhood emphasized the difference between women and men, while for African-American women, motherhood served as a touchstone of racial equality—an equality that contained and respected the different needs and responsibilities of this group of women as mothers. Boris notes further that when (white) policy makers and reformers spoke of mothers, it was usually white women they had in mind; black women seldom benefited from protective legislation and other measures intended to safeguard motherhood.[19]

European historians have tended to minimize the subtext of race as a factor in social politics, despite a vast literature pointing to discursive links between imperialism and reform. As Alisa Klaus demonstrates in her comparison of French and American pronatalism in the late nineteenth and early twentieth centuries (chapter 5), in both countries eugenicist considerations underlay debates over birth policies, though racial themes were more explicit in the American rhetoric. However, even within European states, anxieties about racial and ethnic diversity (particularly visible in large urban centers like Paris, London, and Manchester) converged with class issues, including the social-welfare rights of laboring people. Racial and ethnic heterogeneity *and* class tensions complicated attempts by reformers to use welfare programs to construct national identity and social solidarity. London's sprawling East End, for example, was the *locus classicus* of British social-reform endeavors. But it was also literally the port of arrival and home for tens of thousands of Irish, Jewish, and "coloured" immigrants whose very existence challenged prevailing representations of Englishness.[20] Furthermore, many women devoted to social motherhood and reform at home, including Mary Carpenter and Eleanor Rathbone in Britain, also strongly advocated their own white middle-class conceptions of how to improve the lives of indigenous women in the colonies. European reformers' encounters with different ethnic and racial groups—colonial "others"—at home and on their travels were integral to their larger vision of society and social welfare and constitute an important area for future research.[21]

Reformers' ambivalence about race was complicated by racially motivated pronatalist policies which often created openings for women, both volunteer and professional, to develop services in the field of maternal and child health. Racial concerns also created a favorable climate for Australian feminists seeking to establish women's rights to "maternal citizenship" in post–World War I Australia. With its scant white population of only four million, leaders of the new nation were eager to increase their numbers relative to the Aborigines; accordingly, the new Labor government passed the Maternity Allowance bill as early as 1912.[22] But, as Marilyn Lake shows (chapter 11), racial anxieties were not strong enough to offset Labor men's objections to women's demands for "maternal citizenship."

The Origins of Maternalist Movements

The roots of maternalist movements lie in the early nineteenth century when women in many Western countries began to organize in the name of social reform, reclamation, and moral purity. Essential to this mobilization was the rise of domestic ideologies stressing women's differences from men, humanitarian concerns for the conditions of child life and labor, and the emergence of activist interpretations of the gospel (which varied from country to country and included evangelicalism, Christian socialism, social Catholicism, and the social gospel).[23] Women's moral vision, compassion, and capacity to nurture came increasingly to be linked to motherliness. Once embedded within a political framework, these private qualities became the cornerstone of the public discourses we identify as maternalism.

These discourses linked religious activism and domesticity to one another in a curiously unstable matrix of mutually reinforcing yet contradictory values. On the one hand, women were enjoined to cultivate their womanhood within the home; but on the other hand, they were urged to impress Christian values on their communities through charitable work. Inevitably, the practice of some women's lives as charitable workers conflicted with the dictates of domesticity.

Maternalist discourses were marked not only by national histories but also by their specific political and rhetorical contexts. In the United States, nineteenth-century women activists could draw on a rich legacy of domestic ideologies which historians have named "the cult of true womanhood" and "republican motherhood" in constructing maternalist visions of women and the state.[24] Working in organizations that were sex-segregated by choice, female reformers initially sought to avoid any association with politics, which, they feared, would compromise their putative moral purity and hence undermine the rationale for their womanly mission.[25] By mid-century, however, they became increasingly sophisticated, and many women shifted tactics from "moral suasion" to direct political action.[26] But they continued to claim for themselves a kind of moral superiority rooted in their differences from men. For example, Florence Kelley, a key Progressive reformer, insisted that women possessed special insights into issues of social justice and social welfare and at the same time contended that women's differences from men entitled them to special protection.[27]

Not all American maternalist reformers believed that it was the responsibility of the federal government to aid and protect women. The noted Boston Brahmin and antisuffragist Elizabeth Lowell Putnam called upon her home state to pass pure-milk laws, but opposed any form of federal programs on behalf of women and children. She claimed that the U.S. Children's Bureau, established at the behest of women activists in 1912, "is merely a clever way, because appealing, of granting power to the federal government and taking it away from individual states, which is the great way in which the Soviet government works in getting control of its people, particularly the young—by putting the many in the control of the few."[28]

The British case also illustrates the ways in which women joined notions about their motherly social tasks to different political agendas. Many pro- and antisuffrage activists of both sexes justified their positions in terms of the peculiar moral insights that stemmed from women's domestic and maternal roles. F. W. Hatton Reed deployed separate-spheres rhetoric for suffragist ends. Reed insisted that the stance that "woman's sphere is the home, is one of the greatest arguments in favor of granting her full equality with man." Women's part in safeguarding the "welfare of the child" proved that "in the interests of posterity . . . woman should have no inferior place in our system of society."[29] Antisuffrage women, including Mary Ward and Violet Markham, infused their construction of domesticity with a strong dose of civic maternalism. They urged women to extend their housekeeping out into the municipal arena by seizing opportunities to serve in local government as elected and appointed officials and social-welfare organizers and workers. At the same time, however, they warned that the parliamentary franchise would pollute women by implicating them in the violent business of wars and empire. The first decades of the twentieth century in Britain were distinguished by particularly intense skirmishes between pro- and antisuffrage women activists over the political meaning of motherliness as each group claimed to represent the embodiment of the "womanly" and "motherly" woman.[30]

For some activist women, commitment to maternalist goals sometimes came into conflict with other political agendas and loyalties. In 1929, Margaret McMillan stunned her socialist and Labour friends by openly supporting the parliamentary bid of the Conservative-party candidate, Lady Astor, who had lent her voice and her pocketbook to innovative schemes in maternal and child welfare. McMillan's apostasy was all the more painful because she seemed to be turning her back on fellow Labour and socialist women who had been supporting maternalist policy initiatives for decades. As Thane shows, they had formulated a platform that included women's suffrage, freedom of choice regarding work inside or outside the home, higher wages for male heads of households, and extensive benefits for mothers. Moreover, in 1929, they were rejoicing in the triumphant appointment of one of their leaders, Margaret Bondfield, to the cabinet-level post of minister of labour.

The contest to control maternalist rhetoric was perhaps most intense in the French Third Republic, due to anxieties over depopulation and the perception of military weakness in the aftermath of crushing defeat in the Franco-Prussian War. Maternalism took many forms among French women depending upon whether it was linked to conservative Catholic ideologies, the philanthropic traditions of the active but small Protestant minority, republicanism, socialism, or one of the late-nineteenth-century variants of feminism.

Until the 1880s, two groups of Catholic women had traditionally dominated the care of mothers and children within their communities: Catholic nuns and well-to-do Catholic laywomen.[31] Bonnie Smith's study of the *bourgeoises* of the Nord illustrates that these women saw charity as an organic and natural extension of their domestic roles as mothers and as Catholics.[32] Subscribing to an explicitly antimodern, anticapitalist world view, these *dames patronnesses* established crèches, kindergartens, and maternal-aid societies. Such women lived very public lives but refused to see themselves as engaging in politics.

In the 1880s, the leaders of the Third Republic, as part of their ongoing struggle against the Church, actively sought to undermine the hold of Catholic women on social welfare. Abandoning the moralistic prejudices against unmarried mothers that had characterized the work of Catholic maternalists, advocates of this new, modern ideology recognized all mothers and children as vital resources for the Republic.[33] Their efforts not only increased intervention by male professionals pursuing scientific and bureaucratic initiatives, but also created an opening for women committed to advancing motherhood within a context of Republican ideology and female emancipation.[34] This did not, however, lead to professional opportunities for women. As Klaus contends, male Republicans continued to stress the importance of women solely as "the natural agents of . . . charity."

Catholic women, though marginalized during this period, nonetheless continued to promote maternal and child welfare, reemerging as a vocal and potent political group in the early twentieth century with *La Ligue patriotique des femmes françaises* (the Patriotic League of French Women). Unlike their Catholic predecessors, League women felt compelled to enter politics even as they sought to uphold women's traditional subordination to men.[35] At approximately the same time, a cadre of elite, moderately feminist Protestant French women laid the foundations for the interdenominational *Conseil national des femmes françaises* (National Council of French Women) by targeting associations "that concerned themselves with the lot of women or of children."[36] Thus French women who openly opposed one another on fundamental issues such as suffrage or married women's waged labor often found themselves in apparent agreement over the need to expand and improve maternal and child welfare. As Pedersen argues, it was only under the extreme conditions of the 1930s that the common ground of maternalism shared by secular French feminists and social Catholic women finally eroded.

Maternalism was perhaps the most significant thread tying together the disparate women's movements in Germany from the 1880s until the 1920s. Ann Taylor Allen argues that the "overwhelming majority of feminist leaders in the 19th century" embraced the concept of "spiritual motherhood." Allen aptly insists that "far from the reactionary affirmation of traditional subservience which some feminist historians have denounced, the nineteenth-century glorification of motherhood was initially a progressive trend. . . ."[37] Shortly after the 1848 revolution, Henriette Breymann, a leader of the kindergarten movement, wrote:

> I foresee an entirely new age dawning for women [*sic*] when she will be the center of the home and when she . . . will bring to the broader community a quality which until now has been

entirely lacking—the spirit of motherhood in its deepest meaning and in its most varied forms.[38]

Breymann linked her vision of women to liberal reforms in the
education of women and children.[39]

Breymann could not have predicted the varied meanings and
forms motherhood would take in Germany over the next seventy
years. By the end of the century, maternalist women had linked
motherhood to sex reform, socialist reconstruction of the state
and society, suffrage, and a wide range of state welfare policies
and programs. Alice Salomon, who, along with Jeannette Schwerin, pioneered the development of professional social work in
Germany, literally built on the foundations laid by Breymann
when she established the *Soziale Frauenschule* (Social Work
School for Women) in Breymann's Pestalozzi-Froebel Haus in
Berlin. Salomon demanded the vote and aggressively pushed for
state intervention: "We asked not for privilege for preferential
laws, but for an adjustment to women's greater vulnerability arising from specific organic functions imposed upon them by
nature."[40] Salomon's maternalist social-welfare agenda, as Sachße
shows, was inextricably bound up with her consensual vision of
social relations. The daughter of a wealthy assimilated Jewish
family, she envisioned a motherly state that aimed not at transforming class relations, but at transcending the conflicts between
classes through the bonds of motherhood (chapter 3).

German Socialist women, while divided among themselves,
denounced Salomon and the bourgeois feminist movement as
collaborators with an exploitative system.[41] Women's emancipation could never be achieved, nor the rights of mothers and children secured, without transforming the class underpinnings of
the relationship between working-class clients and middle-class
women social reformers. Lily Braun, a renegade from the aristocracy and a leader of the ethical-socialist *Bund für Mutterschutz*
(League for the Protection of Motherhood), enunciated a passion-
ate brand of maternalism that challenged the male-centered foundations of her society. Braun insisted that women—as women,
not only as socialists and workers—had essential contributions
to make to society. She argued that just as women received "the
seed" from men in creating life, so, too, male-dominated societies
needed to receive the seed of women's distinctive gifts to civilization.[42] Although August Bebel's *Women under Socialism* was the

bible of socialist women and the Social Democratic party (SPD) was the most powerful political advocate for women's emancipation in pre–World War I Germany, Braun believed that even the German socialist movement was implicitly part of the "hitherto purely masculine culture" she sought to feminize.[43]

Braun and the other socialist women who founded the *Bund für Mutterschutz* called for a new sexual ethics and birth control for women to give them direct control over their reproductive labors. The *Bund* demanded a wide range of redistributive state programs, including maternity insurance,[44] extended terms of indemnified and mandatory leave from work before and after parturition, child care, and legal advice for mothers. It even succeeded in its demand to extend state maternity rights to unmarried mothers.[45]

Many of these demands were first put forward by Ellen Key, a Swedish writer and educator whose vision linked motherhood with sexual fulfillment and individual freedom and gave maternalism a distinctly modern tone. While Key herself was world-renowned, the nineteenth-century women's movement in her native Sweden was among the weakest of any Western society. The reasons for this were both economic and cultural. Industrialization and urbanization came relatively late to Sweden, and this delayed until the late nineteenth century the development of a strong middle class with its concomitant transformation of female roles and emphasis on domesticity. Moreover, the high moral rhetoric that often accompanied maternalist declarations did not sit well with Sweden's indigenous culture. Sweden was marked by a "relatively shallow Christianization."[46] Thus, as Donald Meyer has noted, "whereas in the United States popular, lay-generated religious life offered old identities in a time of change to women in particular, in Sweden this recourse proved of far less avail."[47]

By the mid-nineteenth century, a few Swedish women began to articulate a doctrine of female moral superiority and social renewal that placed the family at its center, but they failed to mobilize their sex in great numbers or to define a distinct female sphere. Women constituted the majority of the Swedish Temperance Society, but this organization lacked the political and moral clout of the American WCTU. The Frederika Bremer Society took up a wide range of women's issues, including suffrage, social purity, and women's economic and civil rights. However, its strict moralism deterred younger women from joining; and some criticized the class implications of its training and employment programs for women.

Ellen Key eschewed the straitlaced sexual principles of her female Swedish predecessors. Recasting sexual morality, she claimed that "[c]hastity consists in the harmony between the soul and the senses, and [that] no sexual relationship is moral without such relationship."[48] Since marriage was no guarantee of chastity, women should not submit to the "sexual slavery" that a legal union entailed. At the same time, however, women should have the right to choose motherhood freely, no matter what their marital status. This meant that they should have access to birth control, but if they chose motherhood, neither they nor their children should suffer from the stigma of illegitimacy. For Key, motherhood was important to women not as the rationale for social entitlement but as their chief avenue toward individual fulfillment.

In Sweden, Key generated a good deal of notoriety and debate through her books and through the "dozens"—small groups of women who formed to discuss Key's ideas as well as their own experiences and political views.[49] In a period when social democracy was emerging as a political force in Sweden, the "dozens" for the first time brought middle-class and working-class women together as social equals. But the idiosyncrasies of Key's own philosophy prevented her followers from moving from discussion to social action. Furthermore, her views generated animosity and controversy among Anglo-American feminists, some of whom Key openly criticized. For example, she rejected Charlotte Perkins Gilman's ideas for communal child care, and insisted that "if the destruction of . . . homes were the price the race must pay for women's attainment of full human dignity and citizenship, then the price would be too high."[50] Such words delighted ardent pronatalists and eugenicists like Dr. Caleb Saleeby in Britain who quoted Key in their tirades against the "manly" feminists undermining the British race and empire.[51]

Even abroad, Key's effectiveness was somewhat circumscribed. According to one contemporary American observer, Key "has always occupied an isolated position, and her lack of associative discipline is reflected in the impractical quality of many of her ideas. Her genius and her incompetence together have made her the 'wise fool' of the woman movement."[52] It was not through her own efforts, but through the efficient and determined organization of the *Bund für Mutterschutz* that her ideas were eventually translated into legislative demands and influenced campaigns for social-policy reformers in many countries in the 1910s and 1920s.

One of those countries was Australia, where women's political culture resembled that of European and American women in certain respects but appeared unique in others.[53] Influenced in part by the American Women's Christian Temperance Union, which was imported into Australia around 1885, the "woman movement" called for "Home Protection" and drew on familiar maternalist values such as female spirituality and the restorative powers of domesticity. But movement members also fully shared Australian men's strong commitment to democratic principles and stressed education and opportunities for women.

Many of women's reform efforts brought them up against their society's well-entrenched masculine labor tradition—one that was so apparent that nineteenth-century propagandists unabashedly referred to Australia as the "working man's paradise." Even so, the woman movement managed to become a vital force in Australian politics. After nearly twenty years of arduous campaigning, women won early suffrage victories (first in South Australia in 1894 and then federally in 1902). WCTU members lent crucial support to gigantic petition drives, collecting 30,000 signatures in Victoria and 11,000 in South Australia. The woman movement also claimed credit for the appointment of women to public positions which would otherwise have fallen into men's hands, such as those of factory inspectors, hospital physicians, prison guards, and police and welfare officers. Among their other accomplishments, women counted legislation raising the age of consent, reforms in child-custody laws, the establishment of state systems of infant- and maternal-welfare clinics staffed by women, from about 1914 on, and the Maternity Allowance of 1912.

In all of these campaigns, maternalist rhetoric figured prominently, but it was difficult for the woman movement to retain its cohesiveness and autonomy once suffrage had been won. Rose Scott, leader of the New South Wales Womanhood Suffrage League, claimed that enfranchisement "heralds to a world oppressed with poverty, suffering, and sin, the advent of the mother-woman's world—the wide loving heart and sheltering arms."[54] She and other "nonparty feminists" advised women to remain aloof from party politics so they could continue to support women's issues. Most women, however, responded positively to invitations to join the existing parties.

Though early enfranchisement thus had the effect of weakening women's autonomous organizations, maternalist politics continued to drive women's politics. It was women in the Labor party who took up the *Mutterschutz* idea and began calling on the state to support mothers, no matter what their marital status. Extension of the Maternity Allowance to mothers of illegitimate children was condemned by the WCTU, but applauded as a class victory by Labor women.

Maternalism proved a fragile foundation on which to build coalitions, not only because women were divided among themselves on many key issues, but because they lacked the political power to maintain control over maternalist discourses and policies. Male politicians used maternalist rhetoric, but often merely as a cloak for paternalism. Their real interests seldom lay in establishing or expanding women's rights and opportunities or even strengthening the family as a goal in itself. From the mid-nineteenth century onward, legislators passed a variety of measures that singled out women for special protection by the state. Protective legislation limited or prohibited women's labor-force participation by dictating hours, wages, and working conditions.[55] Despite the humanitarian and maternalist language that accompanied the passage of such bills, "limiting legislation" effectively diminished women's earnings by barring them from employment without compensatory benefits. As feminist scholars have noted, the men who led the campaigns for limiting legislation such as the Mines Act of 1842 in Great Britain and the 1892 labor legislation in France "protected" women in order to reduce the threat of competition from female workers, shore up the family wage, and compel women to remain within their homes.[56] Female activists, by contrast, typically demanded "redistributive" welfare measures that compensated women for lost wages as well as providing direct medical and social services. Such measures left open the possibility of maternal employment. For working women, the differences between "limiting" and "redistributive" welfare measures were stark. Limiting legislation buttressed the gender-biased dual-labor market, while redistributive forms mitigated some of its worst consequences.[57]

By the early twentieth century, many male politicians had become aware of the inefficacy of limiting legislation and they too began to call for redistributive measures. But they tended to do so not for women themselves, but on behalf of infants, the race, and the nation. Republican Emile Rey, during debates in the French Senate over mandatory maternity leaves, echoed Frédéric Le Play's conservative prescriptions for women even as he argued for radically redistributive policies.[58] He insisted that the French state should offer noncontributory and universal allowances to all needy women, not just those who were waged workers, for performing the labor of producing and nurturing children. But Rey was not motivated by generous concern for women. Instead he wished to prevent those who were not already employed outside the home from abandoning the *"foyer"* for the workshop merely to gain benefits. Rey equated women's work outside the home with "immorality."[59]

Did it make sense for women to support men like Rey, who, despite their explicit paternalism, promised to redistribute substantial resources to mothers? In 1915, Katharine Anthony advised her sister feminists to heed the example of their German counterparts and take a pragmatic or opportunistic approach to maternalist politics. The great expansion of benefits to mothers in Germany, she confessed,

> relied in great measure upon good masculine reasons which the masculine mind will understand. The spectacle of official diplomacy working out official reasons for granting a feminist demand is an exhibition from which watchful feminists may learn a great deal, if indeed it doesn't make them too furious to think.[60]

What were the implications of the trade-off suggested by Anthony between gaining feminist demands in the area of child and maternal welfare while accommodating the "masculine mind"? Were the stakes for conceding control over maternalist discourses to men higher in terms of women's long-term political power than Anthony imagined? What were the tangible results of women's activism on their political identities; on maternal- and child-welfare policies and programs; and, more generally, on the state itself?

The Paradoxical Legacies of Maternalism

The essays in this volume make it possible for us to begin to answer some of these questions, first on a country-by-country basis, and then, within a cross-national, comparative framework. American women claimed the political space occupied by state agencies, churches, and state bureaucracies in France and Germany to transform their voluntary charity into a kind of shadow welfare state, an entity that Sara Evans has dubbed "the maternal commonwealth."[61] In contrast to the loose, decentralized "state of courts and parties" that characterized the American polity in the last quarter of the nineteenth century,[62] the private-sector maternal commonwealth became increasingly centralized during this period, as hundreds of local women's voluntary organizations formed national associations. By 1912, maternalist reformers had gained a foothold in the federal government, with the establishment of the U.S. Children's Bureau.[63]

The very existence of the Children's Bureau testifies to the unusual power and vigor of women's higher education and women's movements in the United States and, more generally, to their authority as social-policy experts.[64] But their bureaucratic power was ghettoized and did not translate readily into a federal program of redistributive maternal- and child-welfare benefits. In a 1919 letter transmitting the Bureau's comprehensive international study of maternity benefits, Bureau Chief Julia Lathrop noted poignantly that the report had been compiled "in the hope that the information might prove useful to the people of one of the few great countries which as yet have no system of State or national assistance in maternity—the United States."[65] In 1921 Congress did pass the Bureau-sponsored Sheppard-Towner maternal- and infant-health bill, but refused to renew it in 1929. Another Bureau-supported measure, the Child Labor Amendment, passed Congress in 1924, but could not garner adequate state support for ratification. Ironically but not surprisingly, the *absence* of federal redistributive infant- and maternal-welfare laws in the United States coincided with the *presence* of the only female-controlled state bureaucracy in the world. Despite these affronts to the Children's Bureau and its maternalist allies, American women became entrenched in several branches of the federal bureaucracy, on state boards of charity, and in local and state welfare agencies, where they were sometimes able to campaign successfully for state-level maternalist policies.[66]

Although the British state was somewhat stronger and more centralized than its American counterpart, both societies shared an enduring distrust of centralized government and a traditional reliance on local and private forms of welfare provision. Mixed-sex and all-female voluntary associations in Great Britain were broad-based and influential, addressing a vast panoply of social needs in the pre–World War I period.[67] Many of these organizations later became auxiliaries of the state as they were called upon to help administer maternal- and child-welfare measures. But British women, unlike their American counterparts, never gained an exclusive foothold in the central state, even though both the Majority and Minority Reports of the Poor Law Commission of 1909 called for the creation of a children's ministry which, presumably, would have been run by female activists.[68]

Thane's essay (chapter 10) warns us against an overly sanguine assessment of American women's achievements compared to those of their peers in Great Britain.[69] She argues for the salience of political parties as vehicles for British women activists. In the interwar years, the British Labour party increasingly incorporated into its platform maternalist social-policy measures championed by the Women's Labour League and later the Women's Sections, with tangible electoral benefits to the party and material benefits to women. In her survey of several British provincial towns, Thane concludes that "Labour was most electorally successful when it promoted social-welfare policies" and that women in particular "voted for social-reform parties." For better or for worse, women, in their roles as voters as well as policy makers, must take their share of responsibility for the making of the post–World War II British welfare state. After all, "[w]omen were a majority of voters in the general election of 1945 which brought labour its first ever outright-landslide victory and a majority of the women who cast their votes voted Labour."

Compared to English and American women, French women played more circumscribed roles in shaping social policy. To an extraordinary degree, the French regarded family matters as a public concern, far too important in the eyes of men to be left to women. Male politicians often initiated social-welfare policies targeting women and children, and typically they headed private as well as public social-welfare agencies. In her important study on women and protective labor legislation in France, Mary Lynn Stewart concludes that "feminists played a peripheral role in the campaign for hours standards."[70]

However, as Klaus argues (chapter 5), on the grass-roots level and in a wide range of organizations, French women did participate in public and private social-welfare provision. Their activities in voluntary associations, unlike those of their English and American counterparts, were often heavily subsidized by public funds from the central state (in the case of parochial activities the Church provided funds) as well as from progressive departments (like the département de la Seine) and communes (like the commune of Villiers-le-Duc). Well into the twentieth century, French women were far more likely to participate in maternalist activities than join feminist organizations even though maternalism did not necessarily further their emancipation as a sex.

Despite the relative weakness of women's social-action movements in France, Susan Pederson notes that "it was in France, . . . and not in Britain, Germany, or even the United States, that policies most closely resembling the endowment of motherhood were realized." However, Pedersen, in her study of the UFCS, a leading women's organization demanding endowment of motherhood for unwaged mothers, denies that the UFCS can be meaningfully called a "social feminist" organization and further questions its impact on the ultimate adoption of an "*allocation pour la mère au foyer*" by the Daladier government in 1938. "[I]nsofar as UFCS pressure had been effective, it had been exercised through the medium of their pronatalist friends," for whom declining birth-rates, the rise of National Socialism in Germany, and the economic crisis of international depression—and most emphatically not women's social and economic rights—were paramount. As Klaus cogently explains, while a few women "articulated a distinctive woman-centered approach to maternal and infant welfare," most "served goals defined by male politicians and physicians, often working under the direction and influence of men." Both Klaus's and Pedersen's essays suggest that while French pronatalism proved a potent force for galvanizing generous maternal- and child-welfare provision, French women paid a high price for these gains in terms of long-delayed political and social rights.

German women in the late nineteenth century, like those of the other three nation-states, also drew upon a legacy of private charitable work in maternal and child welfare. But their freedom to initiate policy was profoundly limited by an ever more entrenched state bureaucracy and a system of education which made it difficult for women to acquire necessary skills and training.[71] The precocious development of state welfare programs under Bismarck and the mandarin workings of the exclusively male civil service that it sheltered narrowed the range of issues and power available to German women.[72]

Yet the essays by Quataert and Sachße also show that the bourgeois German woman's movement played a key role in establishing the programmatic foundations of *Sozialfürsorge* (social relief), which, unlike alms and private charity, was rooted in the social rights of citizens and was preventive in aim.[73] As a wide range of new social problems confronted the rapidly expanding urban centers of Germany, bourgeois feminists called for female emancipation based on women's motherly roles as welfare providers in society. They not only organized the national *Bund Deutscher Frauenvereine* (League of German Women's Associations), but also initiated policies and programs through organizations like the *Mädchen und Frauengruppen für soziale Hilfsarbeit* (the Girls' and Women's Groups for Social Assistance Work). Some bourgeois German feminists were trained by the leading male proponents of social science in the *Verein für Sozialpolitik* and embraced its new discourses, which stressed a systematic and objective approach to social problems. Sachße shows that bourgeois feminists' holistic critique of industrial capitalism existed in uneasy tension with their faith in the necessity of using "professional-bureaucratic means" to realize their goals. World War I offered German women social-welfare workers unprecedented opportunities to "prove their female responsibility for the nation and the utility of their work for the Fatherland." But these goals, Sachße avers, must be set against their increasing subordination to the requirements of warfare. The bourgeois women's movement changed, he concludes, "from a tool of social criticism and female emancipation to an active support of the social and political status quo."

Until the turn of the century, Sweden most resembled Germany, in that its strong government left little room for women's benevolent and welfare activities. According to a centuries-old tradition, *byalags* (communes) took local responsibility for the poor. Moreover, the weakness of middle-class development meant that few women were in a position to challenge the government's monopoly.[74] It was not until women initiated discussion groups and conferences through the Social Democratic party just after the turn of the century that they began to articulate a vision of social welfare that would meet the needs of female workers, mothers, and children.[75] For many years Social Democratic men simply turned a deaf ear; at one point, the women became so enraged that they removed their newspaper from the party aegis and began to publish independently. But in the late 1920s, as the party grew strong enough to make a bid for coming to power, male Social Democrats began assiduously to court the female vote, and women finally had an opportunity to make their voices heard in policy debates.

White Australian women occupied an ambiguous political position. Though the parties moved quickly to mobilize them once they had gained suffrage, party affiliation did not carry full privileges for women. As long as their party was in power, Labor women had a certain amount of access to the state but limited ability to dictate the direction of policy, since the movement was so clearly male-dominated. Conservative women, working through the Australian Women's National League (with 54,000 members in 1914, the largest nonlabor political organization in the country), had great influence on the Liberal and Nationalist parties but little interest in challenging the status quo.

Though the ranks of the autonomous woman movement were depleted, Australian activist women had not abandoned their maternalist visions. Emboldened by the extension of the Motherhood Allowance to all mothers regardless of marital status, Labor women hoped to make a feminist, maternalist politics the basis for women's freedom and independence from men. After the Great War, they saw their opportunity. But the 1920s "test case" described by Marilyn Lake in chapter 11 ended in failure; women's claim for rights based on "maternal citizenship" was firmly rejected. Like their Swedish Social Democratic counterparts, Australian Labor women could count on only limited support from a party whose first priority was to strengthen the rights of working men.

Women in nineteenth-century France, Germany, Great Britain, and the United States, joined by their Swedish and Australian counterparts in the twentieth century, affected the shape and tenor of emerging welfare states. But there were important and enduring differences in the character of women's maternalist movements as well as their political power. These essays suggest that, in the first group of countries (France, Germany, Great Britain, and the United States), the strength and range of women's private-sector welfare activities often varied inversely with the strength of the state. "Strong states," defined as those with well-developed domestic-welfare bureaucracies and long traditions of government intervention, such as France and Germany, allowed women less political space in which to develop social-welfare programs than "weak states" like the United States and, to a lesser degree, Great Britain, which allowed women's voluntary associations to flourish. We are also forced to confront a paradox only visible at the comparative level: in the first group of four countries, those where women's social-action movements were strongest granted the least generous state-welfare benefits for women and children in the period *before* 1920. We are not saying, however, that the more active women were *within* their countries the fewer benefits they received. Far from it. Without women's initiatives within each of the countries surveyed, there would have been even fewer benefits.

The strength or weakness of the central state is particularly pivotal in Sklar's analysis (chapter 1). Her essay reads like a roman à clef in reverse, as she eliminates all those institutions and structural factors in male political culture (courts, parties, a labor movement, strong central government, etc.) that might have inhibited the growth and power of women's political culture in the United States during the Progressive Era. For Sklar, the vacuum created by the weakness of the American state was filled by female reformers and their organizations. She offers a subtle account of the distinct but interlocking male and female political cultures which together created the American state. American women were not merely the fortuitous beneficiaries of a weak state, they also built powerful institutions for women's higher education, were closely linked to the emerging social sciences, and knew how to exploit their power as consumers. While foregrounding the significance of class and class conflict in American life, Sklar argues that gender did the work of class in building and shaping social welfare in the Progressive Era United States.

Women's extrastate maternalist activities also helped to shape maternal- and child-welfare policies in Great Britain. Pat Thane argues that the Victorian "state system" was built upon close cooperation between an elaborate voluntary and local government apparatus and an efficient central-state administration. Seth Koven takes up this theme and argues that women's activities in the voluntary "borderland" were a site of welfare-program and policy innovation and functioned as a de facto form of state capacity in Victorian and Edwardian Britain (chapter 2). However, the very success of the central state in negotiating the terms of its relationship with local government and voluntary associations makes Thane wary of calling the British state "weak"; instead she offers the term "minimal state" (chapter 10). In what sense, she asks, can a state be called "weak" when it exerted such decisive, albeit often subtle and intermittent, influence over voluntary and paid agents of authority in the localities? Thane's critique of the categories of strong and weak states draws attention to the problematic issue of defining the boundaries of the state—particularly once the links between state formation and women's extrastate activities are taken into account. Despite Thane's useful criticisms, we feel that in order to make comparisons *between* state systems, some kind of vocabulary is needed which contrasts the widely differing status and authority of central state-welfare bureaucracies in different nation-states.

In Germany, as Quataert argues, "the bureaucratic apparatus that permeated society proved a formidable barrier to all manner of grass-roots pressure, including that of women." Thus Germany, with the strongest state, had politically ineffective women's movements but offered the most comprehensive programs for women. French and German women made more concrete gains in terms of social provision, yet they lacked the degree of bureaucratic and political power enjoyed by their British and American counterparts. In France and Germany, women had trouble gaining footholds in the state itself, even at the lowest levels of the civil service.[76] Their restricted avenues to the civil service also denied them political leverage, with the result that they had little voice in the legislative process.

British and American women were far more vocal. They used their positions as factory, health, and school-board inspectors to organize women workers and more generally promote women's trade unionism. In addition to highly visible positions within the Children's Bureau, American women worked as statisticians and analysts in state labor bureaus, where they gathered data vital to their public-reform campaigns. Though they succeeded in establishing public programs at the municipal and state level throughout the 1910s and 1920s, there were no permanent federal entitlements for women and children until the New Deal broke through Americans' resistance to the idea of national social provision in the 1930s. As Sklar and Hobson recount (chapters 1 and 12), by this time the strong maternalist coalition of the Progressive Era had broken down. Older organizations lost their grass-roots supports, contracted, or disappeared altogether, while many younger women, especially those in business and professions, embraced individual rather than collective solutions to social problems. Female reformers in America, Hobson shows, were thus unable to defend the economic rights of working mothers during the depression. They played only a minor role in formulating key social security measures that were to determine the shape of the American welfare state for decades to come.

In the development of maternal- and child-welfare legislation, Germany and France repeatedly led the way in the range and amount of benefits they provided mothers and children.[77] From 1883 onward, German women received assistance (*Wochengeld,* or confinement money) from the state to compensate for their lost earnings during mandatory maternity leaves. The length of these leaves and the categories of women eligible to receive them were extended several times between 1880 and World War I, eventually reaching eight weeks and covering agricultural laborers as well as factory workers. From 1893 on, French women had the right to free medical treatment during confinement and, after 1911, paid maternity leave and a nursing bonus.[78]

British women received fewer benefits, and what they had often took the form of limiting rather than redistributive protective legislation. From 1891 until 1911, Britain prohibited postnatal employment for four weeks, but offered no compensatory payments. In 1911 the wives of insured workers and women insured in their own rights were finally granted a lump-sum payment, usually 30s. at confinement, to address this hardship. Initially, the benefit was paid to the husband, but after strenuous lobbying by groups including the Women's Cooperative Guild, mothers gained direct control over these funds.[79] Confusion and skepticism over what constituted genuine incapacity to work due to pregnancy intensified deeply engrained objections to public support for maternal welfare in Britain. For several years after the Insurance Act was passed, the approved societies charged with administering it, fueled by the anxieties of their male members as well as a looming fiscal crisis caused by an actuarial miscalculation of the extent of women's perinatal illness, usually denied women's claims for sickness benefits during pregnancy.[80]

The United States provided neither federal maternity benefits nor medical care for mothers and children. Under the Sheppard-Towner Act of 1921, public-health nurses could offer maternal-

and infant-health education, but no direct services. The U.S. was, however, the first country to offer widows' and mothers' pensions (albeit only at the state level until 1935).[81] Since payment levels in most states were calculated to support children but not their mothers, these early pension plans did not prohibit maternal employment; this restriction came later, when the federal government took over provisions as Aid to Dependent Children under the Social Security Act of 1935.[82]

In Sweden and Australia, many early reforms benefiting women were passed without active lobbying on their part. These measures included the rights to education, property, and employment granted Swedish women in the mid-nineteenth century, and Old Age and Invalid Pensions and wage regulation for Australian women in the early twentieth century.[83] Australian women did, however, claim credit for a number of other benefits. Yet women in both countries had difficulty making inroads into left-wing political parties or the governments they controlled. Australian women, for example, were denied positions or promotions in the upper echelons of the educational bureaucracy until the late 1920s, even though the ranks of schoolteachers were largely populated by women.[84] Similarly, Swedish women were kept at the margins of government for decades. As Hobson shows, however, when they were finally invited to join government commissions in the 1930s, their presence made a significant difference in the ways that policies were formulated and their outcomes for women.

A comparison of women's rhetorical strategies in the two societies is also instructive. When radical Australian feminists tried to transform motherhood into a new form of citizenship, they were denied by a Labor government that regarded the endowment of motherhood as a threat to male employment prerogatives and the family (read "men's") wage. But when Swedish women couched demands for employment rights for married women and mothers in a more traditional discourse, arguing that maternal employment was the key to family stability (and thus in the interest of the nation as a whole), they were able to win social policies that allowed women to combine waged work with the roles of wife and mother. Swedish activists thus inscribed a broadened concept of motherhood in the foundation of what was to become one of the most progressive of welfare states.

While the degree of state strength affected the growth and character of women's movements, it cannot explain their political successes and failures. Female reformers using maternalist arguments alone could seldom compel states to act. They were more likely to be effective when their causes were taken up by male political actors pursuing other goals such as pronatalism, control of the labor force, or political hegemony. The decades before World War I were supercharged with nationalist agendas and anxieties around depopulation, degeneration, and efficiency as states vied for military and imperial preeminence. As the essays by Klaus and Lake demonstrate, these, and then the war itself, prompted legislators to establish many programs that might not have received state support under other conditions.[85] In Sweden, too, as Hobson points out, the perception of a population crisis in the mid-1930s created a receptive climate for the passage of social policies favorable to women. Whatever the precipitating factors, in all of these cases the programs passed owed their very existence to the models, organization, and momentum created by female activists.

Conclusions

A review of current research demonstrates that welfare-state development was deeply influenced by maternalist reformers and their philosophies, commitments, and social-welfare experiments. But their success was always qualified by prevailing political conditions. Without maternalist politics, welfare states would surely have been less responsive to the needs of women and children, for female reformers raised issues—or raised them in specific ways—that seldom occurred to male politicians. Indeed, many men felt that only women could identify and respond to these needs. Yet women activists were compelled to rely on these same politicians to gain state support for their programs and often had to wait until a national crisis such as war or class conflict created an opening for their initiatives.

To different degrees, depending upon the availability of political space in the national states we are examining here, maternalism was one of women's chief avenues into the public sphere. Women demonstrated that a strong commitment to motherhood did not necessarily limit or weaken their political participation, but instead transformed the nature of politics itself. Paula Baker's observation about the United States holds true for other countries as well: by identifying and insisting on issues of gender-based needs, women challenged the male monopoly on public discourse and opened it up to discussions of private values and well-being.[86] It was not the case that male political actors, unsolicited, instigated state encroachments on family life; rather, female political actors demanded that states take up the concerns of women and children.[87]

For many female activists, the political process which culminated in the passage of protective and welfare legislation for women and children functioned, in an exaggerated fashion, as a kind of Weberian "iron cage": they found dissonance between means and ends, their own motives and ultimate policy outcomes. The translation of maternalist measures into state policy also meant that poor and working-class women, always at a disadvantage because they lacked direct representation, were even further removed from the sites of policy making. As social work and related health fields became professionalized and services moved into state-run agencies, middle-class women carved out new niches for themselves within or in partnership with the state. In these new positions, however, women frequently found themselves at the bottom of organizational hierarchies, their voices diminished in policy discussions with male bureaucrats and politicians. To offset their liability to marginalization, the younger generation of American activists consciously jettisoned maternalism, which they characterized as unsystematic and unscientific.[88]

The weight of these essays, along with the wealth of new research published elsewhere over the past few years, compels revision of historical conceptualizations of maternalist activities, state development, and the relationship between them in the late nineteenth and early twentieth centuries.[89] When viewed from the perspective of maternalist politics, women's charitable institutions and organizations take on new significance as components of networks of benevolence as well as sites of state welfare-program and policy formulation, experimentation, and implementation. Women's campaigns for maternal and child welfare drew attention to the special needs of women and children in an industrializing world. Joining humanitarian appeals to thorough research and investigation, they contributed to the political momentum needed for reform. Maternalist women not only played important roles in promoting the growth of publicly funded welfare programs but were quick to exploit the new opportunities statutory agencies offered them.

Women of different classes and political orientations saw in motherhood the potential for accommodating and challenging (sometimes simultaneously) the male order and the basis for female social entitlement. Using a variety of rationales, they claimed that the state should provide financial support for mothers. German women—socialists, social democrats, and middle-class reformers alike—were among the first to formulate a demand for maternity insurance beginning in the late nineteenth century. Under the aegis of the *Bund für Mutterschutz,* they waged an international campaign to extend benefits to all women, regardless of marital status. With Ellen Key, they believed that only state support could emancipate women from the "sex slavery" to which they were condemned by the financial dependence on men that motherhood entailed.[90] Though they used less inflammatory language, British and Australian feminists had similar goals in mind when they lodged claims for an "endowment of motherhood" in the 1910s and 1920s; both groups sought universal support for mothers of young children.

American women's demands were more circumscribed. Campaigning for mothers' and widows' pensions in the 1910s and 1920s, they contended that mothering, like soldiering, was a form of service to the state. Yet they asked the state to support only those mothers who could not depend on adult-male breadwinners (widows, divorcées, deserted wives, etc.).[91] Legislation formulated along these more limited lines eventually passed not only in the U.S., but in Britain and Australia as well. According to Susan Pedersen, "Maternalist, 'separate but equal' ideology was pressed into service in the creation of policies encoding dependence, not the value of difference."[92]

These essays chart the histories of women's wanderings toward a "newly born" "mother world" they have long imagined but not yet entered. In the interwar years, the more radical formulations of motherhood endowment built on but also reconceptualized the legacy of prewar maternalist movements. While most of these campaigns were political failures when first put forward, they remain important expressions of the subversive potential of claims based on the social and economic value of motherhood joined to women's freedom to define for themselves their relationships to family and work force.[93]

Notes

Portions of this essay first appeared as "Womanly Duties: Maternalist Politics and The Origins of Welfare States in France, Germany, Great Britain, and The United States, 1880–1920," *American Historical Review* 95 (1990): 1076–1108.

1. *Westminster Review* (April 1908): 445.

2. Mary Beard, *Woman's Work in Municipalities* (New York, 1915), vi. On Beard, see Nancy Cott, *A Woman Making History* (New Haven, 1991).

3. Two British examples include Lucy Re-Bartlett, *The Coming Order* (London, 1911), 116–17, and Honnor Morten, *From a Nurse's Notebook* (London, 1899), 152–53.

4. Emilia Kanthack, *The Preservation of Infant Life* (London, 1907), 28.

5. Bré outlined her vision in *Das Recht auf Mutterschaft* (1904). For a discussion of this work and its relationship to the socialist *Bund für Mutterschutz* (League for the Protection of Motherhood), see Ann Taylor Allen, "Mothers of the New Generation: Adele Scheiber, Helene Stocker, and the Evolution of a German Idea of Motherhood, 1900–1914," *Signs* 10 (1985): 418–38.

6. Charlotte Perkins Gilman, "New Mothers of a New World," *Forerunner* 4 (1913): 149. For a discussion of Gilman's views of motherhood, see Ann J. Lane, *To Herland and Beyond: The Life and Work of Charlotte Perkins Gilman* (New York, 1990), esp. chaps. 9 and 10.

7. By women's movements we mean those expressly aimed at shaping and changing the conditions of women's lives, sometimes but not always sympathetic with the goals of political feminism. By movements of women, we refer to organizations and campaigns initiated and managed by women which did not seek to change women's status.

8. Our definitions are similar to Karen Offen's for "familial feminism" in "Depopulation, Nationalism, and Feminism in Fin-de-Siècle France," *American Historical Review* 89 (1984): 654, and for "relational feminism" in "Defining Feminism: A Comparative Historical Approach," *Signs* 14 (1988): 119–57. We prefer to use the term "maternalism" for this set of ideas, however, because we are mindful of Nancy Cott's caution against conflating all forms of women's activism under the umbrella term of feminism or one of its variants. See Cott, "What's in a Name? The Limits of 'Social Feminism'; or, Expanding the Vocabulary of Women's History," *Journal of American History* 76 (1989): 809–29. Elsewhere, Cott has specifically criticized Offen's use of "relational feminism" to identify all women activists who sought to extend or apply the values of domesticity and motherhood, particularly in the nineteenth century, contending that the term is both confusing and often inaccurate. See Cott, "Comment on Karen Offen's 'Defining Feminism: A Comparative Historical Approach,' " *Signs* 15 (1989): 203–5.

9. For example, Theresa McBride argues that "the consensus of male trade unionists before 1914 was that women's work was a necessary evil, and that women undercut male wages by increasing competition for jobs." Theresa McBride, "French Women and Trade Unionism: The First Hundred Years," in Norbert Soldon, ed., *The World of Women's Trade Unionism: Comparative*

Historical Essays (Westport, Conn., 1985), 37. On the paternalistic attitudes of leading British trade unionists such as Ben Tillett, see Sheila Lewenhak, *Women and Trade Unions: An Outline History of the British Trade Union Movement* (London, 1977), 91. On the strained relationship between the Labour party and the Women's Labour League, especially during its formative years, see Christine Collette, *For Labor and for Women: The Women's Labour League, 1906–1918* (Manchester, Eng., 1989), 35. On women and the *Parti ouvrier français*, see Marilyn J. Boxer, "Socialism Faces Feminism: The Failure of Synthesis in France, 1879–1914," in Boxer and Jean H. Quataert, eds., *Socialist Women: European Socialist Feminism in the Nineteenth and Early Twentieth Centuries* (New York, 1978), 79; Charles Sowerwine, *Sisters or Citizens? Women and Socialism in France since 1876* (Cambridge, Eng., 1982); and Steven Hause with Anne R. Kenney, *Women's Suffrage and Social Politics in the French Third Republic* (Princeton, 1984), chaps. 2 and 3. For an account of the relationship between women and earlier forms of socialism in France, in particular Saint Simonism, see Claire Goldberg Moses, *French Feminism in the Nineteenth Century* (Albany, N.Y., 1984), chap. 3. On a similar phenomenon in England in the 1830s, see Barbara Taylor, *Eve and the New Jerusalem* (New York, 1983), chap. 4.

10. We have used the categories public and private to highlight their permeability. Other feminist scholars have pointed out that the strict gender division between public and private which many social theorists take as a given is, in fact, a social construction. For an extended discussion of the evolution of this dichotomy, see Jean Bethke Elshtain, *Public Man, Private Woman: Women in Social and Political Thought* (Princeton, 1984), chap. 4, and Joan Landes, *Women and the Public Sphere in the Age of the French Revolution* (Ithaca, N.Y., 1988). Landes argues that the extension of male political rights through republican ideology during the French Revolution "depended upon women's domesticity and the silencing of public women of the aristocratic and popular classes" (2).

11. For a general discussion of this phenomenon, see Nancy Fraser, "The Struggle over Needs: Outline of a Socialist-Feminist Critical Theory of Late Capitalist Political Culture," in Fraser, *Unruly Practices: Power, Discourse, and Gender in Contemporary Social Theory* (Minneapolis, Minn., 1989); for a specific comparative case study, see Jane Jenson, "Paradigms and Political Discourse: Protective Legislation in France and the United States before 1914," *Canadian Journal of Political Science* 20 (1989): 235–58.

12. For the rich tradition of women's voluntary activities in the U.S., see Ann Firor Scott, *Natural Allies: Women's Associations in American History* (Urbana, Ill., 1991).

13. States also relied on other forms of private-sector welfare initiatives, including those emanating from churches and business. On the role of business in the French welfare system, see Laura Lee Downs, "Women, Welfare Supervisors, and the Boundaries of Difference in French Metalworking Factories, 1917–1935," in Dorothy O. Helly and Susan M. Reverby, eds., *Gendered Domains: Rethinking Public and Private in Women's History: Essays from the Seventh Berkshire Conference on the History of Women* (Ithaca, N.Y., 1992).

14. Miriam Dixson, *The Real Matilda: Woman and Identity in Australia, 1788–1975* (Auckland, NZ, 1976); Richard J. Evans, *The Feminists: Women's Emancipation Movements in Europe, America and Australasia, 1840–1920* (London, 1977). Marika Lindholm, "Swedish Feminism, 1845–1945: A Conservative Revolution," *Journal of Historical Sociology* 4 (1991): 121–42, also criticizes earlier studies of Sweden.

15. For an interesting account of reform activities by working-class Latinas, see Nancy A. Hewitt, "Charity or Mutual Aid? Two Perspectives on Latin Women's Philanthropy in Tampa, Florida," in Kathleen D. McCarthy, ed., *Lady Bountiful Revisited: Women, Philanthropy, and Power* (New Brunswick, N.J., 1990), 55–69. Hewitt points out that class divided these women from middle-class Latinas, although they could unite around some issues.

16. Scholars like Jane Lewis have rightly pointed out that interpersonal forms of welfare are often based on the assumption that the individual is morally culpable for her/his poverty; see Lewis, *The Politics of Motherhood: Child and Maternal Welfare in England, 1900–1939* (London, 1980), 18–19. The female founders of social work rejected this equation, at least in theory. While they complained about working-class mothers' neglect of their children, reformers were often acutely aware of the burdens faced by working women.

17. Ignota [Elizabeth Wolstenholme Elmy], "Women in International Conference," *Westminster Review* (November 1904): 539.

18. Robyn Muncy puts it well in her discussion of social control: "Clients were not passive victims in these relationships but less powerful partners whose interests sometimes meshed with those of their privileged associates and sometimes did not." Muncy, *Creating a Female Dominion in American Reform, 1890–1935* (New York, 1991), 110. For a nuanced discussion of cross-class, cross-ethnic relations between Anglo nurses and Hispanic and Native American clients in one case, see Sandra Schackel, *Social Housekeepers: Women Shaping Public Policy in New Mexico, 1920–1940* (Albuquerque, N.M., 1992), chaps. 2, 3, and 5.

19. For other analyses of the influence of race on American social policy, see Gwendolyn Mink, "The Lady and the Tramp: Gender, Race, and the Origins of the American Welfare State," in Linda Gordon, ed., *Women, the State, and Welfare* (Madison, Wis., 1990), 92–122, and Gordon, "Black and White Visions of Welfare: Women's Welfare Activism, 1890–1945," *Journal of American History* 78 (1991): 559–90.

20. For an engaging oral history of life in the Jewish East End, see Jerry White, *The Rothschild Buildings: Life in an East End Tenement Block, 1887–1920* (London, 1980). Middle- and upper-class Jewish women took a special interest in reform efforts for their co-ethnics in both England and the U.S.; see Linda Gordon Kuzmack, *Woman's Cause: The Jewish Woman's Movement in England and the United States, 1881–1933* (Columbus, Ohio, 1990). See also Lara Marks, " 'Dear Old Mother Levy's': The Jewish Maternity Home and Sick Room Help Society, 1895–1939," *Social History of Medicine* 3 (1990): 61–88.

21. For recent work in this area see Susan Pedersen, "National Bodies, Unspeakable Acts: The Sexual Politics of Colonial Policymaking," *Journal of Modern History* 63 (1991): 647–80. See also the following essays from Nupur Chaud-

huri and Margaret Strobel, eds., *Western Women and Imperialism: Complicity and Resistance* (Bloomington, Ind., 1992): Barbara N. Ramusack, "Cultural Missionaries, Maternal Imperialists, Feminist Allies," 119–36; Antoinette M. Burton, "The White Man's Burden," 137–58; Nancy L. Paxton, "Complicity and Resistance in the Writings of Flora Annie Steel and Annie Besant," 158–76; and Dea Birkett, "The 'White Woman's Burden' in the 'White Man's Grave': The Introduction of British Nurses in Colonial West Africa," 177–90. See also Ann Laura Stoler, "In Care of the Mother, in Care of the State: European Poor Relief and the Racial Politics of Imperial Rule," paper delivered at Conference on Feminism, Imperialism, and Race: India and Britain, University of Cincinnati, Cincinnati, Ohio, 23 October 1992; and Catherine Hall, *White, Male and Middle Class: Explorations in Feminism and History* (New York, 1992).

22. For a discussion of policies toward the Aborigines in one state, see Helen James, *In Her Own Name: Women in South Australian History* (Netley, S. Austral., 1986), 177–80. James points out the hypocrisy inherent in these policies; while the government paid lip service to protecting families and the mother-child bond among whites, it defended the practice of removing Aboriginal children from their mothers in order to educate them in special centralized schools.

23. Dorothy George linked this phenomenon, which she called the "new humanitarianism," to her optimistic assessment of early industrial capitalism in Britain. See *England in Transition: Life and Work in Eighteenth-Century England* (London, 1931). On the impact of evangelicalism on women's position, see Jane Rendall, *The Origins of Modern Feminism: Women in Britain, France and the United States, 1780–1860* (New York, 1984), chap. 3.

24. The term "cult of true womanhood" was first used by Barbara Welter in her essay by the same name in *Dimity Convictions: The American Woman in the Nineteenth Century* (Athens, Ohio, 1976). Linda Kerber identified the ideology of Republican Motherhood in *Women of the Republic: Intellect and Ideology in Revolutionary America* (Chapel Hill, N.C., 1980), chap. 5.

25. Maternalist ideologies were closely linked to new notions of respectability which, according to George Mosse, arose with the nationalisms of late-eighteenth- and early-nineteenth-century Europe. See *Nationalism and Sexuality: Middle-Class Morality and Sexual Norms in Modern Europe* (Madison, Wis., 1985). chap. 1.

26. See Lori D. Ginzberg, *Women and the Work of Benevolence: Morality, Politics and Class in the 19th-Century United States* (New Haven, 1990), chap. 5. In *Women in Public: Between Banners and Ballots* (Baltimore, 1990), Mary P. Ryan challenges the notion that all early-nineteenth-century women reformers eschewed politics and state involvement. In the 1820s and 1830s, she points out, female moral reformers in New York City "were not averse to seeking either police power or state funds to support their cause" (100).

27. See Florence Kelley, "Should Women Be Treated Identically with Men by the Law?" *American Review* 3 (May–June 1923): 277.

28. Elizabeth Lowell Putnam, "Note on the Children's Bureau" (n.d. [1929?]), Elizabeth Lowell Putnam papers, Schlesinger Library, Radcliffe College, box

3, folder 57. Putnam's remark draws attention to the fact that anti-Soviet backlash was particularly strong in the U.S. and contributed to the overall hostility to federal welfare measures. For more on Putnam's distinctive brand of maternalism, see Sonya Michel and Robyn Rosen, "The Paradox of Maternalism: Elizabeth Lowell Putnam and the American Welfare State," *Gender and History* 4 (1992): 364–86.

29. F. W. Hatton Reed, "Woman and the State," *Westminster Review* (December 1908): 641.

30. See Lisa Tickner, *The Spectacle of Women: Imagery of the Suffrage Campaign, 1907–14* (Chicago, 1988), esp. 153–226.

31. See Olwen Hufton, "Poverty and Charity: Revolutionary Mythology and Real Women," in *Women and the Limits of Citizenship in the French Revolution* (Buffalo, N.Y., 1992), and Claude Langlois, *Le Catholicisme au féminin: Les Congrégations françaises à supérieure générale au XIXe siècle* (Paris, 1984), pts. 2 and 3. For a discussion of the early context of social Catholicism, see Katherine A. Lynch, *Family, Class, and Ideology in Early Industrial France: Social Policy and the Working-Class Family, 1825–1848* (Madison, Wis., 1988).

32. See Bonnie Smith, *Ladies of the Leisure Class: The Bourgeoises of Northern France in the Nineteenth Century* (Princeton, 1981), chaps. 4 and 8, and also Margaret H. Darrow, "French Noblewomen and the New Domesticity, 1750–1850," *Feminist Studies* 5 (1979): 41–65.

33. Feminists like Marie Deraismes linked women's emancipation to the protection of the family and the Republic; see Moses, *French Feminism*, chap. 9. On shifting attitudes toward illegitimacy and women's social-welfare entitlements in the Third Republic, see Rachel Fuchs, "Preserving the Future of France: Aid to the Poor and Pregnant in Nineteenth-Century Paris," in Peter Mandler, ed., *The Uses of Charity* (Philadelphia, 1990).

34. See Moses, *French Feminism*, chaps. 8 and 9, and Hause with Kenney, *Women's Suffrage and Social Politics*, chap. 2.

35. The League's first president, Baroness de Brigode, great-granddaughter of Lafayette, asserted, "Next time we will check the color of the ballots a bit more carefully, for it affects our children's future." Anne-Marie Sohn, "Catholic Women and Political Affairs: The Case of the Patriotic League of French Women," in Judith Friedlander, Blanche Wiesen Cook, Alice Kessler-Harris, and Carroll Smith–Rosenberg, eds., *Women in Culture and Politics: A Century of Change* (Bloomington, Ind., 1986), 242.

36. Hause with Kenney, *Women's Suffrage and Social Politics*, 38.

37. Ann Taylor Allen, "Spiritual Motherhood: German Feminists and the Kindergarten Movement, 1848–1911," *History of Education Quarterly* 22 (1982): 319–20.

38. Henriette Schrader-Breymann, quoted in Allen, "Spiritual Motherhood," 323–24.

39. Not all of her contemporaries were so progressive. One, Amalie Sieveking, saw her motherly work as entirely compatible with women's traditional place in society. See Catherine M. Prelinger, "Prelude to Consciousness: Amalie

Sieveking and the Female Association for the Care of the Poor and Sick," in John C. Fout, ed., *German Women in the Nineteenth Century: A Social History* (New York, 1984), and Prelinger, *Charity, Challenge, and Change: Religious Dimensions of the Mid-Nineteenth-Century Women's Movement in Germany* (Westport, Conn., 1987), chap. 4.

40. Alice Salomon, *Character Is Destiny*, typescript autobiography, 66–67. The Leo Baeck Institute in New York City has a copy of this manuscript, but we must thank Irmela Gorges for sending a complete photocopy from Berlin. Originally written in English, the autobiography has, ironically, been translated into German and published as *Charakter ist Schicksal: Lebenserinnerungen* (Basel, 1983).

41. See Jean Quataert, *Reluctant Feminists in German Social Democracy, 1885–1917* (Princeton, 1979).

42. Lily Braun, "The Female Mind," in Alfred G. Meyer, ed. and trans., *Selected Writings on Feminism and Socialism by Lily Braun* (Bloomington, Ind., 1987), 188.

43. Braun's simultaneous embrace of maternalism and socialism earned her the vituperation of Clara Zetkin, who refused to call herself a feminist because it suggested that women's battle for emancipation could be separated from the struggles of the proletariat to overthrow capitalism. For Braun's response to Zetkin's charges, see her "Left and Right," in Meyer, *Selected Writings*. Jean Quataert discusses the Zetkin-Braun controversy in "Unequal Partners in an Uneasy Alliance: Women and the Working Class in Imperial Germany," in Boxer and Quataert, eds., *Socialist Women*, 130–35.

44. See Lily Braun, *Mutterschaftsversicherung* (1906).

45. Katharine Anthony, *Feminism in Germany and Scandinavia* (New York, 1915), 139.

46. Donald Meyer, *Sex and Power: The Rise of Women in America, Russia, Sweden and Italy* (Middletown Conn., 1987), 70. The religious practices of rural Swedes often diverged considerably from those dictated by the central church, and evangelicalism made little headway. Rural heterodoxy led, among other things, to general sexual tolerance, including widespread acceptance of out-of-wedlock pregnancy (49–50; 172–73).

47. Ibid., 50.

48. Ellen Key, *The Renaissance of Motherhood*, trans. Anna Friess (New York, 1914), 89.

49. For other interpretations of Key, see Cheri Register, "Motherhood at Center: Ellen Key's Social Vision," *Women's Studies International Forum* 5 (1982): 599–610, and Torborg Lundell, "Ellen Key and Swedish Feminist Views on Motherhood," *Scandinavian Studies* 56 (1984): 351–69.

50. Ellen Key, *Renaissance*, 150.

51. Dr. C. W. Saleeby, *Woman and Womanhood: A Search for Principles* (London, 1911), 60–63.

52. Anthony, *Feminism*, 213–14.

53. For the following discussion, we are indebted to Marilyn Lake, who provided essential information and guidelines for understanding Australian women's history. Ultimately, however, the interpretation is our own. See also Bettina Cass, "Redistribution to Children and to Mothers: A History of Child Endowment and Family Allowances," in Cass and Cora V. Baldock, eds., *Women, Social Welfare and the State in Australia* (Sydney, 1983); Peter Beilharz, "The Labourist Tradition and the Reforming Imagination," and Lorraine Wheeler, "War, Women and Welfare," in Richard Kennedy, ed., *Australian Welfare: Historical Sociology* (South Melbourne, 1989); and John Macnicol, "Welfare, Wages and the Family: Child Endowment in Comparative Perspective, 1900–50," in Roger Cooter, ed., *In the Name of the Child: Health and Welfare, 1880–1940* (London, 1992).

54. Rose Scott, *Woman's Sphere*, 10 October 1902; quoted in Kay Daniels and Mary Murname, comps., *Uphill All the Way: A Documentary History of Women in Australia* (St. Lucia, Austral., 1980), 272.

55. These campaigns were led by men like Lord Shaftesbury, Richard Waddington, and Gustave Dron, whose ostensible motives were benevolent and humane, although the consequences of their work were economically damaging for women and ultimately reinforced male control over workplace and family structures. On Waddington and Dron, see Mary Lynn Stewart, *Women, Work, and the French State: Labour Protection and Social Patriarchy, 1879–1919* (Kingston, Can., 1989), 31–36.

56. See Jane Humphries, "Protective Legislation, the Capitalist State and Working Class Men: The Case of the 1842 Mines Regulation Act," *Feminist Review* 7 (1981): 1–33, for the response of working-class miners, men and women, to this legislation in England. See Stewart, *Women, Work, and the French State*, 202, on women's strikes against the implementation of protective laws in France. On working women's resistance to protective laws in Germany, see Jean Quataert, "Social Insurance and the Family Work of Oberlausitz Home Weavers in the Late Nineteenth Century," in Fout, *German Women*, 270–89, and her essay in this volume.

57. Examples of redistributive legislation include the 30-shilling maternity allowance in Britain that was part of Lloyd George's 1911 social-insurance scheme, the 1913 Strauss Law in France, and the various state-level mothers' and widows' pension measures passed in the United States from 1906 on.

58. On the almost Byzantine debates and political machinations over this issue, see Mary Lynn McDougall [Stewart], "Protecting Infants: The French Campaign for Maternity Leaves, 1890s–1913," *French Historical Studies* 13.1 (1983): 70–105, and Jane Jenson, "Gender and Reproduction; or, Babies and the State," *Studies in Political Economy* 20 (Summer 1986): 9–46. The debate can be followed in the minutes of the Senate, *Journal Officiel*, 9 March and 3 December 1912. As McDougall notes, while France was late in passing a mandatory maternity leave, it was not from lack of interest in the issue or from lack of a tradition of state intervention in maternal and child welfare.

59. Emile Rey, *Séance du 8 mars 1912, Journal Officiel, Senat*, 609.

60. Anthony, *Feminism*, 132.

61. Sara Evans, *Born for Liberty: A History of Women in America* (New York, 1989), chap. 6.

62. The phrase is Stephen Skowronek's; see Skowronek, *Building a New American State: The Expansion of National Administrative Capacities, 1877–1920* (New York, 1982), pt. 2.

63. See Molly Ladd-Taylor, "Hull House Goes to Washington," in Noralee Frankel and Nancy S. Dye, eds., *Gender, Class, Race and Reform in the Progressive Era* (Lexington, Ky., 1991), and Muncy, *Creating a Female Dominion.*

64. See Lela Costin, *Two Sisters for Social Justice: A Biography of Grace and Edith Abbott* (Urbana, Ill., 1983); Ellen Fitzpatrick, *Endless Crusade: Women Social Scientists and Progressive Reform* (New York, 1990); and Muncy, *Creating a Female Dominion,* chap. 3.

65. Julia Lathrop, Letter of Transmission, in H. Harris, *Maternity Benefit Systems in Certain Foreign Countries,* U.S. Children's Bureau Bulletin no. 57 (Washington, DC, 1919), 2.

66. On the next generation of women in the federal government, see J. Stanley Lemons, *The Woman Citizen: Social Feminism in the 1920s* (Chicago, 1973); Susan Ware, *Beyond Suffrage: Women in the New Deal* (Cambridge, Mass., 1981), and *Partner and I: Molly Dewson, Feminism, and New Deal Politics* (New Haven, 1987); and Muncy, *Creating a Female Dominion,* chap. 4. Muncy notes that, at the urging of the Children's Bureau, by late 1921 forty-five states had established child-hygiene divisions; forty-two were directed by women and all were largely staffed by female public-health nurses and other officials (119). A useful study of women's state-level activities is Schackel, *Social Housekeepers;* she shows that while New Mexican women had a certain amount of latitude, they were subject to the vicissitudes of local and state politics, as well as federal directives.

67. See Anne Summers, "A Home from Home—Women's Philanthropic Work in the Nineteenth Century," in Sandra Burman, ed., *Fit Work for Women* (London, 1979), 33–63, for a fine-grained study not only of the class tensions between middle-class women philanthropists and their clients in England, but for the role of philanthropy in shaping women's sense of power and public identity.

68. For a reassessment of these reports and their best-known women authors, Beatrice Webb and Helen Bosanquet, see Jane Lewis, "The Place of Social Investigation, Social Theory, and Social Work in the Approach to Late Victorian and Edwardian Social Problems: The Case of Beatrice Webb and Helen Bosanquet," in Martin Bulmer, Kevin Bales, and Kathryn Kish Sklar, eds., *The Social Survey in Historical Perspective* (Cambridge, Eng., 1991).

69. See Theda Skocpol and Gretchen Ritter, "Gender and the Origins of Modern Social Policies in Britain and the United States," *Studies in American Political Development* 5,1 (1991).

70. Stewart, *Women, Work, and the French State,* 96. For an alternative interpretation, see Alisa Klaus, *Every Child a Lion: The Origins of Infant Health Policy in the United States and France, 1890–1920* (forthcoming, Ithaca, N.Y.), chap. 3, which addresses a range of issues and movements that are marginal to

Stewart's study. Klaus offers a fine study of women's maternal and child-welfare activities including the *Société de charités maternelles* and its conflicts with officials of the Third Republic. She also stresses the interventionist and paternalistic role of the medical community, which Stewart sees as insignificant.

71. See James C. Albisetti, "The Reform of Female Education in Prussia, 1899–1908: A Study in Compromise and Containment," *German Studies Review* 8 (1985): 11–41, "Could Separate Be Equal? Helene Lange and Women's Education in Imperial Germany," *History of Education Quarterly* 22 (1982): 301–17, and *Schooling German Girls and Women: Secondary and Higher Education in the Nineteenth Century* (Princeton, N.J., 1989).

72. See Fritz Ringer, *The Decline of the German Mandarins: The German Academic Community, 1890–1933* (Cambridge, Mass., 1969), esp. chap. 3.

73. See Christoph Sachße and Florian Tennstedt, *Geschichte der Armenfursorge in Deutschland*, II: *Fursorge und Wohlfahrspflege 1871–1929* (Stuttgart, 1988), and Sachße, *Mutterlichkeit als Beruf* (Frankfurt, 1986).

74. The account that follows is drawn, with modifications, from Lindholm, "Swedish Feminism"; Richard Evans, *The Feminists: Women's Emancipation Movements in Europe, America and Australasia, 1840–1920* (Totowa, N.J., 1977), 69–75, and Meyer, *Sex and Power*, passim.

75. Ann-Sofie Ohlander, "The Invisible Child? The Struggle for a Social Democratic Family Policy in Sweden, 1900–1960s," in Gisela Bock and Pat Thane, eds., *Maternity and Gender Policies: Women and the Rise of the European Welfare States, 1880s–1950s* (London, 1991), 60–72.

76. German women inspectors were viewed as little more than functionaries, and had no police authority, while male inspectors had full powers. See Jean Quataert, "A Source Analysis in German Women's History: Factory Inspectors' Reports and the Shaping of Working-Class Lives, 1878–1914," *Central European History* 16 (June 1983): 99–121. Quataert focuses on the role of inspectors in imposing bourgeois behavior norms on the working class, but she also considers the roles of male and female inspectors. For the British case, see Mary Drake McFeely, *Lady Inspectors: the Campaign for a Better Workplace, 1893–1921* (Oxford, Eng., 1988), esp. chap. 7, on the inspectors' prosecutions of offenders.

    The position of French *inspectrices* resembled that of their German counterparts: They were often denied powers to investigate conditions or to enforce codes, and their authority and discretionary powers were severely limited. Because of educational and other bureaucratic requirements, they were unlikely to be promoted. See Stewart, *Women, Work, and the French State*, 89–93.

77. For extraordinarily comprehensive and useful data about maternal- and child-welfare bills, their implementation, and policy implications, see International Labour Office, Studies and Reports, esp. *The Law and Women's Work: A Contribution to the Study of the Status of Women* (Geneva, 1939), series 1, no. 4; *Women's Work under Labour Law: A Survey of Protective Legislation* (Geneva, 1932), series 1, no. 2; and the *International Survey of Social Services* (Geneva, 1933), series M, no. 11. Another useful source is

Edward Fuller, comp., *An International Year Book of Child Care Protection* (London, 1924).

78. Women were also given a nursing bonus for the first twelve weeks. In addition to up to eight weeks of paid pre- and postpartum maternity leave, French women received a nursing allowance of half a franc per day for four weeks.

79. The Guild was also responsible for the initial inclusion of a maternity benefit in the 1911 Insurance Act. Under the leadership of Margaret Llewelyn Davies, the Guild was the largest and most politically adept organization representing working-class mothers in England. Davies claimed, "The Guild has . . . made a notable contribution to breaking down class and sex disabilities in public life." Davies, *Life as We Have Known It* (1931; rpt. London, 1977), xiv. The lobbying of women's groups like the Women's Cooperative Guild forced the government to acknowledge the sex-based distribution of resources within the family and pay mothers directly.

80. This miscalculation was, in fact, an artifact of women's own underreporting of illness during the period when they were not covered and felt compelled to work, no matter what the state of their health. Once benefits were available, they acknowledged their illnesses more openly. See Pat Thane's study of the attitudes of male trade unionists and friendly societies to the emergence of welfare legislation, "The Working Class and State Welfare in Britain, 1880–1914," *Historical Journal* 27 (1984): 877–900. Also see Sonya Rose, "Gender Antagonism and Class Conflict: Exclusionary Strategies of Male Trade Unionists in Nineteenth-Century Britain," *Social History* 13 (1988): 191–208. On administration of the Act, see Harris, *Maternity Benefit Systems*, 78–9.

81. However, as Susan Pedersen points out, the criteria for mothers' and widows' pensions were more restrictive than those for the "endowment for motherhood" envisioned by British feminists (but never passed in its original form). While the endowment would have granted universal support to mothers of young children, American mothers' and widows' pensions, as well as the British version that was eventually passed in 1925, predicated payments on the *absence* of a male breadwinner. See Susan Pedersen, "The Failure of Feminism in the Making of the British Welfare State," *Radical History Review* 43 (1989): 105. See also Jane Lewis, "Models of Equality for Women: The Case of State Support for Children in Twentieth-Century Britain," in Bock and Thane, *Maternity and Gender Policies*, 73–92. On the arbitrary and often discriminatory administration and distribution of American pensions, see Joanne Goodwin, "Gender, Politics and Welfare: Mothers' Pensions in Chicago, 1900–1930" (Ph.D. diss., University of Michigan, 1991).

82. See Molly Ladd-Taylor, "Mothers' Pensions: Payment for Childrearing or Charity for Children?" paper presented to the Conference on Women's History and Public Policy, Sarah Lawrence College, June 1989.

83. See Lindholm, "Swedish Feminism," 124–25; Jones, *In Her Own Name*, 165; and Evans, *Feminists*, 59.

84. Daniels and Murname, *Uphill*, 250–51.

85. Deborah Dwork captures the irony of this political fact in the title of her book, *War Is Good for Babies and Other Young Children: A History of the Infant*

and Child Welfare Movement in England, 1898–1918 (London, 1987). On Britain see also Anna Davin, "Imperialism and Motherhood," *History Workshop* 5 (1978): 9–65. For France, see Offen, "Depopulation, Nationalism, and Feminism." War could also lead to a situation in which men were favored over women by virtue of their service as soldiers. On the inadequacy of provisions in Germany, see Karin Hausen, "The German Nation's Obligation to the Heroes' Widows of World War I," in Margaret Higonnet, Jane Jenson, Sonya Michel, and Margaret Weitz, eds., *Behind the Lines: Gender and the Two World Wars* (New Haven, 1987), 126–40.

86. Paula Baker, "The Domestication of Politics: Women and American Political Society, 1780–1920," *American Historical Review* 89 (1985): 620–47.

87. For a critical interpretation of this development in the context of the United States, which holds female activists responsible for state incursions into the family and the private sphere, see Christopher Lasch, *Haven in a Heartless World: The Family Beseiged* (New York, 1979).

88. This shift was led by Julia Lathrop, Grace and Edith Abbott, and Sophonisba Breckinridge; see Muncy, *Creating a Female Dominion*, 102–3. In *Heroes of Their Own Lives*, Linda Gordon labels early maternalist efforts as feminist, insofar as they were linked to a comprehensive critique of male domination in society (32–34), and argues that "[t]he decline of feminist influence in social work, particularly after World War I, meant not only the decreased visibility of family-violence problems altogether but also their redefinition in ways that were disadvantageous to victims [women and children]" (292). While her conflation of maternalism and feminism seems problematic (see n. 2 above), the transformation in social welfare that she identifies is striking.

89. For a critique of existing welfare-state models, see Seth Koven and Sonya Michel, "Womanly Duties: Maternalist Politics and the Origins of Welfare States in France, Germany, Great Britain, and the United States, 1880–1920," *American Historical Review* 95 (1990): 1080–84.

90. Anthony, *Feminism*, 118.

91. See Ann Shola Orloff, "Gender in Early United States Social Policy," *Journal of Policy History* 3 (1991): 249–81, and Michel's contribution to this volume for a critique of Orloff.

92. Pedersen, "The Failure of Feminism," 105.

93. See Wendy Sarvasy, "Beyond the Difference versus Equality Policy Debate: Postsuffrage Feminism, Citizenship, and the Quest for a Feminist Welfare State," *Signs* 17 (1992): 329–62.

1

The Historical Foundations of Women's Power in the Creation of the American Welfare State, 1830–1930

Kathryn Kish Sklar

One of the most exciting features of the new stream of scholarship on women and the creation of the American welfare state during what has been called the "watershed" of American history between 1880 and 1920 has been its tendency to draw large conclusions about the relationship between the political activism of white middle-class women and that of other social groups. For example, through comparisons of white and black women welfare activists, Linda Gordon and Eileen Boris have demonstrated the significance of race as a factor structuring women's reform opportunities. Reform efforts by black and white women rarely overlapped, partly due to racist beliefs that excluded black women from white women's organizations, partly due to the crippling effects of black disfranchisement, partly due to the concentration of African Americans in the South, where ninety percent lived in 1890. Between 1890 and 1920, most white women focused their reform activism on the effects of industrialization in the north, usually implementing programs that required the cooperation of municipal, state, or federal governments. Since black workers, male and female alike, were excluded from industrial work until World War I, and since African Americans generally did not have access to state remedies for social problems either in the North or the South, black women reformers followed a different path, pursuing voluntary activity exclusively, and expressing more concern over issues affecting life in the rural South, especially lynching. Not until the 1920s, and then in the South rather than the North, did white and black women social reformers begin to work together.[1] So the story of white women's reform activism is a race-specific story in which their access to the resources of the state expressed their relatively privileged position in a race-segregated society.

This essay examines other features of American life that help us explain the power that middle-class women exercised in the white polity between 1890 and 1920 as they channeled the resources of the state in new directions. Some historians have offered critical assessments of their efforts, pointing to the limitations of their moral vision and their social methods. Some have praised them. All have agreed that women were central to the process by which the American social contract was recast and state and federal governments assumed greater responsibility for human welfare.[2]

Intriguing questions about this process remain unresolved, however. We can describe it better than we can explain it. To an extent unequaled elsewhere, middle-class American women were crucial and central to the responses state and federal governments made to social pressures created by massive immigration and rapid industrialization and urbanization.[3] Nowhere else did protective labor legislation focus so extensively on women workers, and nowhere else were women so extensively involved in its enactment. Nowhere else did women reformers design and administer a major government bureau responsible for the health and welfare of the nation's infants and children. Every national polity developed its own version of what became known in the 1940s as "the welfare state." Why in the United States was so much of the path to the welfare state blazed by middle-class women?

This essay offers a simple answer to that question. Women's activism was crucial because it served as a surrogate for working-class social-welfare activism. For complex historical reasons that derived partly from the political culture of middle-class women, partly from American political culture generally, women were able to provide systematic and sustained grass-roots support for social-welfare programs at a time when the working-class beneficiaries of those programs could lend only sporadic support.[4] Of course not all middle-class women participated in this effort. Middle-class women were an extremely diverse group. Some were uninterested in legislation benefiting working people, some were eventually persuaded to support such statutes, and some led the way in campaigns for "industrial democracy." This essay focuses on that vanguard and the women who provided it with grass-roots sustenance.[5]

In their analyses of the prominence of American women in social-welfare provisions, historians have emphasized the gendered qualities of their efforts, characterizing their achievements and their methods as "maternalist."[6] In many ways that term rings true, but it does not go far enough. It fails to capture the class struggle that shaped the creation of the American welfare state, and the role middle-class women played in that struggle. Using gender as a substitute for class strategies, women championed more than motherhood. True, their agenda advanced middle-class notions of gender and family relations, focusing as it did on bettering the lives of women and children. True, their leaders tended to benefit personally from the reform upsurge of 1890–1920, moving as they did into new jobs and positions of power that they themselves created. Yet their story embraces more than motherhood and self-interest. Responding to horrific conditions spawned by industrialization—conditions that threatened to poison middle-class as well as working-class life—large numbers of middle-class women sought to improve the welfare of working people generally. Work (and its obverse—unemployment) set the framework within which they viewed social problems and posed solutions. Family life and motherhood were part, but only part, of that framework.

Deindustrialization in the 1980s and 1990s has generated some of the same social traumas that attended industrialization in the 1880s and 1890s. Civil disorder, massive immigration, urban transformation, poverty, homelessness, and an intractable political malaise characterize both periods. Yet beginning in the 1880s, growing in the 1890s, and flourishing between 1900 and 1915, prodigious political mobilization by middle-class women formed the largest coalitions that broke through the malaise and restructured American social and political priorities at the municipal, state, and federal levels. How and why they did so are questions that require a multitude of answers. This essay uses broad strokes to sketch the chief variables involved in that restructuring, some of which remain part of our political culture today.

Welfare and Work: Two Sides of the Same Coin

"Welfare" carries quite different connotations today than it did when the word first entered into common usage in the 1920s.[7] Today "welfare" refers primarily to single mothers who receive Aid to Families with Dependent Children through the program that built "mothers' pensions" into the Social Security Act in 1935. That program, instituted by a combination of male-dominated state "relief" programs and women's political culture, initially benefited chiefly "deserving" widows, but it expanded significantly in the mid-1960s in response to protests raised by the National Welfare Rights Organization against the exclusion of black, divorced, and unmarried mothers.[8] In the 1980s AFDC became the chief problematic feature of American "welfare" policy. Even though federal and state governments maintained many programs designed to assist those in need or to help them remain or become self-supporting, including agricultural subsidies and student loans as well as compensation for large investors in failed savings and loan institutions, current debate about "welfare" focuses on AFDC.[9]

Those who laid the foundations for the "welfare state" between 1880 and 1920 had a different perspective. For them, workers, not mothers, formed the chief focus of social legislation. Contemporary debate about how to alleviate social problems arising from industrialization revolved around wage-earning men, women, and children. "Mothers' pension" plans were one of the least-contested consequences of a larger policy debate about the regulation of the modern workplace and the intervention of the state in relation between capital and labor.[10] Then, as now in the United States, the relatively unregulated workplace produced much higher rates of injuries and deaths than were common elsewhere.[11] In tracing the origins of the American welfare state, feminist scholars have focused on the antecedents of AFDC or "mothers' pensions," but they have often overlooked the larger context within which mothers' pensions emerged—the large population of widows and orphans created by industrial injuries. "Make fewer widows!" one leading woman reformer declared when asked for her opinion on mothers' pensions.[12] Her harsh but realistic reply shows us that there is more to the story of the emerging American welfare state than the "maternalism" that historians have called its chief characteristic.

Therefore, if in studying the origins of social-welfare policies before 1935 we confine our inquiry to the antecedents of AFDC or mothers' pensions, we miss a crucially important feature of the emerging welfare state as it was seen by those who helped create it. Their concerns about the problematic features of the industrial workplace were expressed in the unemployment benefits incorporated within the Social Security Act and the two other major New Deal statutes by which Congress hoped to promote social stability in the mid-1930s: the National Labor Relations Act (1935), which protected the rights of workers and union organizers and created mechanisms for mediating labor disputes; and the Fair Labor Standards Act (1938), which limited the legal length of the working day to eight hours, established a national minimum wage, and set minimum standards of job safety and health. This New Deal legislation, flawed as it was in design and implementation, culminated forty years of struggle by women and men concerned about the oppressive potential of the industrial workplace.[13]

In the 1920s "welfare legislation" was a protean term that conveyed different meanings to different people, but above all it implied labor legislation. The term gained currency among women activists in 1922 during the struggle between opponents and advocates of the proposed Equal Rights Amendment to the U.S. Constitution. At that moment "welfare legislation" became part of reform discourse precisely because it evoked the welfare of wage earners as well as other forms of social protection.

Early in 1922 the exact wording of the Equal Rights Amendment had not yet been determined; its supporters and opponents were locked in a debate over whether the strategy of so sweeping an assertion of sexual equality would nullify all gender-specific legislation that women reformers and women's organizations had fought so hard to implement between 1890 and 1920. Leaders on both sides of the debate were forced to summarize their positions.

Opposing the amendment, Florence Kelley, fiery general secretary of the National Consumers' League (NCL), issued a pamphlet, "Twenty Questions about the Proposed Equal Rights Amendment," in which she listed recent social legislation that the amendment threatened, including labor legislation for women. "What safeguards will wage-earning women have to compensate the disadvantages which they everywhere tend to suffer in competing with men—i.e., longer hours and lower wages?" Kelley asked. Also threatened were mothers' pensions: "The laws providing for

widows' pensions are clearly discriminations in favor of women."
The amendment also imperiled pathbreaking maternal health legislation. "Will the amendment destroy the Sheppard-Towner Act
. . . for the Promotion of the Welfare and Hygiene and Maternity
and Infancy?" In the same vein she asked "What will become of
the dower rights that women now have in many states?"[14]

Kelley's list combined quite diverse entities. Relics of the prein-
dustrial era, "dower rights" were oldest. Women's hour and wage
legislation, beginning in Massachusetts in 1874, and mothers'
pensions, first launched in Illinois in 1911, represented more
recent efforts to remedy some of the negative effects of industrialization. Even newer, more innovative, and representing the high
point of the achievements of women's political activism, the 1921
Sheppard-Towner Act allocated federal funds for the purpose of
reducing the nation's high rates of infant and maternal mortality,
which exceeded those of almost every European country.[15]

On the other side of the debate, responding to these protesta-
tions, amendment supporters in the National Woman's party
(NWP) lumped these diverse laws together under the heading
"welfare legislation." Alice Paul, NWP president, wrote to a supporter in the summer of 1921: "Our amendment is not yet in shape
for introduction, that is, it has not yet been approved by certain
people who are interested in welfare legislation."[16] Journalists
reporting on the debate and lawyers advising each side followed
Paul's linguistic lead. In February 1922 a *New York Times* story
treated protective labor legislation and "welfare legislation" as
interchangeable concepts, writing that "advocates of welfare legislation met with little opposition at a hearing today on the Minimum Wage Commission bill."[17] Even those who opposed the
amendment began to use "welfare legislation," as a convenient
catchphrase for all social legislation benefiting girls and women.
Freda Kirchwey, associate editor of *The Nation*, told Florence
Kelley that she was pressuring the NWP on the question "Why
do they not include a reservation making it clear that their amendment does not apply to welfare legislation?"[18]

Nevertheless, Florence Kelley of the National Consumers'
League and Ethel Smith, head of the Women's Trade Union
League, never used or even commented on the term "welfare
legislation." They shunned the term because, even at this early
date, it had acquired a paternalist tinge. Rather than the rights of
working people or the well-being of the whole society, by 1920

"welfare" invoked paternalistic management policies that acknowledged workers' needs but did not contribute to workers' empowerment. For example, an 1899 book studying "employers' welfare institutions" called them "a dividend to labor," saluting the capitalist-dominated marketplace rather than notions of social justice.[19] In 1908 the business-dominated National Civic Federation set up a Women's Department, which grew out of the Federation's "Welfare Department." Members of the Women's Department "hunted for welfare work" when they visited stores, hotels, and factories. To them that term meant "lunch-rooms, rest-rooms, and proper dressing rooms."[20]

Kelley and Smith believed that society owed more substantial protections to women—especially hours and wage legislation. Women needed protective laws to help them overcome the disabilities arising from their unequal power in the workplace and in society, and to enable them to fulfill maternal responsibilities. The National Consumers' League and the Women's Trade Union League viewed these laws as essential rather than expendable, as more akin to rights than to benefits, and the phrase "welfare legislation" did not quite convey that meaning. Although "rights" and "welfare" had not yet become dichotomous terms, "welfare legislation" blurred the distinction Kelley and Smith were developing between customary forms of charity and the rights of certain citizens to social protection—a distinction between public assistance and social justice, between the imposition of solutions from above and a dialogue between citizens in power and citizens in need.[21] "Welfare legislation" did not imply a set of rights won in industrial battles between capital and labor. So when supporters of the Equal Rights Amendment extended the term to embrace the industrial legislation women reformers had won in their battles with manufacturers on behalf of wage-earning women and children, they trivialized that legislation and diminished the significance of its potential loss.

Reformers like Florence Kelley and Ethel Smith had another serious reason for avoiding the term "welfare legislation." It was part of a linguistic trend around 1900 that detached the word "welfare" from the human recipients with which it had historically been linked. "Child welfare," "the welfare and hygiene of maternity and infancy," "the health and welfare of wage-earning women," "human welfare," and "social welfare" were expressions with honorable histories in which the emphasis lay on the beneficiaries—the child, the woman wage earner, the human, the society.[22] But by naming no recipient, the phrase "welfare legislation" emphasized the process of relief itself—governmental action rather than human need. This shifted the debate into more abstract discourse—discourse that subtly disadvantaged reformers and favored their critics, for, in a polity based on principles of limited government, as the American polity most assuredly was, it was one thing to extend state protection to exploited children or wage-earning women, and it was quite another to justify state responsibility for social welfare in the abstract.

Although Florence Kelley might have resisted the term "welfare state" if she had lived long enough to hear it, she was part of the process that built it. In 1922, if not in 1992, "welfare legislation" was commonly understood to embrace provisions for the well-being of working people as well as other forms of state aid. Despite the cold shoulder she and Ethel Smith gave to the term, it expressed a larger historical truth: before 1930 the protection of industrial workers formed an integral part of social-welfare legislation.

This broader definition of "welfare" carries an important implication for our analysis of women in the creation of the welfare state, for it requires us to enlarge our discussion of men's and women's political cultures to include the forces that generated protective labor legislation for men, women, and children. Although this expansion of scope complicates our inquiry, it is ultimately salutary, since it illuminates the class considerations that helped generate the American welfare state.

One striking peculiarity of the process by which the welfare state emerged in the United States before 1930 was the degree to which widespread mobilization of middle-class women on behalf of legislation to improve the working conditions of wage-earning women became an entering wedge for the extension of state responsibility to wage-earning men and to other aspects of women's lives (such as maternal health.) In this way the grass-roots civic organizations of middle-class women became crucial vehicles for social-justice reform between 1890 and 1920. Their initiative, their leaders, their strength in numbers, and their concern for the welfare of working women and children sustained fundamental changes in the nation's polity by establishing the constitutionality of state intervention on behalf of working people.[23]

This essay examines the historical evolution of women's agency in American welfare legislation. It first explores the social origins of the mass-based, autonomous political activism of middle-class women before 1860, and how that activism emerged in interaction with American political culture. It then analyzes key characteristics of the male polity in the United States before 1900 that invited women's political participation long before they could vote: traditions of limited government; the nation's decentralized political structure; the place of working-class voters within the male polity; the early introduction of universal white-male suffrage; and the power of unregulated capital. Finally, the essay explains how women's and men's political cultures came together so creatively after 1900 to lay the foundation for the American "welfare state."

The Sociopolitical Origins of Middle-Class Women's Political Culture

Historians have often emphasized the ideological components of women's participation in American public life—"Republican Motherhood" being the key concept—but this approach has inadequately appreciated the even more fundamental structural factors that sustained women's presence in the polity.[24] The two most remarkable features of the political activism of white Protestant middle-class women after 1900—its massive grass-roots scale and its institutional autonomy—emerged during the transforming social changes of the antebellum era. To understand that later period we need to account for the emergence of women's political culture before 1860.

Between 1830 and 1860 white middle-class American women constructed vital and autonomous political institutions on the basis of their ability to speak for the needs of women of other races and classes. Their efforts were part of the process of class development during this period of rapid economic and social change, bolstering the emerging hegemony of middle-class values and institutions, especially with regard to family life. During these decades middle-class women established their independence from male authority and defined their own gender-specific goals. In this way they became an autonomous political force, not merely an extension of male-dominated class imperatives.[25]

The best example of the prodigious scale and institutional independence of antebellum women's associations—the American

Female Moral Reform Society (AFMRS)—boasted four hundred forty-five local auxiliaries in 1839, mostly in New York and New England, which meant that one existed in almost every village and hamlet. This was the formative period of middle-class women's political culture. Building on values generated within American evangelical Protestantism, voluntary associations supplied a focus and resolution for the conflicting meanings in women's lives. Although ministers sometimes aided in the launching of local branches, Society members achieved a remarkable degree of independence from male authority.[26] In their campaign against prostitution, for example, the Boston Female Moral Reform Society declared in an annual report in the mid-1830s, "Our mothers, our sisters, our daughters are sacrificed by the thousands every year on the altar of sin," and asked, "Who are the agents in this work of destruction? Why, our fathers, our brothers, and our sons."[27] Not all women's groups expressed so fierce an independence from the men in their own class, but social and political conditions in the United States before 1860 fostered mass-based and politically autonomous women's organizations to a degree that was unknown elsewhere.[28] Similarly, social, economic, and political conditions created by the deeply entrenched system of slave labor in the United States generated a potency and autonomy among women abolitionists that was unknown in England. For example, when American antislavery societies sent seven women delegates to the World Anti-Slavery Convention in London in 1840, the British organizers of the conference refused to seat them, and British women abolitionists, also left out of the proceedings, endorsed the exclusion of their American sisters.[29]

To explain the vitality of middle-class women's social activism in this era, we need to consider how it was fueled by fundamental aspects of male political culture. Most important was a widespread commitment to limited government. After 1776 this commitment dismantled the traditional merger of church and state. Religious "disestablishment" steadily withdrew tax support from churches, thereby greatly enhancing the power of the laity, upon whom ministers now had to rely for financial backing. Since a majority of the laity were women, and since most Protestant churches were self-governing congregations, in contrast to the hierarchically governed Church of England in Great Britain, this change substantially augmented women's social authority, especially their ability to forge autonomous pan-Protestant organizations independent of ministerial direction.[30]

Women's organizations profited from the extension of universal white-male suffrage, albeit indirectly. By the 1830s and 1840s the few remaining limitations on white-male suffrage were abolished, and "the age of the common man" eroded class-based patterns of political deference.[31] While this process was far from complete, it did preclude trends that in England channeled women's energies toward the male-dominated objective of the expansion of male suffrage. There many politically active women joined the Chartist movement, where they devoted their energies to the advancement of universal male suffrage. Although some Chartist leaders paid homage to the rights of women, women's issues never became a major focus of the movement.[32] British restrictions on the political participation of Quaker and other non-Anglican men meant that insofar as the female relatives of these men were politically active, they championed the rights of male dissenters rather than the female-specific agendas more common in the United States. In 1853 a British abolitionist explained to her American friend:

> I find very few people who are aware that with you all *white men* are on a legal equality & that consequently our class restrictions, religious disabilities, landed propertied monopolies etc. etc. all the host of oppressions under which we groan resolve them-selves with you into distinctions of *sex* or of color. If the English public had this key to the enigma they would be a little more merciful to the transatlantic Amazons as they suppose all the advocates of woman's rights to be.[33]

Due to the early introduction of universal white-male suffrage in the United States, distinctions of sex and race became relatively more salient within the polity than distinctions of class. Women's rights "Amazons" were merely the most visible expression of the formation of a vibrant, autonomous women's political culture in the United States. Far from a fluke created by a few visionary women, that culture was deeply rooted in American social and political realities.

Class Themes in the Political Culture of Urban Men, 1870–1900

Opportunities for the expression of women's political activism multiplied after 1870, when traditions of limited government in the United States curbed forces that in England and Europe aided in the creation of welfare legislation. Traditions of limited government had three consequences. They undercut the development of problem-solving governmental agencies and bureaucracies; they promoted the power of professional politicians within the two major political parties; and they invested an uncommon degree of authority in the judiciary branch of government.

Although a few governmental bureaus, such as the U.S. Department of Labor, brought together experts and collected data capable of guiding public policy in attacking social problems created by rapid industrialization, explosive urban growth, and massive immigration, for the most part such expertise remained sequestered in universities, private foundations, and voluntary organizations. Whereas British and German governments were prominent employers of men trained in the new social-science methods of collecting and analyzing data about social problems, this was not the case in the United States, where most social scientists ended up in academic jobs that kept them on the political sidelines.[34]

The failure of civil-service reform in the U.S. illuminates the process by which male middle-class experts were shut out of policy-making positions. Civil-service reform was the top priority of the elite "Mugwump" movement of the 1880s, which succeeded in obtaining the passage of the Civil Service Reform Act in 1883. Yet the effects of the act were negligible.[35] In England civil-service management of public policy was successfully instituted as a way for university-trained elites to retain their control of government despite the growing enfranchisement of working-class men.[36] In the United States this maneuver was not possible because universal white-male suffrage had already recast political life in ways that gave to professional politicians—the men who maintained the heart and soul of the American polity, the two-party system—the power to block civil-service reform. The fundamental design of the American national government as a limited government—with its system of checks and balances among the executive, legislative, and judicial branches, and its federal structure that allocated significant authority to the states—fragmented power so completely that some additional integrative mechanism was required for the system to function as a whole. Political parties supplied that mechanism. In the United States the popular will was constrained not by a civil-service elite, but by men who shaped the agendas of the Democratic and Republican parties.[37] This became even more true after the demise of the People's party and the Populist Movement in 1896.

Increasingly in the last quarter of the nineteenth century, especially in American cities, Democratic politicians were oriented toward working-class, immigrant constituencies, and Republicans toward powerful economic interests, neither of which embodied the desires of middle-class men and women for government more responsive to their interests.[38] Josephine Shaw Lowell, the most politically powerful woman in New York City, wrote to a friend in 1886 that she wished all "decent people would come out of your disreputable party, as we have come out of our disreputable party, and let us all join to make a decent one of our own!"[39] Such criticism of "politics as usual" grew steadily between 1890 and 1920, giving rise to municipal-reform regimes that waxed and waned in many American cities, some of which arose from within the major parties, some of which formed "fusion" movements with party discontents, some of which expressed the growing strength of municipal socialism. A few states, particularly Wisconsin and Minnesota, and to some degree New York, implemented statewide reform programs, including the passage of labor and other social-welfare legislation, but only in 1912 with the Progressive party's unsuccessful presidential campaign in support of Theodore Roosevelt did this reform impulse achieve national scope.[40] By that time many of the key characteristics of the emerging American welfare state had already taken shape.

Notably lacking in this milieu was a strong national political movement representing the class-specific interests of urban working people. Strong self-help traditions continued to promote fraternal lodges, ethnic organizations, and church groups that sustained vast mutual-support networks.[41] But these groups were most successful at the local level, coordinating the resources of neighborhoods, cities, and counties; they rarely undertook autonomous campaigns on behalf of state or national legislation beneficial to wage earners. The Socialist Party of America, founded in 1901 and headed by Eugene V. Debs, did provide a serious national forum for policies benefiting working people when it reached its peak in 1912, the year it won one-third of the vote within the American Federation of Labor to replace Samuel Gompers as president, and the year it attracted six percent of the vote in the presidential election.[42] Yet the socialist upsurge did not prevent the wider political process from undercutting class-specific strate-

gies among working-class men. Because universal white-male suffrage preceded industrialization, political class consciousness did
not evolve, as it had in England, in response to the exclusion of the
industrial working class from political rights.[43] On the contrary,
individualistic ideologies appealed to all segments of the political
spectrum. Although American political life did not foster the kind
of cross-class dialogue and mediation found in Europe or
England, political parties did respond sensitively to ethnic diversity. Both political parties, especially the Democratic party,
attracted the loyalty of immigrant men by appealing to their ethnic
and gender identities rather than their class identity. For example,
the first Italian elected to municipal government in Chicago in
1885 represented the ethnic rather than the class identity of the
city's earliest Italian neighborhood.[44] Partly for these reasons,
organized labor did not emerge as a formidable political force in
the Progressive Era.[45]

In addition to blocking the establishment of problem-solving
bureaucracies and to fostering the entrenched power of the two
major parties, traditions of limited government also enhanced the
power of the nation's courts, and, through them, the power of
unregulated capital. The empowerment of courts, especially their
ability to limit the authority of popularly elected bodies by overrul-
ing legislative actions, was a key element in the design of limited
government in the United States. In the 1880s and 1890s that
power began to be applied systematically to repress organized
labor and overturn legislative strategies designed to benefit working people. Following a pattern of repression begun with the use
of state militias and the national guard to combat strikes in the
1870s and 1880s, courts began during the 1893 Pullman strike to
issue antistrike injunctions. Injunctions rendered strikes illegal
and justified the use of armed force to suppress them.[46]

Moreover, by the mid-1880s courts had begun to overrule prolabor statutes passed by state legislatures.[47] Although legislatures
might respond to the needs of working people, courts could block
their initiatives. Thus conservative judicial opinion sharply constrained the ability of legislatures to devise social policies to alleviate some of the undesirable effects of industrialization,
urbanization, and immigration. The effects of that process on
organized labor were profound. When the New York Supreme
Court ruled 1881 legislation banning the production of cigars in
tenements unconstitutional, Samuel Gompers, head of the fledgling American Federation of Labor, decided that "the power of the

courts to pass upon the constitutionality of the law so complicates reform by legislation as to seriously restrict the effectiveness of that method."[48] The power of the courts to block prolabor legislation steered Gompers and other labor leaders into strategies that avoided political solutions for labor problems. The American Federation of Labor retained an active political presence in state legislatures in order to obstruct the passage of antilabor statutes, and after 1900 cooperated with the National Civic Federation, but labor's chief initiatives lay in "pure and simple unionism," which meant keeping clear of entangling political alliances and concentrating on direct negotiations with employers.[49]

This labor strategy emerged at a time when many large companies, such as U.S. Steel, already maintained their own legions of strikebreakers. The power of unregulated capital mixed with the aspirations of American industrial workers to precipitate widespread civil disorder and death-dealing violence. At Homestead, Pennsylvania, in 1894, in Pennsylvania anthracite coalfields in 1902, at Ludlow, Colorado, in 1913, and many other locations, conflicts between labor and capital were solved through armed struggle.[50] Class war was expressed less through armed insurgencies like the Paris Communie of 1870 and more through direct clashes between labor and management, clashes that labor seldom won. For example between 1877 and 1914 the proportion of strikers who were *injured* in labor conflicts in late-nineteenth- and early-twentieth-century France was roughly the same as the proportion *killed* in such conflicts the United States.[51] The violent repression of American industrial workers delayed union organizing in industries like coal and steel until a full generation after its emergence in England. Before the Wagner Act finally extended state protection to union organizing in the mid-1930s, middle-class men and women reformers tried to solve labor conflicts peacefully through arbitration, but no governmental mechanisms forced employers to participate.[52] Partly as a consequence of the hegemony of unregulated capital (backed by hired guns, state militias, local police, and the courts), the political muscle of elite reformers like Henry Demarest Lloyd, middle-class politicians like John Peter Altgeld, and radical labor organizers like Eugene Debs was significantly attenuated.[53]

The intensity of class warfare in the United States was an important feature of the context within which the American welfare state originated. In that context neither organized labor nor middle-class male reformers were able to build a federal welfare state. The American Federation of Labor became deeply cautious and endorsed only the most limited state intervention in capital-labor relations. The American Association for Labor Legislation failed to work effectively with organized labor at the state or national level to advance workers' health insurance or old-age pensions. In this context, however, women reformers were able to obtain state interventions in capital-labor relations on behalf of wage-earning women and children. Policies toward the "dependent" classes of wage-earning women and children set precedents for state intervention that later could be extended to wage-earning men and to non-wage-earning women and children. Both organized labor and middle-class male reformers relied on large infusions of aid from middle-class women to legitimize such interventions.

Stalemate in Men's Political Culture

Before 1920 the embattled position of organized labor within the American polity undercut labor's ability to shape the emerging welfare state. Furthermore, compared to their European and British equivalents, key groups of middle-class and upper-class men also played a diminished role in the passage of welfare legislation in the United States. The political activism of the most likely group of middle-class social planners—male social scientists—was sharply curtailed at a crucial moment by a wave of political repression that swept American universities between 1886 and 1894. Henry Carter Adams at Cornell, Richard T. Ely at Wisconsin, and Edward W. Bemis at the University of Chicago were among the many university social-science faculty who were either fired or threatened with firing for advocating "radical" ideas. Ely typified the accommodationist response to this threat when he recanted his Christian Socialism during a trial staged by the University of Wisconsin Board of Regents in 1894, declared himself "a conservative rather than a radical," and withdrew from the American Institute of Christian Sociology, which he had helped found in 1893. "Objectivity" replaced advocacy in the work of most male social scientists.[54] After this wave of repression passed, Richard Ely and other social scientists reemerged as relatively conservative experts capable of advising legislators about the efficacy of social and labor reforms, but not as leaders of a crusade for social justice. Ely himself became president of the American Association for

Labor Legislation in 1907, a group of experts who sometimes wielded substantial lobbying power with state legislatures, but never again did he work closely with popular social movements.[55]

Industrialists themselves constituted another group who elsewhere stimulated the creation of state welfare policies but in the United States did not. In Germany, for example, industrialists often supported public initiatives for working-class health and welfare because they were threatened by a highly politicized labor force and, in a context of falling birth rates, had to be concerned about the survival of a population large enough to sustain industrial growth. Yet putting aside the more advanced Bismarckian notions of social insurance, in the United States even such elementary social indices as high rates of infant and maternal mortality or extraordinarily high rates of occupational deaths and injuries prompted less anxiety among industrialists because the labor force was not politically mobilized and the colossal scale of European immigration guaranteed an abundant labor supply.[56] In this context American industrialists often took the lead in instituting welfare legislation that benefited business (such as workmen's compensation plans that ended costly court settlements arising from occupational injuries), but energetically fought legislation that primarily aided workers, such as shorter hours, minimum wages, unemployment plans, and social security pensions.[57]

County-based gentry were another group that in England made significant contributions to the development of state strategies for remedying social problems arising from industrialization, but in the United States did not do so. Lord Shaftesbury in the mid-nineteenth and Winston Churchill in the early twentieth century both criticized the noxious effects of industrialization from radical perspectives engendered in part by their aristocratic place in the social order. In the United States Theodore Roosevelt embodied the equivalent of this tradition but also demonstrated its relative weakness. Although born into a wealthy rural Dutch-American family and educated at Harvard and Columbia, Roosevelt could acquire no electoral sinecure. His choice of a political career obliged him to enter the rough-and-tumble world of machine politics; compromises with the Republican-party bosses were essential to his electoral success. Around 1900 when he became an important ally of men and women social reformers, Roosevelt drew his ideas from them rather than from an aristocratic critique of American industrial society.[58]

Historians once believed that political bosses met the social-welfare needs of urban immigrant constituencies, but recent scholarship challenges that assumption. While municipal governments did dispense most nonfederal state spending before 1940, and hundreds of patronage-based jobs were distributed on the basis of party loyalty, taxes remained low and social services rudimentary. Partly due to a lack of imagination among party bosses, partly due to the restraining influence of the tax-conscious middle-class, urban political machines did not meet their constituencies' needs for positive government. They distributed food at Christmas, and mediated between members of their constituencies and social-service agencies.[59] Sometimes they championed pure-milk campaigns, supported woman suffrage, and welcomed the construction of new schools, but most machine politicians were fiscal conservatives who, except in the business of getting votes, shunned policy innovations. Moreover, machine coalitions reinforced the power of capital by blocking pressures from below that might challenge its hegemony.[60]

Thus policies to help the working poor survive the negative effects of industrialization went against the grain of American political structures, and crucial groups that advanced those policies elsewhere were hobbled in their attempts to do so in the United States. These circumstances created unprecedented opportunities for women reformers. When they moved into the political arena in large numbers in the 1890s, women became crucial catalysts, forming effective coalitions with men and with them constituting a new majority of politically active middle-class people in support of systematic changes in the political status quo. Men in every social group capable of advancing social legislation—lawyers, labor leaders, social scientists, industrialists, party politicians, middle-class male reformers, and even socialists—worked closely with middle-class women and their class-bridging organizations to achieve what men had not been able to accomplish separately.

The Flowering of Middle-Class Women's Political Culture, 1860–1900

The same forces that limited men's power to solve social problems actually promoted the power of women's political culture. This paradigm first became visible during the Civil War in the United States Sanitary Commission, the semipublic organization created to care for Union troops, their wounded, and their families. Stepping into the gap created by the lack of a standing army, women Sanitary Commission volunteers raised the funds that sustained northern state militias in the field, reformed the delivery of food and medical services, and even administered pension programs after the war.[61]

In the 1870s middle-class northern women propelled autonomous, mass-based women's organizations into the nation's political mainstream. This was the development stage of women's political culture. By far the most important organization, the Woman's Christian Temperance Union (WCTU), formed in 1874, carried women's pan-Protestant voluntarism into a new scale of political activism and a new depth of cultural meaning for its participants. Organizing their locals geographically to coincide with congressional districts, the WCTU endorsed woman suffrage as early as 1879. Through its "do everything" policy the Union became an umbrella organization with thirty-nine departments in 1896, twenty-five of which dealt wholly or mostly with nontemperance issues. In Chicago in 1889 the Union built a twelve-story "Woman's Temple" to serve as a national headquarters, hotel, and office building. Moving into openings created by American traditions of limited government, WCTU members generated a wide range of needed social services. In Chicago alone they maintained

> two day nurseries, two Sunday schools, an industrial school, a mission that sheltered four thousand homeless or destitute women in a twelve-month period, a free medical dispensary that treated over sixteen hundred patients a year, a lodging house for men that [before 1890 had] provided temporary housing for over fifty thousand men, and a low cost restaurant.[62]

The WCTU created new opportunities for middle-class women's social activism in a social environment that was absorbing massive numbers of recent European immigrants and a political environment where municipal, state, and national governments offered little if any assistance to needy men, women, and children.[63]

We gain insight into the reciprocal relationship between the WCTU and its social and political environment by noting that the British Women's Temperance Union remained a smaller, more scientific group of relatively elite women that did not swell into an umbrella organization, did not massively mobilize British women, and did not fill public-policy needs disregarded by men. The British group lacked the militancy and the hegemonic power that flowed from the "Christian" identity of the WCTU. "We have had no wonderful crusade in England—no such baptism of power and liberty," a British woman temperance worker wrote in 1883.[64] Much more than was the case in the United States, class structures dominated British political life and tended to channel women's activism into male-dominated struggles. Between 1830 and 1900 British women participated in a wide range of male-dominated movements from Chartism to Fabian socialism, and they built their own institutions, such as the Women's Cooperative Guild and the Women's Trade Union League, but the scale of autonomous organization expressed by the "White Ribbon Army" of the WCTU had no British equivalent.[65]

At the same time, other changes in American life democratized access to higher education and opened institutions of higher learning to women on an unprecedented scale. By 1880 more than forty thousand women were pursuing higher education, and one out of every three undergraduates was female.[66] The feminization of the teaching profession generated these high statistics. Historically controlled by local rather than state or national governments, public schools vastly increased in number between 1800 and 1880 as the Euro-American population spread across the continent. In the competition among neighboring towns for settlers and other commercial advantages, the number or quality of village schools could define the difference between a potential county seat and a permanent backwater. The feminization of the teaching profession occurred in this context of unprecedented demand for teachers, because women were cheaper (and, many argued, better) than the traditional schoolmaster. Since women usually did not remain in the schoolroom after marriage, the female teacher was a resource that required constant renewal. This was accomplished through the widespread admission of women to normal schools, colleges, universities, and other institutions of higher learning, especially land-grant institutions that offered teacher training.[67]

Analysts of the nineteenth-century American state have noted that its principal power lay in its ability to give away its chief resource—land. The Morrill Land Grant Act of 1862 made public lands available to states to create public institutions "open to all" for "the liberal and practical education of the industrial classes." Responding to the pressure to admit women, by 1870 eight state universities did so—Iowa, Wisconsin, Kansas, Indiana, Minnesota, Missouri, Michigan, and California. By 1890 the number of female undergraduates had risen to about 56,000, or 36 percent of the total.[68] The founding of elite women's colleges, including Vassar (1865), Smith (1875), and Wellesley (1875), lent greater visibility to this trend. As Vida Scudder wrote in 1890,

> It is impossible to deny, in the presence of the amazement with which our great women's colleges are still viewed by visitors from distant lands, that we do embody a type, in some respects hitherto unknown. We stand here as a new Fact—new, to all intents and purposes, within the last quarter of a century. Our lives are in our hands.[69]

When the American welfare state began to emerge in the 1890s, a sizable second generation of college graduates was mobilized for action.

Tens of thousands of urban middle-class women put their education to use in the women's club movement. In 1890 the General Federation of Women's Clubs (GFWC) drew together a vast network of local women's organizations, which since 1869 had emerged as the secular equivalent of the WCTU. Generating an effective intermediate level of organization through state federations, and channeling women's energies into concerted political action, the GFWC became the chief voice of "organized womanhood" after 1900. By 1910 it represented 800,000 women, some of whom could vote in local elections, and most of whom had at least some influence on the male voters in their families.[70] Even more remarkable than their formidable numbers was the impressive range of topics women's clubs explored. By 1890 these extended far beyond what might be expected to be their class-specific or gender-specific interests, or even the issues raised by the National American Woman Suffrage Association. For example, the Chicago Women's Club in the early 1880s, under its motto "Nothing Human can be Alien to Us," discussed such political questions as "Free Trade," "The Eight Hour Day," and "Bismarck and His Policy." They circulated petitions in 1886 for state legislative bills to place the treatment of women in public institutions under the supervision of women and city-council ordinances to

add more women to the Board of Education. In response to Eleanor Marx's tour of the United States in 1887, members debated
"Socialism and the Home." Two years later a club member spoke
on "The Influence and Results of Merely Palliative Measures of
Reform."[71]

Ellen Henrotin exemplified the active social conscience and
rapid growth of the club movement among middle-class women.
Married to a prominent banker who became president of the
Chicago Stock Exchange, Henrotin organized the more than thirty
congresses held in connection with the Chicago Columbian Exposition in 1893. Based on her enormous success there, in 1894
she was elected president of the General Federation of Women's
Clubs.[72] During her four-year tenure the number of affiliated wom-
en's clubs doubled, and its "industrial division" forged close alliances with other reform-minded women's organizations. In 1898
the Federation resolved:

> That each club in this Federation shall appoint a standing com-
> mittee whose special duty it shall be to inquire into the labor
> conditions of women and children in that particular locality.
> That each state federation shall appoint a similar committee
> to investigate its state labor laws and those relating to sanitation
> and protection for women and children.[73]

Each committee was expected "to influence and secure enforcement of labor ordinances and state laws." A national committee
collected local reports and presented them at national conventions.[74]

Opposed to the employment of mothers of young children, the
Federation energetically campaigned for the passage of state
mothers' pensions laws.[75] Its rhetoric critiqued industrialization
from the perspective of exploited women and children. The Federation's official history in 1912 expressed the moral outrage that
regularly aroused hundreds of thousands of women to social
action. "Probably the most piteous cry which has reached the ears
of the mothers of the nation is that which goes up from the little
children whose lives are sacrificed to the greed of manufacture,"
it noted in a chapter on "Federation Ideals." Although the "advent
of machinery" had been a great blessing to some, it also increased
"the labor of women and little children."[76] The Federation took a

broad view of that increase, seeing it in the context of an ongoing
social struggle.

> Each day newspapers thrill the blood of the people with the
> pitiful details of labor disturbances; and the public stand aghast
> at the manifestations of the wrongs visited upon innocent and
> guilty alike, due to the helplessness of the laborer on the one
> hand and oppression by the manufacturer on the other.[77]

Politically aware, willing to experiment, and eager to undertake
cross-class initiatives, large numbers of middle-class women were
not mirror images of their fathers, husbands, and brothers but
drawing on common political traditions, structured their own
forms of political action.[78]

The gendered components of American social science made it
relatively easy for college-trained women to think of themselves
as policy experts. By the time Progressive women reformers
encountered social science in the 1880s, it was already thoroughly
gendered—in a woman-friendly way. During that decade women
were prominent in three of the five departments of the American
Social Science Association: "Education," "Public Health," and
"Social Economy." Franklin Sanborn, head of the Social Economy
department in 1887, characterized it as "the feminine gender of
Political Economy" because it was "very receptive of particulars"
and dealt with "Social Welfare."[79] Women responded to this conge-
niality in social science by forming their own social-science organizations as well as by joining those led by men. In New York in
the early 1870s they formed the New York City Sociology Club, the
Women's Progressive Association, and the Ladies' Social Science
Association.[80] By the 1890s women reformers confidently used
social-science tools in ways that permitted them to engage in
reform activity on an equal basis with men without surrendering
the "feminine" qualities that differentiated them from men. Moreover, leading women social scientists, like Florence Kelley and
Jane Addams, who were sustained by female institutions like Hull
House and undeterred by the repression experienced by their male
colleagues in universities, continued throughout their lives to affiliate closely with popular social movements, particularly those
dominated by women.

Just as important as education and social science in drawing
middle-class women into public activism was the growth of their

consciousness as consumers. This consciousness reflected the unprecedented market in consumer goods and the emergence of a consumer culture that linked producers, sellers, and buyers. Waves of immigrants who entered industrial and manufacturing jobs between 1880 and 1900 lifted most northern native-born working-class Americans into white-collar work, creating a large and relatively new group of middle-class consumers.[81] New forms of marketing emerged, visible in the size and number of advertisements in popular magazines and the scale and diversity of department stores. Consumer culture had two striking effects on women within the older, well-established middle class. It made them more conscious of their relatively elite position within emerging middle-class consumer culture; and it highlighted the contrast between their relatively privileged lives and the lives of women who toiled to produce consumer goods. The National Consumers' League and its scores of local branches embodied the new consciousness of middle-class consumers.[82]

Amplifying the trends that deepened and intensified the potential for political activism among middle-class women, a vanguard of talented leaders emerged within the social-settlement movement. Choosing to live in working-class, immigrant neighborhoods, this vanguard acquired potent leadership skills for cross-class cooperation with working-class women, and the ability to speak for the welfare of their entire society, not merely for the needs of women and children, or for the interests of their own class. In the United States the social-settlement movement built on and consummated social trends that had steadily enlarged women's public activism since 1830: religious or moral values that justified women's activism; the gender-specific autonomy of women's organizations and institutions; women's access to higher education; and their use of social science as a reform tool.[83]

A product of the Social Gospel movement, settlements drew on the religious roots of women's justifications of their public power. Although Addams did not permit any religious instruction at Hull House, Italians in the neighborhood treated her like a modern-day nun. After an Italian workingman paid her streetcar fare, the driver explained: "any of them would do it for you as quick as they would for the Sisters."[84] Nevertheless, the primary tone of women's settlements was secular and professional. For hundreds of young women between 1890 and 1920, the question, "After college, what?" was answered with a few years of settlement work before marriage.[85] Moreover, for dozens of talented college graduates like Jane Addams, Florence Kelley, Julia Lathrop, Alice Hamilton, Grace Abbott, and Mary Simkhovitch, settlement life sustained lifelong careers in reform activism. In many ways settlements served as the equivalent of graduate schools where women gained professional training in a supportive and innovative milieu, and of academic apprenticeships where women learned to practice their specializations—Addams and Simkhovitch in settlement work itself, Kelley in labor legislation, Lathrop in social-welfare administration, Hamilton in occupational medicine, and Abbott in immigrant welfare and child welfare. Settlements situated women to make the most of their new methods of social-science analysis. They could collect social data and use it to design remedies for social problems just as well as any university professor.[86]

Although women's settlements received money from wealthy male benefactors and some settlements were sustained by church funds, the leading women's settlements were emphatically autonomous institutions whose destinies were shaped by their founders and the resident communities they nurtured. Hull House, by far the most important women's settlement, was supported primarily by women donors. Others were sustained by women's colleges. Lillian Wald maintained her own independent course at the Henry Street Nurses' Settlement despite disagreements with her chief benefactor, Jacob Schiff.[87] These independent institutions permitted women reformers to draw upon male assistance without succumbing to their control.

Nevertheless, the new empowerment of women reformers through the social-settlement movement did not turn women into men. Indeed, the more women acquired power and resources, the more they did so as women. Women and men remained highly differentiated—socially, politically, and economically. Women's very prominence within the American social-settlement movement reflected that difference, since for them settlements served as a substitute for the political, professional, academic, and religious careers from which they were excluded by reason of their gender. In England settlements were attractive to women for the same reason, but men were most visible because settlements became training centers for public office and the civil service. In the United States, where political parties remained the chief route to public office, men who were attracted to settlement life tended to be ministers trying to combine a religious calling with social action—a smaller and less dynamic group than the throng of reform-minded American settlement women.[88]

The years between 1900 and 1920 marked the maturation of the political culture of middle-class women. Able to vote in only a few states before 1910, excluded by law from public office in most states, and perceived as outsiders by lawmakers in Congress, and in state and municipal governments, women had to find ways to overcome these gender-specific "disabilities" if they were to affect public policy.[89] They did so by drawing on the most fundamental and enduring features of women's political culture—the strength of its grass-roots organizations, and the power of its moral vision.

Structured representationally, women's organizations, even those with strong national leaders like the National Consumers' League, gave great weight to the views of state and local affiliates. This sparked grass-roots initiative. It also fostered belief in democratic processes and the capacity of large social organizations— like state and federal governments—to respond positively to social needs. Whereas the predominant moral vision of men's political culture tended to regard the state as a potential enemy of human liberty, the moral vision of women's political culture viewed the state as a potential guarantor of social rights.

The grass-roots strength and moral vision of women's political culture resided in groups like the General Federation of Women's Clubs, the multitude of local and state organizations affiliated with the Federation, the National American Woman Suffrage Association, the Woman's Christian Temperance Union, the National Council of Catholic Women, the National Council of Jewish Women, the National Consumers' League, the National Women's Trade Union League, the Young Women's Christian Association, the Congress of Mothers, the League of Women Voters (after 1920), and (before 1925) even the Daughters of the American Revolution and the National Federation of Business and Professional Women's Clubs.

To a remarkable degree the creation of the American welfare state before 1930 was due to the endorsement these predominantly middle-class women's associations gave to the expansion of governmental responsibility for the welfare of able-bodied wage earners and their families. They lobbied for legislative interventions in the relations between capital and labor to protect those they viewed as the weakest and most exploited by the forces of industrial capitalism. Shorter hours, higher wages, safer work sites would, they thought, create sounder citizens and a better society. Many of these organizations were explicitly class-bridging, such as the Women's Trade Union League, the National Consumers' League, and the YWCA. All invited the influence of the vanguard of reform leadership concentrated in the social-settlement movement. All cooperated closely with a variety of men's groups.

White Middle-Class Women and Men Create the Welfare State

The distinction between white middle-class women's and men's political cultures expressed deeply rooted gender-specific social structures and cultural values. Yet while this distinction maintained firm differences between women's and men's public endeavors, it also established the preconditions for close cooperation between women and men. Gender differences meant that since women could accomplish some things that men could not, and men could achieve some of what women could not, together they might produce what neither could realize separately. Common goals made it possible for groups of women and men to work together, but differences in their institutional settings, their constituencies, and their beneficiaries meant that cooperation between them could produce spectacular rewards.

Above all, women needed access to the institutional power and positions of public authority that men held, and men needed the grass-roots support that women could mobilize. Thus the National Congress of Mothers drew on the help of juvenile-court judges to launch a successful campaign for state mothers' pensions laws between 1910 and 1915.[90] The National Consumers' League relied on prominent male attorneys to argue their cases before the U.S. Supreme Court. The General Federation of Women's Clubs worked with state superintendents of education and other state and municipal officials in designing and implementing their legislative agendas.[91] And during the early stages of the effort to found the United States Children's Bureau, Lillian Wald and Florence Kelley reached Theodore Roosevelt only through the intervention of Edward T. Devine, professor of sociology at Columbia University, director of the New York School of Philanthropy, and head of the Charity Organization Society in New York.[92]

Other instances of male-female cooperation, though less prominent, alert us to the significance of this dominant pattern of wom-
en's grass-roots organizations and official male expertise.
Sometimes, for example, women's grass-roots strength combined
with that of men. This was the case with child-labor reforms,
which were passed exclusively at the state level before 1938, and
were generally endorsed by organized labor as well as by women's
organizations. This dual support for child labor statutes may
explain why they were implemented and enforced more extensively than any other form of early social-welfare legislation. For
example, after the Illinois Manufacturers' Association succeeded
in its 1895 suit to overturn eight-hour legislation for women as a
violation of employees' right to contract, they tried to deflect the
ensuing public censure by declaring their "hearty support" of
existing child-labor regulations.[93]

Apart from Wisconsin and a few other states where the elector-
ate supported expanded governmental responsibility, male
reformers had a harder time than women reformers in locating
grass-roots backing for greater state responsibility. Sometimes
male reformers worked closely with organized labor, but labor
often proved uncooperative in efforts to enlarge state accountability for social welfare, leaving these reformers without popular
support for their legislative agendas. The best example of sustained cooperation between middle-class men and organized
labor, the National Civic Federation and the American Federation
of Labor, proposed only a limited range of programs for government action. Although they collaborated extensively, their effect
on the creation of the welfare state was limited to the advocacy
of workmen's compensation and a few other programs on which
business and labor could agree.[94]

What happened when measures gained the support of neither
male nor female grass-roots organizations? Good examples were
unemployment insurance and old-age-pension proposals, which
languished in legislative committees until the economic disaster
of the Great Depression demonstrated their necessity. When I. M.
Rubinow, head of the American Association for Social Security,
sketched the history of unemployment insurance, he noted that
although "the Scientific Societies (economic, sociologic, statistical, political and labor legislation)" promoted plans similar to the
one implemented in England in 1911, and successfully inaugurated one in Wisconsin in 1921, popular support for a national

measure developed only as a result of "the obvious overwhelming force of the depression."[95] Until 1932 representatives of organized labor opposed unemployment benefits, exclaiming "a job not a dole!"[96]

The questions then become: "What was it about the combination of women's grass-roots activism and small groups of male experts and leaders that accounted for their success at passing welfare legislation before 1930?" "What did this partnership accomplish and what does it tell us about the forces that created the American welfare state?" The success of these forces was limited. For example, their effort to outlaw child labor through a constitutional amendment failed, as did their attempts to create unemployment insurance nationally—two reforms that became possible only after the devastating depression of the early 1930s— and they failed to establish state-sponsored health care for workers, an issue that continues to bedevil the American polity in the 1990s. But their efforts built a foundation on which it was possible to construct the "New Deal" of the 1930s.

On their own the enormous numbers of women who supported protective labor legislation for women and children, who demanded schools large enough to accommodate the burgeoning population of immigrant working-class children, and lobbied state governments for mothers' pensions for poor widows constituted a vital political force. Linked in various capacities with the full range of male-dominated political groups who advocated some sort of social-welfare legislation after 1900—from municipal socialists to the National Civic Federation—they tipped the balance of the political process heavily in favor of such legislation. Middle-class women remained central to the debate about the welfare of working people—job-related health perils, the length of the working day, the need for a "living wage"—that absorbed the nation's courts, its legislative bodies, and public-opinion forums at the height of American industrialization between 1900 and 1920.[97]

Middle-class white northern women were merely the largest, most prominent (because most elite), and most vocal group of women to address the needs of poorer, working-class people. Similar class-bridging motivations inspired the activism of black club women in the North and South who, through the National Association of Colored Women and its multitude of affiliated organizations, ministered to the needs of black migrants who had left their rural homes.[98] In the same way, German-American Jewish women, through the National Council of Jewish Women, the Henry Street Settlement, the Hebrew Immigrant Aid Society, and other organizations, aided recent Eastern European Jewish immigrants.[99] White women differed from African-American women in their ability to use the state to remedy social problems, but otherwise the dynamic was similar: women took the lead in remedying social problems. Self-interest motivated all three groups, since they each wanted to avoid the threat to their middle-class security posed by the poverty, disease, illiteracy, and degradation of their poorer counterparts. But they were also committed to visions of social justice that transcended their own class interests. Black women did not have access to state remedies, but departing from earlier "Lady Bountiful" methods, Protestant and Jewish women pioneered in the use of the state to heal what they saw as dangerous social divisions. "Maternalism" describes only part of their agenda.

Fueled by a conviction of the positive difference that women could make in the public domain, in terms of both gender relations and class relations, the political culture of middle-class women grew mightily in the 1890s, just after the post-Haymarket repression of the late 1880s dramatically reduced the willingness of skilled workers to aid in the organization of unskilled workers. In many ways middle-class women took over as a popular political force where the pre-Haymarket labor movement, including the Knights of Labor, left off. In the "anti-sweatshop" campaigns of the 1890s, for example, newly formed consumers' leagues worked alongside needle trade unions to pass regulatory legislation and create investigative agencies. Between 1900 and 1920, when women's organizations reached the peak of their power, they cooperated closely with the AFL on some fronts, especially the organization of women's unions through the Women's Trade Union League, but otherwise developed their own cross-class agendas, mobilized their own constituencies, and pursued their own lobbying strategies. Political officeholders, ranging from local school superintendents to the president of the United States, knew women constituted an interest group unlike any other in their ability to speak for the nation's welfare.[100]

While the sex-segregated autonomy of women's political culture kept them from being absorbed into men's reform associations, the social breadth of their undertakings created unprecedented opportunities for female experts like Florence Kelley and Lillian

Wald. "In the lesser household of the home, in the larger household of the city, the aim is the same—to work out the highest good
to all concerned, the advancement of humanity," one commenta-
tor wrote about women's political culture in 1894. "Intelligent
women are everywhere studying civics and the social problems of
the day."[101] They were also following the leadership provided by
an unprecedented generation of talented, college-trained women
who headed their organizations at the national, state, and local
levels.

Not surprisingly, in this context Jane Addams became the pre-
eminent woman and probably the preeminent citizen of her era
through her ability to articulate the new values she called "social
democracy." In the United States, in contrast to Europe, this term
expressed ethical reformism rather than revolutionary political
insurgency, but those carrying its banner, women as often as men,
marched at the forefront of social change.[102] Occupying a place
on the executive boards of almost every reform organization in
the Progressive Era, including men's groups like the American
Association for Labor Legislation as well as women's groups like
the National Consumers' League, and mixed groups like the
National Child Labor Committee, Addams embodied the aroused
conscience of middle-class women and their readiness to take
collective action, not only in the name of womankind, but in the
name of democracy and social justice.[103]

Perhaps the most fundamental characteristic of the emerging
welfare state was the effort to provide minimum standards for
living and working conditions. Early labor legislation for women
was central to that effort, as were the strategies and discursive
shifts by which gender did the work of class. In *Lochner v. New
York* (1905), the U.S. Supreme Court reaffirmed its commitment
to abstract notions of workers' contract rights, making health the
only avenue for arguments designed to limit the exploitation of
workers through long hours.[104] Therefore in *Muller v. Oregon*
(1908) Louis D. Brandeis, a prominent Boston attorney, and Josephine Goldmark, NCL research director, justified state intervention by emphasizing women's physiological weakness.[105] Less
often noted by historians, but no less important, were similar
efforts by Brandeis, Goldmark, and the NCL in 1916 in *Bunting
v. Oregon*, which successfully defended the limitation of men's
working hours by emphasizing men's physiological weakness.
Florence Kelley, for example, rallied public opinion to support

Oregon's law "to the end that the present wholesale using up and wearing out of fathers of families in the manufacturing industries may be checked."[106] As Kelley later wrote, the Bunting decision "took a long step forward" in American judicial history by upholding the constitutionality of the regulation of the workplace of "men in private industry in a non-injurious employment."[107] This precedent smoothed the way for the Wagner Act and the protection of unions in 1935 as well as the regulation of hours and wages in the Fair Labor Standards Act.[108]

Historians usually attribute the judicial breakthrough in the court's decision in *Muller v. Oregon* to female-specific health-related arguments. Certainly those arguments were key. Also important, however, was the position of the NCL within the larger American polity, which enabled it to challenge the Supreme Court's ruling in *Lochner v. New York* against the regulation of nominally noninjurious workplaces. That position had two crucial characteristics: the close coordination between national and local consumer leagues; and the fact that *Lochner*'s endorsement of workers' contract rights shut out challenges by men's groups, either working-class or middle-class. Only through the wedge of gender could freedom of contract be breached.

The close relationship between the NCL's national office and its far-flung locals, particularly, in this case, the Oregon Consumers' League, facilitated its oversight of the progress of Oregon's hours law through the state and federal judicial systems. "Nothing has shown so clearly as [the Muller decision] the value of the National Consumers' League as a clearing house for information and center for effective cooperative effort," the 1909 NCL annual report declared. "The Consumers' League of Oregon sounded the note of warning that the ten hours law of that state was in danger of annulment, and with it the legislation of many states embodying the same principle."[109] Josephine Goldmark and her brother-in-law, Louis D. Brandeis, responded to that warning by arguing the case before the Supreme Court on the basis of sociological evidence, an innovation with enormous consequences for American jurisprudence during the remainder of the twentieth century.

As general secretary from the NCL's founding in 1898 till her death in 1932, Florence Kelley spent half her life on the road, traveling from local to local, solving problems, exhorting members to greater efforts in the implementation of the NCL's national priorities, and knitting the NCL together with other women's organizations at the local, state, and national levels.[110] The NCL had more than sixty locals at the height of its power around 1910. Continuing the historical pattern within women's organizations of strong grass-roots activism, every major city and every northern state felt the League's influence, especially when, as was usually the case, it drew on the support of the General Federation of Women's Clubs and other women's organizations. By contrast, the NCL's closest male equivalent, the American Association for Labor Legislation (AALL), founded in 1906 by John Commons of the University of Wisconsin and headed by his student John Andrews, preferred to remain an elite group of experts without local affiliates. Rather than tolerate the lack of coordination, the dissension, and programmatic variation that locals introduced, AALL leaders deliberately disbanded the few that sprang into existence around 1907.[111] The vitality of women's grass-roots organizations, a fundamental characteristic of women's political culture, accounts at least in part for the NCL's success in establishing legal standards in the American workplace.

Women's collective action in the Progressive era certainly expressed a maternalist ideology, as historians have frequently pointed out. But it was also sparked by a moral vision of a more equitable distribution of the benefits of industrialization, and the vitality of its relatively decentralized form of organization. Within the political culture of middle-class women, gender consciousness combined with an awareness of class-based injustice, and talented leaders combined with grass-roots activism to produce an impressive force for social, political, and economic change. Issues regarding women and children wage earners captured the imagination of tens of thousands of middle-class women between 1890 and 1920, so much so that gender—women's organizations and female-specific legislation—achieved much that in other industrializing nations was done through, and in the name of, class. Women did what Florence Kelley called "the nation's work" by reaching beyond the betterment of their own class to shape a new social compact for the society as a whole.[112]

The End of an Era

The commitment of women's organizations to "welfare legislation" waned considerably in the 1920s. In that decade of paradigmatic change for middle-class women, nineteenth-century notions that valued gender differences gave way to twentieth-century presumptions about the similarity of the sexes.[113] Along with this undermining of "maternalist" motivations, the political climate underwent a sea change: social reform in general and efforts to achieve more equitable distribution of social resources in particular met determined resistance. Florence Kelley and Jane Addams were slanderously attacked as members of a communist conspiracy. American religious life, which between 1890 and 1920 had nurtured social-justice convictions and fostered a "Social Gospel" discourse shared by middle-class and working-class churchgoers, also underwent a sea change. New forms of fundamentalism among poor Protestants and a business-promoting positivism among middle-class Protestants both discouraged commitments to social justice.[114]

Women's organizations persisted, but many lost their interest in social legislation, and their belief that women brought unique capacities to public life diminished. The membership of the General Federation of Women's Clubs no longer provided grass-roots support for social legislation. Though still at the forefront of social-justice campaigns for working people, the National Consumers' League evolved into a much smaller organization. Without the grass-roots support that had sustained their class-bridging campaigns before 1920, the power of the U.S. Children's Bureau steadily ebbed. Female social workers turned away from the broader goals of social reform to embrace therapeutic social work with its focus on the individual and on psychological motivations.[115] These changes within women's political culture coincided with the end of Progressive reform in men's political culture and marked a sharp swing to the right in the nation's political climate.[116] Thus concluded thirty years of nation building by women, and three decades of productive interaction between women's and men's political cultures.

The Progressive Era formed a watershed in the history of state recognition of its responsibility for human welfare. Before 1880 that responsibility was extremely limited, but by 1920 the foundations had been laid for the construction of a modest welfare state. Women were central to that striking transition. In many ways their organizations filled gaps left by American traditions of limited government and other features of male-dominated polity. Taking advantage of those structural opportunities, they used gender-

specific legislation and gender-based moral imperatives as surro-
gates for class-specific laws and visions. As a result, the interaction
between women's and men's political cultures combined to produce changes that neither group could have achieved alone. In
countries with stronger traditions of state authority, women did
not encounter equivalent opportunities and men did not rely so
heavily on their talents.

What conclusions can we draw about the centrality of women
in the construction of the American welfare state? The strength
of social-justice and class-bridging efforts within middle-class
women's organizations illuminates the vitality of American civic
culture between 1890 and 1920, and the ability of that culture to
envision a better society and to take effective action to implement
that vision. The crucial significance of women within American
grass-roots democracy was never better demonstrated.

Women's organizational heyday between 1890 and 1930
brought a new and vital constituency into American political life
at a time when women's political perspectives and resources were
urgently needed. When the crushing effects of the nation's worst
economic crisis prompted a "New Deal" in American public policy,
many of their achievements were incorporated into national law.
Women ceased to engage in autonomous political action on behalf
of expanded state responsibility, but they worked effectively
within the Democratic party to overcome, however temporarily,
some of the deleterious effects of American traditions of limited
government.[117]

Yet, weighing the outcome of women's efforts, the cup can
appear half full or half empty, depending on one's perspective.
Lacking the power to dominate the American polity, women could
not themselves institute a strong welfare state. From this perspective the cup seems half empty. Some historians have viewed the
American welfare state as a failure and attributed its shortcomings
to the women who did so much to create it, and the gender-specific
policies they pursued.[118] Yet, seen from another perspective, the
cup appears half full. Women's grass-roots organizations and their
network of leaders were responsible for many pathbreaking innovations that men could not achieve. The American Association
for Labor Legislation, for example, gave up on its efforts to create
state-sponsored programs of workers' health insurance in 1920,
but in 1921 a broad coalition of women's organizations succeeded
in creating a federally sponsored program for infant and maternity

health, the Sheppard-Towner Maternity and Infancy Protection Act, which many state governments sustained after federal funds ceased in 1927.[119] Women's gender-specific and child-specific strategies aimed to aid all working people, not merely the "truly needy." Rather than isolating poor women, activists envisioned a better society in which poverty could be ended. In the 1990s the Children's Defense Fund shows that their strategy remains a necessary if not sufficient surrogate for class-specific action in a polity that remains deeply hostile to class legislation.

Today, as we near the end of the twentieth century, persisting traditions of limited government empower those who discredit social-justice programs, and the lack of class-based politics erodes the power of those who advocate such programs. Today, during the height of deindustrialization, these problems seem even more grave than they were during the height of industrialization, since the nation is losing jobs that seem unlikely to return. Moreover, welfare policies today have become inextricably combined with attitudes toward race and social justice for African Americans. One hundred years ago gender served as a surrogate for class. Today class is still less prominent than gender and race in the minds of those who design American welfare policy.

Between 1890 and 1930 middle-class women changed American public policy, but they could not and did not change the fundamental nature of the state itself, or alter the character of the male-dominated polity. Nevertheless their legacy amounts to more than the policies they embraced. Their example reveals the enduring efficacy of their methods—grass-roots organizations and class-bridging visions—for those who aspire to change American public policy.

Notes

For their extremely valuable comments on earlier versions of this essay I am grateful to Eileen Boris, Thomas Dublin, Estelle Freedman, Linda Gordon, Michael Merrill, Sonya Michel, and Seth Koven.

1. Linda Gordon, "Black and White Visions of Welfare: Women's Welfare Activism, 1890–1945," *Journal of American History* 78 (1991): 559–90, and Eileen Boris, "The Power of Motherhood: Black and White Activist Women Redefine the 'Political,' " in this volume. For the distribution of the black population in 1890, *Historical Statistics of the United States, Colonial Times to 1970*, part 1 (Washington, D.C., 1975). The exact statistic is 90.28 percent. For black migration after 1915, see James R. Grossman, *Land of Hope:*

Chicago, Black Southerners, and the Great Migration (Chicago, 1989), and Carole Marks, *Farewell—We're Good and Gone: The Great Black Migration* (Bloomington, Ind., 1989). Exceptions to this pattern of separate racial paths included the National League for the Protection of Colored Women, which consisted predominantly of white women and formed an important organizational basis for the creation of the National Association for the Advancement of Colored People in 1909. See "Mary White Ovington," in Edward James, Janet James, and Paul Boyer, eds., *Notable American Women: A Biographical Directory*, 3 vols. (Cambridge, 1971). Florence Kelley was one of several white women reformers in the Progressive Era who worked closely with African-American reformers. At Kelley's memorial service in 1932 W. E. B. DuBois praised her "clear sight and unfaltering courage" on race questions. "DuBois on Florence Kelley," *Social Work* 2.4 (1966): 98–100. For cross-race interaction after 1920, see Jacquelyn Dowd Hall, *Revolt Against Chivalry: Jessie Daniel Ames and the Women's Campaign against Lynching* (New York, 1979), 59–106.

2. This rapidly growing literature is summarized in Seth Koven and Sonya Michel, "Womanly Duties: Maternalist Politics and the Origins of Welfare States in France, Germany, Great Britain, and the United States, 1880–1920," *American Historical Review* 95 (1990): 1076–1108. See also Kathryn Kish Sklar, "A Call for Comparisons," *American Historical Review* 95 (1990): 1109–14, and Linda Gordon, "Social Insurance and Public Assistance: The Influence of Gender in the Welfare Thought in the United States, 1890–1935," *American Historical Review* 97 (1992): 19–54.

3. Paula Baker, in "The Domestication of Politics: Women and American Political Society, 1780–1920," *American Historical Review* 89 (1984): 620–49, argues that women's power increased due to the growing importance of interest-group politics and of what had formerly been viewed as "women's issues"—clean water, urban sanitation, industrial education. Yet Baker's analysis does not explain why women were more influential in the creation of the American welfare state than was the case in Europe or England.

4. In their use of the term "culture" during the past twenty years historians have been influenced by Glifford Geertz, *The Interpretation of Cultures* (New York, 1973). Geertz emphasized the cognitive components of culture—a process that produces meaning and signification. Raymond Williams, *The Long Revolution* (New York, 1961), 41–42, defined the analysis of culture as "the clarification of the meanings and values implicit and explicit in . . . the organization of production, the structure of the family, the structure of institutions which express or govern social relationships, the characteristic forms through which members of the society communicate."

For a definition of "political culture" see Jean H. Baker, *Affairs of Party: The Political Culture of Northern Democrats in the Mid-Nineteenth Century* (Ithaca, N.Y., 1983), 11–12, which relies on Verba and Pye's definitions of political culture as "the system of empirical beliefs, expressive symbols, and values which defines the situation in which political action takes place." This view of political culture also embraces "the life histories of the individuals who make up the system," and public events and private experiences that become "the collective expression of a political system." Lucian W. Pye and Sidney Verba, *Political Culture and Political Development* (Princeton, 1965): 8 (Verba) and 513 (Pye). I am viewing political culture, like class relations in E. P. Thompson's *The Making of the English Working Class* (London, 1963), as a process rather than a thing, not so much as a body of shared beliefs as a set of shared arguments or debates. As such political culture is constantly changing.

Insofar as women inhabited different "political systems" from men, they also maintained different political cultures. By "women's political culture" I mean the political culture specific to a particular group of women in a particular time and place when they come together outside the home. In this case the particular group of women are northern, Protestant, white, and predominantly middle-class.

It is useful to distinguish three levels of political culture that often coexist within any group of women: first, women's collective action outside their families; second, collective activity that expresses a female consciousness or awareness of women's actions undertaken *as women;* third, group activity with the explicit goal of advancing the rights or interests of women.

For an early discussion that dichotomized politics and culture in women's history, see "Politics and Culture in Women's History: A Symposium," *Feminist Studies* 6 (1980): 26–64. A recent example of comparative women's and men's political cultures is Paula Baker, *The Moral Frameworks of Public Life: Gender, Politics, and the State in Rural New York, 1870–1930* (New York, 1991).

5. For example, differences between middle-class women of socialist and mainstream political persuasions on the passage of mothers' pensions laws have been analyzed in Sherry Katz, "Dual Commitments: Feminism, Socialism, and Women's Political Activism in California, 1890–1920" (Ph.D. diss., UCLA, 1991), 510–20.

6. By "maternalism" historians have meant the female version of paternalism, the assumptions women reformers made about women's nature, and the policy strategies they devised to provide social protection for women's maternal responsibilities. One of the most thorough discussions of "maternalism" is Theda Skocpol, *Protecting Soldiers and Mothers: The Politics of Social Provision in the United States, 1870s–1920s* (Cambridge, 1992). Historians of women have debated the extent to which "relational" values of women activists can be called "feminist." See Karen Offen, "Defining Feminism: A Comparative Historical Approach," *Signs* 14 (1988): 119–57, and Nancy F. Cott, "Comment on Karen Offen's 'Defining Feminism,'" *Signs* 15 (1989): 203–5.

7. All scholarship in this field uses the term "welfare" anachronistically. Relying on English usage, Raymond Williams gives 1939 as the date when the term "welfare state" first entered the English vocabulary. See his *Keywords: A Vocabulary of Culture and Society* (New York, 1976), 281. For some useful definitions of "welfare," see Barbara Nelson, "The Origins of the Two-Channel Welfare State: Workmen's Compensation and Mother's Aid," in Linda Gordon, ed., *Women, the State, and Welfare* (Madison, Wis., 1990).

8. For a summary of mother's pensions statutes before 1913, see Edward T. Devine, "Pensions for Mothers," *The American Labor Legislation Review* 3

(1913): 191–201. See also Joanne Goodwin, "An American Experiment in Paid Motherhood: The Implementation of Mothers' Pensions in Early Twentieth-Century Chicago," *Gender & History* 4 (1992): 323–42; and Theda Skocpol, "An Unusual Victory for Public Benefits: The Wildfire Spread of Mothers' Pensions," in Skocpol, *Protecting Soldiers and Mothers.*

9. For a cogent definition of "welfare" as embracing more than AFDC, see Theodore R. Marmor, Jerry L. Mashaw, and Philip L. Harvey, *America's Misunderstood Welfare State: Persistent Myths, Enduring Realities* (New York, 1990). Nelson, in "The Origins of the Two-Channel Welfare State," broadened and critiqued the definition of welfare as "income-tested, noncontributory programs financed through the general revenue" (147).

10. Ann Shola Orloff argues, in "Gender in Early United States Social Policy," *Journal of Policy History* 3 (1991): 249–81, that mothers' pensions were the antecedents of survivor's insurance, not AFDC.

11. In steel making in Allegheny County, Pennsylvania, for example (admittedly at the extreme end of the spectrum), between July 1906 and June 1907 526 men died as a result of industrial injuries, an average of ten a week. Crystal Eastman, *Work-Accidents and the Law* (New York, 1919), ii.

12. Florence Kelley said this to highlight the high rate of industrial injuries in the United States, but she did not actually oppose mothers' pensions. An exception to the rule, Barbara Nelson's article, "The Origins of the Two-Channel Welfare State," discusses the connections between mothers' pensions and workmen's compensation.

    This comparison of women and men reformers differs from that offered by Gordon in "Social Insurance and Public Assistance." Focusing primarily on the Social Security Act of 1935, Linda Gordon highlighted the difference between the discourse of "rights" associated with "male" welfare benefits and the discourse of "needs" associated with "female" welfare benefits, the former being both substantially and culturally superior to the latter, the latter arising from the casework methods affiliated with women's charitable undertakings. This essay, encompassing labor legislation as well as the Social Security Act and taking a larger view of the interaction of men's and women's political cultures, argues that the critical difference between those two political cultures lay in the degree to which each drew on grass-roots support or scientifically based expertise.

13. This reform-history literature is vast. A classic in the field is Sidney Fine, *Laissez-Faire and the General Welfare State: A Study of Conflict in American Thought, 1865–1901* (Ann Arbor, 1956); an example of recent scholarship is Stanley Vittoz, *New Deal Labor Policy and the American Industrial Economy* (Chapel Hill, N.C., 1988). Eileen Boris has shown gender to be a basic component of this legislation. See Boris, "(En)gendering the New Deal Order: Labor Standard's Alternative Stream," paper delivered at North American Labor History Conference, October 1991, and Boris, *In Defense of Motherhood: The Politics of Industrial Homework in the United States, 1880s to 1980s* (Cambridge, forthcoming.)

14. Florence Kelley, *Twenty Questions about the Federal Amendment proposed by the National Woman's Party* (New York, 1922). For more on Kelley, see

Louise Wade, "Florence Kelley," in *Notable American Women;* Dorothy Rose Blumberg, *Florence Kelley: The Making of a Social Pioneer* (New York, 1966); and Josephine Goldmark, *Impatient Crusader: Florence Kelley's Life Story* (Urbana, Ill., 1953).

15. For women's hours legislation, see Kathryn Kish Sklar, " 'The Greater Part of the Petitioners Are Female': The Reduction of Women's Working Hours in the Paid Labor Force, 1840–1917," in Gary Cross, ed., *Worktime and Industrialization: An International History* (Philadelphia, 1988), 103–34. For Sheppard-Towner, see Molly Ladd-Taylor, "Hull House Goes to Washington: Women and the Children's Bureau," in Noralee Frankel and Nancy Schrom Dye, eds. *Gender, Class, Race and Reform in the Progressive Era* (Lexington, Ky., 1991), 110–26.

16. Alice Paul to Judith Hyams Douglas, Washington D.C., 5 August 1921, National Woman's Party Papers, Library of Congress, box 5. See also Nancy F. Cott, "The Equal Rights Amendment Conflict in the 1920s," in Marianne Hirsch and Evelyn Fox Keller, eds., *Conflicts in Feminism* (New York, 1990), 44–59.

17. *New York Times,* 23 Feb. 1922.

18. Freda Kirchwey to Florence Kelley, The Nation, 20 Vesey St., New York, 11 Jan. 1922, National Consumers' League Papers, Library of Congress, box C-4, "ERA Corres., 1922."

19. Nicholas Paine Gilman, *A Dividend to Labor: A Study of Employers' Welfare Institutions* (Boston, 1899). The paid position of "welfare manager" emerged in stores and factories in the first decade of the twentieth century to forestall legislation regulating the commercial and industrial workplace, or, where these laws were already passed, to supervise their implementation, and to placate consumers concerned about the welfare of wage-earning women and children. "Welfare work" was a term coined to describe the labor of "welfare managers." See, for example, William H. Tolman, *Social Engineering: A Record of Things Done by American Industrialists Employing Upwards to One and One-Half Million People* (New York, 1909), iii, and Stuart D. Brandes, *American Welfare Capitalism, 1880–1940* (Chicago, 1976), 21, 23. H. M. Gitelman has convincingly argued in "Welfare Capitalism Reconsidered," *Labor History* 33 (1992): 5–31, that welfare capitalism brought workers few benefits and that these were chiefly implemented as a strategy of increasing profits.

20. Marguerite Green, *The National Civic Federation and the American Labor Movement, 1900–1925* (Washington, D.C., 1956), 283, and Mrs. J. Bordon Harriman, *From Pinafores to Politics* (New York, 1923), 89.

21. For example, in *Some Ethical Gains through Legislation* (New York, 1905), Florence Kelley called hours laws for women "the statutory recognition of a right" (145). For a compelling analysis of rights and needs as dichotomous terms, see Nancy Fraser, "Women, Welfare, and the Politics of Need Interpretation," in Fraser, *Unruly Practices: Power, Discourse, and Gender in Contemporary Social Theory* (Minneapolis, Minn., 1989), 144–60.

22. For example, Florence Kelley used the term "welfare" in very specific ways, writing in her "Twenty Questions" pamphlet: "Why, indeed, should wage-earning women not be permitted to continue to get protective laws for their own health and welfare . . . ?" (6).

    Advocates of legislation for wage-earning women and children suffered a setback when the term "welfare legislation" came into widespread use in the early 1920s, but they had no alternative catchphrase to offer. Proponents of mothers' pensions referred to "the endowment of motherhood," opponents of child labor spoke of "the child's right to leisure," and advocates of laws limiting working hours called them "the statutory recognition of a right," but the concept of welfare entitlements had not yet emerged. Older notions about charity and newer attitudes about the state's responsibility to provide for the working poor intermingled. For example, some child-labor laws, written with the assumption that education was the child's chief route out of poverty, nevertheless exempted widows' children from compulsory-education statutes so they could help support their families. This exception enraged Florence Kelley, but it gratified more conservative child-welfare advocates. This theme is mentioned in Orloff, "Gender in Early U.S. Social Policy."

23. This interpretation of protective labor legislation for women as an entering wedge for the extension of state responsibility to other groups is particularly true of Florence Kelley, the single most effective campaigner for such legislation, and other leaders with whom she worked. See my forthcoming book, *Florence Kelley and Women's Political Culture: "Doing the Nation's Work,"* *1830–1930* (New Haven, 1994). This interpretation can be found in many of the first generation of historians who considered the issue. See especially Elizabeth Brandeis, "Labor Legislation," in John Commons, *History of Labor in the United States,* vol. 3 (New York, 1935; rpt. 1966), 399–700. Since 1970 historians of women have usually emphasized three other factors: the advantages male unionists gained from such legislation when it had the effect of excluding women from their trade; the acceptance of legislative strategies for women by most women trade unionists; and the imposition of middle-class values, which kept women and children out of the paid labor force, on working-class women and children. The most complete exploration of these factors can be found in Alice Kessler-Harris, *Out to Work: A History of Wage-Earning Women in the United States* (New York, 1982), 180–214. These interpretations are not mutually exclusive. By emphasizing the earlier one I am urging historians to see women's efforts in their largest social, political, and economic context.

24. On "Republican Motherhood," see Kathryn Kish Sklar, *Catharine Beecher: A Study in American Domesticity* (New Haven, 1973), 151–68, and Linda Kerber, *Women of the Republic: Intellect and Ideology in Revolutionary America* (Chapel Hill, N.C., 1980), 165–88.

25. The extensive writings on the vitality of northern middle-class women's political activism before 1860 include: Carroll Smith–Rosenberg, "Beauty, the Beast, and the Militant Woman: A Case Study in Sex Roles and Social Stress in Jacksonian America," *American Quarterly* 23 (1971): 562–84; Mary Ryan, *Cradle of the Middle Class: The Family in Oneida County, New York,*

1790–1865 (Cambridge, 1981); Susan Porter Benson, "Business Heads and Sympathizing Hearts: The Women of the Providence Employment Society, 1837–1858, *Journal of Social History* 12 (1978): 302–12; Nancy Hewitt, *Women's Activism and Social Change: Rochester, New York, 1822–1872* (Ithaca, N.Y., 1984); and Lori D. Ginzberg, *Women and the Work of Benevolence: Morality, Politics, and Class in the Nineteenth-Century United States* (New Haven, 1990). White southern women lacked the corporate traditions of religion and community that women drew on in the North and therefore could not speak for the welfare of the whole nearly so effectively. See Suzanne Lebsock, *The Free Women of Petersburg: Status and Culture in a Southern Town, 1784–1860* (New York, 1984).

26. Smith-Rosenberg's "Beauty, the Beast, and the Militant Woman" remains the best treatment of the AFMRS. Their work was partly political since their goals included obtaining the passage of laws about seduction. See also Barbara Berg, *The Remembered Gate: Origins of American Feminism: The Woman and the City, 1800–1860* (New York, 1978), and Hewitt, *Women's Activism and Social Change.*

27. Quoted in Nancy F. Cott, *The Bonds of Womanhood: "Woman's Sphere" in New England, 1780–1835* (New Haven, 1977), 152.

28. Historians have emphasized the similarities between the AFMRS and Josephine Butler's later attack on the Contagious Diseases Act in England between 1870 and 1886, which also befriended prostitutes. Seeking to curb venereal disease in the nation's armed forces, the Contagious Diseases Act required "any woman who goes to places of public resort, and is known to go with different men," to register with the police and undergo regular medical examination. See Judith R. Walkowitz, *Prostitution and Victorian Society: Women, Class, and the State* (Cambridge, 1980), 80. Yet one crucial difference between these two expressions of cross-class solidarity reveals a great deal about the different bases for women's political activism in the two nations after 1870. The Ladies National Association for the Repeal of the Contagious Diseases Act opposed an activist state. The American Female Moral Reform Society opposed the voluntary actions of men. American political traditions, especially the commitment to limited government, rendered initiatives like the Contagious Diseases Act impossible at the national level and highly unlikely at local levels of government. However similar the AFMRS and the LNA might look to us today, the two groups were responding to and shaped by quite different political environments. In England an activist government tended to draw women into agendas determined by men. In the United States traditions of limited government drew women into public-policy gaps untended by men.

29. See Kathryn Kish Sklar, " 'Women Who Speak for an Entire Nation': American and British Women Compared at the World Anti-Slavery Convention, London, 1840," in Jean Fagan Yellin and John C. Van Horne, eds., *An Untrodden Path: Antislavery and Women's Political Culture* (Ithaca, N.Y., 1993).

30. Surprisingly little has been written on the process of religious disestablishment. An exception is John D. Cush, "Notes on Disestablishment in Massa-

chusetts, 1780–1833," *William and Mary Quarterly* 26 (1969): 169–90. For the effects of disestablishment, see Nathan O. Hatch, *The Democratization of American Christianity* (New Haven, 1989); Donald Scott, *From Office to Profession: The New England Ministry, 1750–1850* (Philadelphia, 1978); and Ann Douglas, *The Feminization of American Culture* (New York, 1977).

31. Chilton Williamson, *American Suffrage from Property to Democracy, 1760–1860* (Princeton, 1960). For British suffrage see Neal Blewett, "The Franchise in the United Kingdom, 1885–1918," *Past & Present* 32 (1965): 27–56.

32. The fullest treatment of the topic is Jutta Schwarzkopf, *Women in the Chartist Movement* (New York, 1991). See also Dorothy Thompson, *The Chartists: Popular Politics in the Industrial Revolution* (New York, 1984).

33. Elizabeth Pease to Maria Weston Chapman, 10 Jan. 1853, s.A.9.2.p.4, Boston Public Library. See also Sklar, " 'Women Who Speak for an Entire Nation.' "

34. For this comparison see especially Lawrence Goldman, "A Peculiarity of the English? The Social Science Association and the Absence of Sociology in Nineteenth-Century Britain," *Past & Present* 114 (1987): 133–71; Dorothy Ross, *The Origins of American Social Science* (Cambridge, 1991); and Irmela Gorges, "The Social Survey in Germany before 1933," in Martin Bulmer, Kevin Bales, and Kathryn Kish Sklar, eds., *The Social Survey in Historical Perspective* (Cambridge, 1992), 316–39.

35. See Ari Hoogenboom, *Outlawing the Spoils: A History of the Civil Service Reform Movement, 1865–1883* (Urbana, Ill., 1961).

36. See Stephen Skowronek, *Building a New American State: The Expansion of National Administrative Capacities, 1877–1920* (Cambridge, 1982), 48.

37. The classic comment on the role of political parties in the American polity is James Bryce, *The American Commonwealth* (London, 1888), 2 vols. See also Skowronek, *Building a New American State*.

38. Richard L. McCormick, in *The Party Period and Public Policy: American Politics from the Age of Jackson to the Progressive Era* (New York, 1986), noted: "By the early 1900s the party period's practice no longer matched the country's social circumstances" (221).

39. Josephine Shaw Lowell to Mrs. Charles Fairchild, Southampton, 17 July 1886, Josephine Shaw Lowell Papers, New York Historical Society. However, the Independent Republican or Mugwump movement was distinctly unfriendly to women's political participation. See John G. Sproat, *"The Best Men": Liberal Reformers in the Gilded Age* (New York, 1968), 252–53.

40. Examples of a vast literature are David P. Thelen, *The New Citizenship: Origins of Progressivism in Wisconsin, 1885–1900* (Columbia, Md., 1972); Thomas R. Pegram, *Partisans and Progressives: Private Interest and Public Policy in Illinois, 1870–1922* (Urbana, Ill., 1992); Richard L. McCormick, *From Realignment to Reform: Political Change in New York State, 1893–1910* (Ithaca, N.Y., 1981); and Richard Stephen Skolnik, "The Crystallization of Reform in New York City, 1890–1917" (Ph.D. diss., Yale University, 1964).

41. See, for example, Mary Ann Clawson, *Constructing Brotherhood: Class, Gender, and Fraternalism* (Princeton, 1989); Thomas J. E. Walker, *Pluralistic*

Fraternity: The History of the International Worker's Order (New York, 1991); Maximilian Hurwitz, *The Workmen's Circle: Its History, Ideals, Organization and Institutions* (New York, 1936); Margaret Galey, "Ethnicity, Fraternalism, Social and Mental Health," *Ethnicity* 4 (1977): 19–53; Terance O'Donnell, *History of Life Insurance in Its Formative Years* (Chicago, 1936); Michael R. Weisser, *A Brotherhood of Memory: Jewish Landsmanshaftn in the New World* (New York, 1985); M. Mark Stolarik, "A Place for Everyone: Slovak Faternal-Benefit Societies," in Scott Cummings, ed., *Self-Help in Urban America: Patterns of Minority Business Enterprise* (Port Washington, N.Y., 1980); and Elsa Barkley Brown, "Womanist Consciousness: Maggie Lena Walker and the Independent Order of Saint Luke," *Signs* 14 (1989): 921–29.

42. Nick Salvatore, *Eugene V. Debs: Citizen and Socialist* (Urbana, Ill., 1982), 264–67. See also Dorothy Ross, "Socialism and American Liberalism: Academic Thought in the 1800's," *Perspectives in American History* 11 (1977–78): 5–80.

43. Selig Perlman, *A Theory of the Labor Movement* (New York, 1928), 167, was the first to note the negative effects of the ballot on American working-class political consciousness. See also Richard Oestreicher, "Urban Working-Class Political Behavior and Theories of American Electoral Politics, 1870–1940," *Journal of American History* 74 (1988): 1257–86. For the British contrary example, see Maureen Tomison, *The English Sickness: The Rise of Trade Union Political Power* (London, 1972).

44. Bessie Louise Pierce, *A History of Chicago*, vol. 3: *The Rise of a Modern City, 1871–1893* (Chicago, 1957), 360.

45. The classic discussion of this topic around which much debate has swirled is Werner Sombart, *Why Is There No Socialism in the United States?* (1906: rpt. White Plains, N.Y., 1976).

46. See Gerald G. Eggert, *Railroad Labor Disputes: The Beginnings of Federal Strike Policy* (Ann Arbor, 1967), and William E. Forbath, *Law and the Shaping of the American Labor Movement* (Cambridge, 1991), 59–97.

47. Forbath, *Law and the Shaping of the American Labor Movement*, 37–58.

48. Samuel Gompers, *Seventy Years of Life and Labor*, 2 vols. (New York, 1925), 1:194. See also Boris, *In Defense of Motherhood*, chapter 1.

49. See Michael Rogin "Voluntarism: The Political Functions of an Antipolitical Doctrine," *Industrial and Labor Relations Review* 15 (1962): 521–35, and Leon Fink, "Labor, Liberty and the Law: Trade Unionism and the Problem of the American Constitutional Order," *Journal of American History* 74 (1987): 904–25.

50. One classic description is Selig Perlman and Philip Taft, "Class War on a Grand Scale," in *Labor Movements: History of Labor in the United States, 1896–1932*, vol. 6 (New York, 1935), 189–208. See also Jeremy Brecher, *Strike!* (Boston, 1972); Nick Salvatore, *Eugene V. Debs: Citizen and Socialist* (Urbana, Ill., 1982); and Ronald L. Filippelli, ed., *Labor Conflict in the United States: An Encyclopedia* (New York, 1990).

51. In the U.S. 2 of every 100,000 striking workers were killed. In France 3 per 100,000 were injured. See Forbath, *Law and the Shaping of the American*

Labor Movement, 106, and James Holt, "Trade Unionism in the British and U.S. Steel Industries, 1888–1912: A Comparative Study," *Labor History* 18 (1977): 3–35.

52. Women were prominent in efforts to achieve industrial arbitration. See Josephine Shaw Lowell, *Industrial Arbitration and Conciliation* (New York, 1893), and Jane Addams, *Twenty Years at Hull House* (New York, 1912), 218. Between 1901 and 1905 fewer than 8 percent of strikes were settled with joint agreement or arbitration. U.S. Commissioner of Labor, *Report* (Washington, D.C., 1906), 36–37, 425–71. See also Gerald Friedman, "Worker Militancy and Its Consequences: Political Responses to Labor Unrest in the United States, 1877–1914," *International Labor and Working Class History* 40 (1991): 5–17.

53. See Henry Demarest Lloyd, *Henry Demarest Lloyd and the Empire of Reform* (Philadelphia, 1963); Harry Barnard, *Eagle Forgotten: The Life of John Peter Altgeld* (Secaucus, N.J., 1938); and Salvatore, *Eugene V. Debs.*

54. Mary O. Furner, *Advocacy and Objectivity: A Crisis in the Professionalization of American Social Science, 1865–1905* (Lexington, Ky., 1975), 150–58.

55. See Richard Ely, *Ground under Our Feet: An Autobiography* (New York, 1938), and Ross, *The Origins of American Social Science,* 138.

56. The absence of social conscience among leading industrialists was captured in the phrase "Robber Barons." See Matthew Josephson, *The Robber Barons: The Great American Capitalists, 1861–1901* (New York, 1934). Although the large fortunes accumulated in the nineteenth century by Carnegie, Rockefeller, Mellon, and others later endowed philanthropic foundations, with the exception of the Russell Sage Foundation they did very little to shape welfare policies before 1920. For that exception, founded by Margaret Olivia Sage, see John M. Glenn, Lillian Brandt, and F. Emerson Andrews, *Russell Sage Foundation, 1907–1946,* 2 vols. (New York, 1947). For campaigns against infant mortality see Richard Meckel, *Save the Babies: American Public Health Reform and the Prevention of Infant Mortality, 1850–1929* (Baltimore, 1990).

57. See Edward Berkowitz and Kim McQuaid, *Creating the Welfare State: The Political Economy of Twentieth-Century Reform* (New York, 1980); David Brody, *Workers in Industrial America: Essays on the Twentieth-Century Struggle* (New York, 1980), chapter 2; and Stuart Brandes, *American Welfare Capitalism,* chapters 1 and 14. An older consensus view of the topic can be found in Morrell Heald, "Business Thought in the Twenties: Social Responsibility," *American Quarterly* 13 (1961): 126–39.

58. On conservative reform in England, see F. M. L. Thompson, *English Landed Society in the Nineteenth Century* (London, 1963); Paul Smith, *Disraelian Conservatism and Social Reform* (London, 1967); and José Harris, *Unemployment and Politics: A Study in English Social Policy, 1886–1914* (Oxford, 1972). For Roosevelt's reform style see Howard Lawrence Hurwitz, *Theodore Roosevelt and Labor in New York State, 1880–1900* (New York, 1943). The natural source of conservative anti-industrial opinion in the United States lay in the South, but in this post–Civil War era that region was politically discredited and absorbed in its own recovery problems.

59. The best summary of this is Lizabeth Cohen, *Making a New Deal: Industrial Workers in Chicago, 1919–1939* (Cambridge, 1991), 62–64.

60. See David P. Thelen, "Urban Politics: Beyond Bosses and Reformers," *Reviews in American History* 7 (1979): 406–12; Jon Teaford, "Finis for Tweed and Steffens: Rewriting the History of Urban Rule," *Reviews in American History* 10 (1982): 201–4; M. Craig Brown and Charles N. Halaby, "Machine Politics in America, 1870–1945," *Journal of Interdisciplinary History* 17 (1987): 587–612; Terrence J. McDonald, *The Parameters of Urban Fiscal Policy: Socioeconomic Change and Political Culture in San Francisco, 1860–1906* (Berkeley, 1986); Jon Teaford, *The Unheralded Triumph: City Government in America, 1870–1900* (Baltimore, 1984).

61. See Ginzberg, *Women and the Work of Benevolence*, 133–73. For the implications of the lack of such developments in the South, see George Rable, *Civil Wars: Women and the Crisis of Southern Nationalism* (Urbana, Ill., 1989).

62. Ruth Bordin, *Woman and Temperance: The Quest for Liberty and Power, 1873–1900* (Philadelphia, 1981), 98.

63. In the 1893 depression, for example, the city had little to offer thousands of homeless unemployed people (mostly men) who thronged the lakefront. See, for example, the *Chicago Tribune*, 27 August 1893, "Clash with a Mob."

64. Bordin, *Woman and Temperance*, 29. See also Brian Harrison, *Drink and the Victorians: The Temperance Question in England, 1815–1872* (Pittsburgh, 1971).

65. This conclusion about British women's social activism is based on a wide range of writings, including Jill Liddington and Jill Norris, *One Hand Tied behind Us: The Rise of the Women's Suffrage Movement* (London, 1978); Walkowitz, *Prostitution and Victorian Society;* Jean Gaffin and David Thoms, *Caring and Sharing: The Centenary History of the Co-operative Women's Guild* (Manchester, Eng., 1983); Martha Vicinus, *Independent Women: Work and Community for Single Women, 1850–1920* (Chicago, 1985); Patricia Hollis, *Ladies Elect: Women in English Local Government, 1865–1914* (Oxford, Eng., 1987); Jane Rendall, ed., *Equal or Different: Women's Politics, 1800–1914* (Oxford, Eng., 1987); Deborah Dwork, *War is Good for Babies and Other Young Children: A History of the Infant and Child Welfare Movement in England, 1898–1918* (London, 1987).

66. Barbara Miller Solomon, *In the Company of Educated Women: A History of Women and Higher Education in America* (New Haven, 1985), 63. For higher education among British and European women, see Vicinus, *Independent Women;* James C. Albisetti, *Schooling German Girls and Women: Secondary and Higher Education in the Nineteenth Century* (Princeton, 1988); and Karen Offen, "The Second Sex and the Baccalauréat in Republican France, 1880–1924," *French Historical Studies* 3 (1983): 252–86.

67. See Kathryn Kish Sklar, "The Founding of Mount Holyoke College," in Carol Ruth Berkin and Mary Beth Norton, eds., *Women of America: A History* (Boston, 1979), 177–201; Richard M. Bernard and Maris A. Vinovskis, "The Female School Teacher in Ante-Bellum Massachusetts," *Journal of Social History* 10 (1977): 332–45; Solomon, *In the Company of Educated Women,*

46–47; Polly Welts Kaufman, *Women Teachers on the Frontier* (New Haven, 1984); and Nancy Hoffman, *Woman's "True" Profession: Voices from the History of Teaching* (Old Westbury, N.Y., 1981).

68. Solomon, *In the Company of Educated Women,* 63.

69. Vida Scudder, "The Relation of College Women to Social Need," *Association of Collegiate Alumnae Publications,* series 2, no. 30 (October 1890): 2–3.

70. Mary I. Wood, *The History of the General Federation of Women's Clubs* (New York, 1912), 353. See also Estelle Freedman, "Separatism as Strategy: Female Institution Building, 1870–1930," *Feminist Studies* 5 (1979): 512–29.

71. Chicago Women's Club Minutes, Chicago Women's Club Papers, Chicago Historical Society. See also Amalie Hofer Jerome, *Annals of the Chicago Woman's Club for the First Forty Years of Its Organization* (Chicago, 1916). (Although historians of women have identified a contrary trend, in the 1890s the club changed its name from "Women's" to "Woman's.")

72. See, "Ellen Martin Henrotin," *Notable American Women.* For an illuminating window on her associative world, see Ellen M. Henrotin, "The Attitude of Women's Clubs and Associations toward Social Economics," *Bulletin* of the Department of Labor, no. 23 (July 1899), Washington, D.C.

73. Wood, *History of the General Federation of Women's Clubs,* 111.

74. Ibid.

75. See Skocpol, "An Unusual Victory for Public Benefits," and Orloff, "Gender in Early United States Social Policy."

76. Wood, *History of the General Federation of Women's Clubs,* 309.

77. Ibid.

78. For an explicit contrast between women's and men's political cultures, see Maureen Flanagan, "Gender and Urban Political Reform: The City Club and the Woman's City Club of Chicago in the Progressive Era," *American Historical Review* 95 (1990): 1032–50.

79. The other two departments were "Jurisprudence," and "Finance." *Journal of Social Science* 16 (1882): 98, quoted in Thomas Haskell, *The Emergence of Professional Social Science: The American Social Science Association and the Nineteenth-Century Crisis of Authority* (Urbana, Ill., 1977), 137. Limited in its purview as it might be, the Social Economy Division of the American Social Science Association became the chief arm of the Association's efforts to influence public policy. In 1881 Sanford said that the Association's "work of agitation and indoctrination" sprang out of "our department of social economy." *Journal of Social Science* (Nov. 1881): 33.

80. William Leach, *True Love and Perfect Union: The Feminist Reform of Sex and Society* (New York, 1980), 317.

81. Herbert Gutman was working on this interpretation at the time of his death. See Herbert G. Gutman, *Power and Culture: Essays on the American Working Class* (New York, 1987), 339.

82. See, for example, Susan Porter Benson, *Counter Cultures: Saleswomen, Managers, and Customers in American Department Stores, 1890–1940* (Urbana, Ill., 1986), and Louis L. Athey, "The Consumers' Leagues and Social Reform, 1890–1923" (Ph.D. diss., University of Delaware, 1965).

83. See Kathryn Kish Sklar, "Hull House as a Community of Women Reformers in the 1890s," *Signs* 10 (1985): 657–77.

84. Addams, *Twenty Years at Hull House,* 85.

85. See Sklar, "Hull House as a Community of Women Reformers"; Joyce Antler, " 'After College, What?': New Graduates and the Family Claim," *American Quarterly* 32 (1980): 409–34; and John P. Rousmanière, "Cultural Hybrid in the Slums: The College Woman and the Settlement House, 1889–1894," *American Quarterly* 22 (1970): 45–66.

86. Most settlements were Protestant. For Catholic or Jewish settlements, see Allan F. Davis, *Spearhead for Reform: The Social Settlements and the Progressive Movement, 1890–1914* (New York, 1987), 15. Of the forty settlements founded in Chicago between 1889 and 1910, two were sponsored by Catholics, three by Jews, and two by universities. See Robert A. Woods and Albert J. Kennedy, eds., *Handbook of Settlements* (New York, 1911). For the positive effect of Jane Addams's example on Catholic laywomen, see Mary J. Oates, "The Role of Laywomen in American Catholic Philanthropy, 1820–1920," *U.S. Catholic Historian* 9 (1990): 249–60. For welfare work among black women, see Gordon, "Black and White Visions of Welfare." For social science in the settlements, see Kathryn Kish Sklar, "Hull House Maps and Papers: Social Science as Women's Work in the 1890s," in Bulmer, Bales, and Sklar, *The Social Survey in Historical Perspective*, 111–47. Settlements also gave rise to graduate schools for training social workers. See Mina Carson, *Settlement Folk: Social Thought and the American Settlement Movement, 1885–1930* (Chicago, 1990), 122–38; and Robyn Muncy, *Creating a Female Dominion in American Reform, 1890–1935* (New York, 1991), 66–68.

87. Kathryn Kish Sklar, "Who Funded Hull House?" in Kathleen McCarthy, ed., *Lady Bountiful Revisited: Women, Philanthropy and Power* (New Brunswick, 1990), and Carson, *Settlement Folk,* 184.

88. Women with a stronger religious commitment than most settlement residents were drawn into the home and foreign-mission movement. See Patricia R. Hill, *The World Their Household: The American Woman's Foreign Mission Movement and Cultural Transformation, 1870–1920* (Ann Arbor, 1985). A survey of American settlement head residents and residents in 1896 showed that a majority of head residents were women, 66 percent of residents were women, and 75 percent of settlement clientele were women. Julia Lathrop, "What the Settlement Work Stands For," in Isabel C. Barrows, ed., *A Report of the National Conference of Charities and Correction, 1896* (Boston, 1896), 106–10, 166–76. For British settlements, see Seth Koven, "Culture and Poverty: The London Settlement House Movement, 1870–1914," (Ph.D. Diss., Harvard University, 1987); and Standish Meacham, *Toynbee Hall and Social Reform, 1880–1914: The Search for Community* (New Haven, 1987).

89. Women's "disabilities" was the term that both sides of the ERA argument used to summarize women's particular political situation in 1920.

90. Skocpol, "An Unusual Victory for Public Benefits."

91. See, for example, the reprint of an address by William Allen in Wood, *History of the General Federation of Women's Clubs*, 353–72.

92. Muncy, *Creating a Female Dominion*, 40–41.

93. 3 March 1895. Minutes, Illinois Manufacturers' Association, IMA Papers, Chicago Historical Society.

94. See Marguerite Green, "The National Civic Federation and the American Labor Movement, 1900–1925," (Ph.D. diss., Catholic University, 1956).

95. Isaac M. Rubinow, *The Quest for Security* (New York, 1934), 430. See also Udo Sautter, *Three Cheers for the Unemployed: Government and Unemployment before the New Deal* (Cambridge, 1991), and W. Andrew Achenbaum, *Old Age in the New Land: The American Experience since 1790* (Baltimore, 1978), 127–42.

96. Quoted in Rubinow, *The Quest for Security*, 432. See also Rubinow, 100–102; Sautter, *Three Cheers for the Unemployed*, 208–14. Another example along the same lines was worker's compensation for job-related injuries, which neither organized labor nor women's organizations adopted as a top priority. Reformers/experts like John Andrews of the American Association for Labor Legislation had to do their best in advancing the issue against the well-organized opposition of insurance companies. Employers were not united on the question, however, and some, seeking to avoid costly court settlements arising from industrial injuries, shaped state compensation plans to their advantage. New York was typical. See Robert F. Wesser, "Conflict and Compromise: The Workmen's Compensation Movement in New York, 1890s–1913," *Labor History* 11 (1971); 345–72, and Robert Asher, "The Limits of Big Business Paternalism: Relief for Injured Workers in the Years before Workmen's Compensation," in David Rosner and Gerald Markowitz, eds., *Dying for Work: Workers' Safety and Health in Twentieth–Century America* (Bloomington, Ind., 1989), 19–34. The absence of grass-roots support either delayed the adoption of these measures far beyond the time of their implementation in Great Britain or resulted in plans that gave workers substantially less than equivalent British and European programs.

97. The pages of *The American Labor Legislation Review* (1911–1942) are filled with this debate.

98. See Rosalyn Terborg-Penn, "African-American Women's Networks in the Anti-Lynching Crusade," in Frankel and Dye, *Gender, Class, Race and Reform in the Progressive Era*, 148–61; Deborah Grey White, "Race, Class and Gender: Black Women in the Twentieth Century," paper presented at SUNY Binghamton, April 1992; Boris, "The Power of Motherhood; and Gordon, "Black and White Visions of Welfare."

99. See Faith Rogow, "Gone to Another Meeting: A History of the National Council of Jewish Women" (Ph.D. diss., SUNY Binghamton, 1989), and Doris Groshen Daniels, *Always a Sister: The Feminism of Lillian D. Wald* (New York, 1989), 36–41.

100. See Sklar, "Hull House as a Community of Women Reformers in the 1890s"; "In Defense of Motherhood," chapter 2; and Henrotin, "The Attitude of Women's Clubs and Associations toward Social Economics." Commissioned by the Department of Labor in 1899, Henrotin's survey of 2,110 clubs and 132,023 members affiliated with the General Federation of Women's Clubs, found that 33 percent of the responding clubs engaged in "practical work" related to "sociology, political economy, or philanthropy," and most planned to inaugurate such activities.

101. Mary E. Mumford, "The Place of Women in Municipal Reform," *The Outlook* 49 (31 Mar. 1894): 587–88.

102. This distinction between American and European expressions of social democracy draws on James T. Kloppenberg, *Uncertain Victory: Social Democracy and Progressivism in European and American Thought, 1870–1920* (New York, 1986), 199–224.

103. Standard sources by Addams on social democracy are "The Subjective Necessity for Social Settlements" and "The Objective Value of a Social Settlement," in (no editor) *Philanthropy and Social Progress* (New York, 1893), 1–56; *Democracy and Social Ethics* (New York, 1907); and *Twenty Years at Hull House* (New York, 1910). See also Carson, *Settlement Folk*, passim.

104. See Sidney G. Tarrow, "Lochner versus New York: A Political Analysis," *Labor History* 5 (1964): 277–312.

105. See Sybil Lipschultz, "Social Feminism and Legal Discourse: 1908–1923," *Yale Journal of Law and Feminism* 2 (1989): 131–60, and "The Brandeis Brief," in Goldmark, *Impatient Crusader*, 143–59.

106. Florence Kelley, "Hours and Wages," *Survey* 37 (30 Dec. 1916): 358. See also Anson Rabinbach, *The Human Motor: Energy, Fatigue and the Origins of Modernity* (New York, 1990).

107. Florence Kelley, "The Courts and Labor Laws," unpublished manuscript, n.d., Nicholas Kelley Papers, New York Public Library.

108. Vivien Hart, "Minimum Wage Policy and Constitutional Inequality: The Paradox of the Fair Labor Standards Act of 1938," *Journal of Policy History* 1 (1989): 319–43, and Eileen Boris, "Homework Regulation and the Devolution of the Post-War Labor Standards Regime," in Christopher Tomlins, ed., *Labor Law in America: Historical and Critical Perspectives* (Baltimore, forthcoming). See also J. Joseph Huthmacher, *Senator Robert F. Wagner and the Rise of the Urban Liberalism* (New York, 1968), for the background of New Deal labor policy.

109. *National Consumers' League, Tenth Report, for Two Years Ending March 2, 1909* (New York, 1909), 22.

110. See annual reports of National Consumers' League, NCL Papers, Library of Congress.

111. See, for example, John Commons to Henry W. Farnam, 25 Dec. 1909, American Association for Labor Legislation Papers, Cornell University, reel 2.

112. Florence Kelley's phrase, "the nation's work," appeared in "A Decade of Retrogression," *The Arena* 4 (1891): 365–72.

113. See Nancy F. Cott, *The Grounding of Modern Feminism* (New Haven, 1987).

114. As an example of the pre-1920 links between reform and religion see Herbert G. Gutman, "Protestantism and the American Labor Movement: The Christian Spirit in the Gilded Age," in Gutman, *Work, Culture and Society in Industrializing America: Essays in American Working-Class and Social History* (New York, 1976), 79–118, and Susan Curtis, *A Consuming Faith: The Social Gospel and Modern American Culture* (Baltimore, 1992). For the post-1920 absence of such links see Robert Moats Miller, *American Protestantism and Social Issues, 1919–1939* (Chapel Hill, N.C., 1958).

115. Muncy, *Creating a Female Dominion*, 124–57; Anne Firor Scott, *Natural Allies: Women's Associations in American History* (Urbana, Ill., 1991), 173; Daniel Walkowitz, "The Making of a Feminine Professional Identity: Social Workers in the 1920s," *American Historical Review* 95 (1990): 1051–75. For the effect of women's diminished power on mothers' pensions laws, see Christopher Howard, "Sowing the Seeds of 'Welfare': The Transformation of Mothers' Pensions, 1900–1940," *Journal of Policy History* 4 (1992): 188–227.

116. See "The Spider Web," in J. Stanley Lemons, *The Woman Citizen: Social Feminism in the 1920s* (Urbana, Ill., 1973), 209–27, and Cott, *The Grounding of Modern Feminism*, 242–59.

117. See especially chapter 1 in Christopher Lasch, *Haven in a Heartless World: The Family Besieged* (New York, 1977).

118. Lloyd F. Pierce, "The Activities of the American Association for Labor Legislation in Behalf of Social Security and Protective Labor Legislation," Ph.D. diss., University of Wisconsin, 1953, 254–94, and Muncy, *Creating a Female Dominion*, 93–123.

119. See Susan Ware, *Beyond Suffrage: Women in the New Deal* (Cambridge, Mass., 1981).

2

Borderlands: Women, Voluntary Action, and Child Welfare in Britain, 1840 to 1914

Seth Koven

Introduction

One of the most striking features of social welfare in Victorian and Edwardian Britain was the powers granted to local agents of authority, far from Whitehall, who wielded enormous influence over the type of services and resources available to the poor in their communities. Well into the twentieth century, a great deal of public-welfare legislation that intervened in the heretofore private affairs of individuals and families was permissive, and not mandatory. The decision to adopt this so-called "enabling" legislation was left to the discretion of local ratepayers and executed by local authorities working in concert with existing voluntary organizations. As a consequence, the history of social welfare in Britain is as much the story of local government, private voluntary societies, and individual initiative as it is the story of the emergence and growth of central state bureaucracies and directives.

The local and voluntary character of Victorian social welfare profoundly affected not only the nature of the British state, but the relationship of men and women both to the state and to the construction of social welfare. While British historians have exhaustively argued the causes and nature of the so-called "Victorian Revolution in Government," these same scholars have been much less attentive to the roles women played as policy makers, care providers, and clients in the construction of British welfare policies and programs. This oversight stems partly from the fact that these histories have been written from the records of the official central state run by male bureaucrats and politicians. These studies have failed to look closely at those places where women were most influential: in their localities as elected and appointed officials and as leaders and rank-and-file members of voluntary societies that addressed every conceivable social problem. In their zeal to trace the origins of central government, they have minimized the role of local government, and hence of women as well.

Many leading state-welfare bureaucrats in the twentieth century openly acknowledged the pivotal role of voluntary initiative in forging the welfare state. Sir Hubert Llewellyn Smith, at the twilight of his illustrious career of public service in 1937, rejected out of hand the notion that the growth of state welfare was incompatible with the continued vigor and expansion of the voluntary sector. "Only rarely can a hard and fast line of demarcation be drawn" between public and voluntary action. "It is a much more fruitful conception," he continued, "to regard the two realms of public and private service as being united rather than separated by a borderland zone within which both may act freely in cooperation."[1] William Beveridge echoed this sentiment in his study *Voluntary Action* (1948) published a few years after his famous "Beveridge Report," which has traditionally been viewed as the cornerstone of the modern welfare state in Britain.[2]

Voluntary associations were merely convenient stepping stones for men like Smith and Beveridge as they sought and gained direct access to power within the official central state. Historians of social welfare have reproduced Smith and Beveridge's views by describing voluntary associations as pressure or lobbying groups on the state or as training grounds for careers in public office and the civil service.[3] These accounts overlook the differing significance and function of voluntary associations for men and women, for enfranchised and disenfranchised social actors. The most obvious difference is the fact that no female actor was allowed to follow Smith and Beveridge's paths to power within the central state bureaucracy. As a consequence, many women in the decades before they gained the vote necessarily saw their work in voluntary associations as the most efficacious and sometimes only arena for their engagement in public life and social policy.[4]

Victorian middle-class women's voluntary associations linked the private, female world of household and family to the public, male-dominated world of politics.[5] Their voluntary associational activities depended upon but ultimately challenged the distinction between the state as the site of public political life and civil society as the location of private productive and reproductive activities. In their roles as social reformers, activists, workers, and consumers, women moved between the supposedly discrete spheres of public and private, revealing the artificiality of bipolar constructions of these categories.

This essay explores the varying ways in which women gained power and political expertise, but were also constrained by their work in private-sector voluntary associations. My examples are drawn from the history of child welfare in Britain from the mid-nineteenth century until World War I. My choices deliberately highlight the diversity of ideological and political commitments women brought to bear on the state as voluntary workers: Mary Carpenter's genteel, nonconformist political program to rescue juvenile delinquents from the adult penal system; the progressive-conservative, antisuffrage civic maternalism of Mary (Mrs. Humphry) Ward; and the radical socialist-feminist child-welfare work of Margaret McMillan. The case study approach permits me to illuminate the particular ideological and political contexts in which these women developed their ideas about gender and social welfare and to delineate subtle distinctions between the ways in which individual figures accepted and challenged Victorian conventions of nurture and motherhood. The case studies demonstrate the ways in which the practice of women lives—and the ideologies that galvanized them to act—transformed the "borderland" from a place of passage between two discrete realms (state and civil society) into an arena of women's own self-activity and construction. Significantly, the case studies also underline the limits of voluntary action and maternalism for women as political actors.

The "Useful Power" of Ladies: Mary Carpenter, Juvenile Punishment, and the State

Mary Carpenter's work for the ragged and criminal children of Bristol in the 1840s and 1850s made her an international celebrity.[6] It also secured her a place in the pantheon of "eminent" women constructed by twentieth-century feminists anxious to reclaim a usable past to suit their own political needs.[7] Her career as the architect of a national system of juvenile reformatories is emblematic of women's powers to initiate social-welfare policies that were later subsidized or absorbed by the state; it also serves as a cautionary tale underlining the obstacles women faced in their encounters with the mid-Victorian state.

Carpenter's personal background encapsulates most of the sources of women's activism that historians have identified as crucial to the mobilization of Victorian women's movements.[8] She was a nonconformist, educated to become a governess and school teacher. Within evangelical and nonconformist circles, it was not unusual for women to devote themselves to social welfare, in particular child reclamation and prison reform. Men and women from these circles also became leaders in the antislavery movement. Antislavery societies in England and America in the 1830s provided models of associational activity which women used to launch their own careers as public figures. Many Victorian women reformers, including Carpenter, adopted the moral fervor and language of Christian redemption that were so essential to the success of their abolitionist societies to legitimate their participation in the male world of politics.[9]

Mary Carpenter's young-adult life coincided with important changes in the character of the British state. Beginning with the passage of the Regulation of Mines Act in 1842, the state increasingly claimed the right to regulate the access of women and children to the labor market. The 1842 act purported to "protect" society's most vulnerable and dependent members from exploitation by industrial capitalism. As many scholars have rightly observed, "protection" cloaked male bourgeois anxieties about laboring men's positions within their families and working-class women's independence as wage earners. These scholars stress the repressive and patriarchal character of early state-welfare legislation. However, the assumptions underpinning factory legislation in the 1840s also provided middle-class women with opportunities to extend the scope of their public activism.

From the 1840s onward, a complex and enduring set of relationships emerged between children, women, and the state in Great Britain. These relationships delimited but also defined a specifically female sphere of knowledge and power which middle-class women used to shape public policy through their private, voluntary activities.[10] The Victorian state welcomed benevolent women activists to use voluntary networks on the local level to develop and execute innovative programs on behalf of women and children. Such efforts promised to curtail public expenditure, a cherished goal of reformers since the passage of the New Poor Law. This work also reinforced domestic ideals in two ways. It channeled middle-class women's activism into a traditionally female area of expertise, while providing mechanisms by which middle-class women could impose their domestic ideals on working-class women and children. Fiscal parsimony and domesticity were arguments calculated to appeal to men across the political spectrum in Victorian Britain. Not surprisingly, activist women selectively deployed such arguments in their public utterances.

In effect, an unstated and unacknowledged quid pro quo evolved in the 1840s. Women social reformers accepted (or, for strategic reasons, chose not to challenge) a gender-based division of labor and knowledge by focusing their claims to shape social-welfare programs to traditionally female spheres of competence. In return, the state implicitly allowed women to claim the space to develop an activist, associational culture which contributed to the strength and diversity of late-Victorian and Edwardian women's movements. While voluntary associations were particularly receptive to women, they rarely functioned as sites of an autonomous or exclusive female political culture. Many voluntary associations, like the Charity Organisation Society, included men in important positions of leadership; later in the century, even single-sex organizations, like women's settlements, had close ties to male supporters and operated within larger social and political structures dominated by men.

This was the setting in which Carpenter launched her first independent venture in 1846, a privately financed and run "school for ragged children" in the Lewin's Mead slum of Bristol. Linking the liberation of Africans from the oppression of slavery with her mission on behalf of the poor children of Bristol, Carpenter opened the school on the anniversary of the abolition of slavery in the British dominions.

Carpenter was well aware that the school's opening also inaugurated a new life for herself, a personal liberation from the stultifying prospects she faced as a middle-class spinster. Four years-later, she founded a reformatory school outside Bristol at Kingswood, the former home of John Wesley, the founder of Methodism. With the financial backing of her friend Lady Byron, she later opened a girls' reformatory at Red Lodge, the venture to which she principally devoted herself from 1854 to 1860. Sitting in her study at Kingswood, she read the words that the great man Wesley had etched into the glass pane: "God is here." Carpenter was a demanding and at times dictatorial woman. Her fellow workers may well have wondered if she had not taken Wesley's words too literally.

As she embarked on public work for poor and criminal children in the 1840s, Carpenter felt a heightened sense of individual worth stemming from her emerging female political self-consciousness.[11] She was motivated not only by duty but by the love she gave and received from the children.[12] This love satisfied emotional needs she believed were specific to women. Nearly thirty years later, she reflected upon "how much the useful power and influence of woman has developed. . . . Unattached ladies such as widows and unmarried women have quite ample work to do in the world, for the good of others, to absorb all their powers."[13] Carpenter saw herself as a public mother, a "mothers [sic] in heart, though not by God's gift on earth."[14] Despite her resolutely single life,[15] the family and women as mothers within it were central to her conception of herself and her work.[16]

Carpenter's stance was far from unique. Single women engaged in social work during the Victorian and Edwardian periods consistently extolled the family as the "natural" unit in which women belonged.[17] Some consciously chose to eschew family life and marriage.[18] Others simply lacked the option of marriage and became part of the growing corps of "redundant" women. These were the "useful women" whose labors Carpenter admired and for whom she herself later served as a conspicuous role model. Spinsters like Carpenter, by living unhusbanded but public lives, threatened Victorian society's vision of marriage as the natural foundation of social order. At the same time, this threat was vitiated by the way in which Carpenter and other "glorified spinsters" defined their roles as preservers, nurturers, and moralizers of a family-based society. One might also speculate that Carpenter's awareness of her anomalous position as a spinster in the public eye made her all the more zealous to present herself as otherwise conventional. An anonymous writer in *MacMillan's Magazine* perfectly captured the ambiguities of the position of women like Carpenter. While they were committed to purifying society, "like meteors, they wander free in inter-familiar space, obeying laws and conventions of their own." The author's language betrays the desire to frame spinsters discursively within the boundaries of the familiar. But the passage also intimates that this new class of person, the glorified spinster, cannot be contained or understood within the known universe of social experience.[19]

The Ragged School was a voluntary enterprise over which Carpenter had complete control. Carpenter, like the philanthropist Octavia Hill after her, opposed state-initiated welfare schemes. Her embrace of the principles of voluntarism was part and parcel of her inherited nonconformist distrust of all forms of government interference. She accepted state funding as an unfortunate necessity,[20] but insisted that its worst consequences could be mitigated by leaving the actual work in the hands of voluntary workers who alone were "the best means of supplying to the child the parental relation." Carpenter articulated an argument about the interdependent relationship of state and voluntary action in Britain whose echoes we still can hear today in policy debates: The face-to-face caring work of state welfare was left to voluntary workers, usually women, whose ministrations softened the impersonality and institutional rigidity of official masculine bureaucracies. The state intervened, Carpenter contended, merely so that children could be "restored to the natural condition of a family, and brought under individual influence."[21] In terms of her own life, Carpenter's work for children can be viewed as the means by which she, as a single woman, "restored" herself to the "natural condition of a family."[22]

With the publication of her widely acclaimed book *Reformatory Schools for the Children of the Perishing and Dangerous Classes and for Juvenile Offenders* in 1851, Carpenter suddenly captured a national audience for her work and ideas.[23] The book elaborated her case for the creation of a state-run institutional apparatus to rehabilitate juvenile offenders through education, love, and moral discipline free from the corrupting influence of hardened adult criminals.[24] The next year, she and Matthew Davenport Hill organized the first national Conference on Juvenile Delinquency at Birmingham.[25]

Carpenter's response to the tremendous success of her book and the role she insisted on playing at this conference illustrate her disquiet with her fame. Anxious not to violate notions of genteel womanly behavior, she refused to read her own paper or even speak at the conference she had organized. Authorship provoked a crisis of gender identity. "I used to think that I had more a masculine than a feminine nature, but I feel more and more than my essence is womanly in a peculiar degree."[26] The imperative "need to speak" on behalf of children enabled Carpenter to claim her own voice and her own womanliness. However, Carpenter's gratifying discovery of this voice and identity was accompanied by a self-imposed invisibility and silence at the Conference on Juvenile Delinquency that underscored her commitment to the restrictive conventions of female behavior of her class. Carpenter, like most middle-class female social reformers in Victorian Britain, anxiously negotiated the contradictions between the publicness of her life and her commitment to essentially domestic and bourgeois ideals of womanliness.

Just as Carpenter zealously struggled to conform to accepted norms of female behavior, her programs for the rehabilitation of boys and girls emphatically promoted gender-specific behaviors, values, and skills. Boys, she insisted, "are to be fitted for an independent, enterprising life, very frequently exposed to hardships and the inclemency of the weather; as much liberty should be allowed as is found prudent. . . ." Girls, by contrast, "are to be prepared for the home, either as domestic servants, or themselves hereafter the mothers of the next generation,—the wives who will be the blessing or the bane of their partners in life . . . must be prepared for the natural restraints of the home."[27] Neither of the choices for which Carpenter prepared her girls—full-time motherhood on the one hand or domestic service on the other—was likely to satisfy their needs. It was unrealistic to expect that many of the girls would later be able to eschew paid employment to be exclusively mothers and wives. Given the girls' record of lawlessness and high spirits, it was painfully wishful to imagine that many would be willing or able to satisfy the deferential expectations Victorian mistresses placed on household servants.[28]

In 1852, Carpenter overcame her distaste for public address and testified before the House of Commons Select Committee on Criminal and Destitute Children.[29] It is evidence of her stature that so many of her ideas were incorporated into the 1854 act, which established the foundations of a national system of juvenile reformatories.[30] More than any of her male fellow workers, Carpenter had defined the need for a new kind of educational, and not punitive institution specifically for children of the "pershing and dangerous classes" and aroused public interest in the matter. The 1854 act represented the consummation of years of labor by

Carpenter. It also signaled a defeat for some of her most cherished principles. Despite her ardent protests, all juvenile offenders were still sent to prison for at least fourteen days, and hence exposed to the demoralizing influences of adult criminals.

While Carpenter helped to shape and define the discourse and goals of juvenile reformatories, her success at attracting public notice diminished her control over the movement. As her ideas were taken up by politicians, all of whom were male, she was increasingly distanced from both the process and the outcome of the legislation. For Carpenter, "women's rights" meant the right to shape policy in areas for which women were especially well suited by virtue of being female. It was a mistake, she insisted, to confuse "women's rights" with the parliamentary suffrage.[31]

In the years following the passage of the Reformatory Act, Carpenter's experiences, both day-to-day at the girls' reformatory at Red Lodge and with Her Majesty's Inspectors on their occasional visits, must have given her pause to ponder the limits of her own powers and of her "women's rights." Just as women reformers were pushed farther and farther from the center of policy making as their voluntary initiatives were taken up by male political actors and debated, so too did they have to relinquish some of their authority over the operation of their voluntary institutions to male bureaucrats once they accepted state funding and supervision.

Carpenter's journals from these years underscore her recognition of the erosion of her authority that accompanied her triumph as an architect of state policy. Like a Victorian recasting of *Pilgrim's Progress*, the journals are full of penetrating and merciless self-reflection combined with unshaken confidence in the rightness of her motives and methods. Apollyon took many forms in Carpenter's pages: sometimes the girls themselves; at other times the matrons and female staff who refused to "love" and "discipline" the girls in the ways proscribed by Carpenter; and sometimes the male inspector of reformatories, Sydney Turner, who humiliated Carpenter in private conversation and in public reports.

Carpenter's journals are a powerful indictment of the inefficacy of her personal management and the difficulties of applying her techniques of Christian love and moral suasion to the all too worldly girls who were sent to Red Lodge. She entered Red Lodge "with the prayers that the house might be holy to the Lord."[32] However, within a short time, one girl fled to Cheltenham and ended her frolic in prison. Another responded to Carpenter's loving regime by setting Red Lodge on fire. By late August of 1857, Carpenter allowed the matron to use a rod to discipline a girl.[33] Even with this violation of her principles (the first of many), Carpenter made no progress in establishing order at Red Lodge. To make matters worse, Carpenter scared off several matrons who, she noted, had left "from a fear of my returning to the management of the School and rectifying the many abuses that had crept in."[34] Carpenter's relations with her own female staff appear to have been at least as tumultuous as those with the girl inmates.

While the world continued to applaud her efforts, Her Majesty's Inspectors offered Carpenter even less encouragement than the matrons and girls themselves. Sydney Turner, the former manager of Redhill Reformatory who was appointed the first inspector of reformatory schools, wrote the *First Report*. His opening remarks contain a thinly veiled critique of female philanthropy. The Reformatory Acts

> have already done away with much of the looseness and irregularity and insubordination that used to be met with. A manly, straightforward, and strengthening tone pervades the discipline, far more just and useful to the young offender than the sentimentality and petting and indulgence that might formerly be often complained of. . . . [T]heir management is more systematic and mere kindness superseded by intelligent and gentle firmness.[35]

Turner's language is not difficult to decode. If intelligent, gentle firmness is manly, then kindness, sentimentality, petting, and indulgence are feminine. It is precisely these words Turner chose to use in his report on Carpenter's work at Red Lodge. "The discipline was perhaps on the side of kindness and indulgence. Miss Carpenter has not been so successful as she wished in engaging really efficient assistants but she does a great deal herself."[36] The *Second Report* likewise recalled Turner's contrast between desirable masculine and undesirable feminine management. "The present matron is kind, serious and well-meaning, but hardly sufficiently firm."[37] Thus Carpenter, perhaps the foremost expert on juvenile delinquency and reformatories in the country, was forced to read humiliating reports which criticized her own efforts for being insufficiently masculine.

The dénouement of Carpenter's ambiguous triumph as architect of a national system of juvenile reformatories came in 1859 and 1860. Throughout the 1850s, conditions at Red Lodge had deteriorated for both children and staff. The appointment in 1859 of a new matron, Mrs. Johnson, finally brought order to the institution. Johnson commanded Carpenter's begrudging respect and the obedience of the girls. While Carpenter praised Johnson's success, she was vexed by Johnson's insistence on charting an independent course.[38] Tensions between Carpenter and Johnson came to a head during several of Sydney Turner's periodic inspections.

In her journal, Carpenter dramatically set the stage for what must have been one of the most painful encounters of her life. "All seemed going on fairly until near the end of the month [January 1860] Mr. Sydney Turner came. I had not had any unpleasantness with the Matron, Mrs. Johnson, and thought she was comfortable." To Carpenter's astonishment, Turner informed her that "Mrs. J was extremely uncomfortable! and that I shackled her improperly etc etc he had been eliciting from her numerous grievances which he most improperly, I thought, had listened to." Carpenter recorded in dismay that Turner "seemed to support her in everything against me. . . . Mr. T. spoke to me in an overbearing way which I am sure he would not have done to a gentleman."[39] Despite the affront to her sensibilities, Carpenter successfully stood her ground. She threatened to give up her certificate, which brought with it the authority and financial backing of the state, rather than yield control over the principles and management of Kingswood.

This episode reveals not only Carpenter's weaknesses and style as a manager, but also the shifting locus of power between female social-welfare reformers and male state officials. Carpenter's choice of words suggests that she was offended by Turner's behavior on the basis of her sex as well as her class. Turner, in her eyes, had clearly failed to act the part of a gentleman. By directly soliciting Johnson's views and supporting her against Carpenter, Turner violated the managerial and social hierarchies that governed relations between women and girls at Red Lodge.

The expansion of women's voluntary associations and their incorporation into state-funded programs led to an increase in the numbers and types of social-welfare-sector jobs available to women from a variety of backgrounds. Carpenter's tense relations with her staff illustrated that the growth in women's paid social-welfare work generated conflicts among women—and not only between women and male officials—along institutional, professional, and class hierarchies.[40] In this instance, the bonds of womanliness failed to create gender solidarity that transcended differences between women.

By the end of 1860, Carpenter withdrew from the management of Red Lodge—and, in effect, relinquished her authority to Turner and Johnson. Turner's *Third Report* praising the change in chief matron must have left little doubt in Carpenter's mind that the state, acting through its exclusively male agents, now exercised control over the institution that she had created and championed.

As the century progressed, female reformers consistently invoked the legacy and achievements of Mary Carpenter in justifying their own public activities. It is therefore important that we come to terms with this legacy. First, Carpenter demonstrated to her successors the compatibility (perhaps even desirability) of representing herself as a nurturing, social mother while at the same time pursuing innovative child-welfare policies and political power. For Carpenter, this was not only a useful rhetorical tactic but also the means by which she came to understand herself. Second, her voluntary work for the ragged and criminal children of Bristol in the 1840s, along with her moral authority and eloquence as a polemicist, proved very effective in establishing her credentials as a policy expert and public champion of child welfare. By deploying a heartfelt yet skillful strategy of defining spinsterhood as a social and motherly vocation, she was able to counterbalance anxieties about spinsters as dangerous and redundant burdens on families and society.

Carpenter's story also reveals the limits of her own power and authority as a woman. Once the question of juvenile reformatories became a matter of national controversy, the formulation and implementation of a national policy rested in the hands of members of Parliament and civil servants. Carpenter could not and did not determine the parameters of the debate. More poignantly, she could no longer dictate the terms by which her own reformatories at Kingswood and Red Lodge were administered and how they were evaluated by male inspectors. Inspection and funding proved a potent, if piecemeal, means by which the state asserted its control over the management of juvenile reformatories. As Sydney Turner made clear, the state rewarded "manly firmness" and condemned feminine kindness. Carpenter's career illustrates a recurring theme in the history of women's voluntary social-welfare activities and the state: women's power and control over welfare programs were inversely related to the degree of state involvement and funding.

No doubt some of Carpenter's problems in the management of Red Lodge must be explained as products of her own personal foibles. But it is also indisputably true that by accepting state funding for their voluntary enterprises, women (as well as men) had to contend with an added layer of male administrative authority that distanced them from the site of ultimate decision making. This distance was more significant for women than for their male counterparts in the voluntary sector because, lacking full rights of citizenship, they were definitionally excluded from the official political and bureaucratic mechanisms of the male state. Even when women first gained entry to central state bureaucracies as factory inspectors in the 1890s, they did so under the rubric of separate spheres: women's inspectorial powers were limited to regulating the working lives of other women. As policy innovators in the voluntary sector, Victorian women's encounters with the state were fraught with the contradictions of their status as noncitizens. Yet Carpenter, like her even more famous contemporary Florence Nightingale, never systematically developed her ideas about the relationship between sex, social work, and suffrage. As more women publicly debated the nature and limits of their own citizenship in the 1880s and 1890s, later female social-welfare innovators like Mary Ward and Margaret McMillan felt compelled to reconcile their views on suffrage with their self-representation as social mothers engaged in women's work.

Mary Ward, Civic Maternalism, and State Welfare

Carpenter's life and work provide a point of departure for analyzing the strategies, motives, and achievements of two very different women, Mary (Mrs. Humphry) Ward and Margaret McMillan. Taken together, these important figures in the history of child welfare allow us to chart the shifting political and social contours of the "borderland" of female social-welfare reform and voluntary activity in Victorian and Edwardian Britain.

Ward had close personal and intellectual ties to Mary Carpenter's world of female activism, philanthropy, and nonconformity. Estlin Carpenter, Mary Carpenter's nephew and biographer, and James Martineau, the leading Unitarian theologian of his day and an intimate friend of the Carpenter family, were vocal supporters of Mary Ward and her religious and social schemes. Mary Carpenter's unease with her public life and her acceptance of many of the class and gendered conventions governing the behavior of Victorian "ladies" resonated in Ward's own life and attitudes. Throughout her life, public speaking as well as writing caused Ward enormous anxiety and physical pain. Both women worked within norms of middle-class female behavior which their own life experiences as public advocates for social reform appeared to contradict.

Ward is today best remembered as a leader of the movement *against* female suffrage, and, as such, is typically dismissed as an anomalous reactionary.[41] Such a view is difficult to reconcile with her lifelong advocacy of expanding women's access to higher education and their roles in public life and debate.[42] Ward developed her ideas about the state, women (or, more accurately, well-to-do women), and their social obligations against the background of her own privileged though hardly pampered life. While Ward never felt financially secure, few of her contemporaries were as well placed by birth to transcend the legal and social obstacles to women's participation in public life. Ward was the granddaughter of Thomas Arnold, the niece of Matthew Arnold, and the aunt, mother-in-law, or sister-in-law to a staggering panoply of late-Victorian and Edwardian writers, thinkers, politicians, and do-gooders.[43] Her private social circle merged imperceptibly into the world of politics. Ward's dinner parties, like Beatrice Webb's, were forums for high-minded conversations and political lobbying— only the food was apparently more abundant and better prepared than the meals provided by her abstemious Fabian friend.

Ward's notorious "Appeal against Female Suffrage," published in 1889, is best remembered as a plea for women to avoid partisan involvement in the male politics of the central state and empire.[44] Imperial politics, she insisted, rested upon the unwomanly sanction of force. Ward's vision of politics was profoundly undemocratic and asserted that women could neither participate effectively within a male-defined system of politics nor hope to "feminize" national politics.

But there is another dimension to the "Appeal" which forcefully claimed for women equal but different rights to engage in public, political debate.[45] It called upon women to take up the active public obligations of citizenship by which Ward meant "the participation of each individual in effort for the good of the community."[46] Her conception of the sphere of womanly duties extended out from the home to public work in the community in voluntary associations, social work, and local government. Millicent Fawcett, leader of the suffragists, adroitly but unhistorically implied that the work of women social reformers logically went hand in hand with support for women's suffrage when she paid Ward a backhanded compliment in 1910. Ward, she insisted, was a "social reformer who had somehow wandered into the wrong camp."[47] This was simply untrue.

Ward's labors as a social reformer, child-welfare advocate, and opponent to suffrage were all closely intertwined and grew out of what I term "civic maternalism." My use of this term merits some elaboration because it is at once quite specific and fairly broad. I use it to designate a set of rhetorical strategies, attitudes, and ideas about the ways in which women's motherly capacities to love, nurture, and care for others were linked to the imperative to deploy these gifts within their local communities and municipalities. Civic maternalism was far from an exclusive ideology or discourse and at no point defined a political or social movement as such. Rather, the language of civic maternalism allowed men and women across the political spectrum, who espoused widely differing views about women, the state, and society, to form powerful but transitory coalitions on specific issues.

Ward's civic maternalism echoed Carpenter's ideas about women's obligation to extend the values of motherliness to society as a whole and was based on two assumptions. The first was that women, by virtue of their maternal gifts (not the fact of being mothers), were equal to but different from men. As Ward explained in 1908, "Women are not undeveloped men but diverse. . . . Difference not inferiority—it is on that we take our stand."[48] The second was that women needed to exercise these gifts not only within the family in the nurturance of husbands and children, but in their communities as public mothers. Ward's expansive conception of motherhood led her to demand the extension of women's formal political powers within local government and to urge women to participate in the rich civic life of voluntary associations committed to social welfare.

Ward's maternalism served rather different needs in her life than Carpenter's. By framing her social-welfare work within the rhetoric of maternalism, Carpenter developed a more womanly personal identity. This was not the case with Mary Ward. The name by which Ward was widely known to her adoring reading public and to a less adulatory posterity—Mrs. Humphry Ward— ostensibly signified her roles as Victorian wife and mother. There was, however, very little that was motherly or wifely about Mary Ward when judged by the conventions of her time and class. Throughout her married life, she found other women to run her household affairs (the first helper was her sister-in-law, Gertrude, who fled the Ward household to pursue mission work as an Anglican sister in India).[49] Her husband, Humphry, never fully accepted living in the shadow of his celebrated spouse. The Wards' friends and detractors alike seemed to have enjoyed noting the extent to which Mary, and not Humphry, occupied the male position as head of the household. For Ward, the wife and mother, unlike Carpenter, the spinster, maternalism was primarily a public stance.

Ward's Collectivist Road: From "Higher Criticism" to Recreation Schools

The institutional focus for Ward's work in local government and in the voluntary sector was the two settlement houses she founded. While women's historians have long stressed the importance of settlements in mobilizing American women and their movements, they have overlooked their significance in Britain where settlements also were staging grounds for hundreds of women at the forefront of social-welfare politics in the twentieth century, including Eleanor Rathbone, Mary Stocks, and Violet Markham.[50] Ward's first, short-lived settlement endeavor attempted to capitalize on her fame as author of *Robert Elsmere*, one of the best-selling novels of the century. The novel's eponymous hero experiences a crisis of faith which he resolves by establishing a quasi-Unitarian church and social settlement in a London slum. Ward brought her fiction to life by establishing a settlement, University Hall, in

Bloomsbury in 1890. In settlement work Ward sought for herself an ethical substitute for the dogmatic Christianity she could no longer accept after her own careful study of historical evidence. It was also a natural extension of her conception of her own duties as an educated woman.

Despite the fact that several women's settlements had already been founded in East and South London, the residential component of the settlement was all-male. Ward offered no rationale for this decision. She herself was active for the last three decades of her life in managing the settlement, and the childhoods of her two daughters, Janet and Dorothy, were intimately intertwined with their mother's settlement projects.

University Hall was a thoroughly unsatisfactory venture except perhaps for the few nonconformist divines studying at the adjacent Dr. Williams Library. Neither the local poor of Somers Town and St. Pancras nor the young men who lived at the settlement could muster any enthusiasm for the high-minded, academic discourses that eminent Unitarian theologians delivered regularly to small and elite audiences at the settlement. Even the first warden, P. H. Wicksteed, doubted the suitability of using a settlement to promote religious and intellectual work.[51] The residents soon recognized the futility of Ward's conception of settlement work and took matters into their own hands. In a poor district several blocks away, they defiantly established Marchmont Hall, a separate center exclusively for social work.[52] They hoped it would be free from the interference of Ward and her highbrow overseeing committee of theologians and academics.[53] While Marchmont Hall flourished, especially its programs for working-class boys and girls, University Hall languished.

The failure of her religious programs and tensions with male residents led Ward to plan the outlines of a new settlement (also all-male) in 1894, one which would better reflect the needs of the local working class and settlement workers.[54] Her vision of the settlement, named after its patron, Passmore Edwards, demonstrated Ward's pragmatism and flexibility as a social reformer.[55] University Hall had conspicuously failed to attract working-class men, women, and children. By contrast, Ward reported with delight to her father that the first night at the Passmore Edwards Settlement (PES) was "given up to our working folks. . . ." Men and women who never entered University Hall "marched into *their* new palace, staring about them [emphasis added]."[56] In a speech at the new settlement's opening, she acknowledged the impact of experience on her social ideals. In the 1880s, she had spoken of citizenship in terms of the *individual's* duty to contribute to the good of the community. She now sounded a new note: "Certainly the Collectivist motive, or as I prefer to call it, the citizen motive will be here." She paid homage to the "opportunist form" of collectivism of her Fabian friends and colleagues, Beatrice Webb and Graham Wallas, both of whom had served on the executive committee of University Hall.[57] But even as Ward's speech called for the state to assume greater responsibilities in providing for the welfare of its citizens, she maintained her most cherished notions of the potential and the necessity for individual action. Ward approved of state interference, not as the means toward collectivizing industry and private property, but as the necessary vehicle for protecting the freedom of the individual under modern conditions.

> Along these Collectivist roads, under these Collectivist gas-lamps, by the help of these Collectivist trains, and under the restraint of a hundred Collectivist regulations, the individual energy and will plies its business as keenly as ever, only in a way more consistent with a true freedom, more congruous with a true bettering of life.[58]

Ward embarked on her own "collectivist road" innocently enough through her work with and for the poor children of London.

From the founding of University Hall, work with children had been left to middle-class women volunteers under the auspices of the Women's Work Committee.[59] While the male settlement, according to Ward's daughter Dorothy, was full of "differences of opinion, and sorenesses, and troubles generally," the children's side, under the direction of the Women's Work Committee "has gone quite splendidly, and gives us heart for the rest."[60] One of the most significant achievements of the Women's Work Committee was the creation of an Invalid School for Crippled Children in 1899.[61] From the outset, Ward was determined to use it as a prototype for similar schools throughout London. Cooperation with local government authorities, who provided omnibuses, special equipment, and the names of children needing attention, was essential. On opening day, 28 February 1899, Ward was already envisioning a state-funded program on a national scale. "The

Board [the London School Board] are full of interest in the experiment," she wrote to her father, "and it will very possibly be the beginning of a whole system for these crippled and delicate children, not only for London but for the other large towns."[62]

By the end of the year, the London School Board was sufficiently impressed with the achievements of the Women's Work Committee that it proposed to establish four other "cripple schools" in conjunction with local committees modeled on the PES school.[63] The Bristol School Board sent its own representatives to study the PES program and established a similar institution in Bristol. Within a decade, the London County Council had established a city-wide network of publicly funded and run schools on the guidelines established at Passmore Edwards.

The exigencies of working-class life had suggested the need for a publicly assisted welfare program for crippled children. Ward integrated what she learned into her theoretical construction of the relationship between public and private initiatives. In a speech given at the Victoria Women's Settlement in Liverpool, she outlined her aspirations for the future role of settlements.

> Soon I hope they [settlements] will be regarded in every town as not merely useful, but indispensable, as providing just that opening for experimental and volunteer work, for that intelligent observation, and that inventive initiative, which, as preparing the way for the steady advance of the collective and legal methods of social reform, suit our English temper and our present English society. These irregular individualistic experiments are the necessary pioneers and accompaniments with us of all collective action. We don't wait for Governments; we like to force the hand of Governments . . . we like to fling our irregular forces on the enemy . . . to make a hundred experiments and even a hundred mistakes, before we call up the regular battalions and dream of a final decision.[64]

Ward's analysis is extremely perceptive. Her assertion that the voluntary sector was the arena in which welfare-state programs were first tested and then, if successful, "forced" upon the government, is an important model of welfare-state formation. The trajectory from private initiative to public policy, especially in maternal and child health and welfare, often entailed close cooperation between female-dominated voluntary associations, such as Ward's Women's Work Committee, and municipal government. As

Patricia Hollis has amply demonstrated, municipal government in Victorian Britain was itself a partly feminized sector of the state in which some female property holders had the right to vote and hold elected and appointed offices.[65] The intersection between voluntary associations and local government was one of the most innovative and essential sites of social-welfare development and administration in nineteenth-century Britain as well as a fruitful site for the development of women's civic consciousness.

Ward's analysis defines the space in which women, excluded from participation in the state as parliamentary electors and actors, could and did actively help shape public-welfare programs. For women with free time and financial means, voluntary networks like those established through settlement houses permitted them to participate in politics as "public mothers" and "citizens." In the years following the establishment of the Crippled School, the actions of Ward and the Women's Work Committee at the PES indicate that they knew how to exploit the advantages of their status as members of a female voluntary association in shaping public child-welfare policies and programs. Their next two projects—Recreation Schools after official school hours and Summer Vacation Schools during holidays[66]—also entailed close cooperation with local education authorities on behalf of working-class children. The professional and volunteer staff for both schemes was mostly female. At the beginning, Ward privately raised money for salaries, maintenance, and equipment.[67]

Both enterprises were designed to satisfy the play needs of children and parents' needs for childminding. Working mothers who lacked informal family networks had few options in providing after-school and summertime care for their children.[68] They were quick to seize upon the play centers.[69] From the outset, more children were sent to the PES than it could accommodate. As the program was copied in other parts of London, total attendance in all centers soared from 418,113 in 1907 to 1,322,936 only five years later. Costs more than doubled from £2339 to £5403.[70] The interests of settlement workers, mothers, and children all coincided to ensure the popularity of the programs.[71] Its growth made private funding increasingly impractical, so Ward lobbied strenuously to see play centers incorporated into public policy, first on a local and later on a national level.

Even the staunchest advocates of laissez-faire statecraft recognized that crippled children constituted an extraordinary and unfair burden on individual working-class parents.[72] Extending welfare programs to children whose only claims were their poverty raised rather different and more contentious issues—all the more significant at a time when New Liberals, Socialists, and the fledgling Labour party were vigorously calling for a new kind of activist state. Ward was a conservative in her politics, a liberal in her exaltation of the individual, and closely aligned with the Unionists on imperial matters. This made it all the more crucial for her to differentiate the ideological justification for her programs from those of many other contemporary schemes which, like Ward's, expanded the scope of the state's interventions into working-class family life. Ward met this challenge by linking her programs not to the social rights of mothers and children per se, but to contemporary preoccupations with child life, race degeneration, and hooliganism.[73] She claimed that the purpose of the play center movement was to "protect our growing boys and girls from the demoralising influences which at present seem to be inherent in our city life."[74] To justify the extension of the state, Ward harnessed her particular brand of civic maternalism to the imperatives of controlling the development of working-class youths who, she reminded her readers, were imperial Britain's future soldiers and citizens. Ward's own ardent mixture of maternalism and imperialism provided rhetorical camouflage for her social-welfare initiatives that was perfectly attuned to the priorities of most Edwardian politicians and bureaucrats.[75]

The transformation of play centers from a private, voluntary initiative to a national, state-funded program was a slow process and involved several stages. In 1904, Ward approached the London County Council (which had absorbed the functions of the defunct London School Board) to expand the program to eight other areas of London and successfully enlisted its financial support for heating costs, use of classrooms, and infant rooms.[76] While control of the play centers remained firmly in the private sector, LCC financial contributions were accompanied by LCC inspection, conducted mostly by male bureaucrats.

Ward personally persuaded Augustine Birrell, president of the Board of Education, to include in the Education (Administrative Provision) Act of 1907 a clause empowering local education authorities to provide play centers and Summer Vacation Schools.[77] The "Mrs. Ward Clause" further acknowledged that "the problem of wholesome occupation during play-time was bigger than any voluntary association could cope with, and it looked to the fruitful co-operation between the State and the volunteer. . . ." Its language signaled a shift in the relationship between voluntary work and the obligations of the state. However, like other contemporary child-welfare measures such as the Early Notification of Births Act, it was only permissive, not mandatory, legislation.

The play center clause of the 1907 Education Act grew out of and was justified in terms of the language and debates about race and empire that followed the Boer War. But it was the strains of the First World War on family life and, in particular, the perceived erosion of paternal control over households, that ultimately convinced H. A. L. Fisher, president of the Board of Education, to mandate after-school recreation programs in 1916. Fisher's directive was in response to the Home Office Circular (Number 975) which noted the rise of juvenile delinquency "owing to the absence on military service of their fathers, and perhaps even more their elder brothers, the industrial employment of mothers, the darkening of the streets, and other circumstances arising out of the war. . . ."[78]

Ward's advocacy of welfare-state programs for the care of children was the fruit of her settlement experiences. However, without the pressures and anxieties of war, it is doubtful whether she would have lived to see play centers incorporated into a publicly funded and run program. Women, as workers and as mothers, were crucial to the infrastructure of the domestic wartime economy. At a time when social harmony was essential, juvenile lawlessness could not be tolerated. The Home Office circular ultimately proved more compelling than Ward's special pleadings.

While Ward's road toward statism was in many respects peculiar to her own history and political and ideological commitments, it also illuminates more general issues confronting late-Victorian and Edwardian activist women. Like Carpenter, she remained wary of state encroachment and embraced state intervention insofar as it secured individual rights and opportunities. She came to advocate for local and later central-government social-welfare programs after a series of salutary disappointments with programs, residents, and working-class people at University Hall. To her credit, she listened carefully to her various constituents and gracefully abandoned the religious aspirations that had motivated her first settlement in response to her perception of the immediate needs of working-class families. Ward's successes as an architect of child-welfare policies and programs for "cripples" and for after-school and summer recreation only reinforced her conviction that women's power as citizens was not dependent on their right to vote in parliamentary elections.

The story of Ward and the Women's Work Committee of the PES illustrates one typical way in which thousands of women—most, admittedly, less prominent than Mary Ward—used the freedom offered by their voluntary associations to define new social needs and design programs to respond to them. For Ward, unlike Carpenter, developing programs and policies on the one hand and delivering services on the other were two utterly distinct enterprises. As one of the most prolific and best-paid novelists of her time, she had little time and perhaps even less interest in the day-to-day work of providing services for the "cripples" and working-class children who flocked to her schools and centers. And whereas Carpenter's maternalism sprang from deeply rooted personal needs as well as social conviction, Ward's maternalism, perhaps unfairly, seems more opportunistic. Mirroring a configuration of arguments shared by so much of the medical and political establishment of Edwardian Britain, Ward connected the vitality of empire to the social needs of mothers and children. Ward linked maternalism and imperialism not only on the level of discourse, but in public policy as well. One could certainly argue that Ward's appropriation of maternalism, like her antisuffrage stance, was yet another facet of her co-optation by masculine interests. But such a judgment must be balanced with recognition that Ward genuinely saw herself as a lifelong champion of women's rights and interests.

Socialism and Voluntarism: Margaret McMillan in South London

Margaret McMillan cut a very different figure from both Mary Carpenter and Mary Ward.[79] She was a committed socialist who openly struggled to articulate a radical analysis of the interconnectedness of class and gender oppression. Unlike Carpenter and Ward, she flourished as a public figure in politics and was one of late-Victorian Britain's most accomplished platform speakers. Despite McMillan's obvious differences from Carpenter, she, like Ward, built upon the work and traditions that Carpenter helped to establish. Though both spinsters, McMillan and Carpenter were deeply attracted to the language and ideology of public mother-hood and committed their lives to child welfare.

During the first two decades of her public life, McMillan was well known for her contributions to the socialist Independent Labour party and for her work, not in the voluntary sector, but as an elected member of the Bradford School Board in the 1890s.[80] Late-Victorian socialism in Bradford, with its support for wom-en's rights, the close personal ties between its male and female members, and the easy access to diverse publics it made available to women through the socialist press, provided an exceptionally supportive environment for the nurturance of McMillan's political identity.[81] Her self-assurance and skill as a female politician in Bradford were very evident in her unapologetic manipulation of her male school-board colleagues in 1897 in securing one of her greatest triumphs, the erection of school baths at public expense. The *Labour Echo* offered a blow-by-blow account of debate within the school board, and highlighted McMillan's witty and ferocious dispatch of her male opposition.[82]

The passage of the Education Act of 1902 abolished the system of school boards, which had been important bastions for women in local government, and left McMillan in search of new work. She decided to join her older sister Rachel, who had qualified as a sanitary inspector and was employed not far from London. The metropolis was in many respects a much less promising arena for a socialist woman used to life on the platform and in the school boardroom. In London, McMillan never had the opportunity to match her audacious Bradford triumphs as a politician; in fact, she never again served as an elected public figure. Instead, she was forced to turn to other, more traditionally female venues to carry out her programs for the betterment of the working class, and in particular, the welfare of children. "We had resolved to take action," McMillan recalled, "and as no party in London wanted us to stand for anybody, or anything, this action would have to be entirely on our own."[83]

McMillan's experiences both established new precedents for women and confirmed the efficacy of established patterns of wom-en's activism like those developed by Mary Carpenter. Her first attempts to influence child-welfare programs and policies in Lon-don were discouraging but instructive failures. They underscored the very different strategies women needed to adopt when working outside the political system in the voluntary sector, and not, as in Bradford, as an insider with a political constituency and public. Building on her experiments with school baths in Bradford and armed with the promise of £5000 from the American socialist-philanthropist, Joseph Fels, McMillan approached the London County Council with an offer to build and manage a health center attached to one of the schools in Deptford for which she was an unpaid school manager.[84] Fels wrote in high spirits to the LCC, in anticipation that the center would "serve as an object lesson to the whole country."[85] Months passed and neither Fels nor McMillan received notice of any action or interest on the part of the LCC. Apparently, the letter had been mislaid, only the first of many infuriating encounters McMillan would endure with social-welfare bureaucracies and bureaucrats.

When the Education Committee of the London County Council finally turned its attention to the scheme, the results were even less heartening for McMillan and Fels. McMillan was a complete outsider to the LCC—she lacked friends both on the Council itself and within its permanent bureaucracy. Her background, compared to Mary Ward's, was also somewhat disconcerting: a spinster Scotswoman, a socialist, and a supporter of women's suffrage Her proposal did nothing to assuage bureaucratic anxieties. It was written in that almost Carlylean style of lyrical mysticism that she used so effectively in her journalism and in speeches.[86] Instead of remaining close to the technical details of her proposal, she offered glimpses of her social philosophy and vision of the needs of children. She called sleep "a kind of inner washing" and the bathroom "a theatre for genuine physical training and education." The LCC's educational officers closely scrutinized every word and their internal reports indicate that McMillan's language and her lack of attention to details immediately discredited her in their eyes. The educational officers felt that McMillan's lyrical proposal required "some interpretation before executive effect can be given to it." Moreover, the long-term implications of the experiment frightened them because general adoption of the plan would eventually "involve a capital expenditure running into millions. . . ."

McMillan and Fels had deviated from the successful pattern followed by Carpenter, Ward, and others in gaining public funding for their social-welfare projects. They failed to demonstrate the effectiveness and cost efficiency of their program in the private sector *before* bringing it to the LCC. Only after its worth had been demonstrated, the education officers noted, could they consider the health center as an "object lesson . . . available for the instruction of the Council."[87]

The contrasts between McMillan's failure and Ward's triumph are striking in every respect. Ward had played by the rules with consummate skill; McMillan simply did not know them. McMillan pondered this unfortunate episode for years. She consoled herself that at the time, "we were still very naive, very trustful about public bodies."[88] It would prove rather awkward, in the aftermath of this incident, to balance her growing *distrust* in public bodies with her commitment to the principle that such bodies should assume more and more responsibility for ensuring the welfare of citizens.

Chastened but not deterred, McMillan continued to pursue with vigor other schemes and causes. Her work in Bradford had captured the attention of Robert Morant, a former resident at Toynbee Hall, and, in the best and worst senses, the quintessential social-welfare bureaucrat of his age. Few men were better positioned (or more inclined) to create social-welfare legislation by exercising the powers of bureaucracy. He was the permanent undersecretary for education and an architect of key components of Lloyd George's social-welfare policies. Although McMillan never won many reliable friends at the LCC during these years, she formed close friendships and gained the confidence of Morant and several other influential civil servants in Whitehall.

Morant found in McMillan qualities and insights he deeply admired which were conspicuously lacking in his male colleagues at Whitehall. McMillan was a woman of daring vision, not blinkered by the conventions of bureaucracy. She was deeply attuned to the laboring people around her and possessed unmatched hands-on experience in adapting her ideas to the actual welfare needs of clients. McMillan, safely positioned outside the internecine struggles of the civil service, served as a reliable sounding board for Morant. Finally, McMillan gave Morant a useful though indirect link to the Labour party which, after 1906, became an increasingly significant force during that extended prewar Indian summer of the Liberal party.[89] Lacking a political base of her own, the socialist-feminist McMillan necessarily found in the undemocratic but progressive Morant a powerful ally who could help her to advance her ideas.

While McMillan could not cajole the LCC to accept a gift of

£5000 in 1906, only one year later she found herself in a position of extraordinary influence as confidante and informal advisor to Morant on child-health issues. As McMillan's and Morant's goal of mandating the medical inspection of school children came close to realization, Morant confided that *"between* us we shall do something I am sure, if we can avoid raising public hubbub *against* our efforts [emphasis in original]."[90] Morant often enlisted McMillan—a complete outsider, a socialist, and a woman—to advise him on important and confidential decisions about the management and staffing of a key central-state welfare bureaucracy. He generously acknowledged that McMillan "most signally and most effectively embodied in a private individual the best enthusiasm of the most consuming faith, both in the possibilities of medical inspection and in the potentialities of a real honest preventative conscience in the *state* and in the people."[91]

For all that Whitehall remained very much an all-male preserve, McMillan's relationship with Morant gave her exceptional, albeit largely secret, influence over the implementation of one of the cornerstones of child welfare in modern Britain. Morant thrived on behind-the-scenes intrigues (he seems regularly to have written "highly confidential" letters to people outside of his staff) and his relations with fellow male civil servants were often thorny. For McMillan, confidential chats in closed rooms with elite male civil servants must have struck her as a very different style of political activity from the democratic, constituency-centered politics of Bradford socialism. Her close and warm ties to Morant contrasted sharply with her rather distant and at times hostile relationship with the LCC.

McMillan's part in the passage and implementation of the Medical Inspection of School Children was a high-water mark in her work in London. However, her day-to-day activities involved her in a more traditionally female pattern of women's voluntary associational life. They revolved around developing and managing several private-sector, innovative health and educational schemes in Deptford, run with the assistance of women trained in the emerging area of child welfare. Despite her growing prominence as an author in this field, her influence at Whitehall, and the much broader powers granted to local governments by parliamentary legislation, McMillan's relations with the LCC remained tense and often counterproductive. In her correspondence with LCC about her health center and dental clinic in Deptford in the years following her legislative triumph with medical inspection, one can detect uncanny echoes of Mary Carpenter's ambivalence and frustration in the aftermath of the passage of the Reformatories Act. Both women bridled under the constraints of bureaucratic procedures and authority.

In 1911, after several years operating on a voluntary basis, McMillan's dental clinic in Deptford received its first grant—and approval from the LCC. The LCC's Education Committee agreed to underwrite part of the expenses for the clinic for two reasons: first, unlike her proposal in 1905, the Committee noted that the clinic had already been "conducted as a voluntary institution" for several years. Second, the LCC was anxious to use the clinic to test the cost and administrative feasibility of such programs before committing itself on a metropolitan basis.

Within the year, McMillan and the LCC had expanded their partnership to include the health center. However, arrangements were complicated and unsatisfactory from McMillan's point of view. Despite her insistence that the appointment of staff of the center "remain in the hands of myself and of my Committee," the LCC hired some of its own doctors to do its work.[92] Half of the week, the clinic continued to be run as a private voluntary association by McMillan and her staff and committee. The rest of the week, the LCC covered the costs of the doctors and nurses and saw only patients who had been referred by education authorities. They turned away children, even those desperately sick, who lacked the proper forms or whose illness was not specified for treatment on a given morning or afternoon. This absurd policy vastly diminished the center's effectiveness in terms of cost and treatment. To make matters worse, the LCC failed to understand how to gain access to the network of information and mutual aid of Deptford's working-class mothers. "A great many of our worst cases are not found by doctors," McMillan explained, "but one mother tells another and so they come to the Centre."[93]

Almost from the outset, McMillan found intolerable the interference of the LCC and its insistence on placing bureaucratic procedures before the immediate needs of the people. In January of 1912, she inveighed against the "encroachment" of the LCC. "Your organizer, Miss Davies," she noted bitterly to the school medical officer, "proposed to me in a hurried moment when I was busy at the Clinic and did not understand her that *your* voucher card should be used for *my* ear, eye, throat and nose cases. That is not right. You know that I am bearing more than half the expense of all the Medical work and your name should not be on my cards [emphasis added]."[94] Only two days later, she sent another long and angry letter. "A case of rheumatic fever came up on Tuesday ([on a day officially] allotted for eyes . . .) and was sent away without advice though Dr. Eder was actually there to give it. This thing will amount to a scandal unless it is stopped."[95]

These exchanges are notable in two respects. First, they demonstrate that the growth of maternal and child welfare increasingly led to tensions between those women who worked outside the official state, like McMillan, and those who had recently gained positions as official organizers and inspectors within its bureaucracies, like Miss Davies. Second, McMillan clearly experienced dissonance between her public advocacy of making the state a full partner in ensuring the welfare of children and her reluctance to accept its authority in her own work. As McMillan explained to the school medical officer, Dr. W. H. Hamer, the assistance of public authorities threatened to undermine "the real success of the clinic."[96] Ironically, then, while the politically conservative Mary Ward was delighted to see her schemes taken over and expanded by public authorities, the socialist McMillan struggled to keep control of her ventures out of the hands of insensitive and ineffective bureaucrats.

All too often, historians have assumed that Beatrice Webb's journey from volunteer rent collector to Fabian socialist was paradigmatic of the shift from voluntarism to socialism. McMillan's career presents a different trajectory, influenced less by changing ideology than by the force of practical experience in day-to-day work as a social-welfare provider and policy maker. In her superb biography of McMillan, Carolyn Steedman asked whether McMillan, like other Independent Labour party leaders, had moved from socialism to "the arena of welfare philanthropism and progressive liberalism."[97] The answer and its explanation can be found in the relationship between her ideas and aspirations and her actual experiences. At the outset, McMillan's "retreat" to work in the private sector was not a matter of preference but rather a response to her changed political circumstances. Ultimately, while she never abandoned her advocacy of socialism and the role of public bodies in ensuring the welfare of citizens, McMillan came to embrace the voluntary sector as particularly efficacious for furthering her work.

McMillan's decision to work in the voluntary sector not only was the result of political expediency, but also offered her a practical way to respond to the demands of working-class parents and their children in Deptford. McMillan had always assumed that theory and practice needed to inform one another. She insisted that practice, that is, experience with real people and their problems, should precede study of theory. Her hands-on experience working in Deptford only deepened the distrust of "public bodies" awakened in her by the Fels fiasco. If McMillan embodied and helped to define socialists' and the Labour party's vision of maternal and child welfare, she also tenaciously insisted on maintaining the freedom from bureaucratic interference that accompanied women's work in the "borderland" of voluntarism.

At the turn of the century, few would have doubted that Mary Ward's place in history was more secure than Margaret McMillan's. And yet in the decades following their deaths, Ward was posthumously stripped of her status as a great lady, a great writer, and a great Victorian. McMillan, by contrast, was canonized as a visionary savior of working-class childhood. Oddly enough given their opposing views on women's suffrage, the paths of McMillan's and Ward's careers increasingly coincided during the most militant phase of women's campaign for the vote. In the 1890s, they seemed to have very little in common. They came from and turned to very different political and social cultures and spaces to exploit their talents and energies. But in the first two decades of the twentieth century, each invoked maternalism—albeit linked to widely differing visions of women, the state, and society—in justifying women's child-welfare initiatives in the voluntary sector.

Conclusions

Historians of American women have argued that women's social-welfare work functioned as a kind of shadow welfare state. To make such a claim in the case of British women would, perhaps, be exaggerated. However, their range of social-welfare activities and efficiency in raising funds and engaging large numbers of women were by any standards impressive. Without them the British state would have been forced to rely on a more elaborate and expanded structure of centralized welfare to satisfy the growing demands placed on it for public services. Women's voluntary associations contributed to the success and stability of the Victorian and Edwardian state—and they were equally important as sites for the expression and growth of women's civic and political consciousness. In a variety of occupational, health, and educational matters, child welfare in Victorian Britain functioned as the wedge by which new forms of entitlement as well as protective restrictions were opened up to other social groups. In this way, the significance of women's child-welfare work extended beyond the actual policies and benefits they secured for children in promoting a broader sea change in attitudes about the relationship between the state and its citizens.

The unofficial and financially precarious position of women's voluntary associations underscores their marginality from the centers of political, social, and economic power in Victorian and Edwardian Britain. As these few case studies illustrate, however, even the margin could be used as a base for claiming power. From mid-century onward, women exercised authority and initiative in shaping public policy in the traditionally female sphere of child welfare. They not only defined new social needs such as juvenile reformatories, schools for "cripples," and school-health clinics, but created policies, procedures, and institutions to address them. Their creations were sometimes literally absorbed and other times copied and modified by local and central government officials.

Educated middle-class women used voluntary associations to carve out for themselves political identities and a variety of new professions such as health and district visiting and social work. Participation in voluntary societies enhanced middle-class women's lives by enabling them to exercise power outside their homes. "Lady" social-welfare workers invariably represented the exercise of their authority as demonstrations of their motherly love for impoverished children and their sisterly solicitude for unfortunate or feckless working-class women.[98]

The histories of Victorian child welfare published in the 1920s and 1930s focused on the heroic labors of men—mostly doctors and public-health officials—on behalf of ignorant working-class mothers and their offspring. G. F. McCleary's *The Early History of the Infant Welfare Movement* (1933) is quite literally a portrait gallery of eminent men. Such hagiographical accounts have more recently given way to a new feminist orthodoxy that rightly highlights the repressive use of the politics and rhetoric of motherhood by male medical, political, and social-reform activists.[99] This essay

extends and modifies both of these bodies of scholarship by show-
ing how women used maternalist imagery and arguments in
advancing themselves and their visions of child welfare. This chapter illustrates not only the limitations but also the opportunities
that maternalism offered women activists like Carpenter, Ward,
and McMillan. It calls attention to the mutability of maternalism
as an ideological discourse.

However, to notice that the language of maternalism had wide
currency among a diverse and large number of women (and men)
who helped to form welfare policies and programs before World
War I is an important but only preliminary observation. Maternalist discourses did not exist in an ideological or political vacuum.
It would be absurd, for example, to suggest that maternalism by
itself defined the social politics of Carpenter, Ward, or McMillan—
much less determined the emergence of the welfare state in prewar Britain. Maternalism necessarily operated in relation to other
discourses—about citizenship, class relations, gender differences,
and national identity, to name only a few—and in relation to a
wide array of concrete social and political practices. The women
examined in this essay chose to invoke maternalism in making
specific claims about why they as individuals, and women as a
sex, were especially qualified to shape welfare policy and provide
care for working-class children. But, as I have tried to illustrate
through detailed case studies, they made these claims in an effort
to promote widely varying agendas about the position of women
and the obligations of the state.

Stuart Hall, in considering the debate over the welfare state in
Thatcherite Britain, offered some general remarks that can be
usefully applied to the ideological and discursive struggles over
definitions of motherhood and motherliness in Victorian and
Edwardian Britain.

> [I]deological contestation does not take place between fully
> formed, competing world views—theirs and ours. The field of
> ideology is not divided in that way. It's a field in which there
> are many different discourses and social forces in play at the
> same time. Contestation often has to do with the engagement
> around existing ideological symbols and slogans, winning them
> away from connotative chains of association they have
> acquired, which build them into languages that seem to con-
> struct topics so that they deliver an answer that favors one end
> of the political spectrum.[100]

In the cases of Carpenter, Ward, and McMillan, maternalism helped to produce answers that favored a strikingly broad "spectrum" of views about women, the state, and social class. None of these women succeeded in wresting maternalism completely from its moorings in either the "existing ideological symbols" or the "connotative chains of association" surrounding Victorian ideas about motherhood. In fact, none of them, even the radical Margaret McMillan, aspired to such a revolutionary rupture. But each, in her own way, added to and transformed the range of available meanings of maternalism.

Carpenter's maternalism made it possible for her to define herself as a motherly woman, despite her ostensibly unsexed status as a childless spinster. Her vision of social motherhood allowed her to reconcile her deeply rooted nonconformist distrust of the state with expansion of the state's role in regulating and financing juvenile reformatories. It also enabled her to reconcile her class-based ideas of female gentility with her own reluctant engagement in public life. Unlike Carpenter's vision of social motherhood, Ward's "civic maternalism" did not strengthen (and perhaps even threatened) her private identity as wife and mother. She used maternalism to explain why women's essential biological and social differences from men necessarily implied different privileges and duties in the political life of the nation and empire. Hence Ward linked her formulation of maternalism to her antisuffrage views. Margaret McMillan, by contrast, believed that the oppressions of class and gender were bound to one another. Like Ward and Carpenter, she believed that women possessed maternal gifts peculiar to their sex. But women's differences from men made it all the more important in her mind that they have equal political rights with men. How else, she reasoned, could women bring their distinctive contributions to bear fully upon the economic, social, and political problems of the day?

The three case studies also illuminate profound changes in the scope and nature of institutions and opportunities available to British women from the 1840s until World War I. Carpenter's programs for the poor children of Bristol were the work of a lone pioneer. By the early twentieth century, women like Ward and McMillan could and did look to political parties (not just the ILP and later the Labour party), local government, settlement houses, the women's press, women's colleges, and a huge network of local and national voluntary societies to develop and promote their child-welfare schemes. Many of these institutions and settings allowed middle-class women to develop a female social and political culture—one closely tied to the ethos of voluntarism and care giving. However, the case studies presented here have not focused on women's voluntary activities and institutions as parallels to the official male state (though this argument can be made),[101] but rather on the interconnections and interdependence of the two.

From the 1840s onward, the official state sanctioned women's voluntary social-welfare activities as a means to limit state welfare expenditures and promote private initiative. By the first decade of the new century, the ties binding the state and voluntary associations had grown stronger. As the state increasingly intervened in the lives of its citizens, it explicitly acknowledged that preponderantly female voluntary societies were important to the implementation (though not the formulation) of social-welfare measures. Most major child-welfare measures passed between 1906 and 1920 mandated personal, family-by-family home visiting, conducted mostly by women serving as both salaried professional and voluntary agents of the public welfare. Whenever possible, the British state built upon existing networks and institutions in implementing policy instead of creating entirely new ones. Voluntary associations thus functioned as a kind of de facto "state capacity" and eased the way for the relocation and reconfiguration of social-welfare authority between private and public bodies, women and men.

Notes

I would like to thank William Koven, Adele Lindenmeyr, and Sonya Michel for their helpful criticisms.

1. Hubert Llewellyn Smith, *The Borderland between Public and Voluntary Action in the Social Services* (London, 1937), 3.

2. William Beveridge, *Voluntary Action* (London, 1948).

3. See Hugh Heclo, *Modern Social Politics in Britain and Sweden* (New Haven, 1974), in which he offers an analysis in which the work of voluntary societies would fall under his category of "interest groups" or "pressure groups." See also Alex Tyrell, "Women's Mission and Pressure Group Politics in Britain (1825–1860)," *Bulletin of the John Rylands University Library Manchester* 63.1 (Autumn 1980).

4. Pat Thane's essay in this volume, "Women in the British Labour party and the Construction of State Welfare, 1906–1939," calls attention to the impressive numbers of women involved with political parties. Even within

the party most receptive to women, the Independent Labour party (ILP) and later the Labour party, the influence of Labour women was fairly circumscribed for most of the pre–World War I period.

5. For a comprehensive treatment, see Madeline Rooff, *Voluntary Societies* (London, 1957); Frank Prochaska, *Woman and Philanthropy in Nineteenth Century England* (Oxford, 1980); on middle-class uses of voluntary associations, see R. J. Morris, "Voluntary Societies and British Urban Elites, 1780–1850," *Historical Journal* 26,1 (1983): 95–118. On the status of local and women's voluntary associations in welfare state history, see Frank Prochaska, *The Voluntary Impulse: Philanthropy in Modern Britain* (London, 1988), xiv, 25.

6. The major biographies of Carpenter are by her nephew, J. Estlin Carpenter, *The Life and Work of Mary Carpenter* (London, 1879)—hereafter cited as *Life*—which is virtually a primary source of printed letters, and Jo Manton, *Mary Carpenter and the Children of the Streets* (London, 1976), For hagiographic accounts, see Ruby Saywell, *Mary Carpenter of Bristol* (Bristol, 1964), and Margaret Tabor, *Pioneer Women* (London, 1927).

7. I analyze Edwardian and later feminists' misappropriation of Carpenter in "Contextualizing Feminism: Women's Social Action Movements and the Problem of Naming in Victorian Britain," paper presented to the American Historical Association, New York, December 1990.

8. See Jane Rendall, *The Origins of Modern Feminism: Women in Britain, France, and the United States, 1780–1860* (New York, 1984). On evangelical culture, the formation of the middle class, and women's public charity work, see Leonore Davidoff and Catherine Hall, *Family Fortunes: Men and Women of the English Middle Class, 1780–1850* (Chicago, 1987), esp. chap. 10.

9. Carpenter urged "Christian women" not to "fear the difficulties to be contended within this work, the apparent publicity to which it may expose them, or the unwillingness of the other sex to allow them to work." "A true woman will surmount all obstacles by the God-sent strength of her very weakness. . . ." Mary Carpenter, "Women's Work in the Reformatory Movement," *English Woman's Journal* (July 1858).

10. The founding of the Social Science Association in 1857 established an institutional setting for women like Carpenter committed to bringing together women voluntary workers with state bureaucrats in the task of policy formulation.

11. In December of 1846 she confided that she "had more power than I thought, that my individual being was more prized by others than I had thought." Mary Carpenter, December 1846, as cited in *Life*, 107.

12. *Life*, 138.

13. Mary Carpenter to Dr. Guillaume, 12 Feb. 1873, quoted in *Life*, 405.

14. Carpenter, "Women's Work in the Reformatory Movement."

15. For an amusing account of Carpenter's businesslike reserve, see Frances Power Cobbe, *Life of Frances Power Cobbe, As Told by Herself*, with an introduction by Blanche Atkinson (London, 1904), in which she describes the time she lived and worked with Carpenter.

16. When she adopted a young girl of five in 1857–58, she noted gleefully that she had finally become a real mother, without the impediments of marriage and a husband; *Life*, 252.

17. This was a recurring theme in Octavia Hill's many writings; see C. Edmund Maurice, *Life of Octavia Hill, As Told in Her Letters* (London, 1914).

18. Martha Vicinus, *Independent Women* (Chicago, 1985); Sybil Oldfield, *Spinsters of This Parish, the Life and Times of F. M. Major and Mary Sheepshanks* (London, 1984); and Sheila Jeffries, *The Spinster and Her Enemies, Feminism and Sexuality, 1880–1930* (London, 1985).

19. "The Glorified Spinster," *MacMillan's Magazine* (Sept. 1888).

20. For Carpenter's explanation of this seeming violation of the principles of voluntarism and laissez faire, see Mary Carpenter, *Reformatory Schools for the Children of Pershing and Dangerous Classes and for Juvenile Offenders* (London, 1851), vi and 209. See also Carpenter, "Grants from the Committee of Council on Education Solicited for Preventive and Reformatory Schools," where she also calls for state support. Carpenter Papers, Bristol Record Office, 12693/23.

21. Mary Carpenter, *Juvenile Delinquents, Their Condition and Treatment* (London, 1853), 378.

22. Benjamin Kirkman Gray, in his insightful study of philanthropy and the state, concluded that the history of the movement to establish juvenile reformatories was "one of the latest attempts on a large scale to elevate the idol of 'voluntaryism' into a leading principle of politics; among its pioneers it numbered the most fervid mistrusters of the State, who nevertheless were driven to demand State assistance on quite a heroic scale." Gray, *History of English Philanthropy* (London, 1905), 166.

23. The decision to write the book was wrenching, and recalls the cost with which women entered all realms of public debate in early Victorian England, even the relative safety of authorship.

24. See Margaret May, "Innocence and Experience: The Evolution of the Concept of Juvenile Delinquency in the Mid-Nineteenth Century," *Victorian Studies* 17,1 (1973): 7–29.

25. See *Matthew Davenport Hill, Recorder of Birmingham* (London, 1872), chap. 9, esp. 161–68.

26. *Life*, 145.

27. Mary Carpenter, *Suggestions on the Management of Reformatories* (London, n.d.), 8.

28. Carpenter's vision of producing good servants out of girls from the "dangerous" classes was not isolated. In the 1870s the East End social reformer Henrietta Barnett helped to found the Metropolitan Association for Befriending Young Servants, MABYS, which, like Carpenter's work, strove to make poor-law girls into ideal domestic servants.

29. Proceedings of the Select Committee, *House of Commons Papers* (1852), vii, 1ff.

30. On 11 May 1853, Sir J. Pakington, a Committee member, explicitly singled out Miss Carpenter's "able and excellent works upon this subject" during the proceedings. Proceedings of the Select Committee, *House of Commons Papers* (1853), xv.

31. See Carpenter to Sandhurst (31 Aug. 1854) as quoted in *Life*, 204. See also Carpenter's correspondence with John Stuart Mill and Helen Taylor in the Mill/Taylor Papers, vol. 1, 102, 109, and 110, British Library of Economic and Political Science. For a discussion of this correspondence see Harriet Warm Schupf, "Single Women and Social Reform in Mid-Nineteenth Century England: The Case of Mary Carpenter," *Victorian Studies* 18,3 (1974): 316.

32. Mary Carpenter, "Record of the First Year at Red Lodge," Carpenter Papers, Bristol Record Office, 12693/1, vol. 1, 10 Oct. 1854, 1, hereafter cited as *Journals*.

33. She claimed that the rod was "a mere semblance of one [which] could not have really hurt her." *Journals*, vol. 1, Aug. 1857. In July 1859, Carpenter noted that the matron, Miss Swanbourne, had "certainly done harm using the cane," but Carpenter, desperate to maintain order, had done nothing to stop the practice. *Journals*, vol. 2, 12693/2, July 1859, 96.

34. *Journals*, 12693/1, vol. 1, Apr. 1856, 7.

35. Sydney Turner, *First Report of the Inspector Appointed to Visit the Reformatory School of Great Britain*, PP, First Session, 1857–58, vol. 29, 818.

36. Ibid., 835.

37. *Second Report*, 1859, PP 2nd Session, 13, part 2, 33.

38. Carpenter was forced to concede that Johnson was "exercising an excellent influence over her and hopes to bring her permanently under controul [*sic*]. The other girls appear impressed with the measures wch [which] have been found necessary." *Journals*, 12693/2, vol. 2, 2 Sept. 1859, 102.

39. *Journals*, vol. 2, 6 Apr. 1869, 110–11.

40. This is a recurring theme in many of the essays in this volume. Eileen Boris, for example, examines conflict along race and class lines (ch. 6); Sonya Michel discusses tensions between female policy makers and care providers in day nurseries (chap. 8).

41. Some important works on Ward include John Sutherland, *Mrs. Humphry Ward, Eminent Victorian, Pre-eminent Edwardian* (Oxford, 1990); Enid Huws Jones, *Mrs. Humphry Ward* (London, 1973); and Françoise Rives, *Mrs. Humphry Ward, Romancière* (Lille, 1982). See also Jane Lewis, *Women and Social Action in Victorian and Edwardian Britain* (Aldershot, Eng., 1991).

42. On her work as a founder of Somerville College, see Mrs. Humphry Ward, *A Writer's Recollections* (London, 1918), 204.

43. Ward's family circle, including the Macaulays, Trevelyans, Arnolds, Forsters, and Huxleys, superbly illustrates what Noel Annan has so aptly called the "intellectual aristocracy" of Victorian England. Annan, "An Intellectual Aristocracy," in J. H. Plumb, ed., *Studies in Social History* (London, 1956).

44. Ward's cosignatories included Beatrice Webb, Mrs. T. H. Green, and the wives of many prominent social reformers and intellectuals.

45. Ward expressed her own views in the novel, *Delia Blanchflower* (New York, 1914): "Are there not many roads to political equality?—many forms of government within government, that may be tried, before you insist on ruining us [women] by doing men's work in the men's way?" (305).

46. Mary Ward, "An Appeal against Female Suffrage," *The Nineteenth Century* (June 1889): 783.

47. Millicent Fawcett, *Common Cause* (10 Nov. 1910): 498, as quoted in Brian Harrison, *Separate Spheres* (London, 1978), 22.

48. Mrs. Humphry Ward, "The Women's Anti-Suffrage Movement," *The Nineteenth Century* (August 1908): 348.

49. See the Manuscript Diary of Gertrude Ward, Pusey House, Oxford.

50. On the history of women's settlements in Britain, see Seth Koven, *Culture and Poverty* (New York, forthcoming), and Vicinus, *Independent Women*, chap. 6.

51. Philip Wicksteed to Mary Ward, 2 Oct. 1890, University Hall Archives, Mary Ward Centre. Wicksteed lived in Toynbee Hall for several weeks before assuming the position of warden. He found that Toynbee men "take but small interest in either Biblical or directly religious matters." Wicksteed to Ward, 10 Nov. 1890. Wicksteed was a Unitarian minister, an outstanding Dante scholar, and a brilliant economist in the school of Jevons. He was a frequent university extension lecturer.

52. Wicksteed was often forced to mediate between residents and Ward in the first years at the settlement. One resident actually resigned, and several others waged what Wicksteed called "the Monday Mutiny." For details of these controversies, see the University Hall Archives, especially T. Locke Worthington to Mrs. Ward, 21 Feb. 1891; Peel Dawson to Mrs. Ward, 24 Feb. 1891; P. H. Wicksteed to Mrs. Ward, 20 July 1891; and Alfred Robinson to Mrs. Ward, 18 Sept. 1891. Ward made no allusion to these embittered times in her memoirs, *A Writer's Recollections*.

53. Estlin Carpenter, James Drummond, James Martineau, Frances Power Cobbe, and Beatrice Potter sat on the Council of University Hall. The Committee included W. Copeland Bowie, Stopford Brooke, Mrs. J. R. Green, Blake Odgers, and Graham Wallas.

54. In December 1894 she wrote her father that she was pondering a series of letters written by working men to her on "the past and future of the Hall, parts of which I am embodying in the Appeal [for the new settlement]." Mary Ward to Thomas Arnold, 19 Dec. 1894, Ward Papers, Pusey House, Oxford.

55. All that remained of the ambitious program in religious instruction was an annual series of lectures in memory of the Master of Balliol, Benjamin Jowett. Ward's work at the settlement has received only passing attention from her biographers. The only study of the Passmore Edwards Settlement is by James Jeffrey Robinson, "Adult Education and the Urban Working Class: A Study of Continuity and Change at the Mary Ward Centre," (M.A. thesis, Kings College, University of London, 1979).

56. Mary Ward to Thomas Arnold, 12 Oct. 1897, Ward Papers, Pusey House, Oxford.

57. Fabian socialism appeared "opportunist" to Ward and many contemporaries because the Fabians worked within existing state and bureaucratic structures, and, wherever possible, pushed for radical but gradual economic, social, and political reorganization. They aimed to permeate, not overthrow, the state. Ward had long-standing ties with various Fabians. She had known Webb since the 1880s. It was Graham Wallas, more than Webb, who urged Ward to consider collectivist ideas during the 1890s. See Jones, *Mrs. Humphry Ward*, 127–29.

58. Mrs. Humphry Ward, "Social Ideals," typescript speech (October 1897), PES Archives, Mary Ward Centre.

59. The Women's Work Committee, which supervised the activities of a large number of female volunteers, included Mrs. Ward, her daughter Dorothy, her extremely able secretary Bessie Churcher, and, among others, the wives of two former Toynbee residents, Mrs. Ernest Aves and Mrs. E. T. Cook.

60. Dorothy Ward to Sally Norton, 10 Dec. 1904, Ward Papers, Pusey House, Oxford.

61. Ward's scheme was not the first program for crippled children in London. The Invalid Crippled Children's Association was already over a decade old, and settlers at the WUS had established a cobbling workshop for crippled boys, St. Crispin's. Grace Hannam had established her Guild of the Poor Brave Things for handicapped children in conjunction with the Bermondsey Settlement by 1895. The women's branch of Mansfield House, the Canning Town Women's Settlement, had established a crippled school on weekday mornings in 1893.

62. Mary Ward to Thomas Arnold, 28 Feb. 1899, Ward Papers, Pusey House, Oxford.

63. PES Annual Report (1899), 11. I use the term "cripple" in this essay to call attention to Victorian social attitudes toward disability.

64. Mary Ward, typescript (n.d.), Liverpool Speech, circa 1899 2–3, PES Archives, Mary Ward Centre.

65. See Patricia Hollis, *Ladies Elect: Women in English Local Government, 1865–1914* (New York, 1987).

66. The focus of both programs was on play: storytelling and crafts, dancing, music drill, cobbling, gymnastics, coloring, wood shop.

67. An assistant master at the Highgate School, Edmund Holland was the first director of the Vacation School. Ward's secretaries, Bessie Churcher and Eleanor Taubman, also figured prominently in its management.

68. Ward explained the working mother's dilemma in her annual begging letter to the *London Times* of 1907. Working women were forced either to lock their children inside their cramped homes or leave them unattended to the mercy of the streets. While some neglected their children, many were "earning all that the family has to depend on," and could not be blamed for

failing to supervise their children's leisure. Mrs. Ward, letter to the *Times*, 8 Oct. 1907.

69. One woman "pushed forward five little ones—'here they are, Miss, all five of them'—then turning to the visitor—'Now I know they're safe for two hours, and perhaps I can do a bit of cleaning and sewing!' " as quoted in Janet Trevelyan, *Evening Play Centres for Children, The Story of Their Origin and Growth* (New York, 1920), 33.

70. *Ibid.*, 35, 40. Some children attended two or three times a week during the school year, so one child could account for 100 attendances.

71. Ironically, Ward's most outspoken opponents were the aristocratic promoters of the Children's Happy Evening Association who opposed state funding and whose programs were much more limited in scope. Their opposition was really nothing more than jealousy that Ward's program promised to make their own obsolete. See the Davidson Papers, vol. 147, Lambeth Palace, for both Ward's letters to the Archbishop and those of the Happy Evening supporters.

72. The Invalid Children Aid Association, for example, began as an offshoot of the Charity Organisation Society (COS). But its members felt increasingly compelled to break with COS principles because of the extraordinary claims of cripples. For this see Seth Koven, "Remembering and Dismemberment: Crippled Children, Wounded Soldiers and the Great War," paper presented to the Social Science History Association, New Orleans, October 1991.

73. See Mrs. Humphry Ward, *The Passmore Edwards Settlement* (London 1901), 11. On connections between social reform and welfare and the representation of working-class male youths as hooligans, see Seth Koven, "From Rough Lads to Hooligans: Boy Life, National Culture and Social Reform," in Andrew Parker, Mary Russo, Doris Sommer, and Patricia Yaeger, eds., *Nationalisms and Sexualities* (London, 1992).

74. Mary Ward, in preface of Trevelyan, *Evening Play Centres for Children*, xx.

75. See Anna Davin, "Imperialism and Motherhood," *History Workshop Journal* 5 (1978): 61–113.

76. See Paul Thompson, *Socialists, Liberals and Labour, the Struggle for London, 1885–1914* (London, 1967), for a nuanced analysis of London municipal politics and the Progressive party.

77. The clause said specifically that education authorities were empowered to "provide for children attending a public elementary school, vacation schools, vacation classes, play centres, or means of recreation during the holidays or at such other times as the Local Education Authority may prescribe, in the schoolhouse or in some other suitable place in the vicinity."

78. Quoted in Trevelyan, *Paly Centres*, 56–57.

79. Major studies on McMillan include Carolyn Steedman, *Childhood Culture, and Class in Britain, Margaret McMillan, 1860–1931* (New Brunswick, 1990); Elizabeth Bradburn, *Margaret McMillan: A Portrait of a Pioneer* (London, 1989); and Albert Mansbridge, *Margaret McMillan, Prophet and Pioneer, Her Life and Work* (London, 1932).

80. Steedman stresses McMillan's socialism and her links to Bradford in *Child-hood, Culture, and Class.*

81. See Katherine Bruce Glasier, "Margaret McMillan in the Dawn of the I.L.P.," *The New Leader* (10 Apr. 1931): 7, for a brief account of McMillan's impact on Bradford's socialist community in the early 1890s.

82. After one of her sallies during the debate, "Mr. Brereton, pulling up his clerical collar, did what he could to look extremely shocked"; later in the discussion, McMillan was unabashed at the proposed expense of the baths "though Mr. Crow, when uttering it, fixed his gaze upon her in a way that was not, at any rate, suggestive of affection." The article concluded when "Our Margaret . . . rolled her sleeves up, and Canon Simpson looked as if he expected something to happen. Something did happen. Margaret wiped the floor with the Canon, and the Canon seemed hardly to relish the performance. . . . At the conclusion of Margaret's address, there was no more fight left in the Board. . . ." See *The Labour Echo*, "Baths for Bradford Board Schools, Margaret McMillan Triumphs," by the Gatherer [pseud.], 31 July 1897.

83. Margaret McMillan, *The Life of Rachel McMillan* (London, 1927), 108.

84. The proposed center consisted of showers and a swimming bath used in conjunction with a new curriculum of physical education, training in voice and breathing.

85. Joseph Fels to W. Buck, official correspondent, LCC Education Committee, 26 July 1905, EO/PS/2/36, Greater London Record Office, hereafter cited as GLRO.

86. For a good example of this kind of mystical journalistic style, see her critique of nineteenth-century philanthropy, "She Who Must Be Obeyed," The *Workman's Times*, 5 May 1894.

87. McMillan wrote to F. W. Jowett, who would soon be instrumental in the passage of the Administrative Provisions (Feeding of Necessitous School Children) Act, that the LCC "want[s] precedents" and hoped he could show them the bathing arrangements at a school. McMillan to Jowett, 11 Dec. 1905, A1/6. McMillan Papers, Thames Polytechnic, Deptford, hereafter cited as Thames. I wish to thank the Rachel and Margaret McMillan Trust for permission to cite these papers.

88. McMillan, *Life of Rachel McMillan*, 112.

89. On Morant's use of McMillan as a conduit to leading labour men, see Morant to McMillan, 22 Feb. 1912, A1/30, Thames.

90. Robert Morant to Margaret McMillan, 26 June 1907, A1/8, Thames.

91. Morant to McMillan, 22 Dec. 1908, A1/12, Thames.

92. McMillan to LCC, 14 Dec. 1912, PH/SHS/2/87, GLRO.

93. McMillan to Dr. Hamer, 27 May 1913, PH/SHS/2/87/GLRO.

94. McMillan to LCC, 24 Jan. 1912, PH/SHS/2/86, GLRO.

95. McMillan to LCC, 26 Jan. 1912, PH/SHS/2/86, GLRO.

96. McMillan to Dr. Hamer, 11 Feb. 1912, PHSHS/2/86, GLRO.

97. Steedman, *Childhood, Culture, and Class,* 172.

98. The theme of this work as an expression of womanly solidarity transcending class was aptly expressed in a poem a Mrs. Alexander wrote to commemorate elite women's social-welfare work. "Not alms profuse at random thrown, / Not class 'gainst class her lip would teach, / But brave self help, sweet mercy shown, / And free dependence each on each." Mrs. Alexander, "The Work of Woman's Hand," stanza 7, in Angela Burdett-Coutts, ed., *Woman's Mission: A Series of Congress Papers on the Philanthropic Work of Women by Eminent Authors* (London, 1893), 1–3. However, the work of many other historians has challenged such self-representations by pointing out the repressive and disciplinary character of middle-class women's relationships with working-class women.

99. There is a rich literature on this subject. Some of the contributions to it include Elizabeth Wilson, *Women and the Welfare State* (London, 1977); Anna Davin, "Imperialism and Motherhood"; Carol Dyehouse, "Working-Class Mothers and Infant Mortality in England, 1895–1914," *Journal of Social History* 12 (1979): 248–67; and Jane Lewis, *The Politics of Motherhood: Child and Maternal Welfare in England* (London, 1980). For a critical revision of this scholarship, see Deborah Dwork, *War Is Good for Babies and Other Young Children: A History of the Infant and Child Welfare Movement in England, 1898–1918* (London, 1987).

100. Stuart Hall, transcript of questions and answers following his essay, "The Toad in the Garden: Thatcherism among the Theorists," in Cary Nelson and Lawrence Grossberg, eds., *Marxism and the Interpretation of Culture* (Urbana, Ill., 1988) 58.

101. See Kathleen McCarthy, "Parallel Power Structures: Women and the Voluntary Sphere," in McCarthy, ed., *Lady Bountiful Revisited: Women, Philanthropy, and Power* (New Brunswick, 1990).

3

Social Mothers: The Bourgeois Women's Movement and German Welfare-State Formation, 1890–1929

Christoph Sachße

Introduction

Much of the current debate on the crisis of the welfare state in Western industrial countries is devoted to the ways in which welfare-state institutions and provisions discriminate against women.[1] Employment-based social security, instead of compensating for the disadvantages women experience in the labor market, historically has reinforced them. Welfare-state institutions have significantly contributed to defining sex roles. The concept of women as the dependents of men whose place is the family and whose major social responsibility is the breeding and raising of children is widely reproduced by social policies. It has become more and more clear in recent feminist political debate that the welfare state is not a neutral set of social-political institutions and that it has been shaped by gender and class relations.

Women have always been and remain overrepresented among the recipients of poor relief and welfare. But they have also made significant contributions to the formation and development of welfare states. Positioned as both clients and policy makers, women have shaped and influenced welfare policies in ways that reflect their particular concerns and needs as women.[2] Modern social-service professions and systems in many Western societies have largely been influenced by women's movements and concepts of female emancipation. Women in Germany did not have the vote before 1919 and thus could not exert major influence on social legislation on the imperial or state level. Nonetheless, women's movements had decisive impact on shaping the specific forms and concepts of municipal social reform. The German bourgeois women's movement's vision of female emancipation shaped social work as a female profession and in this way contributed to the formation of the specific structures of the German welfare state.

Bourgeois Social Reform in Wilhelmine Germany

The development of social work as women's work in Germany can be understood adequately only within a broader context of late-nineteenth-century social reform. As part of his shift to conservatism and protectionism, Bismarck implemented a series of sweeping social-welfare measures in the 1880s. His program included a system of contributory social insurance, *Arbeiterversicherung* (workmen's insurance), health insurance (1883), accident insurance (1884), and eventually old-age and disability insurance (1889).[3] Although the benefits were initially small and only a minority of workers were covered, Germany was the first country to have two systems of social security side by side: public, municipal relief for the destitute and contributory social insurance for workers. The working-class question (*Arbeiterfrage*) was thereby clearly separated from the traditional question of the poor (*Armenfrage*) by legislation and administrative institutions, though in practice the constituencies of both systems often overlapped. Poor relief did not, as many had predicated, become completely obsolete through the mere existence of social insurance. During the following decades, however, poor relief became the target of far-reaching reforms, which led to the development of new forms of so-called *sociale Fürsorge* (social relief) beyond the sector of traditional poor relief.[4]

Reform of municipal relief systems beginning in the 1890s was one facet of a broader bourgeois reform movement focusing on social policies at the municipal level. Middle-class social reformers were troubled by their increasing perception of the division of contemporary society into antagonistic classes. In response, they called for the middle class to assume social responsibility for the nation as a whole. Social reform, they insisted, was the vehicle by which the lower classes would be integrated into bourgeois society and the "unity of the nation" restored.[5]

Middle-class social reform reflected the ambivalence embedded in a wide range of critiques of contemporary society. *On the one hand*, pessimistic cultural currents influenced the character of social reform, and in particular those movements known as "Life Reform." "Life Reform" comprehended a whole range of movements with diverse goals such as vegetarianism, natural healing, nudism, and the health-food movement. These movements decried the forces of urbanization, science, and technology and offered a critique of capitalism that highlighted the artificiality of society. The different strands of "Life Reform" found common ground in their commitment to living a more "natural way of life" which contrasted the scientific rationality of the Enlightenment with the essential reasonableness of nature. Life Reform attacked urban life as the root of all ill health and social and cultural malaise; it proposed a conscious retreat from the city to reverse the process of rural exodus demanded by modern society. Life reformers exalted a holistic culture of naturalness as an alternative to technical-industrial civilization.[6] *On the other hand*, bourgeois social reformers were critical of the escapist and pastoral aspects of Life Reform that failed to confront the existing realities in Germany's expanding urban sector. While the bourgeois social-reform and Life Reform movements were both highly critical of the social consequences of industrialization and urbanization, bourgeois social reform strove to bring about a more humane restructuring of living conditions of the lower classes *in* the city. These social reformers wanted to integrate the urban poor into bourgeois industrial society by using the tools of modern civilization—rational organization and the scientific analysis and treatment of social problems—to introduce pragmatic reforms. Thus, bourgeois social reform simultaneously expressed both a critique of and a belief in progress.

Bourgeois social reformers put their theories to the test in many of Germany's major urban centers. Cities such as Berlin, Frankfurt, Cologne, and Munich, whose bourgeois elites were imbued with a strong sense of social responsibility and traditions of local self-government, became important centers of social-reform innovation in the 1890s. The liberal, urban academic middle class were the principle social underwriters of reform. Their sense of social obligation, not the organized voices representing the lower classes, was intended to be the motor of societal reform. Their concept of reform was paternalistic. It strove for social reform *without* political democratization and thereby mirrored the specific political, social, and cultural makeup of Wilhelmine Germany.

In practice, bourgeois social reform produced a wealth of new-style institutions and measures for municipal poor relief that recognized special categories of risk distinct from the more general risk of impoverishment. Specialized measures and benefits for the unemployed, public health, and public housing as well as child- and youth-welfare provisions emerged out of the undifferentiated poor-relief system. Personal advice, instruction, and control became ever more distinctly the hallmarks of the new ways in which assistance or welfare was dispensed.[7]

The new measures and institutions of municipal health care established around the turn of the century provided prototypes for the development of social services that redefined traditional poor relief.[8] New public municipal health-care measures were designed primarily to serve groups who were excluded by health insurance typically because they were not employed and hence did not pay contributions. These included infants, small children, school children, pregnant women, and women in childbed (*Wöchnerinnen*). They were designed to deal with physical handicap as well as chronic or contagious diseases such as tuberculosis, venereal diseases, alcoholism. They aimed to prevent, not remedy, disease by providing medical advice and by improving the living conditions of the poor rather than by making medical treatment available.

The centers for medical advice (*Gesundheitsberatungsstellen*), particularly for pregnant women and mothers with infants, stood at the center of public municipal health care. The first of these centers were established in 1905 in Munich and Berlin, and by 1907 there were already 73 of them throughout Germany.[9] Infant mortality was high: the average stood at 27.8 infant mortalities per 100 births between 1870 and 1875 and at 22 per 100 between 1884 and 1893. And the birthrate, too, began to decline by the turn of the century.[10] Thus, the new forms of health care for pregnant women, mothers with infants, and school children have to be understood as part of a "pronatalist" population policy which began to replace traditional neo-Malthusian arguments at the end of the century.

Infant mortality and a declining birthrate became matters of national interest: after all, "population was power."[11] Although the

Kaiser himself proclaimed that "prohibiting women in childbed from work is a matter of improving the race,"[12] infant mortality was generally seen as a problem of maternal ignorance and irresponsibility rather than as a problem of inadequate protection for female workers. Consequently, health care for mothers with infants primarily took the form of maternal education. Mothers' standards and knowledge had to be improved, and their behavior had to be adapted to scientific norms of hygiene. Mothers were taught to nurse their babies themselves and to keep them clean. They were taught that doctors' and health nurses' expert knowledge was superior to traditional forms of caring and advice given by neighbors and grandmothers.[13] Municipal health centers were typically headed by a male physician. But under his supervision were female health nurses who cared for mothers and infants and female health visitors who saw them at home and checked whether the medical advice dispensed was carefully followed.

The new forms of municipal health services nicely demonstrate the shared characteristics that marked all arenas of municipal social reform beginning in the early 1890s. First, the new forms of municipal services claimed to be working on a *scientific* basis and with *scientific* methods. Second, to be put into practice, they needed an organizational and administrative infrastructure. Third, they increasingly required a trained, paid professional (as opposed to voluntary) staff.

The scientific character of social reform formed a new source of legitimacy which set it apart not only from traditional, religiously motivated philanthropy, but also from the outdated, repressive concept of public relief. Bourgeois social reformers' understanding of "science" had several dimensions.[14] Science was understood as an ethical-normative discipline which emphasized the social responsibility of the middle classes for the nation as a whole and legitimated holistic concepts of reform. This concept of science was reflected particularly in the different schools of contemporary political economy (*Nationalökonomie*), among which Gustav Schmoller's "historical school" was the most influential. According to Schmoller's concept, political economy was supposed to be a "moral-political science." Scientific knowledge was at the same time supposed to provide arguments for binding norms for the development of social relations.

The concept of the scientific understanding of public hygiene ran along different lines. It was seen as an empirical discipline within the natural sciences. It claimed not only to analyze social problems with scientific precision, but also to provide scientifically based methods applicable for reform measures. Hygiene became a model discipline for all newly developing arenas of municipal welfare in the last years of the nineteenth century, not just for health services. And it generated a pressure for the professionalization of these arenas. The role of science in bourgeois social reform was multifaceted. On the one hand, it was intended to furnish proof for general bourgeois responsibility for the nation as a whole. On the other hand, it paved the way for the bureaucratization and professionalization of welfare.

The expansion of municipal welfare was part of a far-reaching change in the functions and structures of municipal administration which took place in the cities of Wilhelmine Germany.[15] The extension of the tasks of municipal administration required specialist knowledge, the introduction of specially trained civil servants, and a permanent governmental bureaucracy. Bourgeois social reform was based on a critique of the division of labor, specialization, and the bureaucratization of technical-industrial civilization. The holistic reforms it promoted, however, were to be instituted with the resources offered by scientific rationality, specialized methods, and bureaucratic organization. To that extent, it relied upon the scientific-technical progress of industrial society, whose social consequences were paradoxically the source of deepest concern, in calling for holistic reforms. Here lies the basic tension pervading Wilhelmine concepts of bourgeois social reform: far-reaching, holistic reforms implemented by industrial-bureaucratic means.

The differentiation of various municipal-welfare functions and the establishment of specialized "scientific" methods to meet the needs of the urban poor led to an increasing demand for skilled and trained welfare workers. In the field of health care in particular, there was a consensus that unskilled voluntary visitors were no longer equal to the tasks of modern municipal welfare. And with the increasing demand for special skills and special training, the outlines of a new social-service profession began to take shape. It was the bourgeois women's movement in Germany that combined the different trends of specialization and professionalization in social welfare with its own ideal of "social motherhood" and thus shaped social work as an exclusively female profession.

The Bourgeois Women's Movement and the Concept of "Social Motherhood"

In its early stages in the mid-nineteenth century the aims of the women's movement in Germany had been primarily liberal: equal rights, equal opportunities, equal wages. By the end of the century, however, a new vision of female emancipation developed. After 1894, the *Bund Deutscher Frauenvereine* (League of German Women's Associations), a national umbrella organization including a broad spectrum of women's organizations, became the most important organizational platform of bourgeois women in Germany. Within the *Bund* the wing of the so-called *Gemäßigten* (moderates) fostered the new emancipative ideal.[16] For the *Gemäßigten* equal rights for women were mere egalitarianism, not emancipation.[17] They stressed the particular nature of women, which was to be strengthened and expanded throughout society. Formal equality should not be the aim of the women's movement, they insisted, but rather the development of a specific female culture to enrich the male-dominated structures of industrial society.

At the very center of that culture was "motherhood." Not only mothers were "motherly." Motherhood was the nature of women in general. They proposed an all-embracing feminist ideal of motherhood as the guiding principle for a moral reform of the masculine world of rationality and self-interest, industrialism and specialization. For the German women's movement, motherhood became the incarnation of life and humanity in a technical world of capitalism and bureaucracy, of social disintegration and cultural decay. The task of women's emancipation was not formal equality but the expansion of female culture throughout society. Women's emancipation was women's "cultural mission" (*Kulturaufgabe*), a moral reform of society. And this could only happen by extending women's motherly influence from women's traditional sphere, the family, throughout society. Motherhood had to become "social motherhood."[18]

The concept of "social motherhood" expresses a specifically female variant of contemporary cultural and social criticism. The feminine principle of motherhood was supposed to provide a protective wall of warmth, emotion, and social wholeness against the destructive consequences of industrialization and the widening out of masculine objectivity and technical rationality. The theory of "social motherhood" and women's "cultural mission" intended a *moral* reform of society, not a political one. Women's emancipation, framed in this way, was dissociated from the democratization of society and from equal rights and suffrage for women. It thus illustrates the disconnection of social reform and political democracy typical of bourgeois social reform in Wilhelmine Germany.[19]

The new sectors of municipal social welfare suggested themselves as a field of activity to extend female motherly influence into new spheres of society. Welfare reforms could be understood as substitutes for functions the family could no longer perform. If working-class mothers had to work in the factories, bourgeois social mothers were required to take care of the home, children, and the sick. And, in fact, the relations between the bourgeois women's movement and municipal social reform were close.

In Berlin a new type of women's welfare organization was founded in November 1893, the *Mädchen- und Frauengruppen für soziale Hilfsarbeit* (the Girls' and Women's Groups for Social Assistance Work). The organization of the "Groups" was an initiative of Minna Cauer and Jeannette Schwerin, leaders of the Berlin bourgeois women's movement. The Groups' sponsors included Ignaz Jastrow and Gustav Schmoller, prominent representatives of German *Nationalökonomie* and members in the *Verein für Sozialpolitik,* one of the most influential associations of contemporary social reformers. Eduard Eberty, a Berlin city alderman, also lent his support. He was a well-known member of the *Deutscher Verein für Armenpflege und Wohltätigkeit,*[20] an association of German communes and municipalities, private charity organizations, and individuals engaged in social welfare, which during the 1890s became an important platform of advocacy for municipal social reform. The call for the organizational meeting of the Group was dramatic:

> Economic and cultural distress among large strata of the population of our fatherland, increasing bitterness among vast parts of the people urgently and most definitely call for social assistance work also on the part of women. It can no longer be denied that particularly girls and women of the propertied classes bear serious complicity in increasing this bitterness through their lack of interest and compassion for the opinions and feelings of the impoverished classes, through their lack of any personal contact with these parts of the people.[21]

The idea behind it was quite simple. If there were leisure and abundance for the women of the propertied classes on the one side and stress and privation for working-class women on the other, could there not be some kind of exchange? Why could bourgeois women not share their abundance with their sisters of the working class, who were desperately in need? In an article in the well-known feminist journal *Die Frau*, Emil Münsterberg, who later became head of the Berlin poor administration and who was one of the leaders in the *Deutscher Verein für Armenpflege und Wohltätigkeit*, strongly advocated the idea of social-assistance work as a kind of cross-class gender coalition beneficial to everyone involved.[22] The poor would be helped and integrated in bourgeois society; the rich would be safe from working-class insurrection and, moreover, acquire some useful skills and knowledge.

The concept of a cross-class coalition of women existed more in rhetoric than reality. In fact, the German women's movement was deeply divided. The *Bund Deutscher Frauenvereine* did not accept socialist women's organizations as members. And the socialist women's movement under the leadership of Clara Zetkin was anxious to separate itself ideologically and politically from all bourgeois women's reform policies.[23] Maternalist policies as advocated by the bourgeois women's movement thus developed as a tool of imposing middle-class norms and values on working-class women rather than a movement of women across class lines.

Female charitable work, of course, had a long tradition throughout the nineteenth century. What was new—almost revolutionary—within the Groups in the 1890s was the idea that special training was the indispensable precondition for effective social assistance. From their very beginnings the Groups organized lectures on various subjects in the field of social welfare to teach their members the knowledge and skills required for the new type of "systematic" social work. Max Weber and Theodor Weyl, a leading representative of social hygiene, were among the lecturers in those early years.[24] The combination of practical female social work and specific social work training made the Groups the birthplace of modern professional social work in Germany. It was social education that shaped social work as a female profession.

The most important personality for the development of social-work education in Germany was Alice Salomon.[25] Salomon was born in Berlin on 19 April 1872, the fourth of six children of a wealthy Jewish businessman. She went to school, but education for girls was poor in her day.[26] Professional training was not suitable for young women of her background, and there were no professions that women could engage in. Women like Salomon were expected to wait for and then marry an appropriate young man of a good family. So she learned needlework and housekeeping, a little literature and languages. She ironically summarized the benefits of her early education. "We fed canaries, watered the flowers, made embroideries, played piano, and waited."[27]

In November 1893 she was invited to the organizational meeting of the Groups. Within the Groups, Salomon found a field of activity that brought meaning and substance into her life. She contacted Jeannette Schwerin, who expounded to her the concept of "social motherhood." Schwerin also introduced Salomon to the principles of "social peace" as developed in the social thought of Thomas Carlyle and John Ruskin.

Apparently Salomon's authority within the Groups increased rapidly. In any case, after Jeannette Schwerin's death in 1899, Salomon became chairwoman of the Groups at the early age of 27. She proved equal to the task in all respects. From that moment on, she linked the establishment of the profession of social work with her own remarkable career. She attached most importance to the development of social-work education. As early as 1899, she established a one-year training course, which marks the beginning of systematic social-work training in Germany. Beginning in 1902, Salomon took courses in national economy at Berlin University, as a guest student, since women did not have access to German universities at that time.[28] Here she studied contemporary theories of social reform, including ideas stressing the social commitment of the middle class for the poor and the underprivileged. She completed her studies in 1906 with a doctoral thesis on the origins of wage inequality of men's and women's labor.

Salomon also followed in the footsteps of Jeannette Schwerin in the bourgeois women's movement. In 1900 she succeeded Schwerin as a member of the board of the *Bund Deutscher Frauenvereine*. She was one of the leading organizers of the 1905 International Council of Women Conference in Berlin, and, she was elected secretary of the Council at its meeting in Toronto in 1909.

Salomon's outstanding social-political and feminist achievement was the combination of the women's movement's concept of female emancipation with contemporary bourgeois theories of social reform. Her vision was strongly influenced by British reform ideologies and practices. She was deeply attracted to the social thought of Thomas Carlyle and John Ruskin, who had stressed the importance of the moral reform and personal social commitment of the propertied class itself as indispensable for bridging the social cleavages of industrialization and capitalism. In the English settlement movement—particularly in Toynbee Hall, the famous East London settlement—these ideas had already taken the shape of practical social reform.[29] The residents of Toynbee Hall intended to help the urban poor not through financial aid and material benefits, but through personal commitment and understanding, through living with them and providing them with the fruits of culture as those had been developed and appreciated by the university-educated classes. It was, so to speak, a modernized version of the Scottish theologian Thomas Chalmers's classical slogan, "Not alms, but a friend!"

Certainly, there is much similarity between these ideas and German concepts of bourgeois social reform that Salomon championed. But there is one remarkable difference. While the German version stressed the importance of legislative and administrative reform, the English version insisted on the importance of *personal* commitment and moral reform of the propertied. And it was exactly that idea, which Alice Salomon, who had visited Toynbee Hall during a stay in London, tried to adopt. She amalgamated the concept of "social motherhood" with the English concept of "social peace." The result was an identification of women's emancipation and social reform, a concept of social reform *as* female emancipation. In Alice Salomon's thought, it was the responsibility of women of the propertied classes to struggle for social peace through *personal* social commitment. Women were destined by their motherly nature to transcend class distinction and class struggle through personal social service for the poor. By helping the poor and the underprivileged, they extended their female influence in society, promoted their own emancipation, *and* served the people as a whole (*dem Volksganzen*) by strengthening the unity of the nation. Social work from the perspective of Alice Salomon was not a "profession" but rather a "program" for social reform and female emancipation. She once said that, for her, social work and women's emancipation were exactly the same.[30]

The efforts to establish a new approach to systematic social assistance went hand in hand with strong criticism of the "dangerous dilettantism" of the *Wohlfahrtsdamen* (welfare ladies) who, according to Helene Lange, "used their handkerchiefs to keep away poor people's odor." The Groups, anxious to distance themselves from traditional female charity, favored a deepened understanding of social problems as a basis for systematic social work. Thus, social-work education became part of their work from the very beginning.

Social-work education, in Salomon's formulation, had two main goals. Its first task was to teach professional skills and knowledge that would enable bourgeois women to mold the character and behavior of working-class families; but skills and knowledge were not enough. It also was intended to shape the social character—the "social attitude"—of bourgeois women themselves. Salomon averred that "all social education remains inefficient and unfruitful, if it only teaches people something they did not know before and does not make them something they had not been before."[31]

Consequently, social-work education could never be part of German universities, which were male, patriarchal institutions. Female education needed its own institutional setting. Salomon believed that the *Soziale Frauenschulen* (social women's schools), founded in growing numbers in 1908,[32] could and should serve that function. At the outset, they were not meant to be schools of a lower level, but a female alternative to male university.[33]

Social-work education became an effective tool for monopolizing the various activities in the new fields of municipal welfare as female occupations. Traditional voluntary visiting had been exclusively male. The famous "Elberfelder System," a system of public poor relief first installed in the town of Elberfeld in 1853 and later adopted by many other German towns and cities, had restricted the role of poor visitor to those possessing full citizen's rights, thereby excluding women. Though a number of German towns reluctantly began to admit women as visitors by the end of the century, male visitors continued to oppose women's incursions. Voluntary visiting remained predominantly male until the outbreak of the First World War. The new social occupations around public housing, health, and youth care, however, were seen as particularly appropriate for women's motherly nature. And since only women had the specific knowledge and skills required for these occupations, they developed as female occupations. These newly established forms of female "visiting" coexisted with traditional male visiting of the Elberfeld type.

Social-work education as developed by Alice Salomon, though, was not meant to be training for a salaried job. It addressed a specific class of women: the wealthy, "unproductive" women of the educated classes, who did not care for money but who sought female emancipation through social responsibility. Social work was not a job like others. It was a "vocation," a unique chance for middle-class women to emancipate themselves by helping the poor. So, the concepts of social work and social-work education were closely tied to the peculiar social situation of both the urban bourgeois middle class in imperial Germany and middle-class women.

Bourgeois women's concepts of female social work shared many of the basic contradictions characterizing all concepts of late-nineteenth-century bourgeois social reform in Germany: the tension between holistic reform ideals and professional-bureaucratic means to realize them. In addition, other tensions underpinned the bourgeois women's movement's concept of female social work. First, the "motherly" elements of female emancipation on the one hand sometimes existed uneasily with the requirements of steady and effective help for the poor on the other. If reliable assistance should be provided, some form of stable organization, specialization, and division of labor had to be maintained. Though the concept of "social motherhood" was based on a strong criticism of bureaucracy and specialization, the concept of feminist social work could not completely do without them. And in fact, there was considerable cooperation between local municipal administration and female social workers from the very beginnings of female social work in Germany. Salomon's insistence that social work should be exclusively *voluntary* work for well-to-do women did not go unchallenged. Even in the years before World War I, the number of women engaged in salaried social work began to increase. By 1910 there were about 400 salaried women in municipal social administration in Germany.[34]

Social-work education was also riddled by the tensions between the demands of training and professionalization and its simultaneous aspiration to shape women's social character. Professional training tended to undermine the motivation for what Salomon called "charismatic social work": the motivation not to do a specialized job but to serve "the people as a whole" and thus extend female culture in society. The ethical-feminist aspects of training, on the other hand, tended to undermine the quality of professional skills and knowledge taught at social-work schools, since the quality of education was not just a matter of professional qualification but also a matter of developing the "social character" of women which was almost impossible to evaluate.[35] During the Wilhelmine period, however, the tensions between the social responsibility of the middle class, holistic-feminist elements, and professional as well as bureaucratic aspects within the concept of female social work in Germany remained in fragile balance. The development of new sectors of *sociale Fürsorge* and the beginnings of female social work within them were restricted to a number of major German cities only and thus of little numerical relevance. During the First World War and the Weimar Republic, however, when the system of municipal welfare began to expand rapidly, its contradictions and tensions began to unfold.

Women, War, and Welfare: The Nationalization of the Women's Movement

World War I constituted an important break in the development of welfare in Germany. The war led to a profound restructuring in economic, social, and political relations. State power to intervene in all arenas of society, including poor relief, expanded enormously under the pressures thrown up by the war.[36] Entirely new kinds of groups found themselves in need of support. And entirely new forms of benefits were also introduced. Most men called up for military service at the outbreak of the war left their families without an adequate income. A new arena of "war relief," organizationally separate from traditional poor relief, was developed for these families. It granted benefits at a level above subsistence rates in order to ensure that these dependents of servicemen did not sink into a "lower social stratum or fall into the domain of public poor relief."[37] Thus, "war relief" was clearly distinguished from public poor relief: it was nondiscriminatory and the new benefits were legally guaranteed rights. In the course of the war, war-disabled soldiers and dependents of war casualties also joined soldiers' and sailors' families as groups requiring support. They received pensions regulated by law. Other new-style assistance measures were introduced to promote the rehabilitation and reintegration of disabled veterans and to offer individual care for war widows and war orphans. Finally, measures were created that expanded the social basis of welfare dependents by supporting members of the middle class suffering from the effects of war. To ensure the full citizenship rights of these new classes of welfare recipients, these measures no longer had anything in common with traditional poor relief. New criteria for welfare benefits took into account wartime sacrifices made on behalf of the Fatherland. Social reformer Helene Simon spoke of an "uplifting of assistance in the context of war relief measures."[38] She underlined not only that the material well-being of war victims had improved, but also, that a more intense and personalized care, and a new, nondiscriminatory style of dispensing assistance had come into existence. While the provisions of war-linked assistance were completely organized by municipalities, the costs were to a large extent carried by the central state, the Reich. If public relief was exclusively a concern of local municipalities before the war, the Reich assumed financial and regulatory authority in this realm in the course of the war. For the first time in German history, public assistance was expanded into a comprehensive system of welfare. Many of the demands which social reformers had unsuccessfully put forward before the war were fulfilled in war-related relief programs. However, this development also had its price.

Coming to terms with mass, war-related emergency conditions presupposed the existence of a comprehensive and reliable welfare administration. Bureaucratization and centralization of welfare accordingly progressed in the course of the war. Within the new, rapidly expanding sectors of war relief there was a strong demand for voluntary assistance work. And the women's movement provided a remarkable reserve of qualified workers, many trained in social work, others experienced organizers from the *Bund Deutscher Frauenvereine* or one of its member associations. For them, the outbreak of the war offered opportunities to prove their female responsibility for the nation and the utility of their work for the Fatherland. Female service at the home front seemed to provide a unique opportunity to extend female culture within society and to win social recognition for the women's movement.

The *Nationaler Frauendienst* (National Women's Service or NFD) has to be understood as an attempt to attain these goals.[39] Initiated by Gertrud Bäumer, chairwoman of the *Bund Deutscher Frauenvereine*, local NFD agencies sprang up during the first weeks of war and were administered and controlled by women. They initiated close cooperation with the municipal agencies of war relief and the NFD actually became an important part of the adminstration of war relief. Within its numerous organizations, thousands of women came into positions of public responsibility and public influence, a development the women's movement had long lobbied for unsuccessfully in the prewar period. Women's gains, however, were also accompanied by increasing restrictions on their control over relief: women's work within the NFD became increasingly subordinated to the requirements of warfare, and the NFD itself became more and more part of the war administration.

The expansion of war relief had a decisive impact on the women's movement and the development of female social work. Within the bourgeois women's movement the influence of conservative leaders and organizations increased during the war. Female social work began to change from a tool of social criticism and female emancipation to an active support of the social and political status quo. And the *Bund Deutscher Frauenvereine* increasingly became an annex of the military welfare apparatus.[40] Thus, the extension of female work during the war did not go hand in hand with an extension of female culture in society. On the contrary, it became more and more subordinated to the war machine, the incarnation of male patriarchal structures.

Welfare in Weimar: The Bureaucratization of Social Work

The expansion of public relief into a comprehensive "people's welfare" program was completed during the Weimar Republic. The welfare state became a constitutional compromise between the forces of the Left and those of the Right in the new Republic.[41] The state's assumption of responsibility for the well-being of its citizens coincided with poverty on a scale unprecedented in prewar years. At the same time, in comparison with the prewar period, the infrastructure of the economy dramatically deteriorated. The expansion of the Weimar welfare state thus did not proceed in a well-planned and continuous manner. Rather, crises cast dark shadows on it and mass destitution defined its parameters. Under conditions of extreme social, political, and economic duress, the internal contradictions of Wilhelmine bourgeois social reform inherited by the Weimar Republic's system of social welfare could no longer be kept in check. The new demands confronting state welfare generated momentum for intensified bureaucratization and standardization, hence further widening the gap between the practice of state welfare and its ideological foundations. The Wilhelmine legacy of a distinctly female cultural mission and of bourgeois social responsibility remained unfulfilled promises or disappeared entirely from the rhetoric and reality of Weimar social welfare. Encouraged by increased freedom to criticize public authority, the growth of state welfare in Weimar was, not surprisingly, attended by widespread discontent and criticism.

This was the setting in which female social work expanded rapidly during the Weimar years. In 1925 there were 22,547 social workers in Germany, 21,906 female, 641 male. By 1933 the number of social workers increased to 24,129 (22,229 female, 1,830 male).[42] Social work became a major field of activity for women during the Weimar Republic, but with its numerical expansion the character of female social work completely changed. Alice Salomon's concept of female social work—designed under the particular political, social, and cultural conditions of Wilhelmine Germany—never addressed women in general, as her socialist critics had long maintained. It addressed a specific class of women who, like Salomon herself, came from the wealthy, educated middle class and worked, not for money, but from a sense of social vocation. By the mid-1920s this class of women had almost disappeared. During the war and in particular during the postwar inflation, large parts of the German "Mittelstand" were impoverished. Now, even women from what had been the upper middle class had to work for money. And an increasing number of women from the lower classes, particularly social-democratic working-class women, for whom paid work was an essential priority, surged into the new female service professions. Thus, the "social basis" of Salomon's concept no longer existed.

The organization of social work had changed, too. With citizen's welfare guaranteed in the Weimar constitution, the responsibility for social reform definitely shifted from the upper middle class to the state. Social work became part of public-welfare bureaucracy. Although female social work expanded rapidly within the new sectors of social administration, only a handful of women came into leading administrative positions.[43] Thus, social administration remained under male control. And social work changed from a concept of female emancipation to a male-controlled profession on the lower level of municipal welfare administration.

The character of social-work education also changed. The number of social women's schools had increased rapidly during the war and continued to increase during the Weimar years. By 1913 there were 14 schools in Germany; between 1916 and 1918, 13 more schools were opened; and by 1927 there were 33 social women's schools in Germany.[44] It was no longer a privilege of well-to-do women to go to social women's school to form their motherly nature and social responsibility. From a female equivalent to male universities, the schools of social work in fact changed to training schools of lower level without academic standards. And women with only social-work training could not compete with university-trained women on the labor market. Thus, the ambitious feminist ideal of social-work education produced a system of professional training perceived as vastly inferior to university education.[45]

Although they had little left in common with bureaucratic routine social work in Weimar Germany, the Wilhelmine women's movement's ideals were not explicitly abandoned. The female schools of social work in particular continued to foster the cult of motherhood and *Volksgemeinschaft*, which increasingly became mere rhetoric. The former emancipative ideals successively became conservative professional ideologies, which eventually gave way to Nazi abuse and deformation. As female social work expanded rapidly during the Weimar years,[46] it ironically lost its feminist, emancipationist components. From a tool of female emancipation it turned into a female service profession. Its underlying theoretical concept was transformed from a theory of women's emancipation into an ideology which helped to legitimize the contradictions of a female profession incorporated into "male" bureaucracy and subordinated to male control. The reform ideals stemming from the Wilhelmine period actually contributed to doubts about the Weimar welfare state and the new, democratic nature of the political system. As such, they ironically played a role in creating those conditions of political instability that led to the collapse of the Weimar Republic and the subsequent perversion of the feminist ideals of social motherhood and social reform under the Third Reich.[47]

Notes

1. Elizabeth Wilson, *Women and the Welfare State* (London, 1977); Ilona Kickbusch and Barbara Riedmüller, eds., *Die armen Frauen: Frauen und Sozialpol-*

itik (Frankfurt, 1984); Barbara Riedmüller, "Armutspolitik und Familienpolitik: Die Armut der Familie ist die Armut der Frau," in Stephan Leibfried and Florian Tennstedt, eds., *Politik der Armut und die Spaltung des Sozialstaats* (Frankfurt, 1985), 311–35; Ilona Ostner and Hiltrud Schmidt-Walderr, "Politik mit den Frauen-Über Frauen, Frauenarbeit und Sozialpolitik," in Michael Opielka and Ilona Ostner, eds., *Umbau des Sozialstaats* (Essen, 1987), 155–66. Mimi Abramovitz, *Regulating the Lives of Women: Social Policies from Colonial Times to the Present* (Boston, 1988); Linda Gordon, *Women, the State, and Welfare* (Madison, Wis., 1990).

2. John T. Cumbler, "The Politics of Charity: Gender and Class in Late 19th Century Charity Policy," *Journal of Social History* 14,1 (1980): 99–111; Robyn Muncy, *Creating a Female Dominion in American Reform, 1890–1935* (New York, 1991). Seth Koven and Sonya Michel, "Womanly Duties: Maternalist Politics and the Origins of Welfare States in France, Germany, Great Britain, and the United States, 1880–1920," *American Historical Review* 95 (1990): 1076–1108; Gisela Bock and Pat Thane, eds., *Maternity and Gender Policies: Women and the Rise of the European Welfare States 1880s–1950s* (London, 1991); Linda Gordon, "Social Insurance and Public Assistance: The Influence of Gender in Welfare Thought," *American Historical Review* 97 (1992): 19–54.

3. Otto Quandt, *Die Anfänge der Bismarck'schen Sozialversicherung und die Haltung der Parteien. Das Unfallversicherungsgesetz, 1881–1884* (Berlin, 1938); Florian Tennstedt, "Vorgeschichte und Entstehung der Kaiserlichen Botschaft vom 17 November 1881," *Zeitschrift für Sozialreform*, vol. 27 (1981): 663–710; Friedrich Kleeis, *Die Geschichte der Sozialversicherung in Deutschland* (Berlin, 1928; rpt. Berlin/Bonn, 1981); Walter Vogel, *Bismarcks Arbeiterversicherung* (Braunschweig, 1951); Florian Tennstedt, "Sozialgeschichte der Sozialversicherung," in Maria Blohmke, Christian von Ferber, and Hans Schaefer, eds., *Handbuch der Sozialmedizin*, vol. 3 (Stuttgart, 1976), 385–492; Klaus Saul, "100 Jahre Sozialversicherung: Wirtschafts- und sozialpolitische Grundlagen," *Zeitschrift für die gesamte Versicherungswirtschaft* (1980): 177–98; Michael Stolleis, "Die Sozialversicherung Bismarcks: Politisch-institutionelle Bedingungen ihrer Entstehung," in Hans F. Zacher, ed., *Bedingungen für die Entstehung und Entwicklung von Sozialversicherung* (Berlin, 1979).

4. Karl Flesch, "Sociale Ausgestaltung der Armenpflege," *Schriften des Deutschen Vereins für Armenpflege und Wohltätigkeit*, Heft 54 (Leipzig, 1901). The spelling of the term *sociale Fürsorge* here and elsewhere in this essay differs from modern orthography (*Sozialfursorge*) but reflects contemporary usage.

5. Rüdiger vom Bruch, "Bürgerliche Sozialreform im Deutschen Kaiserreich," in Rüdiger vom Bruch, ed., *Weder Kommunismus noch Kapitalismus: Bürgerliche Sozialreform in Deutschland vom Vormärz bis zur Ära Adenauer* (Munich, 1985), 61–179; E. J. Kouri, *Der deutsche Protestantismus und die Soziale Frage: Zur Sozialpolitik im Bildungsbürgertum* (Berlin/New York, 1984); Christoph Sachße, *Mütterlichkeit als Beruf: Sozialarbeit, Sozialreform und Frauenbewegung, 1871–1929* (Frankfurt, 1986), 49ff.

6. Wolfgang Krabbe, *Gesellschaftsveränderung durch Lebensreform* (Göttingen, 1974); Wolfgang Krabbe, "Die Lebensreform: Individuelle Heilserwartung im industriellen Zeitalter," *Journal für Geschichte* 2 (1980); Janos Frecot, "Die Lebensreform," in Klaus Vondung, ed., *Das Wilhelminische Bildungsbürgertum* (Göttingen, 1976).

7. William H. Dawson, *Municipal Life and Government in Germany* (New York, 1916); Christoph Sachße, *Mütterlichkeit als Beruf*, 49–104; Christoph Sachße and Florian Tennstedt, *Geschichte der Armenfürsorge in Deutschland*, vol. 2: *Fürsorge und Wohlfahrtspflege, 1871–1929* (Stuttgart, 1988), 27–38.

8. For a detailed description of the history of municipal health care in Germany, see Alfons Labisch and Florian Tennstedt, *Der Weg zum Gesetz über die Vereinheitlichung des Gesundheitswesens* (Düsseldorf, 1985).

9. Gustav Tugendreich, *Die Mutter- und Säuglingsfürsorge* (Stuttgart, 1910), 283.

10. Friedrich Prinzing, *Handbuch der medizinischen Statistik*, 2d ed. (Jena, 1931), 18, 375.

11. Anna Davin, "Imperialism and Motherhood", *History Workshop* 5 (1978): 10.

12. Alfons Fischer, *Gesundheitspolitik und Gesundheitsgesetzgebung* (Berlin/Leipzig, 1914), 53.

13. For parallel developments in Britain see Davin, "Imperialism and Motherhood," 9–65.

14. Sachße, *Mütterlichkeit als Beruf*, 95–104; Sachße and Tennstedt, *Fürsorge und Wohlfahrtspflege*, 18–22.

15. Hugo Lindemann, *Städteverwaltung und Municipalsozialismus in England* (Stuttgart, 1897); Karl Bücher, *Die wirtschaftlichen Aufgaben der modernen Stadtgemeinde* (Leipzig, 1898); Franz Adickes, *Die sozialen Aufgaben der deutschen Städte* (Leipzig, 1903); Wolfgang Hofman, "Aufgaben und Struktur der kommunalen Selbstverwaltung in der Zeit der Hochindustrialiaierung," in Kurt G. A. Jeserich, Hans Pohl und Georg Christoph von Unruh, eds., *Deutsche Verwaltungsgeschichte*, vol. 3: *Das Deutsche Reich bis zum Ende der Monarchie* (Stuttgart, 1984); Wolfgang R. Krabbe, "Die Entfaltung der kommunalen Leistungsverwaltung in deutschen Städten des späten 19," in Hans Teuteberg, ed., *Urbanisierung im 19 und 20. Jahrhundert* (Cologne/Vienna, 1983), 373ff.; Wolfgang R. Krabbe, *Kommunalpolitik und Industrialisierung: Die Entfaltung der städtischen Leistungsverwaltung im 19 und frühen 20, Jahrhundert* (Stuttgart, 1985); Jürgen Reulecke, *Geschichte der Urbanisierung in Deutschland* (Frankfurt, 1985).

16. Amy Hackett, The Politics of Feminism in Wilhelmine Germany, 1890–1918 (Ph.D. diss., Columbia University, 1976); Richard J. Evans, *The Feminist Movement in Germany 1894–1933* (London/Beverly Hills, 1976); Richard J. Evans, "Liberalism and Society: The Feminist Movement and Social Change," in Evans, ed., *Society and Politics in Wilhelmine Germany* (London/New York, 1978), 186ff.; Barbara Greven-Aschoff, *Die bürgerliche Frauenbewegung in Deutschland, 1894–1933* (Göttingen, 1981); Sachße, *Mütterlichkeit als Beruf*.

17. Helene Lange, *Das Endziel der Frauenbewegung* (Berlin, 1904).

18. Sachße, *Mütterlichkeit als Beruf;* Irene Stoehr, "Organisierte Mütterlichkeit: Zur Politik der deutschen Frauenbewegung um 1900," in Karin Hausen, ed., *Frauen suchen ihre Geschichte* (Munich, 1983), 221–249; Dietlinde Peters, *Mütterlichkeit im Kaiserreich: Die bürgerliche Frauenbewegung und der soziale Beruf der Frau* (Bielefeld, 1984).

19. The German bourgeois women's movement's concept of "social motherhood" has much resemblance to female reform policies and reform ideologies traditionally summarized under the term of "social feminism" in the United States. Conflating the different forms of female reform policies around maternity, health, and child care under the umbrella term of "social feminism" has become controversial in recent American feminist debate (see the introduction to this volume). In the German case, however, the concept of "social motherhood" was advocated by the *organized* bourgeois women's movement; by women who clearly understood themselves as "feminists" envisioning not only reforms to improve the social situation of mothers and children but an extension of female influence and female culture in society in general. Thus, it seems to be justified to call the concept of "social motherhood" a "feminist" concept. For comparative purposes the term "maternalism" suggested by Seth Koven and Sonya Michel in the introduction to this volume best captures the common characteristics of female reform policies promoting public health and child welfare in different countries.

20. Mädchen- und Frauengruppen für soziale Hilfsarbeit, *Denkschrift anläßlich des zehnjährigen Bestehens* (Berlin, 1903), 10.

21. Ibid.

22. Emil Münsterberg, "Ziele der weiblichen Hilfstätigkeit," *Die Frau* 5 (1898): 420ff.

23. Greven-Aschoff, *Die bürgerliche Frauenbewegung*, 96.

24. Alice Salomon, *20 Jahre soziale Hilfsarbeit* (Berlin, 1913), 65.

25. Alice Salomon, *Charakter ist Schicksal: Lebenserinnerungen* (Weinheim/Basel, 1983); Dora Peyser, "Alice Salomon, Ein Lebensbild," in Hans Muthesius, ed., *Alice Salomon. Die Begründerin des sozialen Frauenberufs in Deutschland* (Cologne/Berlin, 1958); Monika Simmel, "Alice Salomon: Vom Dienst der bürgerlichen Tochter am Volksganzen," in Christoph Sachße and Florian Tennstedt, eds., *Jahrbuch der Sozialarbeit*, vol. 4 (Reinbek, 1981), 366–402.

26. There were female high schools (höhere Mädchenschulen), graduation from which, however, did not provide access to university studies. Most of them were private and curricula were very heterogeneous. They were schools for the cultivation rather than the education of the daughters of the prosperous.

27. Salomon, *20 Jahre soziale Hilfsarbeit*, 3.

28. Only with the major Prussian school reform of 1908 was the diploma from a girls' high school recognized as a credential equivalent to the "Abitur." Simultaneously Prussian universities were opened for women. Other states had preceded: Baden in 1902, Bayern in 1903, Württemberg in 1904, Sachsen in 1906, and Thüringen in 1907.

29. Gerhard Schulze-Gaevernitz, *Zum sozialen Frieden: Eine Darstellung der sozialpolitischen Erziehung des englischen Volkes* (Leipzig, 1890); J. A. R. Pimlott, *50 Years of Social Progress: Toynbee Hall* (London, 1935); Emily Abel, "Toynbee Hall, 1894–1914," *Social Service Review* 53 (1979): 606–32; Asa Briggs and Anne Macartney, *Toynbee Hall The First Hundred Years* (London, 1984).

30. Peyser, "Alice Salomon," 65.

31. Alice Salomon, *Die Ausbildung zum sozialen Beruf* (Berlin, 1927), 204.

32. Salomon, *20 Jahre soziale Hilfsarbeit*, 76.

33. Dieter Goeschel and Christoph Sachße, "Theorie und Praxis in der Sozialarbeit," in Sachße and Tennstedt, *Jahrbuch*, 422–43; Sachße, *Mütterlichkeit als Beruf.*

34. Jenny Apolant, *Stellung und Mitarbeit der Frau in der Gemeinde* (Leipzig/ Berlin, 1910).

35. Goeschel and Sachße, "Theorie und Praxis in der Sozialarbeit"; Sachße, *Mütterlichkeit als Beruf*, 138ff., 250ff.

36. Sachße and Tennstedt, *Fürsorge und Wohlfahrtspflege*, 46–67; Sachße, *Mütterlichkeit als Beruf*, 151–86; Rolf Landwehr, "Funktionswandel der Fürsorge vom 1. Weltkrieg bis zum Ende der Weimarer Republik," in Rüdeger Baron and Rolf Landwehr, eds., *Geschichte der Sozialarbeit* (Weinheim/Basel, 1983), 73–92.

37. Wilhelm Polligkeit, "Wie ist in der Armenpflege und Wohltätigkeit die Übergangszeit nach dem Kriege zu gestalten?" *Zeitschrift für das Armenwesen* (1917): 24.

38. Helene Simon, "Bericht über den Arbeitsausschuß der Kriegerwitwen- und waisenfürsorge, in Stenographischer Bericht über die Verhandlungen des 35. Armenpflegetages des Deutschen Vereins für Armenpflege und Wohltätigkeit am 21. und 22. September 1917 in Berlin," in *Schriften des Deutschen Vereins für Armenpflege und Wohltätigkeit*, Heft 107 (Munich/Leipzig, 1917), 25.

39. Gertrud Bäumer, *Die deutsche Frau in der sozialen Kriegsfürsorge* (Gotha, 1916); Catherine E. Boyd, "Nationaler Frauendienst: German Middle-Class Women in Service to the Fatherland, 1914–1918" (Ph.D. diss., Univeresity of Georgia, 1979); Ursula Gersdorff, *Frauen im Kriegsdienst* (Stuttgart, 1969), 15ff.; Marie-Elisabeth Lüders, *Das unbekannte Heer* (Berlin, 1937), 7ff.

40. Greven-Aschoff, *Die bürgerliche Frauenbewegung*, 149.

41. Ernst Wolfgang Böckenförde, "Der Zusammenbruch der Monarchie und die Entstehung der Weimarer Republik," in Kurt G. A. Jeserich et al., eds., *Deutsche Verwaltungsgeschichte*, vol. 4: *Das Reich als Republik und in der Zeit des Nationalsozialismus* (Stuttgart, 1985), 1–23; Werner Abelshauser, ed., *Die Weimarer Republik als Wohlfahrtsstaat* (Stuttgart, 1987); Sachße and Tennstedt, *Fürsorge und Wohlfahrtspflege*, 77–87.

42. *Statistik des Deutschen Reiches*, vol. 402: *Volks-, Berufs- und Betriebszählung vom 16. 6. 1925. Die berufliche und soziale Gliederung der Bevölkerung des Deutschen Reiches* (Berlin, 1927); *Statistik des Deutschen Reiches*, vol. 453: *Volks-, Berufs- und Betriebszählung vom 16. 6. 1933. Die berufliche und soziale Gliederung im Deutschen Reich* (Berlin, 1936).

43. The most important of them were: Helene Weber, former head of the Catholic social women's school in Cologne, who became a leading executive in the Prussian Ministry of Public Welfare; Gertrud Bäumer, former chairwoman of the Bund Deutschen Frauenvereine, who became a leading executive in the Imperial Ministry of the Interior; Julia Dünner, a leader of the Catholic wing of the women's movement, who became a leading executive in the

Imperial Ministry of Labor; Herta Krauß became head of the welfare department in Köln; Helene Krieger became head of the youth department in Halle.

44. Salomon, *Die Ausbildung*, 8ff.

45. Sachße, *Mütterlichkeit als Beruf*, 250ff.

46. For female labor-force participation in general, see Renate Bridenthal and Claudia Koonz, "Beyond Kinder, Küche, Kirche: Weimar Women in Politics and Work," in Renate Bridenthal, Atina Grossman, and Marion Kaplan, eds., *When Biology Became Destiny: Women in Weimar and Nazi Germany* (New York, 1984), 33–65.

47. See Christoph Sachße and Florian Tennstedt, *Der Wohlfahrtsstaat in Nationalsozialismus* (Stuttgart, 1992), 187–97.

4

Woman's Work and the Early Welfare State in Germany: Legislators, Bureaucrats, and Clients before the First World War

Jean H. Quataert

Introduction

Social Scientists recently have turned to probing the multiple connections between state power, class hierarchies, and gender relations. To be sure, a large literature already exists that describes the reciprocal relationship between the state and the economy and questions the extent of state autonomy from class rule.[1] The inclusion of gender has deepened and enriched this matrix. Unraveling these ties is an empirically rewarding task, one that has considerable theoretical importance and contributes as well to a much-needed comparative dialogue over time and place. For example, in a remarkable study of the consolidation of state power (the imposition of Inca imperial rule in Peru and the subsequent transformation of the Andes into a Spanish colony), Irene Silverblatt demonstrates clearly how gender differences were transformed into gender hierarchies and played a critical role in the consolidation of class relations that underpinned imperial authority. The coming of the Spanish in the sixteenth century undermined further the traditional Andean chain of shared authority by gender; in the new context, men alone were privileged as administrators, decision makers, and public figures. At the same time, metaphors of gender became central to a systematic critique of class relations that challenged Spanish rule.[2] In this study, Silverblatt constructs an historically grounded analysis which demonstrates concretely the rewards of connecting class and gender relations with political power and authority.

Can similar insights inform historical research for other areas that did not experience such dramatic breaks in political authority as transitions to imperial control and later colonial rule? Despite obvious differences, nineteenth century continental Europeans confronted the problematics of state building on many different levels. After mid-century, the new nations of Europe—notably Germany, Italy, and Austria-Hungary—were forged through war out of the complicated and overlapping sovereignties of Central and Southern Europe. Henceforth, rulers were intent on making villagers into nationals. These highly visible events were surrounded by other more subtle changes: beginning first in Western Europe and spreading slowly (and incompletely) eastward, legal norms and codes were transformed that ensured the solidification of bourgeois civil society. In the nineteenth century in Western and Central Europe, state formation resulted from the convergence of industrial development, consolidation of bourgeois civil society, and superimposition of national rules and regulations on local communities. There was nothing abstract about these events. Under state auspices, the bourgeoisie came more and more to ensure its values and economic dominance: the rule of law, private property, sanctity of contract, free exchange of labor, and divisions between public and private spheres.[3] But this power did not automatically guarantee a liberal nation-state, as the example of imperial Germany demonstrates unmistakably.

State formation in the century had profound implications for gender relations as well. The legacy of Enlightenment political philosophy and revolutionary practice constructed a new basis of legitimate authority, the male property-owning citizen freely exercising his political rights and speaking on behalf of his household dependents. While definitions of "real" citizen gradually expanded to include lower-class men, they continued to exclude all women from formal political participation. As one study shows, these public constructions influenced the heart of masculine identity. The rhetoric of middle-class men's politics in early-nineteenth century England, for example, intertwined political rights, power, control, and manliness. That is, notions of masculinity that were being redefined in the century carried with them the right to partake in, and shape, the political world. Other important changes took place in the course of the century that influenced gender identity and relationships in different ways. Spokesmen for an expanded public weal successfully challenged the night-watchman model (which saw the maintenance of law and order, the safeguarding of property at home, and the championing of citizens' rights abroad as the only legitimate functions of the state) and advocated broad intervention into affairs of labor, the uses of urban space, and even the health and wealth of the inhabitants of the nation. Indeed, growing state regulation, particularly with the transition to welfare policies in the late nineteenth century, affected the very core of family life, changing relations between parents and children, husbands and wives, love and labor inside the home.[4] The family had become subsumed in the broader public order, a transformation rich in implications for the construction of femininity as well. Sheila Rowbotham is not alone in speaking of "welfare patriarchy." The modern welfare state establishes rules governing private lives and destitute women find themselves dependent on male authority through both marital ties and welfare provisions. Paradoxically, by assuring a tolerable minimum of existence, the welfare state also gives women a chance for a "war of independence."[5]

The emergence of the welfare state thus offers a particularly instructive case for examining the modern configurations of class, gender, and political rule. After all, welfare policies had the *potential* to reach people in the remotest corners of the realm, at their place of work or home, in the town hall, at the insurance office, or through receipt of a pension check. Indeed, the era of the activist state marks a true watershed in history precisely because of the ways interventionist policies structured class and gender relationships and affected social consciousness. And a framework which explores the relationship between the legislators (policy formulation), bureaucrats (implementation), and clients at the local, state, and national levels is a particularly useful way to look at the problematics.

Such a view immediately uncovers complex and reciprocal lines of causality. For example, legislation is not formulated in a vacuum; certainly by the late nineteenth century, a whole array of interests had coalesced in various (often conflicting) reform movements—women's organizations, socialist parties, trade unions, charity and Catholic reform groups—which buttressed their case for legislative change by "scientific research" and sought to persuade by gathering so-called "objective" facts and figures. In the emerging world of democratic mass politics, social pressure from below decisively shaped decision making from above. But bureaucrats, too, fashion laws in real ways. As any student of bureaucracy knows, administrators, through implementation, exercise hidden power by defining the law's intent in concrete ways, often well beyond the original vision of the legislators themselves. And clients are not passive recipients of decisions from above but seek, in turn, to manipulate the laws in order to gain maximum advantage. This framework has the added advantage of easy adaptability for comparative purposes. Besides, it offers new ways to connect formerly distinct interpretive traditions in the writing of German history.

Contemporary observers and later historians have recognized the pioneering role of imperial Germany in the field of social welfare and protective legislation. Imperial Germany was the first industrializing country in the West to adopt compulsory national pension plans for wage earners. Factory workers obtained health insurance in 1883 and accident insurance in 1884; five years later, the old-age pension scheme was passed. Already in 1878, lawmakers had reformed the industrial codes and expanded protective laws, singling out working women for special attention; that year they mandated a nationwide factory inspectorate to watch over and enforce the new labor legislation. The belief that local communities and groups were obdurately committed to laissez-faire principles and unwilling to challenge local business and political interests led to the creation of an inspectorate, appointed by each state government, representing the larger nation-state down the ladder of the governmental administrative districts. The Zittau (Saxony) Chamber of Commerce in 1888 offered a revealing glimpse into reasons for begrudging compliance by the business community. Only the nation-state, its members agreed echoing the popular view, could ensure uniform development of industrial life and see that all employers share equally in the growing burdens of welfare reform. At the same time, the organization decried the excessive costs of such legislation.[6] While there was no exact identity of view between the German state and the business world, it is clear that a strong, activist state was compatible with the orderly reproduction of capitalist relations.

These unprecedented steps toward governmental regulations initially received mixed reviews. Supporters of the new activist role called the early experiments of the 1870s and 1880s "bold";

the United States consul, for one, was so impressed that he wrote in awe of the "gigantic dimensions" and the "enormous apparatus" that would be needed to enforce the novel insurance system.[7] By contrast, early skeptics in Germany predicted devastating financial burdens that would reduce industry's competitiveness and hinder national progress. Others spoke dourly of breeding apathy among workers and weakening their sense of personal responsibility. The more radical among them pointed to the limits of a reform that failed to address the root causes of poverty and promised to redistribute wealth only slightly. A small group of middle-class feminists wondered aloud whether the protective laws "for women only" might not hurt their market position vis-à-vis men.

By 1911 it was clear to all in the Empire that the dire prognoses of industrial and financial collapse had not materialized. Even the party of working people (the German Social Democratic party) had come to favor the welfare provisions. In addition, the German example was influencing passage of similar legislation in other European countries, most notably Austria, the Scandinavian nations, and Great Britain. The early English reforms, for example, promulgated by the Liberals between 1906 and 1911, were inspired partly by the German model. One contemporary naively credited Germany's low unemployment rates, the cessation of out-migration as well as the rise in longevity for males and females in the early twentieth century to its expanding welfare policies. By the second decade of the twentieth century, welfare had become associated, in the contemporary language, with "unending blessing."[8]

For nearly a century, consensus reigned among German historians concerning the "progressive" nature of the country's social-welfare legislation. Another theme soon took its place in the literature. Historians became fascinated with a seeming paradox: why did Bismarck, a Prussian Junker and staunch conservative, oversee promulgation of such novel and farsighted legislation so early? Social insurance and other forms of state intervention interested German historians only as indicators of elite power (these authors had a simplistic model of influence proceeding in one direction, from the top down). They concluded that Bismarck and his supporters hoped to wean the industrial work force from socialism through welfare capitalism and that, ultimately, they were relatively successful in doing so.[9] In this analysis, welfare policies served to mitigate radical consciousness by increasing worker identification with the state, although *no one* studied the actual impact of the welfare provisions on the lives of the clients, let alone the female groups among them. Similarly, the emerging female profession of social work and the story of middle-class women's involvement with the new welfare agencies received short shrift.[10] The whole topic, in fact, gradually faded out of sight. More recently, in 1981, one hundred years after the introduction of the first insurance bill into the Reichstag, a comparative conference on the century-old welfare state was organized in West Germany. The participants focused on the politics surrounding passage of the legislation and the financial and other details of the program. Once again, the actual impact of such policies on work life was not addressed. In the last several years, too, a reevaluation of the nature and cohesion of the ruling class in imperial Germany has, by implication, involved new discussion of the original social-welfare legislation—but for old purposes, as indications of elites jockeying for power.[11] But the analytic category of gender now has opened entirely novel interpretive spaces and challenged treasured assumptions. This essay explores some of the ways in which women were agents as well as objects in the historical emergence of German state social-welfare policies and programs; it elucidates the ways in which the emergence of social-scientific discourses and surveys, in which women were also special subjects of interest, at once informed and reflected the class and gender agendas of the state.

Women's Work, Social Science, and Bureaucracy

Expansion of the early labor codes and laws in the 1870s had been preceded, as was typical of the era, by a series of inquiries and investigations that centered in good measure on women's work in factories and workshops, a symbol of the new industrial era that many found disturbing. A number of surveys had been initiated by the federal government (the Reichstag) while others were undertaken by a variety of private reform groups, among them the influential *Verein fur Sozialpolitik* (Association for Social Policy).[12] Private interest groups were multiplying in the German body politic by the last third of the nineteenth century, reflecting growing disenchantment with "Manchester liberalism" on the part of legislators and politicians, professors of national economy,

bankers, doctors, priests, and pastors—in short, Germany's educated political male elite. These private organizations vocally pres-
sured for legislative reform and increasingly appropriated the
methods and language as well as the prestige of science and survey
research for their purposes. *Verein* members, including highly
influential theorists like Gustav Schmoller, Werner Sombart,
Alfred and Max Weber as well as Ferdinand Tönnies stood at the
forefront of such endeavors as they grappled with some of the
central problematics of the complex relationship between science
and politics that social research poses. Committed to ameliorating
the worst abuses of the capitalist system while preserving its basic
structure, they applied the larger epistemological debates of the
day—over change, causality, history, and explanation—to the
practical workings of survey research. Over time, the organization
pulled back from explicit advocacy of social-policy legislation for
the benefit of workers (at its early congresses, *Verein* members
passed resolutions and sent them to parliament) in favor of stressing its scientific, objective side. While numerous voices continued
to favor research out of a moral concern for greater social justice
and rights, the center of gravity shifted to those who stressed
"scientific necessities" over "political commitments" and emphasized the importance of devising value-neutral instruments and
methodologies.[13]

The *Verein*'s position partly reflected the efforts of the younger
male generation of scientists both to distance themselves from the
political pressures of the authoritarian German state as well as to
secure university and other official positions, easier to do under
a garb of "neutrality" than advocacy. The end goal, then, was to
establish scientific neutrality but not to withdraw into an ivory
tower. *Verein* members had wide contacts among a variety of
important players influential in shaping the welfare state. The
organization operated essentially as a research hub in the larger
welfare nexus, and its members had ties to legislators on both the
national and state levels as well as to the implementors of the new
laws like factory inspectors, who brought policy and reform to the
local level. Members' circles of associates also included a number
of highly talented and well-trained women involved in the bourgeois women's movement. The *Verein* was predominantly a male
organization, but by the turn of the twentieth century, a number
of academically trained women (Drs. Marie Bernays and Rosa
Kempf, for example) as well as those with experience in running

businesses had joined; its chosen research topics included subjects about and of real interest to women; and women were drawn
into research design and implementation.[14]

The simultaneous development and spread of social-science
tools and methods was hardly unique to Germany. Industrial
capitalism was accompanied everywhere by growing attention
to social research, including new methods of analysis, refined
statistical categories, and greater reliability. As noted earlier, legislative change was shaped partly by the scientific case made for
reform by organized interest groups, academics, and all manner
of experts. The authority and power associated with command
over social-scientific discourses encouraged nonspecialists to
appropriate their vocabulary; so, while social science emerged in
Germany as a tool and discourse of a small male elite, its new
language proved particularly beneficial to the "outsiders" of Germany's authoritarian political structure who gained access to it—
middle-class women and organized workers.

The impact these outsiders—women and laboring people—had
on directly shaping state policy was limited in part by the fact-
gathering mechanisms used in Germany. Whereas in Britain and
the United States, social surveys and official inquiries such as
Royal Commissions interviewed men, women, and sometimes
even children from all walks of life, the subjects of social-scientific
investigations were not consulted directly in Germany. Instead,
German politicians and officials relied on *enquêtes* (questionnaire
surveys), that were sent to Germany's highly efficient, geographically decentralized, and extensive male bureaucracy as well as
to local male officials accustomed to implementing the census.
Official government inquiries and most of those initiated by private organizations were sent to municipal officials and local elites
including elected town councilors, Chamber of Commerce representatives, pastors, teachers, police, and factory owners who
reported on local conditions. Not surprisingly, the results of these
inquiries reflected the concerns and interests of the groups of men
who controlled them to an even greater extent than in Britain and
the United States where women and laboring people were at least
given the opportunity to speak for themselves.[15] In the massive
survey data on women's work which accumulated from the 1870s
on, only in exceptional cases (surveys on home industry, for example, organized by bourgeois feminists or by female factory inspectors) did anyone ask the opinion of the working women
themselves.

The extensive bureaucratic apparatus as well as public reliance on elite opinion also restricted the extent to which women could affect reform legislation, more so in Germany than elsewhere, or so it appears. As the chapter by Kathryn Sklar in this volume demonstrates, the patterns of change that emerged in the United States simply were not duplicated in Germany. In the United States, laws appointing female inspectors and the first steps in labor reform such as child-labor laws, minimum-wage regulations, and health and sanitary measures were grass-roots efforts by educated middle-class women at the state level. Florence Kelley herself, a leading reformer, recognized that the pressures for change "proceeded from people and groups [upward] acting in the interest of philanthropy."[16] That a woman, Florence Kelley, was appointed *chief* factory inspector for the state of Illinois could not have happened in any of the states in imperial Germany. Even the "lady factory inspectors" in England, headquartered in London and supervised by the chief inspector, had considerably more authority and latitude for decision making than their German counterparts. They not only inspected, recommended changes, and issued warnings, but also prosecuted employers in court for violations of the law, a situation unimaginable in the German judiciary. "It is unlikely," writes one analyst of the British case, "that any of the lady inspectors had even been in a courtroom before, and no woman had appeared before a British court as a lawyer, yet May Abraham (a female inspector) conducted some eighty prosecutions during her first year and Lucy Deane prosecuted her first case in Derby only a month after she began work" in 1894.[17] And, in Russia, if I may offer a tentative hypothesis which needs verification, the marked discrepancy between the excessive claims of autocratic rule and its actual weaknesses in practice seems to have left considerable space for middle-class women to organize grass-roots movements at the local level to improve the working and living conditions of the lower social orders.[18]

What made the German case so different? Why did German women have less say in shaping and implementing policy? Where, indeed, did their influence lie? Which administrative levels proved most receptive to arguments made from a "woman's perspective"? In Germany, the bureaucratic apparatus that permeated society proved a formidable barrier to all manner of grass-roots pressure, including that of women. The bureaucratic organization of public life, reinforced by the hierarchical system of higher education, functioned to dampen social change and restrict class mobility. The shaping of the factory inspectorate, symptomatic of the broader bureaucratic picture, illustrates the point fully.[19]

Factory inspectors were state officials with job tenure and pension rights (*Beamte*). Information on their occupational background places them squarely in the educated and professional community of imperial Germany. For example, the first inspector in Baden, Friedrich Woerishoffer, was a railroad engineer; in Württemberg, two senior administrative officials in the state's central department for trade and industry became inspectors. Bavaria established criteria that limited applicants to those with "academic or equivalent" training. Given the class nature of higher education in imperial Germany that discriminated against working-class people, those who had university training almost always came from middle-class and other privileged backgrounds. But the decision to restrict applicants to those with "academic or equivalent" experience also meant that inspectors who came from the technical managerial groups or government service were used to seeing workers "from above." As middle-class men, they also adhered strongly to the separate-spheres philosophy for the sexes. These bureaucrats had considerable say over work life in their jurisdictions and they interpreted the laws from their own class perspective. Inspectors were middle-class males with middle-class biases.[20]

It took several decades to make a successful case for admitting women to the German inspectorate. Initially, the educational requirement had dashed any hopes of having female inspectors; women were denied access to higher education in the German states until well after the turn of the twentieth century. But pressure by women's organizations and the socialist movement by the late nineteenth century was creating a climate favorable to the hiring of female inspectors; the first woman was appointed in the more liberal state of Baden in 1892. Again as a result of the push "from below" by organized labor, a representative of working people was added to the state inspectorates around 1905. However, the choice to "represent" the working class was in every case male.

German women inspectors came out of the same privileged milieu as their male colleagues, although the requirement for academic training was replaced in many cases by "good general education and practical experience in life." The Baden case is instructive. Dr. Elisabeth von Richthofen assumed her position in 1900. Among the first women trained academically, she had studied with Max Weber and was part of Germany's progressive-reform groups. But she left the position after one year due to her marriage. Her successor, Dr. Marie Baum, a chemist, acquired a reputation as a thoughtful and sensitive observer of working-class life. She, too, had close ties with middle-class reformers. In Württemberg, a widow, Mrs. Grünau, became an inspector's assistant; for the Oberlausitz province in Saxony, another widow, Mrs. Marie Merback began her job in 1900. Thus, women shared the class origins of men (but not their family status, being either single or widowed as was the case also in England) but here all similarity stopped. As a middle-class bureau, the German inspectorate divided up tasks by gender. Female inspectors had their own sphere—responsibility for working-class women in home industry and those factories and workshops in which female labor predominated, mainly branches of textiles, apparel, and cigar and brickmaking. The sex-segregated work force of industrial capitalism facilitated such a division of jurisdiction. But it meant that male inspectors increasingly were poorly informed on the conditions of labor of typical female employment. Furthermore, women were not given *Beamte* status but rather assistantships and were placed on quarterly notice. In addition, to lend credibility, their reports typically were published under the head inspector's authorship and not under their own name. And a final characteristic of the women's position reflected concern over the authority inherent in the job itself; as state officials, inspectors had near police power to enforce the law and force change. Unlike their British counterparts, German women inspectors were not granted the power to enforce the law and compel change. In Germany, the right to audit business enterprise remained exclusively in the hands of men.

The detailed rules and regulations governing personnel matters in the German inspectorate left little room for change. Indeed, these highly prescribed and centralized bureaus fit comfortably into the traditional bureaucratic structure of Central Europe—reflecting the time-honored Prussian tradition of "state activism," of widespread belief in a strong, powerful, immediate yet benevolent state to solve the dislocations arising from economic and social development.[21] Two pronounced characteristics of the emerging welfare state—its reliance on "scientifically proven" statistical surveys and the proliferation of bureaus and agencies—were eminently compatible with traditional notions of German statecraft. The belief in value-neutral science perpetuated the self-image of the German nation-state plying a disinterested path between major social classes. Establishment of needs and ameliorative legislative measures easily were hailed as "objective" undertakings in the name of the general good.

The modern bureaucratic structures designed to meet newly uncovered needs for social services operated in a highly supportive political milieu at all the levels of organization. At the level of the individual factory, for example, health-insurance funds were administered by an elected executive committee comprised, typically, of the owner as well as representatives of his white-collar personnel such as treasurers, overseers or shipping clerks, and spokespeople for blue-collar workers, including women. Women voted for and served on these local bodies. The committees handled contested cases over pay between ill workers, hospitals, and doctors; set contributions for pregnancy leaves; and paid claims at death, among other responsibilities.

At the municipal level, the traditional communal charity administration (*Armenpflege*), which had been exclusively a male preserve, increasingly shared the stage with more modern welfare agencies that were being created to oversee crèches, organize foster care, help destitute women in childbed, or educate and train wives and mothers in the latest in domestic science (*Mutterschule*).[22] Each local agency had its provincial and state overseer, which functioned as a court of appeal for final decision making. The higher the administrative level and the more formal the organization, the less room there was for alternative, female voices in actual decision making. Indeed, in Germany, women exercised influence much more on a voluntary or piecemeal than formal basis. For example, in 1901, of 488 women who cared for orphans in Berlin, only a handful were found in paid positions. According to a 1910 survey, in towns with more than 10,000 inhabitants, only 400 women held salaried posts in the local welfare systems; five years later (in part reflecting the crises of war but the proportions nonetheless are indicative), in 45 large towns there were 761 paid female welfare workers next to 10,000 female volunteers.[23]

As Christoph Sachße's essay stresses, it was at the municipal level that middle-class women were able to help mold the institutions that most directly affected welfare clients in their daily lives. The case of the Saxon Oberlausitz, a borderland between Silesia to the east and Bohemia to the south, is highly instructive. In the industrial villages of the south, the lead in helping design welfare efforts and institutions was taken by the wives of mill owners and industrialists. As part of the local elite, their endeavors to shape life in and around the factories was a response to the destabilizing conditions of ongoing industrialization. In this regard, the Oberlausitz example reflected wider political realities at the local level. There, the German middle classes had preserved considerable power, partly by safeguarding highly restrictive voting laws that favored property owners based on levels of wealth. While in former times, the wives of local factory owners and other prominent businessmen in the textile villages of the Oberlausitz might have helped with the accounts, increasingly they turned their newfound "leisure" time to reform work. By late in the century, in their husband's places of business, they had set up a series of special courses and classes designed to promote "domesticity" among women workers. They entered the political realm by claiming that all manner of activities associated with the home could be subjected to "scientific analysis" and rational management and they proved their assertion by seeking to restructure working-class women's lives, health, and behavior, first at the place of gainful employment itself. To buttress their case, they drew on factory inspectors' reports and other "scientific" data. Thus, Frau Preibisch in Reichenau and Frau Müller in Hirschfelde instituted cooking schools for young girls in the local textile mills; in the damask-weaving village of Gross-Schönau there were similar courses organized for cooking, knitting, and sewing. By the turn of the twentieth century, this factory-based instruction was widespread indeed.

For these local reformers, there was no great gap in practice between the public and private realms, and the public world of work became a suitable venue to instill sober German family values and good rational management practices. Middle-class women in Saxony essentially moved from public charity—giving money to the needy through their women's clubs—to social reform, first within the factory gates but increasingly outside as well. They provided the womanpower for the networks of social services that gradually emerged in the villages. Through the women's movement—the Lutheran variety in this case—they instituted day-care centers, kindergartens, and infant schools for working women, "schools" for mothers, and hygienic birthing homes, revealing their growing concern with the plight of their less fortunate working sisters. According to a governmental survey, by 1914, there were 31 infant centers in the greater district of Bautzen alone. These efforts were part of a wider movement of middle-class women to reach across the social gap and, through reform work, cement social harmony between the classes.[24]

Middle-class women were not alone in demanding municipal social reform. In large urban centers like Leipzig, Bremen, Berlin, and Cologne where the working class had established a powerful presence, socialist women also were making inroads into welfare activities. In the decade prior to World War I, they too found the municipality more flexible and willing to bend to their pressures. They became increasingly involved in maternal and infant health care and day-care services; in local housing issues; and in pressuring for local electoral change. For example, in Cologne, the socialist Marie Juchacz worked closely with male municipal welfare officials. Similarly, Helene Grünberg entered the Nuremberg committee for the poor in 1911. Two years later, she joined an infant-welfare bureau that organized meetings at which doctors spoke. That same year she was admitted to the youth court as the social worker for juveniles.[25]

German state welfare programs were originally formulated with implicit expectations about the class and gender characteristics of both policy recipients and executors. Through the criteria established to qualify for assistance, state welfare programs promoted the normative ideal of the regularly employed male as both worker and welfare recipient. So, too, on the local level, the state opened up its offices, agencies, and professions to a particular type of woman—the dedicated middle-class woman. However, the second or third generation of socialist women—women who had been educated through the party, gained a measure of real control over their lives and believed in reform not revolution—could also participate in the local constellation of welfare agencies and activities. Municipal welfare reform thus provided a common ground for activist women with often very different social and political backgrounds and commitments.

Social Science, Gendered Labor, and Welfare in Saxony: The Oberlausitz Weavers

While policy makers and executors, both male and female, tended to envision clients as passive recipients of welfare, the practice of social welfare on the local level does not corroborate such a view. The case of self-employed handweavers, a group of workers in Germany brought under welfare legislation in the 1890s,[26] offers fascinating insights into the dynamic ways in which class, gender, and social-scientific discourses helped to shape the implementation of welfare policies and the distribution of benefits. Such study allows us to begin to uncover how distinct categories of workers were given coverage and to assess the impact of welfare legislation on their lives and on their overall attitudes toward work and family and housekeeping.

Why handweavers were singled out for protection early on is not difficult to understand. Weavers had become emotional symbols in German society for both the political Right and the Left as well as subjects of contemporary research projects designed to reinforce the case for welfare reform. For Germany's right wing, rural weavers were religious and authoritarian people, representatives of a patriarchal way of life fighting valiantly against the encroachment of an alien urban and rationalist culture. In contrast, for the left wing, handweavers symbolized an honorable craft downgraded and destroyed by the dehumanizing impact of capitalism—to the point of collective rebellion and uprising. Indeed, memories of the Silesian weaver revolt of 1844 were kept very much alive in the 1890s in the riveting lithographs of Käthe Kollwitz and the powerful performances of Gerhard Hauptmann's play *The Weavers*.[27]

Weavers also had become the objects of considerable scientific research. For example, the *Verein* itself had commissioned a four-volume detailed study of the various branches of home industry, published in the late 1890s. The organizing principle of the large study was the shared distinction authors made between the so-called "old" and "new" home industries. Gender, however, was the real key in this analysis. The "old" were the traditional rural trades (weaving and clog or tinplate making) in which men were "masters," heads of households, and organizers of production. These were male-dominated home industries, although men's essential labor was supplemented by the work of their wives and dependents, who did the ancillary and necessary preparatory tasks. These descriptions resembled the normative ideal of the family that was beginning to inform much early welfare legislation: a residential unit comprised of a breadwinner and his dependents, whose labor, particularly for the lower classes, might be needed to supplement the family income.

Despite profound differences in the actual organization of the workplace, the *Verein* analysis of the "new" home industries closely mirrored accounts of the "old" industries. The ready-made garment industry, prototypical of new, urban domestic work, was a female-dominated branch in which women and children labored to add to the household wage of husbands and fathers, the chief breadwinners who worked in the petrochemical, metal, and machine industries of Germany's larger cities. The typological division of home industry into male-dominated branches yielded a very similar analysis of the place of women's work in the family economy.[28]

Other affiliates of the *Verein* did actual field research similar to participant observation. For example, Robert Wilbrandt traveled throughout Germany between 1903 and 1904 and reported on the changes transforming weaving districts.[29] While his analysis, perhaps, does not fully reflect the tenor of *Verein* writing, it unambiguously demonstrates the gender biases in the approaches of these middle-class men and the difficulties of using the study's statistics and data without serious qualification.

Wilbrandt, a reformer, in *Die Franenarbeit*, focused on what he called the "social problem" of capitalism which, he argued, emerged most clearly in the case of weaving. He defined the problem as the disastrous effect of the competition of women's work on the life situation of men.

> In this sense, weavers typify the problem of female competition in capitalism . . . and particularly from the perspective of the woman as wife and mother [the woman's "true" profession, according to Wilbrandt] it is to be applauded that the near male monopoly of heavy industry, of iron and coal production, is prototypical of our industrial development rather than the increasing feminization of the textile trade.

Elsewhere in the text he comments that "what makes the transition from handweaving to mechanical factory production one of ongoing poverty is the competition of the sexes," destroying simultaneously the family (22) and masculinity—that is, transforming "real" men (who should be breadwinners responsible for their families) into caricatures of women. Wilbrandt believed that "when the weaver is called to the factory he is transformed from master craftsman into unskilled underling and from a man into a girl" (*aus einem Mann ein Mädchen*) (3).

Wilbrandt's imagery was inflammatory; it played on the emotions and exacerbated the sexual tensions that already existed in the workplace over principles (the woman's "right to work"), job opportunities, and mobility. Wilbrandt claimed to speak in systemic terms as he sought to uncover the shortcomings of capitalism. However, ultimately his analysis suggested that the true problem besetting German industry and society was women's work, the competition of cheap, unskilled female labor which results in men's emasculation and their degradation. The solution, too, was equally clear: return women to their true occupation of wives and mothers at home. Despite Wilbrandt's elaborate veneer of "science" in the tables and statistics of his book, his beliefs about men and women's social and economic roles clearly undermined his claim to have conducted serious and meaningful social-scientific research. Normative assumptions about gender and work infused so-called social-scientific analyses about the effects of capitalism on society which in turn influenced legislators seeking to preserve the status of male breadwinners and the "handicrafts."

In part, social pressure had first turned legislators' eyes to the nation's domestic weaving population. In 1894, the German *Bundesrat* extended disability and old-age pensions to the self-employed in homeweaving (the so-called *Hausgewerbetreibende*). Passage of this amendment elicited no special commentary at the time; it seemed to fit an emerging pattern of expanding insurance coverage. In practice, however, the decision to include homeweavers represented something new. Both the original insurance plans and the protective labor laws had been geared to labor in factories and larger workshops, both easily counted and measured. The 1894 law was one of the first—and until 1914, the most important—to extend insurance into the *home* of the self-employed.

Given working-class women's more tenuous relationship to factory work (but not necessarily to wage labor), the law might have begun to offer large numbers of women the benefits of insurance, which they regularly relinquished when they left the factory for the hearth. The law, furthermore, was straightforward. Written in a gender-neutral vocabulary, it spoke simply of persons who wove and their apprentices (*Hülfspersonal*). But it was precisely in implementing the law that conflict erupted over definitions of women's work, assumptions about gender divisions in occupations, and proper family living arrangements among the lower classes. Ample archival materials on the ensuing controversy, which lasted nearly two decades, exist for the Oberlausitz textile province of Saxony. These documents permit more detailed examination of the complex links between policy formulation, implementation, and client responses. The case study demonstrates the larger truth about welfare provisions: their effects reach far beyond the people's "welfare" and "the public good," for embedded in the laws are explicit assumptions about work, family life, and proper gender roles. And the conflict also says much about the bureaucratic mentality which is an integral part of the increased record-keeping activities of the welfare state. Officials consciously sought to pigeonhole their citizens into assumed generally rational and valid categories, which, in the case of rural handweavers did not reflect the more fluid and ambiguous nature of their work lives.

Despite their seeming simplicity and gender neutrality, the laws concerning handweaving left room for considerable manipulation both by bureaucrats and clients. To qualify for insurance, workers had to be engaged in activity recognized as "real work" by the Industrial Code. Only work as defined in the Industrial Code was covered by the welfare provisions. This code, promulgated most recently in 1869 and implemented by a series of ordinances, provided workers who were covered with such important guarantees as Sunday rest, continuing education for (male) youths, and freedom of contract. It also outlawed exploitative practices such as the truck system.

A series of ordinances qualified the extent of labor regulation more explicitly by excluding two kinds of workers from *all* regulation. The first were those engaged in the female domestic arts of spinning, knitting, and needlework as well as washing and ironing, not because of their ties to home industry but because lawmakers associated such activity with housework. Supplemental wage work done not as a permanent occupation but next to everyday housework was not considered labor and remained unregulated.

The second exempted group consisted of assistants of self-employed homeworkers who were family members. Family members did not qualify as industrial laborers (*gewerbliche Hilfspersonen*) unless they had a separate work contract that stipulated wages. Thus, in the transition to welfare capitalism, legal definitions in Germany ignored the economic cooperation among family members and did not acknowledge the family as a work unit, beyond rewarding the member of the family identified as the breadwinner.

What effect did these assumptions have when insurance was extended to the small, semi-independent family weaving businesses in the south Oberlausitz province? In a detailed survey of the area's weaving households undertaken in conjunction with extension of the pension plan, the wives of male homeweavers appear as "mere assistants" of their husbands (*bloss Gehilfin des Mannes*), even though they had long labor careers themselves as handweavers. Time and time again, the pollsters noted that the wife was merely helping her husband.[30] The statement, however, was normative, not truly descriptive and it reflected the new understanding of a proper family that was spreading in the industrial world of imperial Germany. The insurance survey itself assumed that men were the main breadwinners. Several questions were directed especially to the wife, asking whether her husband worked in home industry *so that* she just provided supplemental labor (*sodass die Ehefrau nur Gehilfin ist*). Indeed, the survey was worded in such a way that it elicited the very answers it expected, since the gender work rules of these "traditional" or "old" home-industry households had been established by scientific research in the first place.

The outcome of disputed insurance claims also reflected beliefs about proper gender work roles. Several types of cases came before insurance officials in the two decades after promulgation of the law. The first concerned weaving families that owned one loom only: then the husband's labor alone was seen as real and insurable. The second involved those couples in which the wife essentially wove throughout the year for the businessman. If the husband worked summers in agriculture or construction (as was often the case in the weakly urbanized province) but wove on the same loom in the winter, then she was judged helping him. More accurately, of course, he was helping her. Nonetheless, his work alone was acknowledged by eventual receipt of a pension. A final case involved families with at least two looms. If the husband and wife worked for one employer and shared an account, he—but not she—was required to join the insurance plan. The legal guidelines stipulated the presence of direct contact between worker and boss for any acknowledged work relationship. The trend in the past decades of the nineteenth century had been to give women their own separate accounts, but this had not yet become universal practice. Historically, joint family employment had been organized under one account and it was most typically in the husband's name. This method of payment reflected the pooled labor of all members of the family. Now this traditional custom was used to dismiss the serious nature of women's labor.

Family members themselves had colluded in the designation of women as supplemental laborers. On one level, the reasons are perfectly understandable. Joining the pension plan cost precious pennies of hard-earned income. Members of these weaving households in the Oberlausitz, dirt poor and living at the margin, were deeply skeptical of the newfangled notion of state pensions that were financed through deductions from their current earnings. They tried to get out of paying the weekly insurance premiums by verbally camouflaging women's productive involvements; the cash then could continue to be used for daily living. Weavers believed that such a stratagem served best what can be called "collective family interests." Besides, the very assumptions in the law had made such subterfuge possible. Weavers knew that state officials would more readily accept the label "supplementary" for women's work than for men's activities. Karl Köhler summed it up beautifully when he said, "my wife is a mere helpmate, as it says in the Imperial law."[31] The designation, however, was a verbal mask and it became a central part of these home-industry families' resistance to the encroachment of state welfare capitalism.

Government officials sought to structure the impact of the new law on an ad hoc basis. Individual members within individual households were required to account for themselves, their work, and their income on official forms or at hearings arranged by insurance and municipal officials. These working people—as individuals and members of households—were adept at maximizing what they saw to be their own private interests. But they also joined together. They used the same language and phrases in separate appeals and sent off joint petitions. They sometimes even acted in concert by refusing contributory payments. For example, the young weavers in Ollersdorf scornfully proclaimed that "we don't earn anything," and defied municipal authorities to prove otherwise.[32] For two decades, in fact, weaver households in the Oberlausitz comprised a loosely organized interest group that challenged the policy making and enforcement prerogatives of the young German welfare state. Pulled into a public arena in this contest, household members tried to defend their life-style in their own language against alien values and middle-class notions of "proper" gender work roles.

More was involved in the controversy than the financial worries that lay at the forefront of worker consciousness. With the advantage of hindsight, it is clear that state policy threatened a way of life and a family ethic that valued both the so-called public and the private contributions of family members, and assigned them in various mixes at different junctures in the domestic cycle. Government policy upset this traditional calculus, applying greater worth to the public sphere and paid labor, and also to male labor, which was clearly the standard for public activity and wage work. While officials, as we have seen, automatically regarded husbands as the family weavers, wives described the household division of labor quite differently. In Auguste Lowe's words, "In the winter, he [her husband, who also was a mason] did the weaving, in the summer I; we shared a loom. . . . During the summer months, weaving was my main occupation. . . ." In addition, in accounting for their work, household members were forced to respond according to formulas on time and income that reflected a growing market mentality and the rigors of the factory bureaucracy— according to categories that policy makers had devised. Officials wanted to know the *exact* financial contribution of each family member, requiring near mathematical precision (for example, husbands contributed two-thirds, two children one-eighth each, or in another case, a wife one-half of the total wage income from domestic manufacture). They also asked women the *exact* amount of time each day spent in *wage* work and *house*work. It was recorded, for example, that Anna Hauptmann worked six hours daily, four days a week, in manufacturing and eight hours daily in housekeeping (she had eight children) while Anna Engler in Jonsdorf was a housewife for thirty hours per week and a weaver for thirty-six. At the same time, correspondence among the educated bureaucrats makes it clear that they scorned these people precisely for their lack of precision, attention to detail, or willingness and ability to keep simple and clear records on their own. As one report noted in 1902, these were barely literate people, "incapable" of doing paper work, not at all used to writing or doing any "demanding mental activity," and hardly even able to put their names to paper. No matter how simple the formulas were, one official predicted, the clients would never successfully master them alone: they had, he added, considerable "distaste" for clerical work (*Widerwille gegen Bureauarbeit*), an ambiguous statement which seems also to acknowledge the active resistance of weavers to filling out the forms.[33]

What is clear is that these bureaucratic calculations were at variance with the values of the older collective family entity. While its members might both have thought of time as money and been aware of paid and nonpaid labor, both types of work activity were seen as vital to the survival of the whole household. In the new formula, however, family labor was redefined and some of it valued (declared "work" worthy of receipt of a pension) and some of it devalued (there were no pensions given for housework or the labor needed to sustain a small family-subsistence plot). It is no wonder that so many people in these weaver households resisted being incorporated into the welfare state. And it is not surprising that women joined in protest, as did forty handweavers in Wittgendorf, who appeared before local health-insurance officials on 13 September, 1894. The handweavers questioned the new definition of time embodied in the law (the factory's standard of "uninterrupted" time), arguing cogently that it hurt their interests. To gear contributions to a specified time and not to output disadvantaged old people, who worked more slowly and women, whose daily routine was divided between child care, agricultural work, and weaving.[34]

Indeed, it was women's diverse contributions in the household that were most negatively affected by the new bureaucratic norms, and many intuitively perceived it, even if they did not fully comprehend the basis for change. As we have seen, a gender perspective challenges the standard assessment of welfare legislation promulgated in the "general good." In reality, application of the law fed into a broader public climate that was devaluing women's multiple work activities. Johanne Walter in Wittgendorf described a full workday, but her busy schedule did not qualify as "proper" work according to government officials. Her husband was a day laborer and two children were in service. She did their laundry and wove a bit at home (receiving 2,70 marks per piece which she estimated took about two weeks to complete). In addition, she took care of her father's house in the village of Dreusendorf some miles away, she sewed all the clothing for her family and repaired it as well (but denied sewing for strangers), and on the family's small plot of land she grew potatoes, rye, or oats and leased a parcel of land for hay. She marketed the agricultural products, except the potatoes.[35]

The impact of the law on the lives of rural householders forces careful assessment of behavior based on a sense of a "collective family interest." In the particular case of handweaving, such "shared interest" worked to the advantage of men in the families. It appears that a sense of shared family commitment and fate was in each case at the base of individual response to the law. If it met perceived family needs, wives camouflaged their wage work at home; as we have seen, the pension laws assumed anyway that men were the real breadwinners, even if they also worked in the home. By siding with wage work that was amenable to exact calculation and by defining women's work as housework, the welfare laws gave men in the families added status and power as well as concrete material advantage later on by receipt of a pension. At the time, widows did not inherit their deceased husbands' pension rights.

Compulsory extension of old-age and disability insurance to handweavers offers a graphic and poignant example of how the politics of sex in Germany became enmeshed in social reform and social welfare at all levels. This was true for decision makers and social scientists, who were determined to promote socially integrative sentiments; for reformers, who saw a model patriarchal working-class family as the basis of uplifting lower-class life; and even for the clients themselves, who aimed to manipulate both the applications of laws and the discourse around women's work to their own perceived benefit.

Equally as important, the interventionist policies contained negative assessments concerning women's multiple domestic roles in so-called wage and housework, in paid and unpaid labor, as well as small-scale agriculture. These very values gradually have become the standards by which society judges the variety of work activities involved in production and reproduction. The monetary and bureaucratic calculations effectively obliterated different ways that householders organized and made sense out of their own lives.

Paradoxically, social-science research, which silenced such patterns in the past, has the potential to capture these once lived historic priorities in the present. Max Weber recognized that "the social sciences belong to those disciplines to which eternal youth is granted . . . to which the eternally onward flowing stream of culture perpetually brings new problems" and the necessity for reinterpretation.[36] New questions, new methods, new politics, indeed, are shaping a new social science which now uncovers these arenas of lost experience. For the scientist, however, there still is the issue of assessment, because behavior based on collective family interests will not necessarily have the same consequences for the men and women in the family. As this case has shown, the gendered political world of lawmaking and implementing has meant that similar motives may in reality work to promote men's independence and women's dependence.

Notes

1. Ralph Miliband, *The State in Capitalist Society* (New York, 1969), and his *Class Power and State Power* (New York, 1983); Karl Polanyi, *The Great Transformation* (Boston, 1957); Bob Jessop, *The Capitalist State* (New York, 1982); Peter B. Evans, Dietrich Rueschmayer, and Theda Skocpol, eds., *Bringing the State Back In* (New York, 1985); Gabriel A. Almond, "The Return to the State," *American Political Science Review* 82 (1988): 853–74; Gary Bonham, "State Autonomy or Class Domination: Approaches to Administrative Politics in Wilhelmine Germany," *World Politics* 35 (1983): 631–51; David Abraham, *The Collapse of the Weimar Republic: Political Economy and Crisis*, 2nd ed. (New York, 1986), specifically 1–41; David Blackbourn and Geoff Eley, *The Peculiarities of German History* (New York, 1985), in particular 241ff.

2. Irene Silverblatt, *Moon, Sun and Witches: Gender Ideologies and Class in Inca and Colonial Peru* (Princeton, N.J., 1987).

3. I am following the line of argument of David Blackbourn and Geoff Eley concerning the significance of the consolidation of bourgeois civil society for nineteenth-century state building. See, Blackbourn and Eley, *Peculiarities*, 90ff. Also, Eugen Weber, *Peasants into Frenchmen: The Modernization of Rural France, 1870–1914* (Stanford, Calif., 1976); George Steinmetz, "The Myth and the Reality of an Autonomous State: Industrialists, Junkers and Social Policy in Imperial Germany," paper presented to a conference entitled The Kaiserreich in the 1990s: New Research, New Directions, New Agendas, University of Pennsylvania, 23–25 February 1990; Hagen Schulze, ed., *Nation-Building in Central Europe* (Lemington Spa, Hamburg, and New York, 1987). Also, consult the collection of Charles Tilly, ed., *The Formation of National States in Western Europe* (Princeton, N.J., 1975), and that of Charles Bright and Susan Harding, eds., *Statemaking and Social Movements: Essays in History and Theory* (Ann Arbor, 1984).

4. Catherine Hall, "Private Persons versus Public Someones: Class, Gender and Politics in England, 1780–1850," in Carolyn Steedman, Cathy Urwin, and Valerie Walkerdine, eds., *Language, Gender and Childhood* (London, 1985), 10–33; Jane Lewis, ed., *Labour and Love: Women's Experience of Home and Family, 1850–1940* (New York, 1986).

5. Sheila Rowbotham, "The Trouble with 'Patriarchy,' " in Raphael Samuel, ed., *People's History and Socialist Theory* (London, 1981), 364–69; Ute Gerhard, *Verhältnisse und Verhinderungen. Frauenarbeit, Familie und Rechte der Frauen im 19. Jahrhundert* (Frankfurt, 1978), 17. Also, Beatrix Campbell, *Wigan Pier Revisited: Poverty and Politics in the 80s* (London, 1984).

6. Zentrales Staatsarchiv, Potsdam (hereafter ZStAP), RMdI, no. 6869: Die Berichte der Handels- und Gewerbekammern, 1881–1890, Bl. 61 (Bericht der Handels- und Gewerbekammer Zittau vom 12 Dezember 1888).

7. United States National Archive, Consular Reports, Germany, no. 89 (Washington, D.C., 1888), 613.

8. G. Zacher, "German Workingmen's Insurance and Foreign Countries," *American Journal of Sociology* 17 (1911): 178, 180; Henry E. Sigerist, "From Bismarck to Beveridge: Developments and Trends in Social Security Legislation," *Bulletin of the History of Medicine* 13 (1943): 373–76; E. P. Hennock, *British Social Reform and German Precedents: The Case of Social Insurance, 1880–1914* (Oxford, Eng., 1987); Peter Flora and Arnold J. Heidenheimer, *The Development of Welfare States in Europe and America* (New Brunswick, N.J., 1981); G. A. Ritter, *Sozialversicherung in Deutschland und England. Entstehung und Grundzüge im Vergleich* (Munich, 1983); W. J. Mommsen, ed., *The Emergence of the Welfare State in Britain and Germany, 1850–1915* (London, 1981); William Harbutt Dawson, *Bismarck and State Socialism: An Exposition of the Social and Economic Legislation of Germany since 1870* (1890; rpt. New York, 1973).

9. Sidney B. Fay, "Bismarck's Welfare State," *Current History* 18 (1955): 2–3; A. Gladen, *Geschichte der deutschen Sozialpolitik bis zur Gegenwart* (Wiesbaden, 1974); M. Stolleis, "Die Sozialversicherung Bismarcks," in H. F. Zacher, ed., *Bedingungen für die Entstehung und Entwicklung von Sozialversicherung* (Berlin, 1979), 387–410; F. Syrup and O. Neuloh, *100 Jahre staatliche Sozialpolitik, 1839–1949* (Stuttgart, 1957); Hajo Holborn, *A History of Modern Germany, 1840–1945* (New York, 1969), 287–93; Florian Tennstedt, *Sozialgeschichte der Sozialpolitik in Deutschland. Vom 18. Jahrhundert bis zum Ersten Weltkrieg* (Göttingen, 1981), 142ff.

10. See Christoph Sachße, "Social Mothers, the Bourgeois Women's Movement, and German Welfare-State Formation, 1890–1929," in this volume, for an extended analysis of bourgeois women's roles in social welfare.

11. Peter A. Köhler and Hans F. Zacher, eds., *The Evolution of Social Insurance, 1881–1981: Studies of Germany, France, Great Britain, Austria and Switzerland* (London and New York, 1982). Otto Pflanze, "Bismarcks Herrschaftstechnik als Problem der gegenwärtigen Historiographie," *Schriften des Historischen Kollegs* (Munich, 1982).

12. Among other government-sponsored inquiries see, Zentrales Staatsarchiv, Merseburg, Rep. 120 BB, 7, 3, no. 2, vol. 1: Beschäftigung der Frauen und Minderjährige in den Fabriken (27 April 18726–29 May 1876); ZStAP, RMdI, no. 6742: Mitteilungen der Bundesregierungen über die Lohnverhältnisse der Arbeiterinnen in der Wäsche-fabrikation und der Konfektionsbranche (7 May 1886–24 July 1886); ZStAP, Reichlandsbund. Pressearchiv, no. 7958. Frauenfrage (9 September 1905–30 June 1907): B1. 37, "Die Heimarbeiterinnen als Frau und Mutter," by the South German Factory Inspector Frl. Dr. Baum, Karlsruhe. The studies sponsored by the *Verein* are published under separate volumes of *Schriften des Vereins für Sozialpolitik*. For example, an early inquiry published in 1873 concerned factory legislation: *Über die Durchführung einer Enquete auf dem Gebiet der Fabrikgesetzgebung, Schriften*, vol. 4.

13. For the history and the methodological debates in the *Verein* see Irmelda Gorges, *Sozialforschung in Deutschland, 1872–1914* (Königstein, 1980); Franz Boese, *Geschichte des Vereins für Sozialpolitik, 1872–1932* (Berlin, 1939); Anthony Oberschall, *Empirical Social Research in Germany, 1848–1914* (New York and Paris, 1965); Dirk Käsler, *Max Weber: An Introduction to his Life*, trans. Philippa Hurd (Chicago, 1988); Max Weber, *Gesammelte Aufsätz zur Sociologie und Sozialpolitik* (Tübingen, 1924); and Max Weber, "Die 'Objektivität' sozialwissenschaftlicher und sozialpolitischer Erkenntnis," *Archiv fuer Sozialwissenschaft* 19 (1904): 22–87.

14. The shifting membership lists of the Association are found in Gorges, *Sozialforschung*. Its research subjects of interest to women included examination of existing factory legislation, investigation of home industry, questions of apprenticeship training, housing, hawking, and consumer cooperatives, among others. As part of a *Verein*-sponsored investigation into the selection and adaptation of workers in large private industries, Marie Bernays researched and wrote *Auslese und Anpassung der Arbeiterschaft des geschlossenen Grossindustrie. Dargestellt an den Verhältnisses der "Gladbacher Spinnerei und Weberei" A-G zu München-Gladback im Rheinland. Schriften des Vereins fuer Sozialpolitik*, vol. 133 (Leipzig, 1910). And Rosa Kempf investigated *Das Leben der Jungen Fabrikmaedchen in München: Die soziale und wirtschaftliche Lage ihrer Familie, ihr Berufsleben und ihre persönlichen Verhältnisse. Schriften des Vereins für Sozialpolitik*, vol. 135 (Leipzig, 1911). The Association's survey net was spread exceedingly wide in contrast, it appears, to fin-de-siècle France; there, the literature on women using the latest "scientific" language and methods focused essentially on sweated labor. I want to thank Kathryn Sklar for referring me to the informative article by Judith Coffin, "Social Science and Sweated Labor: Discussions of Women's Work in Late Nineteenth-Century France," *Journal of Modern History* 63 (1991): 230–70.

15. Oberschall, *Empirical Social Research*, 16–17. The *Verein*'s study of rural laborers had been criticized by social democrats and others precisely because it failed to obtain information firsthand from the subjects under investigation. See, Gorges, *Sozialforschung*, 245–48.

16. Florence Kelley, "Die Weibliche Fabrikinspektion in den Vereinigten Staaton," in *Archiv für soziale Gesetzgebung und Statistik* 11 (1897): 131. I want

to thank Kathryn Sklar for making this material available to me and for sharing ideas on differences between the German and the North American case.

17. Mary Drake McFeely, "The Lady Inspectors: Women at Work 1893–1921," *History Today* 36 (1986): 51. Also see her recently published book *Lady Inspectors: The Campaign for a Better Workplace, 1893–1921* (New York, 1988).

18. See Adele Lindenmeyr, "Voluntary Associations and the Russian Autocracy: The Case of Private Charity," *The Carl Beck Papers*, University of Pittsburgh, no. 807 (Pittsburgh, 1990). On women's roles see Richard Stites, "Women and the Russian Intelligentsia: Three Perspectives," in D. Atkinson, A. Dallin, and G. Warshofsky Lapidus, eds., *Women in Russia* (Stanford, Calif., 1977), 39–62; Barbara Evans Clements, *Bolshevik Feminist: The Life of Aleksandra Kollontai* (Bloomington, Ind. and London, 1979), 40–81; Rose Glickman, *Russian Factory Woman: Workplace and Society, 1880–1914* (Berkeley, 1984); Aleksandra Kollontai, "Three Generations," in *Love of Worker Bees*, trans. Cathy Porter (Chicago, 1978), 182–211.

19. The following points about the German factory inspectorate draw heavily on my article, "A Source Analysis in German Women's History: Factory Inspectors' Reports and the Shaping of Working-Class Lives," *Central European History* 16 (1983): 99–121.

20. This was also true in Britain where inspectors were expected first of all to persuade by "moral argument," a verbal facility not deemed possible among working-class people.

21. For discussions of the activist state in Germany see, among others, Dieter Langewiesche, " 'Staat' and 'Kommune.' Zum Wandel der Staatsaufgaben in Deutschland im 19. Jahrhundert," *Historische Zeitschrift* 248 (1989): 621–35; Lothar Gall, "Zur Ausbildung und Charakter des Interventionsstaats," *Historische Zeitschrift* 227 (1978): 552–70; Wolfgang Köllmann, "Die Anfänge der staatlichen Sozialpolitik in Preussen bis 1869," *Vierteljahresschrift für Sozial- und Wissenschaftsgeschichte* 53 (1966): 28–52. An interesting contrast is Stephen Skowronek, *Building a New American State: The Expansion of National Administrative Capacities* (New York, 1982). Also, Stephen D. Krasner, "Approaches to the State: Alternative Conceptions and Historical Dynamics," *Comparative Politics* 16 (1984): 223–46.

22. Information on the functioning and running of the factory and local (village) health-insurance funds is found in archival collections, Staatsarchiv Dresden, Aussenstelle Bautzen (hereafter B), Amthauptmannschaft Zittau (hereafter AZ), no. 7771 (Betriebskrankenkasse der Fabrik Wäntig, 1908–15); also no. 7870 (Betriebskrankenkasse der Fabrik von Adolf und Wilhelm Glathe, jun. in Mitteloderwitz); no. 8016, Betriebskrankenkasse der Fabrik von H. R. Marx, Seifhennersdorf; no. 8001 (Ortskrankenkasse Seifhennersdorf, 1884); among other references. As far as I am aware, no one has studied these important local and factory institutions. They were an important exception to the general disenfranchisement of women in imperial Germany. For the new municipal institutions, see, ZStAP, Reichlandsbund, Pressearchiv, no. 5749, Mutter- und Säuglingsschutz, Säuglingsfürsorge, Kindergarten, and also RMdI, no. 11976, vol. 4, Säuglingssterblichkeit, Bl. 496–99: Abschrift,

Zusammenfassender Bericht über Mütterschule und Kinder tagheim (Stuttgart, 1921).

23. Ute Frevert, *Women in German History: From Bourgeois Emancipation to Sexual Liberation*, trans. Stuart McKinnon-Evans (Oxford, Hamburg, and New York, 1989), 104.

24. Local newspapers document the women's activities: *Zittauer-Morgen Zeitung*, 3 February 1891, describes a local women's movement's meeting; on 27 January 1903 there is a report on the yearly meeting of the Frauen-Unterstützungsverein (Women's Assistance Association) in Seifhennersdorf and one on 7 March 1903 on its own women's movement meeting. Also, B, Amtsgerichts Zittau, no. 991 (Frauen-Verein zu Olbersdorf mit Eichengraben, 1904), 300. For the survey of child care in the area, B, Kreishauptmannschaft Bautzen, no. 9494 (Kleinkinderbewahranstalte, 1913–1923). Also, Herrad-Ulrike Bussemer, *Frauenemanzipation und Bildungsbürgertum: Sozialgeschichte der Frauenbewegung in der Reichgründungszeit* (Weinheim and Basel, 1958); and James L. Greer, "The Political Economy of the Local State," *Politics and Society* 15 (1986–87): 513–38.

25. Klara Weyl, *Die Frau und die Gemeindepolitik* (Berlin, 1912); Alice Salomon, *Die Ausbildung zum sozialen Beruf* (Berlin, 1927), as well as Hans Muthesius, ed., *Alice Salomon: Die Begründerin des Sozialen Frauenberufs in Deutschland. Ihr Leben und ihr Werk*, Schriften des Deutschen Vereins für Öffentliche und Private Fürsorge (Cologne and Berlin, 1958). For additional information on socialist women's municipal activities, see Jean H. Quataert, *Reluctant Feminists in German Social Democracy, 1885–1917* (Princeton, N.J., 1979), 220–27.

26. The following is a transformed version of issues which I first touched on in the following article, "Workers' Reactions to Social Insurance: The Case of Homeweavers in Saxon Oberlausitz in the Late Nineteenth Century," *Internationale wissenschaftliche Korrespondenz zur Geschichte der deutschen Arbeiterbewegung* 20 (1984): 17–35.

27. Renate Hinz, ed., *Käthe Kollwitz. Druckgraphik, Plakate, Zeichnungen* (Berlin, 1980). For Kollwitz's interest in weavers as artistic symbols see *The Diary and Letters of Käthe Kollwitz*, Hans Kollwitz, ed., and trans. Richard and Clara Winston (Chicago, 1955), as well as Martha Kearns, *Käthe Kollwitz: Woman and Artist* (Old Westbury, N.Y., 1976). Correspondence among conservative government officials betrays their concerns about the demise of an honorable and loyal occupational group, which was their view of handweavers. See the large collections, ZStAP, RMdI, no. 6729–33 (Die Verhänisse der Hausindustrie und der Heimarbeit im Allgemeinen, 1882–1911).

28. *Schriften des Vereins für Sozialpolitik* 39. *Die deutsche Hausindustrie*: vol. 1, Wilhelm Stieda, *Literatur, heutige Zustände und Entstehung der deutschen Hausindustrie* (Leipzig, 1889) and 42, vol. 4, *Berichte aus der Hausindustrie in Berlin, Osnabrück, im Fichtelgebirge und in Schlesien* (Leipzig, 1890).

29. Robert Wilbrandt, *Die Frauenarbeit. Ein Problem des Kapitalismus* (Leipzig, 1906), and also his *Die Weber in der Gegenwart. Sozialpolitische Wanderungen durch die Hausweberei und die Webfabrik* (Jena, 1906).

30. The survey information is found in the following collection, B, AZ, no. 8208–41, Invaliden und Altersversicherung für Heimarbeiter der Textilindustrie in [various villages], 1894–1909. I have developed the case for women's prominent role in homeweaving in the following articles: "Combining Agrarian and Industrial Livelihood: Rural Households in the Saxon Oberlausitz in the Nineteenth Century," *Journal of Family History* 10 (1985): 145–62; "Teamwork in Saxon Homeweaving Families in the Nineteenth Century: A Preliminary Investigation into the Issue of Gender Work Roles," in Mary Jo Maynes and Ruth-Ellen Joeres, eds., *German Women in the Eighteenth and Nineteenth Centuries: A Social and Literary History* (Bloomington, Ind., 1986), 3–23.

31. B, AZ, no. 8238, Invaliditäts . . . Versicherung, Spitzkunnersdorf, Bl. 109 (16 July 1896).

32. B, AZ, no. 8082, Die Krankenversicherungspflicht der Hausgewerbetreibende, 1902–1905, Bl. 34–35 (report concerning Ollersdorf).

33. For Auguste Lowe's remarks, see ibid., no. 8235, Invaliditäts . . . Versicherung, Seifhennersfoff, Bl. 54. (September 1899); also no. 8210, Bertsdorf, Bl. 49 (13 October 1900) and no. 8217 (Jonsdorf, Fragebogen, 1906). For the bureaucratic prejudices against the workers, see, ibid., no. 8082, Die Krankenversicherungspflicht der Hausgerbetreibende, 1902–1905, Bl. 70–76 21 April 1902.

34. Ibid., no. 8241: Invalidatäts . . . Versicherung, Wittgendorf (1895–1908), Bl. 1.

35. Ibid., Wittgendorf, Bl. 17–18.

36. In Käsler, *Max Weber*, 184.

5

Depopulation and Race Suicide: Maternalism and Pronatalist Ideologies in France and the United States

Alisa Klaus

In the late nineteenth and early twentieth centuries, women reformers in France and the United States joined with male physicians, public-health officials, and politicians in a movement to prevent infant mortality. These women's contribution to both private and public infant-health programs in both countries was vital. Their work was a natural outgrowth of the dedication to improving motherhood, the care and education of children, and the home that characterized the moral-reform and charitable work of women in both countries in the nineteenth century. While female activists in the U.S. and France shared a legacy of domestic ideology and a sense of the special role women were destined to play in social reform, the nature of their reform activities and their influence on the development of welfare-state policies differed strikingly.

Bourgeois French women who were recruited to visit the homes of working women to determine their eligibility for government aid were carrying out a policy in which women had no voice. They participated in maternal- and child-welfare work almost exclusively as volunteers; very few would be paid for their work before the 1920s. In contrast, women in the U.S. actively influenced policy at all levels as professionals as well as volunteer activists, and often as public officials. They directed and staffed the U.S. Children's Bureau, authored major pieces of maternal- and infant-health legislation, headed several state and municipal

divisions of child hygiene, and provided professional nursing services for urban maternal- and infant-health programs.

These differences were the result of both structural and ideological factors. In France, the depopulation crisis and the nationalist
pronatalism stimulated by the decline in the birthrate formed
the explicit background for all discussions of maternal and child
health. The French birthrate declined rapidly in comparison with
other European countries beginning around 1800, and by the late
1860s the problem had begun to attract the attention of scholars
and politicians. France's defeat in the Franco-Prussian War
sparked debates about the sources of French weakness, including
depopulation, that continued for over fifty years.[1] French women
active in infant-health work came from both the Right and the
Left; some, but not all, identified themselves as feminists. Because
depopulation was so close to vital concerns of politicians, however, pronatalism was essentially a male-defined, male-controlled
ideology. The voices and autonomy of French women activists
were further limited by institutional structures; hampered by
obstacles to professional education and employment, their organizations constrained by government centralization and bureaucracy and the conflicts between the Catholic church and the
republican state, they lacked the institutional and political power
to shape policy.

Karen Offen has argued that the discourse of French feminists
between 1900 and 1940 was closely intertwined with the profamily
and pronatalist concerns of the republican regime. French feminists, she writes, "advocated putting France's welfare and a reconstituted family ahead of individual or personal needs, in the name
of national solidarity."[2] Women who worked in organizations dedicated to protecting maternal and infant health consistently
defined their work in these terms. A few articulated a distinctive
woman-centered approach to maternal and infant welfare, but
they did not challenge the ideological basis of pronatalism.
Instead, they served goals defined by male politicians and physicians, often working under the direction and influence of men.
Male as well as female activists, however, envisioned bourgeois
women as essential agents of pronatalist policies, and until the
1920s the French government relied heavily on voluntary agencies, often organized, funded, and staffed by women, to implement
its maternal- and infant-health programs.

In the U.S., partly because immigrants more than made up for the decline in the birthrate among the native-born middle class, and partly because the U.S. did not experience a serious military threat in this period, a belief that the nation's survival depended on saving the lives of infants did not guide maternal- and infant-health reform. Instead, ideas about the value of child life to the nation focused on the ethnic composition of the population and the perfection of the physical, mental, and moral health of the nation's citizens. The notion of "race betterment," of which eugenics was an important aspect, pervaded the infant-health movement in the U.S. "Race betterment" owed as much to women's ideas of moral reform and scientific motherhood as it did to social scientists' concepts of economic efficiency and the conservation of human resources or to scientific eugenics.[3] While the major women's organizations sought to improve the race more through educational, environmental, and public-health reforms than through elimination of the unfit through repressive legislation, racism and the ideal of human perfection played a major role in shaping Progressive maternal- and infant-health programs in the U.S. This tendency ultimately contributed to the defeat of the maternalist program in the 1920s, since it left reformers ill-equipped to challenge the racism and hostility to the poor that characterized U.S. social policy making.

A combination of several factors allowed American women to rise to prominence in the field of maternal and infant health in the early twentieth century. First, they drew on an extensive network of female institutions, the fruit of the nineteenth-century women's rights and social-reform movements. In addition, the relatively decentralized nature of the U.S. state, and the reluctance of politicians to support an activist role for the government in social and economic affairs, allowed voluntary organizations and local agencies, where women's influence was strongest, much greater autonomy than in France. The comparison with France also suggests that "race betterment" simply did not provide as compelling a motive for legislative action and intervention by powerful male-controlled institutions as depopulation. While these conditions opened the field to women in the U.S., they also made the battle for enduring public commitment to maternal and child health much more difficult.

In attempting to explain the remarkable achievements of female Progressive reformers in the U.S., historians have stressed the importance of women's voluntary organizations, settlement houses, colleges, medical schools, and hospitals. These institutions provided emotional support, intellectual and social communities, and educational and professional opportunities for a generation of women who became professional reformers.[4] Professional women also worked closely with the hundreds of thousands of women in voluntary organizations which had their roots in domestic ideology and moral-reform movements based in evangelical religion. The leaders of these organizations argued that women needed a political voice in order to exert a distinctive female influence on policies which concerned women and children, the home and family.

Not only did these women successfully campaign alongside male Progressives for the creation of new social institutions and the passage of legislation providing for such measures as factory inspection, the protection of women and children workers, and juvenile courts, but they were frequently appointed to direct and staff the newly created agencies. Maternal and infant health was one area in which by 1919, women held numerous prominent positions in national private organizations and government agencies. The first national meeting on infant mortality was conceived by a woman, Helen Putnam, the president of the American Academy of Medicine; women frequently held offices and spoke at the meetings of the American Association for the Study and Prevention of Infant Mortality, the organization created by the participants in this conference. In 1909 Sara Josephine Baker was appointed first head of the nation's first Bureau of Child Hygiene, in New York City, a position she held for nearly thirty years. As other cities and states created similar agencies in the 1910s, women were often appointed to direct them. Florence Kelley and Lillian Wald were credited with the conception of the U.S. Children's Bureau, and Julia Lathrop became its first chief.[5]

While male public-health officers, pediatricians, and obstetricians played important and sometimes dominating roles in urban infant-health work, the alliances among professional women, female government officials, and national and local women's organizations provided the creativity, labor, and political force for much federal- and state-level work, and for most local measures outside the major cities. The Sheppard-Towner campaign seemed to fulfill activists' vision of a united political force of women.[6]

In contrast, French women's extensive voluntary activity and activism did not translate into official influence in this period, and women were able only rarely even to obtain professional positions in child welfare.[7] The greater degree of central state control over social welfare and education in France placed constraints on the autonomy of voluntary agencies and limited women's access to professional education. In addition, because of the centralization and political position of the Catholic church, insofar as women's reform work was linked to religious impulses it did not lead them to articulate independent political or social positions. Female educational and welfare institutions, under the aegis of Church hierarchy, also lacked independence. Finally, women's loyalties were caught up on both sides of the struggle between the Church and republican politicians for control over social institutions and the loyalty of the nation's citizens.[8]

French Catholic women's organizations, like their Protestant counterparts in the U.S., took up social issues related to the economic and moral protection of women and children. They too argued that their private role gave them the grounds for participation in the public sphere. They did not, however, develop a secular program that reflected their own experience and interests. In the context of republican attacks on the Church, Catholic women's organizations defended religious morality and the institutional power of the Church. The *Ligue patriotique des femmes françaises*, founded in 1902 to defend religious liberty and freedom of education—in other words, to counter the state's attack on Catholicism—became the most powerful women's organization in the country, with four hundred thousand members in 1909. Its program was that of the Church; it attacked the "Jacobin" regime, socialism, and usury, (*"juiverie"*) and fought a prolonged battle against secular education.[9] The group *Action sociale de la femme*, developed a concept of women's social responsibility in areas related to family life and child welfare and formed the *Congrès Jeanne d'Arc*, a coalition of women's charitable organizations. The regulations of this congress stipulated that all members had to be Catholic; the educational work of all its affiliates had to conform to Catholic doctrine, and the program of the congress had to follow a plan approved by ecclesiastical authority.[10]

The centralized institutional structures of both the Church and the state limited French women's access to professional education and status. In their efforts to gain access to the medical profession in the nineteenth century, women in the U.S. benefited from the competitive private system of medical education. As medical colleges proliferated, homeopathic institutions and state universities found it hard to attract competent students and often turned to women as a source of qualified candidates. The fluidity of the system also enabled women, with the assistance of sympathetic men, to organize separate women's medical colleges. Between one-third and one-half of the female physicians trained in the nineteenth century graduated from the women's medical colleges; these schools and the women's hospitals provided opportunities for women to receive clinical experience and obtain teaching positions.[11]

In France, medical training was available only through the centralized, state-controlled system of medical education. While the first woman was admitted to the School of Medicine in Paris in 1865, few followed in her footsteps; only about one in two hundred physicians in France was a woman by the turn of the century, compared with about one in twenty in the U.S.[12] In part this was because even the lycées for girls created under the educational reforms of 1879 did not train girls for the *baccalauréat*, which was the prerequisite for entrance into schools of medicine.[13] The highly structured system of exams and competitions for hospital and clinic appointments and medical teaching positions also constituted a major obstacle to women seeking professional careers. By 1900 women could compete for hospital internships and a few women held official appointments in institutions for children, local welfare bureaus, and girls' schools, and as teachers in nursing schools, but they could not compete for medical teaching positions. While some French women called for the creation of clinics and hospitals staffed by women to provide the clinical training and experience essential to a successful career, they were not successful.[14]

Traditionally, religious orders had provided professional opportunities for women in France. In particular, the nursing orders, especially the Daughters of Charity, had administered hospitals, run pharmacies, and cared for the sick since the seventeenth century. Under the Third Republic these women found themselves under attack; not only did they pose an obstacle to physicians' authority but their religious base brought them into conflict with republican policies. In the late nineteenth century, physicians began to train nonreligious nurses, educated in orthodox scientific medicine and with a clear understanding of their place in the medical hierarchy. The divisions between religious and nonreligious nurses prevented the development of an independent nursing profession in France until after World War I.[15]

Despite the difficulties French women faced in pursuing professional careers, both Catholic tradition and the French state encouraged women's voluntary activity. By 1900 the French government had relied for a century on the charitable activities of wealthy women to aid poor mothers and their infants. France's oldest maternal charity, the *Société de charité maternelle*, had been founded in 1784 by an aristocrat, Mme. Fougeret, to provide assistance to poor married women in their homes. Members of the society visited each recipient in her home, delivering a layette, money at the time of delivery, and an additional gift each month for a year if she continued to care for and nurse her child. The society survived several political revolutions and continued to receive public subsidies throughout the nineteenth century, serving, in the words of one historian, as an "official alms-purse."[16]

Given its moral imperatives—most branches refused, for example, to aid those who could not produce a certificate of religious marriage—and patronage by ecclesiastical notables, the society lost its favored status under the Third Republic. Beginning in 1908 the government instituted a greatly expanded system of subsidies for maternal and infant charities, but the branches of the maternal charity society now had to compete for these funds with a growing number of newer maternal- and child-welfare institutions, many of these also organized by women, often with republican sympathies.[17]

The new policies grew out of the late-nineteenth- and early-twentieth-century discussions of infant mortality as part of the larger crisis of "depopulation." The French birthrate had begun to decline in the late eighteenth century, and by the end of the nineteenth century France had the lowest birthrate in the world. The problem of depopulation was conceived primarily in terms of France's declining international power, particularly in relation to the German military threat. Sociologists, demographers, journalists, physicians, and politicians described depopulation as the source of France's economic stagnation and moral degeneration.[18] Depopulation was consistently invoked as the most compelling rationale for measures to protect maternal and infant health; infant mortality figured prominently, for example, on the agenda of the commission appointed by the minister of the interior in 1902 to study the question of depopulation.[19]

Though politicians on the Right and the Left agreed on the gravity of the problem, they disagreed over its causes and solutions. Conservative Catholic writers, for example, argued that the decline in the fertility rate was the result of the abandonment of religion and traditional morality, while socialists claimed that the hardships suffered by the working class under capitalism were to blame. The Radical Republicans who provided much of the leadership in campaigns for maternal- and infant-health programs saw the declining birthrate as both a moral and an economic problem. The heart of the crisis, they felt, lay in the disintegration of family life and parental responsibility—the consequence of growing individualism in the case of the bourgeoisie, but the effect of oppression in the working class. Bourgeois couples delayed marriage and bore only one or two children in order to provide their homes and families with the expected social and material trappings; bourgeois women neglected to breast-feed out of vanity or social ambition. Economic pressure and oppressive working conditions, on the other hand, made a healthy homelife impossible for working-class families. The hardships working-class women suffered in childbearing as a result of hard work and poverty made them shun motherhood.[20]

Making maternity compatible with wage labor was a primary focus of many French maternal- and infant-health programs. Not only did infants die because their mothers gave up breast-feeding when they returned to work, often placing their infants out to nurse in the country, but the physical suffering and financial burdens made women reluctant to become pregnant in the first place. Since families depended on their incomes, however, legislators tried to make it possible for women to take a maternity leave, to avoid sending their children out to nurse, to continue breast-feeding after they returned to work. Thus, common proposals included maternity leaves, maternity benefits, crèches, breast-feeding breaks for working mothers, nursing rooms in factories, and bonuses for those who breast-fed their infants. Medical supervision was an important component of most of these proposals.[21]

Other legislation focused on protecting the children most at risk—those of single mothers, who had the fewest social and economic resources. Proposals for secret asylums, where a pregnant woman could receive care without revealing her name, and special financial benefits for destitute single mothers, were criticized by some conservative policy makers because they would

reward immoral behavior and promote dependence. Many politicians, however, were willing to sacrifice these moral imperatives
for the sake of the nation's survival. As one group of deputies
summarized, "The protection of the woman, at the time she
becomes a mother, is the surest safeguard of the child's life; fertility is the very condition of the existence of the nation; by protecting
maternity, the nation protects itself and guarantees its power and
its existence."[22]

It is too simplistic, however, to see Radical Republican mater-
nal- and infant-welfare programs as a response solely to demographic imperatives. Recent historians of republican social policy
in this period have seen reforms such as social insurance essentially as part of an effort to defuse working-class discontent and
radicalism.[23] The distinctive role that Radical Republicans envisioned for bourgeois women in public policy suggests that efforts
to regulate reproduction and to promote class harmony were
closely intertwined. In recruiting the voluntary efforts of bourgeois women, leading male physicians and politicians hoped not
only to protect maternal and infant lives and to reawaken the
maternal instincts of bourgeois women themselves, but to contribute to the project of reconciling the working class to the Republic.
A principal strategy of French maternal- and child-welfare policy
before the 1920s, therefore, was the subsidy of private charities
and the incorporation of volunteers in public programs. Subsidies
were also used to encourage specific types of private activities.
Thus, government policies sustained private charities but also
constrained them, since an agency that received public funds was
subject to government regulation.

The new female organizations competing with the *Société de
charité maternelle* were the outgrowth of a women's movement
based on domestic ideology, but they defined a new role for
women in the public sphere. Many of the new organizations had
ties with moderate feminist organizations such as the *Conseil
national des femmes françaises*. This group's political philosophy
coincided generally with that of the Radical Republicans; its program for women's rights aimed at improving the education of
girls and the professional opportunities of women, and protecting
women's working conditions and the welfare of children.[24] The
Conseil, the *Congrès International des droits des femmes*, and the
Congrès des oeuvres et institutions féminines all passed resolutions
urging legislation requiring maternity leaves, state maternity
assistance, breast-feeding rooms in factories, and other forms of
maternal assistance.[25]

The oldest of the non-Catholic charities was the *Oeuvre de l'allaitement maternel*, founded in 1876 by Marie Béquet de Vienne to propagate breast-feeding primarily through the assistance of poor mothers. Like the members of the *Société de charité maternelle*, the benefactors of this organization visited the homes of poor mothers, distributing bread, meat, wine, medicine, fuel, and clothing. In 1892 they also opened a refuge for pregnant women.[26] The *Pouponnière de Porchefontaine*, founded in 1891, was a unique institution, essentially a group wet-nursing establishment. Working mothers could send their children to be cared for at the *Pouponnière*, paying about the same price as they would to a private nurse. The children were cared for by the single mothers who were housed there, each nursing her own child and one other.[27]

Beginning in 1905 women also organized *Cantines maternelles*, which offered free meals for nursing mothers; a woman had merely to show that her breast was producing milk to be admitted. The *Oeuvre nouvelle des crèches parisiennes*, which maintained day nurseries for the children of working women in Paris, was formed by women in 1896.[28] Wealthy women also organized *Mutualités maternelles*, or maternal mutual-aid societies, which offered a form of maternity insurance to working-class women. This was a favorite of republican politicians because it involved a degree of self-help. It also was a charitable institution at the same time, since it relied heavily on donations and was administered not by the members but by a committee of patrons who visited the members' homes and supervised the distribution of benefits.[29]

In addition to the charities they founded, women often made up the bulk of the benefactors of male-run institutions such as the *Association de l'oeuvre sociale du bon lait*, founded by a group of men to provide cheap or free high-quality milk to working-class and poor mothers. Virtually all institutions or charities serving mothers and children had a committee of "dames patronnesses," or lady patrons, whose primary tasks were fund raising, home visiting, and the distribution of benefits.[30]

The lady visitor was incorporated into public policy in 1874 as part of the Roussel Law, which created a system of medical supervision of children placed out to nurse. The legislation provided for the appointment of a local commission which was to include two respectable married women who were to visit the nurses regularly, investigating the hygiene and safety of the homes and overseeing the care they provided.[31] The Strauss Law of 1913, which required women working in commerce and industry to take a two-month maternity leave, allowed for the possibility of women volunteers taking on the task of supervising the recipients in their homes. The legislation provided for case benefits to compensate the workers partially for their lost wages, but a woman could receive the benefits only if she actually rested and cared for herself and her child according to the rules of hygiene. The welfare bureau in each commune was responsible for designating someone to make sure these conditions were fulfilled but it was not necessary, argued the minister of the interior, to create a new class of civil servants for this purpose. Local officials could count instead on the plentiful source of female volunteers from the nation's burgeoning private maternal and infant organizations. He wrote: "Taking advantage of that touching instinct, so strong in the hearts of the women of France, it is impossible not to succeed in creating around poor mothers and their newborns a network of enlightened and active affection which will undoubtedly constitute an effective insurance against infant mortality."[32]

Though overseeing the health of infants, these women were not trained professionals, unlike the visiting nurses who instructed American mothers in their homes. Instead they were considered qualified for their role only by virtue of their class and sex. Though essentially their job was to police the recipients of assistance, their activities were usually described by their male supporters in terms of a secular charitable ideal. Such women were the embodiment of the Radical Republicans' philosophy of solidarism, which emphasized the social obligations of the wealthy to give up some of their wealth in return for the benefits they received from working-class labor.[33] For bourgeois women this duty involved both caring for poor mothers and their children, and bearing children of their own. According to this ideal, bourgeois women were to promote class harmony through their contact with working-class women.

The legislators who supported the Roussel Law in 1874 had hoped that the women on the local commissions would make a significant contribution to erasing the "prejudices and biases which cast such evil ferments into society." In the early twentieth century most French advocates of public maternal and infant welfare shared a belief that public assistance could not completely replace private charity, even if the state had the necessary financial resources.[34] Women, they believed, were the natural agents of such charity; their feminine attributes would enable them to personalize an increasingly bureaucratic welfare system, thus healing the alienation of the working class from the bourgeoisie. In addition, physicians and politicians often voiced the hope that such voluntary activity would restimulate the maternal instinct of bourgeois women and girls.

It is difficult to determine how French bourgeois women viewed their own participation in such organizations, because so often they worked under the supervision of men, under official scrutiny, or under the public aegis of male-dominated organizations. French women involved in these institutions sometimes challenged their relegation to an auxiliary role, however, insisting that the recognition of women's needs and rights was essential and that women should have a greater voice in the making and carrying out of policies. The *Conseil national des femmes françaises*, for example, passed a resolution in favor of resurrecting and expanding the local commissions mandated by the Roussel Law, arguing that male physicians were not qualified to oversee the daily care of children.[35] Béquet de Vienne, speaking at a general meeting of the *Oeuvre de l'allaitement maternel*, complained that male policy makers were unwilling to recognize paternal irresponsibility and women's fears of humiliation and poverty as causes of depopulation. Female juries, she asserted, would understand why single mothers resorted to abortion or infanticide. If the state wanted children, then it must see that pregnant women were surrounded with respect and assistance.[36]

Gabrielle Chapuis, writing in *Féminisme Intégral*, a militant-feminist journal, also connected her call for political rights for women to depopulation. The nation was in danger, she argued, because women had no rights; while instinct pushed them toward maternity, their consciences cried: "Stop! You don't have the right to give life to beings who will not belong to you, that you will not be able to protect. You are a slave, since you depend absolutely on the whims of men. . . . " In the interests of their children, she concluded, women must have the right to manage their finances, administer public funds, and take part in decisions about war and peace and social welfare.[37]

As Karen Offen has argued, such women were making use of the population crisis as a way of drawing attention to and gathering support for women's rights.[38] In debating policies, however, politicians did not refer to the demands of women's organizations but to the resolutions passed by the *Académie de médecine*, the male-dominated *Congrès national de la protection de la première enfance*, and all-male pediatric and obstetric associations. Most often French women acquiesced in viewing their effective role in maternal and infant health in terms of a charitable model rather than an activist one and they accepted the argument that motherhood constituted their preeminent social duty. Women, proclaimed Olga Veil-Picard, president of the *Pouponnière de Porchefontaine*, should "bravely . . . support the nation's defense." They should claim for themselves the privilege of forming the army of "auxiliaries for the propagation of infant hygiene."[39] Pronatalist ideology and state policy thus defined the proper role for bourgeois women in maternal- and child-welfare policy. While this role provided women's organizations with material support and quasi-official legitimacy, it also placed constraints on their autonomy. Given the power of French pronatalism and the structural inhibitions on women's public voice and professional activity, French women were not generally able to transcend this role; they made their mark on the early-twentieth-century maternal- and infant-health movement as volunteers aiding in a national cause rather than as advocates of a distinctive program of their own making.

In contrast, as Molly Ladd-Taylor shows in her article in this volume, women in the U.S. actively campaigned, as part of a consciously female movement, for a maternal- and infant-health program conceived and developed primarily by women. This movement must be understood in the context of the extensive infant-health work in urban areas undertaken by pediatricians, obstetricians, and public-health officials. Milk stations and infant-health clinics in U.S. cities resembled their counterparts in France, though a distinctive element in the U.S. was the emphasis on home instruction by professional public-health nurses. Reformers in the U.S. also failed to see financial assistance as a significant solution to the health problems of the poor, though they did recognize the strong association between poverty and infant mortality. Maternity insurance, a vital issue in French debates, played only a minor role in the U.S. Instead, activists in this country sought legislation that would provide for preventive health services with an emphasis on education.[40] To some extent, differences in the approaches of the two countries to infant mortality can be explained by differences in the demographic and political context. Most obviously, observers in the U.S. did not perceive the kind of population crisis that stimulated and shaped

French pronatalism; Progressive reformers in the U.S. did not face the possibility of a decline in the nation's population. They did, however, fear physical degeneration and the declining predominance of the Anglo-Saxon "race."

It was common for American writers to argue that children constituted a valuable national resource, and historians have often identified children as a central concern of Progressive social reformers.[41] Theodore Roosevelt, for example, linked the nation's military and economic vigor with the strength of the family, and likened motherhood to military service. Advocates of mothers' pensions made the same analogy, insisting that the benefits granted to mothers were not charity but payment for services rendered to society. Some leaders of the conservation movement focused their attention on the value of human resources; in a volume of the report of the National Conservation Commission devoted to human resources Irving Fisher, a Yale social scientist, used economic calculations to estimate the dollar value of children's lives.[42] Despite this rhetoric, however, infant and child mortality never constituted an urgent threat to the nation's survival as it did in France.

Like their French counterparts, physicians and female reformers and politicians in the U.S. argued that the nation had an interest in child health. American reformers, however, were less concerned about the number of future citizens than about the quality and composition of the population. Those who campaigned for maternal- and infant-health programs, like most Progressive reformers, agreed that improving the physical and mental health of the nation's children would improve society or the nation. This general concept was often referred to as "race betterment." The loosely organized race-betterment movement drew on the traditions of evangelical perfectionism and republican virtue as well as the Progressive reformers' argument that the state should make an investment in the reproduction of productive citizens for the sake of national efficiency.

Race betterment was compatible with a variety of political perspectives. For Theodore Roosevelt, a conservative model of the family served his larger goals of economic concentration, efficiency, and U.S. imperialism, while the National Congress of Mothers began with an essentially conservative moral program grounded in religious ideology. The female reformers associated with Hull House and other settlement houses, on the other hand, often voiced ideals of human liberation or human rights, but they too shared a belief that society had an interest in the improvement of its members. Lillian Wald, for example, insisted that even mentally handicapped children had a right to respect, dignity, and education. When they reached adolescence, however, society's right to protect itself took precedence, and the children should be segregated to prevent them from reproducing.[43] No one in the U.S. publicly voiced the opinion that the prevention of infant mortality was dysgenic because it enabled genetically ill-adapted children to survive. Many active in campaigns to prevent infant mortality, however, suggested that "negative" eugenic measures could prevent both illness and social deviance. Abraham Jacobi, a leading pediatrician, and Joseph Neff, head of the Philadelphia Department of Health, for example, argued that the prohibition of marriage among the unfit and even forced sterilization were justified not only to prevent infant deaths from syphilis and tuberculosis, but also to save taxpayers money for prisons, reformatories, hospitals, and asylums.[44] As Charles Richmond Henderson argued in his 1910 presidential address to the American Association for the Study and Prevention of Infant Mortality, society could not neglect the life of any human being, no matter how feeble or unfit. At the same time, once the public took on the responsibility of supporting the "feebleminded" it must then reconcile its humanitarian impulses with "our scientific vision of the progress of the races, which has equal or higher claims on us."[45]

The women's infant-health movement also shared a eugenic vision. The National Congress of Mothers claimed to have originated the race-betterment movement, and discussions of the role played by heredity in spreading disease and deviance figured prominently at the organization's founding convention in 1897.[46] Eugenics was an obvious element of the baby-health-contest campaigns popular among women's organizations in the 1910s. In theory the baby-health contest was an educational event; contestants were examined by a single physician or a panel of specialists and scored on their physical health. Parents received a copy of the score card pointing out the child's defects and making suggestions for improvement. The children were judged, however, on hereditary characteristics, including some that were clearly aesthetic and obviously racist—such as size and shape of their ears, nose, and lips—as well as indicators of nutritional status and other aspects or parental and medical attention.[47]

The contests were not designed to save infant lives; instead they seemed to aim toward the physical perfection of children. The baby-health contest was invented by two Iowa clubwomen purportedly inspired by the effectiveness of the livestock show in improving the breeding of cattle, and frequent analogies with the stock show suggests that selective breeding was indeed in the minds of its organizers and promoters.[48] Some even proposed contests in which children would be scored on the quality of the "parental union." Mary Bates, of the American Baby Health Contest Association wrote: "The sooner we get all of the people to understand the right of the Baby to Better Birth and the right of the community to immunity to degenerate and diseased stock— human,—the better, and every way that carries the lesson will speed the day when we can have scientific elimination before the birth of the unfit, and someday the scientific culture of the fit."[49]

The General Federation of Women's Clubs and the National Congress of Mothers supported "negative" eugenic measures such as the institutionalization of the "feebleminded" and legislation to prevent the marriage of other "defective" people (the usual estimate was that the ten percent of the population in institutions were completely unfit to reproduce). The improvement of genetic stock through selective breeding was not the focus of eugenics in the maternal- and infant-health movement, however. Instead, the emphasis was on education of future parents so that they could improve their health and avoid diseases whose effects could be passed on to their children.

Therefore, in the maternal- and infant-health movement eugenics was usually identified with "education for better parenthood" rather than with calls for repressive legislation. In 1916, for example, when the *New York American* magazine launched a campaign to "teach the women of America to produce better babies," the topics it covered included eugenics, the care of pregnant women, and the care of infants. The program emphasized the importance of health in choosing a spouse and the avoidance of diseases which parents could pass on to their offspring, such as alcoholism, syphilis, tuberculosis, epilepsy, and insanity.[50]

The focus on education was also consistent with the argument of many professional eugenists that inheritance probably depended largely upon the physical condition of the parents at the time of conception and therefore not on the parents' own genetic background. Syphilis, and other infections, malnutrition, and exhaustion in parents affected their children not through "true" heredity but rather through the action of some toxin on the germ cells.[51] This type of eugenics can be seen as a natural outgrowth of the moral-reform tradition of many women's organizations, since the rules of hygiene were consistent with conservative morality.

Thus, those who were devoted to race betterment did not necessarily emphasize the selective breeding of humans and did not espouse the actual elimination of particular racial or ethnic groups. Though some women activists were strongly committed to "negative" eugenics, the women's infant-health movement reflected a wide range of opinions on the subject. Furthermore, some were strongly motivated by concerns other than improvement of the race; the Children's Bureau, for example, sought to meet the often desperate needs of the women who wrote to them for assistance. The campaign for the Sheppard-Towner Act reflected many women's conviction that the day had arrived when they could force men in power to recognize the importance of the work and suffering borne by women in bearing and raising children. It is evident, however, that the popular women's infant-health campaigns reflected the class and racial biases of their mostly white middle- and upper-class members; state and federal policies responded best to these women's demands.

World War I increased interest in infant health; child-health advocates often cited the large number of military recruits who were physically unfit to serve. The war also accentuated the nativism that had always been present in the movement. After the war, several maternal- and child-health reformers lamented the neglect on the part of maternal- and child-health programs of the people of "moderate means," "the Americans, the native women, the old stock people, who are living a rural life." One congressman urged his colleagues to support the Sheppard-Towner Bill as "the only prospect of maintaining a leavening of the native-born," since rural women would benefit most.[52]

There were inherent contradictions in a health program with such strong eugenic elements. Given these contradictions, the notion that society had a compelling interest in protecting child health could not sustain significant political support for maternal- and child-welfare programs once the political power of a united women's movement had subsided in the 1920s. Maternal- and infant-health advocates faced many political obstacles; in particular they had difficulty overcoming the professional interests of the AMA and hostility to government spending on public-welfare programs and government intervention in social life.[53] In addition, because so many of the poor children who were at risk were members of despised racial or ethnic groups, saving their lives was not a priority for politicians in power. The ideology and rhetoric of the women's infant-health movement, based on the goal of perfecting the race, did not offer a challenge to this.

The influence of racism was particularly evident in the case of black children in the South. Though their chances of dying in their first year were twice those of white children, white child-health advocates rarely devoted attention to the special nature of the risks these children faced. Northern white activists occasionally considered the needs of black children in a tentative way. The U.S. Children's Bureau included black children in its study of rural child welfare in North Carolina, for example, and the New York Association for Improving the Condition of the Poor carried out an infant-health campaign in a black neighborhood in 1916. In the South, however, white supremacy shaped all public-health programs.[54]

In the 1910s southern white physicians and public-health officials were engaged in a discussion of whether or not the particular health problems of blacks were the result of genetic inferiority (or at least inability to adapt to a cold climate or urban life), or the result of social and environmental handicaps. In 1914, when the American Public Health Association held its annual meeting in Jacksonville, Florida, and made blacks' health the focus of their discussion, some health officials still maintained that because blacks were unable to adapt to urban life they were becoming extinct; some argued outright that spending money on them was a waste.[55] Though the tendency was increasingly toward a social and environmental explanation for the high death rate of blacks, even those southern health officers who vocally supported public-health work among blacks often simultaneously expressed contempt for and hostility toward them. The standard arguments for public-health work in black communities were that they were dependent on whites and would continue to be, and that because they came into daily intimate contact with whites, their disease, immorality, and ignorance were a threat to all.[56] Though they deemphasized genetic *physical* inferiority, white supporters of such work tended to blame the poor health of blacks on supposed racial behavioral traits such as laziness, immorality, and stupidity rather than on poverty and environment. While infant-health work among European immigrants in the urban North focused on education, the assumption of many white public-health workers in the South was clearly that blacks would not be helped by such programs.

In reality, of course, southern blacks depended not on whites but on the hard work and expertise of black physicians, nurses, philanthropists, settlement houses, and volunteers, especially before the advent of major foundation efforts in southern health in the 1920s. Black women's organizations initiated infant-health programs as part of their larger program of racial uplift. The Neighborhood Union in Atlanta, for example, organized classes in home hygiene and prenatal and infant care, mothers' meetings, visiting-nurse services, and infant and preschool clinics. The Locust Street Settlement in Hampton, Virginia, founded by Janie Porter Barrett, held talks on infant and child care and sponsored an annual Baby Day beginning in 1909. Black women's organizations also played a leading role in national health campaigns such as the annual Negro Cleanup Week.[57] Because racism and the paucity of resources devoted to public health in the South, however, these women, unlike their white counterparts in the North, did not acquire political influence through their work, though they occasionally succeeded in persuading local or county governments to hire black public-health nurses.[58]

On the national level the organized forces of American maternalism successfully campaigned for a maternal- and infant-health program designed by women. This achievement, however, was not a lasting one; the Sheppard-Towner Act did not survive the 1920s.[59] Ironically, though, Americans made a lasting contribution to French maternal- and child-health programs. It was through the work of the American Red Cross and the Rockefeller Commission during World War I that visiting public-health nursing first came to France on a large scale. Upon its departure the Red Cross left over two million francs to stimulate maternal- and infant-welfare work through the establishment of a national school of child hygiene, dispensaries, preventive health services, and visiting-nurse programs; these programs played a major part in shaping the new profession of child-health visitor.[60] Women's role in maternal- and infant-health programs was thus professionalized; these programs were integrated into an expanding pronatalist family policy which included repressive legislation against birth control and abortion as well as new forms of maternal assistance such as breast-feeding bonuses for women receiving maternity benefits, family allowances, and, as part of the new social-insurance system created in 1928, maternity insurance.[61]

These measures were enacted in a distinctly antifeminist climate and, as before the war, women had little voice in their conception. Pronatalism had a dual legacy for French women, however. On the one hand, it reinforced an ideology that defined a narrow social role for women and limited women's ability to control their reproductive lives; the political invisibility of French maternalism can also be traced partly to the heavy investment of many male politicians and intellectuals in pronatalist discourse and legislation. At the same time, however, French public policies provided women's organizations with both resources and legitimacy, created a basis for women's professional work, and materially assisted many women and children. In the long run, French pronatalism proved a more potent force for maternal and infant welfare than American maternalism influenced by race betterment.

A relatively strong position in the medical profession, organizational autonomy, and comparative freedom from male-dominated institutions and government agencies gave women reformers in the U.S. the opportunity and the resources with which to shape public policy. In the long run, however, American activists were unable to overcome the persistent American resistance to a socially activist state and the commitment of the organized medical profession to a private health-care system. In the absence of a demographic or military crisis akin to French depopulation, the lives of the nation's poor children did not have enough political value to compel an enduring public interest in child health.

Notes

1. For general histories of debates over depopulation see Angus McLaren, *Sexuality and Social Order* (New York, 1983); Joseph Spengler, *France Faces Depopulation: Postlude Edition, 1936–1976* (Durham, N.C., 1979); Francis Ronsin, *La Grève des ventres: Propagande néo-Malthusienne et baisse de la natalité française, XIXe–XXe siècle* (n.p., 1980).

2. Karen Offen, "Defining Feminism: A Comparative Historical Approach," *Signs* 14 (1988): 147, and "Depopulation, Nationalism, and Feminism in Fin-de-Siècle France," *American Historical Review* 89 (1984): 673.

3. For an overview of race betterment see *Proceedings of the First National Conference on Race Betterment* (Battle Creek, Mich., 1914).

4. Estelle Freedman, "Separatism as Strategy: Female Institution Building and American Feminism, 1870–1930," *Feminist Studies* 5 (1979): 512–29; Kathryn Kish Sklar, "Hull House in the 1890s: A Community of Women Reformers," *Signs* 10 (1985): 658–77; Ellen Fitzpatrick, *Endless Crusade: Women Social Scientists and Progressive Reform* (New York, 1990), 79–80. For a comparative analysis, see Seth Koven and Sonya Michel, "Womanly Duties: Maternalist Politics and the Origins of Welfare States in France, Germany, Great Britain and the United States, 1880–1920," *American Historical Review* 95 (1990): 1085–86.

5. Robyn Muncy, *Creating a Female Dominion in American Reform, 1890–1935* (New York, 1991), esp. chap. 2; Richard A. Meckel, *Save the Babies: American Public Health Reform and the Prevention of Infant Mortality, 1850–1929* (Baltimore, 1990), 108, 115. For Sara Josephine Baker's career, see her autobiography, *Fighting for Life* (New York, 1939).

6. Stanley Lemons, *The Woman Citizen: Social Feminists in the 1920's* (Urbana, Ill., 1973), 155–58; Molly Ladd-Taylor, *Mother-Work: Women, Child Welfare, and the State, 1890–1930* (Urbana, Ill., forthcoming), and the Ladd-Taylor article in this volume.

7. See for example, Mme. Remember, "Le Vote familial et la repopulation," *Féminisme Intégral* (July 1919).

8. On the relationship between feminism and republicanism in nineteenth-century France, see Offen, "Depopulation, Nationalism, and Feminism," 652; Claire Goldberg Moses, *French Feminism in the Nineteenth Century* (Albany, N.Y. 1984), 229.

9. Anne-Marie Sohn, "Catholic Women and Political Affairs: The Case of the Patriotic League of French Women," in Judith Friedlander, Blanche Wiesen Cook, Alice Kessler-Harris, and Carroll Smith-Rosenberg, eds., *Women in Culture and Politics: A Century of Change* (Bloomington, Ind., 1986), 239.

10. Henri Rollet, *L'Action sociale des catholiques en France*, vol. 2, *1871–1914* (Paris, 1958), 101.

11. Regina Markell Morantz-Sanchez, *Sympathy and Science: Women Physicians in American Medicine* (New York, 1985), 234; Mary Roth Walsh, *"Doctors Wanted: No Women Need Apply"; Sexual Barriers in the Medical Profession, 1835–1975* (New Haven, 1977), xvii.

12. There were 95 female physicians in France in 1900; in 1911, there were 20,809 physicians in France altogether. Walsh, *"Doctors Wanted,"* xvi; "Paris Correspondent," *Lancet*, 29 March 1913, 294; Nancy Woloch, *Women and the American Experience* (New York, 1984), 392.

13. Moses, *French Feminism in the Nineteenth Century*, 233.

14. Deuxième Congrès international des oeuvres et institutions féminines (1900), *Compte rendu des travaux* (Paris, 1902), vol 4: 110, 126, 145.

15. Yvonne, Knibiehler, *Cornettes et blouses blanches: Les Infirmières dans la société française, 1880–1920* (Paris, 1984), chap. 1; Jacques Léonard,

"Femmes, religion et médecine: Les Religieuses qui soignent, en France au XIXe siècle," *Annales E.S.C.* 32 (1977): 889; Colin Jones, *The Charitable Imperative: Hospitals and Nursing in Ancien Régime and Revolutionary France* (London, 1989), chaps. 3–5.

16. Maurice Melin, *L'Assurance maternelle* (Paris, 1911), 172; Comte Albert de Mun, *La Société de charité maternelle de Moulins* (Paris, 1912); Paul Delauney, *La Société de charité maternelle du Mans et ses origines* (Le Mans, 1911); A. Cornereau, "Notice sur la Société de charité maternelle de Dijon," *Mémoires de l'Académie des sciences, arts et belles-lettres de Dijon*, 4th ser., vol. 7 (1899–1900), 414–16.

17. Ministre de l'Intérieur, Circular, 19 September 1908, Archives Nationales, Paris, Fla 3157.

18. For general discussions of depopulation, see Spengler, *France Faces Depopulation*; Angus McLaren, *Sexuality and Social Order* (New York, 1983).

19. Commission de dépopulation, *Séance du 19 janvier 1902* (Melun, n.d.), 2; J. Marie, *De l'assistance publique relativement à l'enfance* (Paris, 1892),40; Charles Delplanque, *Assistance aux enfants du premier âge privés de ressources* (Lille, 1910), 3; Claude Souquet, *Mortalilté infantile de la première année à Toulouse, de 1900 à 1910* (Toulouse, 1911), 7; Henri Bouquet, *La Puériculture sociale* (Paris, 1911), 2–3; G. Variot, *L'Hygiène infantile; allaitement maternel et artificiel; sèvrage* (Paris, 1908), 1; A. Balestre and A. Giletta de Saint-Joseph, *Etude sur la mortalité de la première enfance dans la population urbaine de la France de 1892 à 1897* (Paris, 1901), 42.

20. McLaren, *Sexuality and Social Order*, 171–73.

21. Louis Marin and Paul Strauss, "La Protection de la maternité ouvrière," *Association nationale française pour la protection légale des travailleurs, Compte rendu des discussions*, 7th ser., no. 2 (1912); André Goirand, *De la protection et de l'assistance légales des femmes salariées avant et après leur accouchement* (Paris, 1906), 34; Félix Saporte, *Assistance et maternité* (Bordeaux, 1910), 30; Deborah Bernson, *Nécessité d'une loi protectrice pour la femme ouvrière avant et après ses couches* (Paris, 1899), 107.

22. Chambre des députés, Annexe au procès-verbal de la séance du 23 juin 1910, *Proposition de loi relative à la maternité*; Conseil supérieur de l'assistance publique, *Comptes-rendus*, fascicule no. 37, séance de janvier 1892, 71,90.

23. Sanford Elwitt, *The Third Republic Defended: Bourgeois Reform in France, 1880–1914* (Baton Rouge, 1986), 7; Judith F. Stone, *The Search for Social Peace: Reform Legislation in France, 1890–1914* (Albany, 1985), 23; Mary Lynn Stewart, *Women, Work, and the French State* (Kingston, Ont., 1989), 12–13.

24. Steven C. Hause, *Women's Suffrage and Social Politics in the French Third Republic* (Princeton, N.J., 1984), 36–39.

25. *Congrès international de la condition et des droits des femmes* (Paris, 1901), 92–93; *Deuxième Congrès international des oeuvres et institutions féminines* (1900), *Compte rendu des travaux*, vol. 2 (Paris, 1902), 62; "Voeux émis par la section d'hygiène du Conseil national des femmes françaises," Archives Nationales, F22 446, n.d.

26. *Bulletin de l'Oeuvre de l'allaitement maternel et des refuges-ouvoirs pour les femmes enceintes*, December 1913 and July 1918.

27. *Une Expérience sociale: Société maternelle parisienne la pouponnière* (n.p., n.d.), 23.

28. Cantine maternelle du XVIIIe arrondissement, *Compte rendu*, 1909–10 and 1911; *Oeuvre nouvelle des crèches parisiennes*, March 1904, 10–11.

29. A. Vallin, *La Femme salariée et la maternité* (Paris, 1911), 147; F. Poussineau, "Rapport sur la Mutualité maternelle," *Bericht uber den III. Internationalen Kongress fur Sauglingsschutz (Gouttes de lait)* (Berlin, 1912), 890; *Premier Congrès national de la Mutualité maternelle* (1908); Félix Poussineau, *La Maternité chez l'ouvrière en 1910* (Paris, 1910), 4; Jacques Mornet, *Les Mutualités maternelles* (Paris, 1911).

30. *Bulletin de l'Association de l'oeuvre sociale du bon lait*, October 1909, 141–50.

31. Chambre des députés, *Rapport au nom de la commission chargée d'examiner la proposition de loi Roussel*, 9 June 1874, 118.

32. *Journal Official*, 11 August 1913, 1724.

33. Offen, "Depopulation, Nationalism, and Feminism," 664; Henri Hatzfield, *Du Paupérisme à la sécurité sociale* (Paris, 1971), 271–72. For general discussions of the philosophy of solidarism, see Stone, *The Search for Social Peace*, 27–30; Elwitt, *The Third Republic Defended*, 170–71, 180–83; Jane Jenson, "Gender and Reproduction; or, Babies and the State," *Studies in Political Economy* 20 (1986): 38.

34. Charles Mercier, *Les Petits-Paris: Etude critique et conseils pratiques sur l'hygiène infantile* (Paris, 1898), 174; G. Eustache, *La Puériculture, hygiène et assistance* (Paris, 1903), 255; August Luling, *De la Mortalité des nourrissons en rapport avec la modalité de leur alimentation* (Versailles, 1901), 77; P. Pecker, *La Puériculture par l'assistance scientifique maternelle à domicile* (Paris, 1904), 133.

35. Hélène Moniez, *Les Commissions locales de la protection du premier âge: Rapport présenté au nom de la deuxième section à la Société internationale pour l'étude des questions d'assistance* (Paris, 1904), 1–2.

36. Sicard de Plauzoles, *La Maternité et la défense nationale contre la dépopulation* (Paris, 1909), 88–90.

37. Gabrielle Chapuis, "Dépopulation," *Féminisme Intégral* (April 1913). See also Mme. Mariceau, "Les Femmes administratrices dans établissements publics d'assistance en France," in *Deuxième Congrès international des oeuvres et institutions féminines*, vol. 2, 150–54; C. L. de Ferrer, *Pourquoi voteraient-elles? Cahiers exposant quelques-unes des revendications féministes les plus urgentes à solutionner pour le relèvement de la natalité en France* (Paris, 1910).

38. Offen, "Depopulation, Nationalism, and Feminism," 667.

39. Olga Veil-Picard, *La Puériculture à Porchefontaine* (n.p., 1913), 2.

40. See Meckel, *Save the Babies*, for an overview of the U.S. campaigns to prevent infant mortality. For a more comprehensive comparison of the French and American movements see Alisa Klaus, *Every Child a Lion: The Origins of*

Infant Health Policy in the United States and France, 1890–1920 (Ithaca, N.Y., 1993).

41. Examples include Robert H. Wiebe, *The Search for Order, 1877–1920* (New York, 1967), 169; Meckel, *Save the Babies*, 103; Harold Underwood Faulkner, *Quest for Social Justice, 1898–1914* (New York, 1931), 177; Robert H. Bremmer, *From the Depths: The Discovery of Poverty in the U.S.* (New York, 1956), 213.

42. Theodore Roosevelt, opening address, *First International Congress on the Protection of Children, National Congress of Mothers* (1908), 15; Ladd Taylor, *Mother-Work*, chap. 5; Irving Fisher, "National Vitality, Its Waste and Conservation," in U.S. Congress, Senate, *Report of the National Conservation Commission*, 1909, vol. 3: 673.

43. Lillian Wald, *The House on Henry Street* (New York, 1915), 121–23.

44. Joseph Neff, "A City's Duty in the Prevention of Infant Mortality," *Transactions of the American Association for the Study and Prevention of Infant Mortality* 1 (1910): 154; A. Jacobi, "Address," *Transactions of the American Association for the Study and Prevention of Infant Mortality* 1 (1910): 44–45.

45. Charles Richmond Henderson, "Greetings by the President for 1911," *Transactions of the American Association for the Study and Prevention of Infant Mortality* 1 (1910): 19.

46. *Child-Welfare Magazine* 7 (1914): 248; National Congress of Mothers, *The Work and Words of the National Congress of Mothers* (New York, 1897), especially talks by Mrs. Theodore Birney, Mary Lowe Dickinson, Mrs. Wilbur F. Crafts, and Mrs. H.A. Stinson; Ladd-Taylor, *Mother-Work*, chap. 2.

47. Lucia B. Harriman, "Oregon Mothers Conduct Eugenics Department in State Fair," *Child-Welfare Magazine* 7 (1912): 84.

48. John J. Biddison, " 'Better Babies,' " *Woman's Home Companion*, March 1913, 96.

49. Mary E. Bates to Julia Lathrop, 13 March 1910, Records of the U.S. Children's Bureau, National Archives, Washington, D.C. 4–14–2–3–0.

50. Helen Lowry to Julia Lathrop, n.d., Records of the U.S. Children's Bureau, 14–1–9–2.

51. Meyer Solomon, "Infant Mortality and Eugenics," *Illinois Medical Journal* 23 (1913): 159; Fisher, "National Vitality," 723.

52. R. W. Lobenstine, "Maternity Centers in New York City," in U.S. Children's Bureau, *Standards of Child Welfare: a Report of the Children's Bureau Conferences May and June 1919* (Washington, D.C., 1919), 185; U.S. Congress, House Committee on Labor, *Hygiene of Maternity and Infancy. Hearings . . . on H.R. 12634* (Washington, D.C., 1919), 37–38; U.S. Congress, House Committee on Interstate and Foreign Commerce, *Protection of Maternity and Infancy. Hearings . . . on H.R. 10925* (Washington, D.C., 1920), 57.

53. Lemons, *The Woman Citizen*, 173; Ladd-Taylor, *Mother-Work*, 371–73; Rothman, *Woman's Proper Place*, 151.

54. Frances Sage Bradley and Margaretta A. Williamson, *Rural Children in Selected Counties of North Carolina*, U.S. Children's Bureau, Rural Child

Welfare Series No. 2 (Bureau Publication no. 33) (Washington, D.C., 1918); Meckel, *Save the Babies*, 142. Segregated baby-health contests were held for both black and white children in some communities: Frank D. Loomis, "Indianapolis Baby Week, Oct. 3–9, 1915," Records of the U.S. Children's Bureau, 4–14–2–2–4; letter from Mrs. Dan Lott to Julia Lathrop, 11 June 1917, Records of the U.S. Children's Bureau, 4–14–2–1–4.

55. Edward H. Beardsley, *A History of Neglect: Health Care for Blacks and Mill Workers in the Twentieth-Century South* (Knoxville, Tenn., 1987), 130.

56. William F. Brunner, "The Negro Health Problem in Southern Cities," 183–90; L. C. Allen, "The Negro Health Problem," 194–203; Lawrence Lee, "The Negro as a Problem in Public Health Charity," 207–11; all in *American Journal of Public Health* 5 (1915).

57. Jacqueline Rouse, *Lugenia Burns Hope, Black Southern Reformer* (Athens, Ga., 1989), 71; Cynthia Neverdon-Morton, *Afro-American Women of the South and the Advancement of the Race, 1895–1925* (Knoxville, Tenn., 1989), 108, 119, 145–47, 225.

58. On black public-health nurses in the South, and their difficulties in obtaining training, see Evelyn Pitter, "The Colored Nurse in Public Health," *American Journal of Nursing* 26 (1926): 719–20; Stanley Rayfield, "A Study of Negro Public Health Nursing," *Public Health Nurse* 22 (1930): 525–36; Neverdon-Morton, *Afro-American Women of the South*, 63; Nannie J. Minor, "Status of the Colored Public Health Nurse in Virginia," *Public Health Nurse* 16 (1924): 243–44; Darlene Clark Hine, *Black Women in White: Racial Conflict and Cooperation in the Nursing Profession, 1890–1950* (Bloomington, Ind., 1989), 61.

59. See Ladd-Taylor, *Mother-Work*, chap. 6 on the defeat of Sheppard-Towner.

60. Yvonne Knibiehler, "La 'Lutte antituberculeuse,' instrument de la médicalisation des classes populaires (1870–1930)," *Annales de Bretagne et des Pays de l'Ouest* 86 (1979): 327–28; Emmanuel Perret, *Les Visiteuses de l'enfance* (Trévoux, 1919); Children's Bureau, American Red Cross in France, *Complete Report, August 1917 to April 1919*, Archives of the American Red Cross, 942.11 (box 847); Jules Renault and B. Labeaume, "L'Evolution de la protection de l'enfance," *Bulletin de l'Académie de médecine*, 3d ser., 117 (1937): 769; *Ecole de puériculture de la Faculté de médecine de Paris* (Paris, 1921).

61. Yvonne Knibiehler and Catherine Fouquet, *Historie des mères du Moyen Age à nos jours* (n.p., 1977), 305–8; Ministre de l'intérieur, Circulars, 3 November 1919 and 1 December 1919, Archives nationales, F2 2088; Ronsin, *La Grève des ventres*, 146–47; Françoise Thébaud, "Donner la vie: Histoire de la maternité en France entre les deux guerres," Thèse du 3ème Cycle, Université de Paris-VII, 1982, 86–91, 96–100, 305; David Glass, *Population Policies and Movements in Europe* (Oxford, Eng., 1940), 104.

6

The Power of Motherhood: Black and White Activist Women Redefine the "Political"

Eileen Boris

Yes, it is the great mother-heart reaching out to save her children from war, famine and pestilence; from death, degradation and destruction, that induces her to demand "Votes for Women," knowing well that fundamentally it is really a campaign for "Votes for Children."

—Mrs. Carrie W. Clifford, honorary president of the Federation of Colored Women's Clubs of Ohio, 1915[1]

Good women try always to do good housekeeping. Building inspectors, sanitary inspectors and food inspectors owe their positions to politics. Who then is so well informed as to how these inspectors perform their duties as the women who live in inspected districts and in inspected houses, and who buy food from inspected markets?

—Adella Hunt Logan of the Tuskegee Women's Club, 1912[2]

In the early-twentieth-century United States, women of African descent constructed a political voice that refused to be bounded by the separation of public from private, of work from home. Just as African-American women lived lives that knew no such artificial divisions, so those active in national and local women's organizations drew upon their strength as mothers to argue for a legal equality that recognized their difference as black and female from the dominant white society. They offered an interpretation of political life that emphasized the role of women as saviors of the race, justifying their activity because they were mothers. Indeed, they connected women's rights, unlike men's, to the experience of motherhood.

This language of social housekeeping extended women's realm from the home into the community, city, and nation.[3] By claiming expertise and responsibility for nonfamilial social spaces, black suffragists were redefining the political and demanding votes for women on the basis of their *work* as—rather than their merely being—mothers.[4] Black suffragists' discourse of female difference provided them with a unifying vocabulary, one that coexisted with, indeed complemented, another set of metaphors based on equal rights and universal claims.[5]

In their own context, white women activists in the early twentieth century employed a similar vocabulary. But while analysis of the speeches, writings, and programs of women reformers reveals African-American and Euro-American women sharing language, metaphor, and position in relation to lower-class women of their groups, the power of "motherhood" led to different outcomes for black and white women when it came to status and rights.

This essay asks, What does it mean that black and white activist women both created texts that relied on motherhood as image, experience, and rhetoric to forge a new, more inclusive definition of the "political"? How similar were the social programs that complemented, followed, or explained such linguistic constructs of womanhood as motherhood? What were the political consequences of a discourse that relied on the same central image—the altruistic, protective, and nurturing mother—that was embodied in the dominant male-supremacist and racist culture and the judge-made law of the period, but concurrently harnessed to a reform agenda?

This essay focuses on the African-American women's club movement to illuminate both the texts and contexts of motherhood as a political platform. It suggests the potential compatibility of equality with difference. After analyzing aspects of the black women's club movement, it briefly discusses the use of motherhood by white women reformers who also sought to better the homes of working-class women. It argues that white women shared less with their "clients," a social group distinguishable from themselves by class and ethnicity, than black club women did with the masses of African Americans. That is, racial unity was more important than class difference in the relation of black activist women to those they sought to uplift. Finally, this essay considers how the feminist discourse on motherhood, even as it redefined the subjects and objects of politics in the late nineteenth and early twentieth centuries, never escaped legal definitions of motherhood, as seen in labor legislation which sought to protect mothers, but excluded the paid labor of African-American women. Within the word "mother," as used by many reformers and makers of public policy, lurked the referent "white," the very association fought against by activist black women. Nevertheless, black women challenged Jim Crow laws and public policy in ways that demanded equality on the basis of recognized difference. Equal justice under the law, after all, need not obliterate difference.[6] We can be equal without being identical.

For black women activists, the state was hardly neutral. It often functioned as a negative force, blocking the advancement of the race. From municipal ordinances that hampered black artisans from pursuing their trades to explicit segregation of public facilities and the underfunding of limited social services, southern black women confronted a state that did not act in the interest of mothers, their children, or family life as a whole. They pursued their social reform through institutions of their own making. So did white women. But white activist women were able to transfer their programs to the state, becoming the administrators of new state agencies dedicated to maternal and child welfare. Black women, in contrast, gained few benefits from the emerging welfare state.[7]

The Historical and Political Underpinnings of "Motherhood" in the Early-Twentieth-Century Women's Movement

To explore the political differences underlying the term motherhood for black and white women activists, we must historically situate their discourses.[8] Although Adella Hunt Logan and Carrie W. Clifford expressed themselves similarly to the white women who dominated major national women's groups,[9] few of the leaders in these and other white women's organizations welcomed them as sisters in the women's movement of their day.[10] For Hunt Logan and Clifford were African–American women, and though privileged by education and wealth compared to the masses of their race, they felt the burden of black womanhood and black motherhood during a time that historians usually refer to as the Progressive Era, but which we must reconceptualize as an era of disenfranchisement of all women and black men, and of legalized segregation.[11] Consequently, the practices of women like Clifford and Hunt Logan, as well as their rhetoric, must be understood in the context of the actual conditions of black family life.

At the turn of the century, infant mortality and mothers working outside the home were both more common in the black community than in the white. In Washington, D.C., from 1888 to 1892, the death rate among black children stood at 15 per thousand, nearly three times greater than among whites.[12] As early as the 1870 census, at least three times as many black, compared to white, southern urban women listed an occupation, while by the early twentieth century, up to 70 percent of black women were earning wages at some point during the year, which meant that five times the number of married black, compared to white, women were in the labor force.[13] Reporting on Atlanta, Nashville, and Cambridge, Massachusetts, the United States Department of Labor found that females supported "wholly or in part" nearly 60 percent of black families." Most worked as domestics which led them, according to Lucy Laney at the first Atlanta University Conference in 1896, to "be away from the home all day" so that children received inadequate care from an absent and/or exhausted mother.[14] Nearly all of the 80 percent of southern blacks who were rural lived the poverty-stricken and hard life of the tenant farmer or sharecropper.[15] These women engaged in family labor (reproduction, dependent care, housework, and sex/affective labor), joined in the farm labor, and sometimes worked for wages for white farmers and housewives. Fertility for both rural and urban women was declining at the turn of the century, but still, among African Americans, wives of nonagricultural men had, on average, four to six children, with rural women having about eight, actually fewer than white southern women.[16] Yet the amount of household work under nonmechanized conditions remained staggering.[17]

At the same time, the cultural construction of womanhood took middle-class white women as the norm, even though privileged black women appeared to live by its tenets. A 1908 study by Atlanta University defended the virtue of black women but still gave credence to the stereotype of the "bad," "loose" black woman by arguing that "sexual immorality is probably the greatest single plague spot. . . ." The study did, however, go on to argue that, "[the plague spot's] greatest cause is slavery and the present utter disregard of a black woman's virtue and self-respect, both in law court and custom in the South."[18] Defined by the dominant white culture as breeder and slut, though subjected to sexual harassment, rape, and intimidation, black women existed outside the boundaries of an ideal of womanhood that the very absence of black women shaped.[19] The A and M Women's Mutual Improvement Circle could declare, "[t]he women of our circle recognize (as true women all over the land are doing) that without a better home life, the future of our race is indeed precarious,"[20] ignoring that the dominant culture denied to A and M women inclusion within their own term, "true women." As the educator Anna Julia Cooper declared before the Women's Congress at the World's Columbian Exposition in 1893, "[Although] in the eyes of the highest tribunal in America [the black woman was] deemed no more than a chattel, an irresponsible thing, a dull block, to be drawn hither or thither at the volition of an owner, still the Afro-American woman maintained ideals of womanhood unshamed by any ever conceived." Outspoken women like Cooper defied this denial of the status of mothers, daughters, sisters, that is, women, to African Americans.[21]

Because black women stood outside the boundaries of "true womanhood" as defined by the dominant culture, by being black and descended from slaves (even if their actual ancestors were free), black activists' references to "highest womanhood," to "true motherhood," appeared to subvert a social script written for them by the larger culture that sought to deny them the possibility of nurturing, motherhood, and family maintenance. That is, words that seemed to reflect the hegemonic culture, that seemed to suggest a consciousness steeped in a limited domesticity, in fact challenged that dominant culture.[22]

Thus, through organized self-help, African-American women—the most unequal and the most different in a culture where white men were and are the norm—simultaneously sought equal rights and celebrated their femaleness and their blackness. They sought to advance their race, to uplift black womanhood from the slurs of racism and the legacy of slavery, and they redefined the political and motherhood in the process.[23] They demonstrated that difference need not stand in binary opposition to equality, that, as one feminist has put it, "equality is not the elimination of difference, and difference does not preclude equality."[24] They understood their womanhood as a qualification for citizenship, as a characteristic that enabled them to serve the community rather than as a distinction that hampered participation in the larger social life. They shared such a use of womanhood with those white women who argued that women would bring special values to public life.[25]

Moreover, they showed that equal rights and cultural differences or diversity can coexist. After all, they were, for the most part, strong *race* women, asserting their bonds with black men and children while claiming the same rights for which white women struggled. This maintenance of difference as distinction within the search for equal rights before the law and in social practice predominated, although activist black women shared both Victorian values (such as the work ethic and gentility) and the religiosity associated with white America. Still an equilibrium, not an opposition, between equality and difference existed in the midst of persistent sexual and class divisions within the race, along with racial divisions among women.[26]

Black Women Activists

The National Association of Colored Women

Formed in 1896 from the merger of the National Federation of Afro-American Women with the Colored Women's League of Washington, D.C., the National Association of Colored Women (NACW) unified the philanthropic, self-improvement, and racial-uplift efforts of "bourgeois" black women until the mid-1930s. At that time Mary McLeod Bethune, a former president, founded the National Council of Negro Women and added the support of New Deal programs to the self-help tradition of black America.[27] By then, the NACW had limited its efforts to two major departments, "Mother, Home, Child" and "Negro Women in Industry," with its primary focus on the first of these.[28] Yet from the start, the association had concentrated on the status of black womanhood, the activities of mothers, and the quality of homelife.

Concerned with defending black womanhood from charges of immorality, and discriminated against by the white women's club movement which refused to give credentials to black women at General Federation of Women's Clubs (GFWC) conventions, black women had organized separately but not as separatists. During the first national meeting called by the Boston New Era Club in 1895, Josephine St. Pierre Ruffin declared:

> Our woman's movement is [a] woman's movement in that it is led and directed by women for the good of women and men, for the benefit of all humanity. . . . [W]e ask the active interest of our men, and, too, we are not drawing the color line: we are women, American women, as intensely interested in all that pertains to us as such as all other American women. . . .[29]

Although asserting their sameness with "all other American women," that is, with white women, organized black women would speak for the race:

> [F]or the sake of the thousands of *self-sacrificing* young women teaching and preaching in lonely southern backwoods, for the noble army of mothers who have given birth to these girls, mothers whose intelligence is only limited by their opportunity to get at books, for the sake of the *fine cultured* women who have carried off the honors in school here and often abroad, for the sake of our own dignity, the dignity of our race, and the future good name of our children, it is "meet, right, and our bounden duty" to stand forth and declare ourselves and principles, to teach an ignorant and suspicious world that our aims and interests are *identical with* those of *all good aspiring women.*[30]

As "an army of organized women standing for purity and mental worth," black activists would represent womanhood, a womanhood that was "self-sacrificing," "noble," "*fine cultured*," "good." They would claim a motherhood previously associated with white women but which black women would redefine in universal terms. But they also stood for "colored women," with special interest in applying universal precepts of homelife and womanhood to "the peculiar conditions" of a people only a quarter century removed from slavery and ever caught in the noose of racism through actual lynchings, job discrimination, poverty, and lack of educational opportunity.[31]

Mary Church Terrell best articulated this combination of racial

uplift and social motherhood, identity with the race and upholding of genteel values, in her speeches and writings as first president of the NACW between 1896 and 1901. This daughter of
the South's first black millionaire, graduate of Oberlin College,
speaker of numerous European languages, and first black member
of the District of Columbia Board of Education combined a philosophy of activism grounded in the idea of female difference with
promotion of racial and sexual equality based on rights discourse.
In a 1912 article, she proclaimed the justice of woman suffrage,
comparing the rights due women with those owed black men and
thus linking the disenfranchisement of both to the same sources.[32]
She ended one report on the work of club women with the declaration, "Seeking no favors because of our color, nor patronage
because of our needs, we knock at the bar of Justice and ask for
an equal chance."[33]

A charter member of the NAACP and supporter of desegregation
throughout her life, Terrell advocated civil rights as well as self-
help. Privileged and sometimes seen by outsiders as "white," she
recognized that her class position carried responsibilities to her
race, although she distinguished the respectable and educated
women, of whom she was one, from those she judged with the
larger culture to be ignorant, lazy, and immoral. She was a feminist, a member of the National Women's party, and a maternalist,
a woman who lost three children within days of their births,
who had her daughter Phillis in 1898 in the midst of her NACW
presidency, and who would adopt her brother's daughter seven
years later.[34]

For Terrell, motherhood was felt experience as well as an ideal.
This confession comes in the midst of recounting the tragic series
of infant deaths that marked the early years of her marriage:

> The maternal instinct was always abnormally developed in me.
> As far back as I can remember I have always been very fond of
> children. I cannot recall that I have ever seen a baby, no matter
> what its class, color, or condition in life, no matter whether it
> was homely or beautiful according to recognized standards, no
> matter whether it was clad in rags or wore dainty raiment, that
> did not seem dear and cunning to me.[35]

For white readers, Terrell indirectly refuted the negative impact
that slavery supposedly had on African-American women's mater-

nal feelings. She reminds us of the social circumstances of mothering, of how her ancestors could not always control the conditions of their mothering and how children born even to well-off women, like Terrell, still could fail to receive adequate medical intervention. She ended with the thought that perhaps here was a blessing in disguise.[36] Because upstanding black men, like her Memphis friend Thomas Moss, were being lynched,[37] perhaps it was better that children died. The threat of violent death inured Terrell, the bereaved mother, to her "cruel fate."

As if she had not already clearly linked motherhood and the condition of African Americans, this passage reinforces an earlier one where Terrell reimagines "that parting scene when Emmeline, my grandmother, who was then only a small child, was sold from her mother never to see her again."[38] This sense of poignancy, derived from the conditions of slavery, hangs over Terrell's discussion. Those actual circumstances—in which women bore children as producers of labor power, where motherhood was not necessarily chosen and where the mother-child bond faced the threat of disruption through sale, under the blessing of the law[39]—provide the words "maternal instinct" and "motherhood" with an oppositional quality.

Images of mothers, children, and homes dominated Terrell's NACW speeches and writings. She spoke of the NACW in maternalist terms:

> So tenderly has this child of the organized womanhood of the race been nurtured, and so wisely ministered unto by all who have watched prayerfully and waited patiently for its development, that it comes before you today a child hale, hearty, and strong, of which its fond mothers have every reason to be proud.[40]

At the first Biennial Convention of the organization in 1897, she proclaimed in words repeated in her widely distributed pamphlet, "The Progress of Colored Women":

> Believing that it is only through the home that a people can become really good and truly great, the NACW shall enter that sacred domain to inculcate right principles of living and correct false views of life. . . . [M]ore homes, purer homes, better homes is the text upon which our sermons to the masses must be preached.[41]

Like the authors of the Atlanta University investigations of black life, Terrell recoiled from what she perceived to be the average home "in which the air is foul, the manners bad and the morale worse."[42] Such a home, whether in urban alleys or rural planta-tions, she called "a menace to health, a breeder of vice, and the abode of crime."[43] Surrounded by vice, germs, and dinginess, children suffered. As fitting true mothers, Terrell called upon her "sisters of the Association"

> to rescue them [children] from evil and shame. . . . Listen to the cry of the children, my sisters. Upon you they depend for the light of knowledge, and the blessing of good example. As an organization of women, surely nothing can be nearer our hearts than the children, many of whose lives so sad and dark, we might brighten and bless.[44]

Relying on knowledge gleaned from education and on example, Terrell urged rescue work for the race. The club women would lighten the darkness of the masses. The secular became sacred; the impure, transformed by the "lightness" of the reformers' touch.[45] Terrell's metaphor reflected both the chasm of class within the black community and the effort to lessen that gap through volun-tary efforts.

But unlike their white counterparts, black women activists shared a common heritage with the poor. Like other women with class privilege, they practiced a politics of maternalism, a superi-ority of knowledge that led them to dictate standards for those judged below them. Yet their fate interlocked with the objects of their uplift: "Not alone upon the inmates of these hovels are the awful consequences of their filth and immorality visited, but upon the heads of those who sit calmly by and make no effort to stem the tide of disease and vice will vengeance as surely fall."[46] Racism bound together the "lesser" with the "better," and may have con-tributed to the creation of those very categories,[47] certainly class privilege intensified such divisions. Not surprisingly, "Lifting As We Climb" became the motto of the NACW, a motto which embod-ied the ties of gender and race and reflected a wish to bridge the gulf of class—but on terms set by the club women themselves.[48]

Next to the educated "better" women of the race stood both the masses of mothers in need and the white mothers with power to stymie the efforts of all black mothers. In both cases, Terrell's feminism suggests an incomplete sisterhood, despite appeals to the fairer ladies and expressions of solidarity with the darker masses. Before the 1899 Third National Congress of Mothers, a predominantly white organization devoted to the principles of an "educated" motherhood,[49] she compared the expectations that white and black mothers could have for their children and thus highlighted the difference that racism made for motherhood in consciousness and practice:

> Contrast, if you will, the feelings of hope and joy which thrill the heart of the white mother with those which stir the soul of her colored sister. Put yourselves for one minute in her place, (you could not endure the strain longer) and imagine, if you can, how you would feel if similarly situated—As a mother of the ["weaker" crossed out, and "oppressed" scratched in above] race clasps to her bosom the babe which she loves as fondly as you do yours, her heart cannot thrill with joyful anticipations of the future. For before her child she sees the thorny path of prejudice and proscription which his little feet must tread—She knows that no matter how great his ability, or how lofty his ambition, there are comparatively few avocations in which any one of his race may hope to succeed. . . . So rough does the way of her infant appear to many a poor black mother that instead of thrilling with the joy which you feel, as you clasp your little one to your breast, she trembles with apprehension and despair.[50]

As a representative of black womanhood, she appealed, "In the name of the child of my race, Mothers of the National Congress, I come, asking you to do all in your power by word and deed to give them the opportunities which you desire for your own."[51] By virtue of a shared motherhood, Terrell asked white women to provide equal opportunity for black children by teaching their own children "to be just and broad enough to judge men and women by their instrinsic merit, rather than by the adventitious circumstances of race, or color or creed."[52] Here the experience of motherhood, based on women's difference from men, opens the door to the argument for justice on the basis of universal human qualities.

As Terrell pleaded to the mothers of the men who had power in the land, as she suggested to her Association sisters that they follow the lead of the Mothers' Congress, she pointed out that even white women needed education in motherhood. In her 1897 presidential address she claimed:

> If the women of the dominant race with all the centuries of education, culture and refinement back of them, with all their wealth of opportunity ever present with them, if these women ... felt the necessity of calling a Mother's [sic] Congress that they might be enlightened as to the best methods of rearing children and conducting their homes, how much more do the women of our own race from whom the shackles of slavery have just fallen need information on the same subjects?[53]

Terrell lamented the ignorance of many African-American women (but not her sister club women). These she wished to expose to the knowledge within the grasp of white women, not to imitate whites, but for the betterment of the race.

Into the Home

Black activists took their work directly into the home. While organizations like the white National Mothers' Congress were intellectually organized by the era's thrust toward scientism, black women's own Mothers' Conferences were grounded in the black church. Their membership would somewhat overlap with club movements, like Terrell's, that blossomed around the same time, but Mothers' Conferences probably embraced a wider class of women because of the Conferences' church roots. The Conferences relied on religion to provide the text for education. Respectability became this text's major lesson.[54]

Under the leadership of Sister J. P. Moore of Spelman Seminary of Atlanta, Baptist and African Methodist Episcopal women throughout Arkansas, Tennessee, Alabama, Georgia, and North Carolina established in the early 1890s fireside schools, bible bands, and mothers' clubs out of the belief that "we must have good mothers before we can develop a good race of people."[55] Assuming that mothers were responsible for the moral, religious, and social development of their children, the movement under Sister Moore counseled women to train their children for God, teach them values rather than good dress, and make a happy, clean, comfortable but not luxurious home. The group's *Resolu-*

tions on Improving the House in Which We Live, for example, called for having, if possible, more than the common one-room house of the rural South, separate bedroom areas for boys and girls, and a dining room arranged so the family could sit down and eat together—goals that would be taken up by the NACW. In the various guidelines of the clubs—including the "Mother's pledge"—Victorian values of work and deportment joined with celebrations of the mother-child bond and exhortations to labor for God and the race. For their fireside or home school, mothers were to read to their children *Peep of the Day, Temperance Reader*, and the monthly magazine, *Hope*, especially the "Monthly Talk to the Young." They also were to report monthly to church and quarterly to the fireside headquarters, presumably to discuss their progress in setting "a good pattern for [their] children in their daily life" and in training them for God.[56]

The voices of women on the reconstituted plantations of tenant farmers and wage laborers are absent from the proceedings of the NACW but came through in the minutes of this earlier 1894 Mothers' Conference. One woman confessed,

> I have worked hard all day in the field, and walked five miles to hear this missionary from Sister J. P. Moore's school. I have not seen her, but I love her for the help she has given me through paper *Hope*. All my family loves and reads it daily. It has brought joy and sunshine into my home; it has helped me to give up my frowns and cross words, and be more loving, gentle and sweet.[57]

Another from Wakefield, North Carolina, reported how the mother's pledge made her "give up my snuff," "love my husband better and treat him more kindly," take better care of her children, and be a better housekeeper. "It makes everything go better about the plantation, because we have pledged ourselves to do better."[58] Significantly, "this pledge has greatly improved not only the mothers, but the fathers and the children in our neighborhood."[59] Mothers" clubs represented the work of mothers for the race that extended beyond the confines of the home.

The NACW also placed the establishment of mothers' clubs—along with day nurseries and kindergartens—at the top of its priorities. In such actions we see an acceptance of paid labor for mothers as a necessary reality. We also see both the bonds these privileged black women felt with their less well-off sisters and their sense of distance. Again Terrell expressed this tension. Addressing the NACW in 1899, she explained,

> To our poor benighted ["underprivileged" written above these words in speech draft] sisters in the Black Belt of Alabama we have gone, and have been both a help and a comfort to these women, through the darkness of whose ignorance of everything that makes life sweet . . . no ray of light would have penetrated but for us.[60]

Woven within such professions of concern comes a sense of superiority but also a fear; fear that their sameness (race and gender) would obscure their difference (class and education). This class concern partially lay behind the crusade against the one-room cabin, for morality and modesty, because "a majority of the dominant race . . . insists upon judging the Negro by his lowest and most vicious representatives instead of by the more intelligent and worthy classes."[61] Since "the womanhood of our people" was judged by the state of the masses, Terrell called upon "the more favored colored women," the bringers of light, to influence "their illiterate and unfortunate sisters," the receivers of advice, in whose hands lay the power to shape the homes, and thus, the morals of the race. But she also desired to improve the daily standard of living of those below her.[62]

Mothers' clubs thus not only improved homelife but also turned into a popular vehicle for cross-class association and for social betterment among African-American women. The Ladies Auxiliary of the District of Columbia reported on its mothers' meetings, held weekly in a chapel, with coffee and rolls after short talks: "The mothers are composed of working women, taught to make their own clothing. They are permitted to pay so much per week for the material until paid for and are entitled to the garments they make. They are also instructed how to keep their own houses neat and clean."[63] The Woman's Civic League of the State of Illinois also claimed success: "Mothers have gone out encouraged, homes have been made better and happier; good resolutions have been made and kept by those who had felt almost alone."[64] The Women's Club at Mr. Meigs Institute in Alabama brought together the mothers and daughters among the plantation women to build up their mutual "confidence." It boasted of success: "[T]heir homes are neat and clean, pictures on their walls, flowers growing in the yards, strings no longer are wrapped around the hair, and an air of contentment and a love of house seems to surround their little homes."[65]

Relationship to the Labor Question and Education

Recognizing that the mothers of their race often had to leave their children to work, the club women accepted the working mother as a worthy mother.[66] They understood how racism and discrimination ensured the inadequacy of most black men's wages, making wage earning a necessity for thousands of black mothers.[67] Labor issues, then, became an area for club work. As Terrell explained,

> So many families are supported entirely by our women, that if this movement to withhold employment from them continues to grow, we shall soon be confronted by a condition of things, serious and disastrous indeed. It is clearly the duty of this, the only organized body of Colored women in the country to study the labor question, not only as it affects the women, but also as it affects the men.[68]

NACW-sponsored mothers' clubs advocated the establishment of training schools to promote domestic science and manual training courses. So did Nannie Helen Burroughs, corresponding secretary to the Baptist Women's Convention.[69] If blacks were well trained, it was believed, whites could not use the excuse that they lacked proper skills or were unable to produce quality workmanship. But this concern with vocational education never meant that the club women saw such schooling in opposition to liberal arts. Rather, they viewed both as necessary, indeed, as interconnected.[70]

Education for motherhood and housekeeping never meant training for domestic service alone, but belonged to an understanding of women's role that merged the public with the private. Indeed, Burroughs justified her program of "Bible, Bath, Broom, Clean Lives, Clean Bodies, Clean Homes," by observing that "[t]he crux of our economic and social crisis or problems is in the Negro home."[71] An educated mother could turn from housekeeping for the family to housekeeping for wages, but it was expected that she would clean her own home as professionally as she would another's. Indeed, the respect that black activists gave housewives is evident in their eligibility for membership in the National Association of Wage Earners, for which Burroughs, Bethune, and other leaders of the NACW were officers in the early 1920s.[72]

Local clubs practiced a larger social motherhood that provided necessary services to the community. They established kindergartens, old-age homes, working girls' lodgings, social-purity projects, female protective leagues, orphanages, and settlements.[73] Such actions were political. As educator Lucy C. Laney noted at the 1899 Hampton Negro Conference, "Women are by nature fitted for teaching very young children. . . . In the kindergarten and primary school is the salvation of the race."[74] Between 1892 and 1898, the Woman's League of Washington, D.C., for example, organized seven kindergartens serving more than a hundred children. It opened a "mending bureau" to provide sewing for the poor and conducted classes in tailoring. Like white women's clubs, it sought to establish a "diet kitchen" to provide pure milk for infants and thus curb the alarming black infant-mortality rate in the nation's capital.[75] Club women in Providence, Rhode Island, organized a day nursery for mothers "who must go out to work —to leave their little ones to be cared for, instead of having them roam the streets uncared for."[76] Other locals, such as the Progress Study Club of Kansas City, combined philanthropy with self-improvement, setting up free kindergartens and devoting one afternoon a month to their own efforts at art needlework and lace making.[77] The Little Rock branch offered instruction in the vocational and liberal arts, including an industrial department with an exchange bureau through which women and girls could offer their handicraft for sale, a training department to improve the skills of domestic workers, and literary meetings for children to direct their reading out of the belief "that if we succeed in forming a taste for pure literature in the home, . . . we will have protected its sanctity from violation."[78]

Applying their education to the home, especially to lower mortality rates, the women of A and M College, Normal, Alabama, formed the Women's Mutual Improvement Circle. Like the Tuskegee Women's Club, this club of college women (teachers, students, and faculty wives) attempted to induce women from the community to hear talks on sanitation, general health, the mother-child relationship, child development, and related matters. Cooking and sewing classes, along with friendly visiting, brought the ideal of educated motherhood to the black belt for the purpose of individual but also race improvement.[79] A "Mothers' Reception" of the Colorado State Federation summarized the major themes of all the NACW affiliates, ranging from "Ventilation and Sanitation" to "The Mother's Influence in the Home." It advocated patience instead of whipping and called for "pure mothers for pure children."[80]

Relationship to the Fight against Segregation and Racial Violence

Finally, the club work of black women needs to be considered in the context of the violence and social degradation suffered by all African Americans. From the start, the programs of the NACW addressed Jim Crow laws, the convict-labor system, chain gangs—which imprisoned children—and disenfranchisement. These issues grew from positive action by a hostile state. Thus black women usually were fighting the state, rather than courting it.

Even before the organization of the movement, club founder and militant journalist Ida Wells Barnett attacked the segregated trains, which, affronting the dignity of black women, required them to leave the Ladies Coach for the (men's) smoking car or third-class passenger car (for "promiscuous" male and female lower sorts). After being forcibly removed from her usual seat in 1884, Wells Barnett sued the Chesapeake and Ohio Railroad, challenging the Supreme Court's "nullification" of the 1866 Civil Rights bill.[81] Club women continued to protest what they labeled as improper public accommodations, such as unisex train waiting rooms and bathrooms for "colored." The issue of lynching, as reported by Wells Barnett, stimulated some of the early gatherings of black women. By the 1920s, the NACW was lobbying for anti-lynching bill and child-labor amendment. Here were the topics of politics, as usually defined, which black women as the social mothers of the race claimed as their own. As Anna Julia Cooper proclaimed, "Only the BLACK WOMAN can say 'when and where I enter, in the quiet, undisputed dignity of my womanhood, without violence and without suing or special patronage, then and there the whole *Negro race enters with me*."[82]

"$acred Motherhood:" White Women Reformers and the Courts

The centrality of motherhood to the arguments and programs of white women reformers at the turn of the century is better known. Since the 1840s, the women's movement "believed in both sexual equality and a gender-defined society." Prominent reformers of the Progressive Era "did not see feminism as a rejection of domesticity, but rather as an extension of woman's role and power within the home into the larger society."[83] As one young trade unionist put it, "A woman is the mother: whether she has children or not her mission is to work for the good of the race."[84]

Certainly the iconography of the National Women's Trade Union League (NWTUL) projected a safe and improved motherhood as the goal of reform. Its 1903 emblem pictured in front of a burst of sunrise, a symbol of hope and victory, a classically draped mother and child and a warrior woman reaching out to each other in a handclasp, with the League's demands written in the space between them. These demands—"The Eight Hour Day, A Living Wage, To Guard the Home"—reveal how interconnected home and work, family and society were in the minds of women reformers. Only through shorter hours, higher wages, and generally improved working conditions would motherhood be protected and homelife secured. This policy contrasted with the ethos of industrial capitalism, with its emphasis on commercialism and profits. White women activists offered an alternative vision of a nurturing society, a vision projected from the social experience of women—as defined by such women—onto the entire society. The NWTUL adopted an even more powerful image: "$acred Motherhood," a portrait of a mother running a foot-powered sewing machine in a tenement while nursing her baby. The League made a postcard of this picture which it used to raise milk money for the children of strikers and to publicize the plight of women workers during the great Chicago garment strike of 1910–1911.[85]

Such visual texts emphasize how the social-welfare measures which historians link to progressivism were sold through appeals to maternalism on the part of women who represented the mothers of "the race," that is, the human—which, in general dialogue, was often equated with the white—race. As Frances Perkins, later secretary of labor under Franklin Roosevelt, recalled, success in gaining legislation came from behaving so as to remind politicians "subconsciously of their mothers."[86] Such images also suggest how the larger culture substituted paeans to motherhood and child life for any adequate resolution of the conflict between capitalist development and the real needs of mothers and children. White reformists often offered the definition of motherhood understood by white Protestant middle-class women to working-class ethnic women as a goal toward which to strive.

Yet actual implementation of programs produced a more complex understanding of motherhood, one shaped by recipients and not merely by reformers. To take one example, those fighting tenement homework and sweated labor believed that waged labor had no place in real homes; it degraded motherhood, childhood, and family life. Immigrant women, in contrast, regarded making artificial flowers, sewing garments, and the hundred other activities they performed for wages at home as enabling them to fulfill their duty as mothers and sought to convince judges and investigators to allow them to continue such labor at home. The reformers got their laws, but homeworkers defied them and the hidden nature of such labor made regulation difficult until changing economic conditions and unionization rid most trades of homework. At the same time, immigrant women often used child-protection services for their own ends, especially to break down the power of husbands and fathers. Further evidence of "clients" shaping social services comes in the form of letters from rural and urban, poor and middle-class women, all of whom influenced the programs of the Children's Bureau.[87]

Motherhood became contested terrain, the ground upon which white women reformers battled industrialists as well as sought to impose their notions of homelife onto the immigrant working class. White women's clubs in the late nineteenth century reacted to the pollution of the environment in which their own homes were situated by fighting for pure food and milk and other forms of consumer protection against the shoddy, contaminated products of trusts. They carried forward their project to women from other classes, but from the start they were mothering the world rather than attempting to maintain the home separate from the world. In doing so, they not only relied upon their own voluntary organizations, establishing model projects, but lobbied the state for such measures as tenement-house reform, pure-food and drug laws, maternal and infant welfare, schools, even laws against prostitution and public sexuality. Although disenfranchised like their

African-American counterparts, white women had access to white men who wielded power in their communities through economic, if not political, prowess. Even when fighting machine bosses and corrupt political parties, white women reformers looked to the state as the appropriate arena to carry out their agenda. They viewed the state as a terrain for struggle.[88]

African-American women viewed the state less as a potential friend and more as a roadblock, indeed as an enemy, to the advancement of the race. First, most African-American activists still were in the South where state and local governments actively enforced segregation and at best ignored the exploitation and terrorization of the black masses. Even when it came to services for whites, the South failed to invest in public provision; the region had, as one historian has explained, "smaller administrative capacities."[89] In an important sense, channels open to white women did not exist for black activist women. Self-help was a necessity. But the lines between community institutions and state services in practice were more complex. Black women raised funds for public institutions earmarked for their people, institutions underfunded by the state. With political institutions for whites only, they relied upon their schools, churches, and fraternal organizations to meet community needs.

The voluntary effort that turned into a public program in the urban North, when directed by white women for the immigrant working class, remained part of the community work of black women in the South—with the benefit of control but also the burden of strained resources. Even in the North, African Americans were only beginning to carve a place in the political system. Yet black club women were avid suffragists; after they gained state suffrage in Illinois, they would provide the foot soldiers, as well as crucial votes, in the election of Chicago's first black congressman.[90]

Like black club women, white women activists sought to improve the homes of poorer, less educated women. Their understanding of the pains and difficulties of maternity allowed some to identify with the plight of poorer women, but many viewed working-class and immigrant women as "the other" in need of a transformative education.[91] We can see this most blatantly in the Americanization campaign that reached a feverish pitch with World War I. The YMCA's Edith Terry Bremer argued, "to America the 'Immigration problem' is a great 'problem' of homes." Following this lead, the Federal Bureau of Naturalization argued in *Suggestions for Americanization Work among Foreign-Born Women*, "America is no better than its homes" and the mother "determines the kind of home and the health and happiness of the family." The General Federation of Women's Clubs (GFWC) pledged to "carry the English language and American ways of caring for babies, ventilating the house, preparing American vegetables, instead of the inevitable cabbage, right into the new homes." In this light, the work of visiting nurses and social-settlement mothers' clubs took on a multiple identity, expressive of the alternative ethos of women reformers, their understanding of the material conditions of women's lives, and the solving of urban problems by imposition of the "American way." In one sense, women reformers were modernizers, rather than merely Americanizers. If they were unable to adapt old-world practices to the industrial city, they would attempt to eradicate them.[92]

Perhaps the power of motherhood reached its rhetorical heights in the women's peace movement, also of the World War I era. Founders of the Women's Peace party (WPP) in 1915 (of which Mary Church Terrell was a member) believed that women's qualities as women—their actual or potential motherhood, their ability to talk things out rather than resolve disagreements through violence—generated a desire to preserve life. Women pacifists criticized American foreign policy on the basis of their experience with nurturing and their expectation of what it took to perform that act. Motherhood, then, provided a moral basis for action, a direction for politics.[93]

If the discourse of white women reformers promised a new vision of the industrial city, indeed a new world, it failed to escape its ties to the dominant culture's conception of womanhood as embodied in the law. As Justice Bradley wrote in his famous concurring opinion in *Bradwell v. Illinois*[94] during a time when Congressional Reconstruction held sway, but racism kept black women from being included in the idea of "woman,"

> [T]he civil law, as well as nature herself, has always recognized a wide difference in the respective spheres and destinies of man and woman. Man is, or should be, woman's protector and defender. The natural and proper timidity and delicacy which belongs to the female sex evidently unfits it for many of the occupations of civil life. The constitution of the family organiza-

tion, which is founded in the divine ordinance, as well as in the nature of things, indicates the domestic sphere as that which properly belongs to the domain and functions of womanhood.[95]

The sexual division of social life became embedded in labor-standards legislation in part because Bradwell set up women as a special class to which the equal-protection clause failed to apply; the right to contract did not apply because women were treated as a class of dependent persons. The famous Brandeis brief in *Muller v. Oregon*[96] also reflected preexisting understandings of woman's place and female difference. The arguments of Josephine Goldmark of the National Consumers' League (NCL), who researched much of the brief, reinforced the idea that women were different from men. But her arguments that women were weaker than men sprang from the reality that women working in factories were injuring themselves and, because they were unorganized, had no recourse outside the law. For Goldmark, using women's alleged "weakness" was a practical tactic in seeking to ensure that the law would improve the lives of these otherwise unprotected, suffering workers.[97]

Significantly, the decision in *Muller* justified maximum hours for women on the basis of protecting motherhood; women carried with them responsibility for "the well-being of the race."[98] *Muller* represented the sanctification of motherhood which had existed for nearly a century alongside women's attempts to increase their power through their position as mothers. However, the hours laws upheld in *Muller*, as well as attempts at minimum wage bills and exclusionary legislation like night-work laws, applied only to limited groups of women because the legislation exempted from coverage agricultural, nonprofit, and usually domestic workers (though not necessarily the black-dominated occupation of laundresses in laundries). That these were the very jobs held by women of color further suggests how the term "mother" in the judge-made discourse referred to white women.[99] Laws which protected immigrant working women who labored outside the home, then, did not apply to the women on the plantation who were the chief target of efforts by the NACW to uplift the race.

Conclusion

Nearly a century ago, black activist women understood the complex relation between gaining civil rights and maintaining one's heritage, culture, and self-determination. Their referents to justice and difference might not appeal to those who see both "justice" and "difference" as constructed by universalistic male dominance.[100] For African-American women did not discredit motherhood as a female experience shaped by male demands; rather, they based their political programs as well as their epistemology on their own understanding of it. Many traditional African cultures privileged the mother-child bond.[101] Yet the circumstances first of slavery and then of poverty forced many mothers to work away from their children, despite their preferences. Thus, black women, even NACW members, favored mothers' earning wages at home, an activity which white women reformers fought as a social evil but Italian immigrant mothers embraced as fulfilling their maternal duty.[102] If they were privileged and recognized their class, they knew how race and racism shaped their lives for better and for worse.

White women reformers did not have to defend their reputations as mothers, as black women activists often did, because the dominant culture found in them the prototype for "woman," and "mother."[103] White women could use dominant cultural conceptions as a political tool for exposing the gaps between sentimentality and reality, as embodied in the image of "$acred Motherhood." But, working to improve the actual conditions of mothers and children, as did the black women's clubs, white women still ran up against a difference standard defined by men, including white male judges.

In the case of white activist women, the male dominance of the time shaped the understanding of both difference and equality, which helps to explain the disappointing impact of white-activist efforts.[104] Women's culture, an alternative set of values based on women's perceptions and experiences as mothers, failed to transform the relations between the sexes or usher in an era of gender justice. Its understanding of motherhood—equated with peace and social nurturance—fed into the hegemonic culture's equation of motherhood with biology and female dependence on men. This ideological equation remained even though women reformers actually reduced such dependence through programs that substituted dependence on the state and social-service institutions for dependence on a husband, father, other male relative, or lover.[105] Thus the concept of women as mothers or potential mothers justified limiting women's labor-market options but did not necessarily elevate the value of motherhood or nurturing, even though women reformers valued such activity. Social programs would protect working women, but not immigrant mothers working in the home as industrial homeworkers or African American mothers working in other women's homes as domestic servants. Such home-based waged labor was invisible. Home and workplace remained separate spheres, with housework not considered real work and industrial homework dismissed as an avocation. The male values of the workplace became conflated with the whole of social life.[106]

The work of bourgeois black women must also be evaluated in the context of unequal power relations. To deny the reality of patriarchy, or male power over women, would be to romanticize black male-female relations and to ignore the power of ruling-class white men over all other groups in the society. Yet black women's reliance on motherhood, a status and experience disrupted and denied to their mothers and grandmothers, challenged the subordination of African Americans. Like their white counterparts, African-American women addressed the actual needs of mothers and children. Even though their own classism, along with the racism and sexism of others, sometimes stymied their efforts, the history of black activist women at the turn of the century suggests that justice and difference can coexist under the banner of self-determination, if not liberation. This history may encourage us to replace an equality standard that fails to incorporate the historic position of African Americans and of women with a justice standard that incorporates the ethics of care.

The history of African-American activist women also cautions us against a linear history of women reformers and the state. Their more holistic community approach, where civil rights activity and social provision appeared interlocked,[107] came both from a self-help ideology and from political necessity. Their history reminds us that the movement from voluntary to state service was not inevitable in the early twentieth century, forcing us to reevaluate the terms upon which other groups of women, more privileged in race and class, made that transition from private program to public responsibility.

Notes

I would like to thank the participants at the Fourth Annual Conference on Feminism and Legal Theory, Adele Logan Alexander, Sharon Harley, Nelson Lichtenstein, Nancy Hewitt, the editors of the *Yale Journal of Law and Feminism*, especially Stephanie Cotsirilos, and Sonya Michel for their comments. This article is a revised version of the one that appeared under the same title in *Yale Journal of Law and Feminism* 2 (Fall 1989): 25–49.

1. Mrs. Charles W. Clifford, "Votes for Children," *The Crisis* 10 (August 1915): 185.

2. Adella Hunt Logan, "Colored Women as Voters," *The Crisis* 4 (September 1912): 242–43. For more information on Adella Hunt Logan, see Adele Logan Alexander, "Black Women at Tuskegee: Building a Foundation, 1895–1920," paper presented at the Conference on Afro-American Women and the Vote, University of Massachusetts, Amherst, 1987.

3. For discussions of social housekeeping, see Dolores Hayden, *The Grand Domestic Revolution* (Cambridge, Mass., 1981); Marlene Wortman, "Domesticizing the Nineteenth-Century City," *Prospects: Annual of American Cultural Studies* 3 (1977): 531–72. For the merging of public and private in the lives of women of color, see Evelyn Nakano Glenn, "Racial Ethnic Women's Labor: The Intersection of Race, Gender and Class Oppression," *Review of Radical Political Economics* 17 (1985): 86–108.

4. For an analysis of the women's movement building out of the "dailiness" of life, see Bettina Aptheker, *Tapestries of Life: Women's Work, Women's Consciousness, and the Meaning of Daily Experience* (Amherst, Mass., 1989).

5. For a fine discussion of the competing claims of difference and equality within both the women's movement and the feminism of the 1910s, see Nancy Cott, *The Grounding of Modern Feminism* (New Haven, 1987), 3–50. To emphasize difference or the mother metaphor, as I do in the above paragraphs, should not be understood to mean that African-American women neglected justice arguments, as we shall see. For example, see Adella Hunt Logan, "Woman Suffrage," *Colored American Magazine* 9 (1905): 487–89.

6. For one discussion of the problem of formal versus substantive equality, see Richard A. Wasserstrom, "Racism, Sexism, and Preferential Treatment: An Approach to the Topics," *UCLA Law Review* 24 (1977): 581–622.

7. For these points, see Eileen Boris and Peter Bardaglio, "Gender, Race, and Class: The Impact of the State on the Family and the Economy, 1790–1945," in Naomi Gerstel and Harriet Gross, eds., *Families and Work* (Philadelphia, 1987), 132–51; and Robyn Muncy, *Creating a Female Dominion in American Reform, 1890–1935* (New York, 1991).

8. See, for example, Chris Weedon, *Feminist Practice and Poststructuralist Theory* (New York, 1987), 24–25. See also Mary Poovey, "Feminism and Deconstruction," *Feminist Studies* 14 (1988): 51–65; Linda Alcoff, "Cultural Feminism versus Poststructuralism: The Identity Crisis in Feminist Theory," *Signs* 13 (1988): 405–36; Teresa de Lauretis, "Feminist Studies/Critical Studies: Issues, Terms, Contexts," in de Lauretis, ed., *Feminist Studies/Critical Studies* (Bloomington, Ind., 1986), 5–19. For African-American women, see Hazel V. Carby, *Reconstructing Womanhood: The Emergence of the Afro-American Woman Novelist* (New York, 1987), 16–17; and Evelyn Brooks

Higginbotham, "African-American Women's History and the Metalanguage of Race," *Signs* 17 (1992): 251–74.

9. Among such organizations were the National American Women's Suffrage Association (NAWSA), the General Federation of Women's Clubs (GFWC), and the National Consumers' League (NCL).

10. For the history of African Americans and suffrage, see Rosalyn Terborg-Penn, "Afro-Americans in the Struggle for Woman Suffrage" (Ph.D. diss., Howard University, 1977); and Terborg-Penn, "Disenchanted Black Feminists: Prelude and Postscript to the Passage of the Nineteenth Amendment," in Lois Scharf and Joan M. Jensen, eds., *Decades of Discontent: The Women's Movement, 1920–1940* (Westport, Conn., 1983), 261–278. See also Angela Davis, *Women, Race and Class* (New York, 1981), chaps. 4, 7, and 9.

11. For a survey of this period that links Progressive electoral reforms with Jim Crow segregation, see Nell Painter, *Standing at Armageddon: The United States, 1877–1919* (New York, 1987).

12. George G. Bradford, "Reports from the City of Washington," in "Mortality among Negroes in Cities," *Atlanta University Publications* 1 (1896): 15–16.

13. Jacqueline Jones, *Labor of Love, Labor of Sorrow: Black Women, Work, and the Family* (New York, 1985), esp. 65–66, 105.

14. Butler R. Wilson, "General Summary," in "Social and Physical Condition of Negroes in Cities," *Atlantic University Publications* 2 (1896), reports on the Department of Labor study, 6; Lucy Laney, "General Conditions of Mortality," in "Mortality among Negroes in Cities," 36.

15. Jones, *Labor of Love*, 72, 73–79.

16. Ibid., 83–84, 107.

17. See "Mortality among Negroes in Cities"; "Social and Physical Condition of Negroes in Cities"; Jones, *Labor of Love*, 65–66, 71–78, 91–118, for general demographic and social conditions.

18. W.E. Burghardt Du Bois, ed., "The Negro American Family," *Atlanta University Publications* 13 (1908): 37–42.

19. Hazel Carby is quite helpful in articulating this point. See *Reconstructing Womanhood*, 30. On the history of violence against black women, see Jacquelyn Dowd Hall, " 'The Mind That Burns in Each Body': Women, Rape, and Racial Violence," in Ann Snitow, Christine Stansell, and Sharon Thompson, eds., *Powers of Desire: The Politics of Sexuality* (New York, 1983), and Davis, *Women, Race and Class*, chap. 11.

20. Folder, "National Association of Colored Women, Mss. Reports to 1899 Convention," Mary Church Terrell Papers, carton 23, Library of Congress.

21. Anna Julia Cooper at the World's Fair, quoted in Louise Hutchinson, *Anna J. Cooper: A Voice from the South* (Washington, D.C., 1981), 88.

22. White, Protestant, educated women reformers, on the other hand, forged an alternative ethos against industrial capitalism, yet fed into the dominant

sex/gender, class, and racial systems. Their social policies, when translated into law and public policy, ultimately reinforced labor-market segmentation because, in part, they never escaped their status as the referent to true womanhood; their arguments merged into those of courts and male-dominated legislatures. For greater elaboration of this argument, see Eileen Boris, "Reconstructing the Family: Women, Progressive Reform and the Problem of Social Control," in Nancy Schrom Dye and Noralee Frankel, eds., *Gender, Class, Race, and Reform in the Progressive Era* (Lexington, Ky., 1991), 73–86.

23. Like that of their white counterparts, black activists' appeal to motherhood also implied a certain, somewhat ambiguous, differentiation of class since black activists distinguished themselves from their less privileged sisters even while asserting their bonds.

24. Joan W. Scott, "Deconstructing Equality-versus-Difference: Or, The Uses of Poststructuralist Theory for Feminism," *Feminist Studies* 14 (1988): 33, 38. The "equality versus difference" debate which has polarized feminists in recent years dichotomizes our political choices in ways that key segments of the women's movement of 1900 avoided.

25. Cott, *Grounding*, 31–32.

26. For the history of such black women activists, see Cynthia Neverdon-Morton, *Afro-American Women of the South and the Advancement of the Race, 1895–1925* (Knoxville, Tenn., 1989); Jacqueline Rouse, *Lugenia Burns Hope, Black Southern Reformer* (Athens, Ga., 1989); Anne Firor Scott, "Most Invisible of All: Black Women's Voluntary Associations," *Journal of Southern History* 56 (February 1990): 3–22; Beverly Jones, "Mary Church Terrell and the National Association of Colored Women, 1896 to 1901," *Journal of Negro History* 67 (1982): 20–33. Jones calls such women "conservative" rather than "feminist" because they geared their programs and rhetoric to motherhood. In doing so, she superimposes a contemporary definition of the term feminist onto the turn-of-the-century movement. For more on this matter, see below.

27. For a summary of the NACW, its founding and activities, see its publication, *National Notes*, Mary Church Terrell Collection, folders 249, 240, 251, boxes 102 and 103, Moorland-Spingarn Research Center, Howard University. For secondary accounts, see Stephanie J. Shaw, "Black Club Women and the Creation of the National Association of Colored Women," *Journal of Women's History* 3 (Fall 1991): 10–25; Paula Giddings, *Where and When I Enter: The Impact of Black Women on Race and Sex in America* (New York, 1984); Wilson Jeremiah Moses, *The Golden Age of Black Nationalism, 1850–1925* (New York, 1988), 103–31; Elizabeth Davis, *Lifting as They Climb: The National Association of Colored Women* (privately printed, 1933). See also Angela Davis, "Black Women and the Club Movement," in *Women, Race and Class*, 127–36. No adequate biography of Bethune exists. Her New Deal role, as the head of the unofficial black cabinet, is discussed in Nancy J. Weiss, *Farewell to the Party of Lincoln: Black Politics in the Age of FDR* (Princeton, N.J., 1983).

28. Davis, *Lifting*, 97–103.

29. "Address of Josephine St. P. Ruffin, President of Conference," in Davis, *Lifting*, 18.

30. Ibid., 18.

31. For the condition of the former slaves, see John Hope Franklin and Alfred Moss, Jr., *From Slavery to Freedom*, 6th ed. (New York, 1988), 224–90; Arnold Taylor, *Travail and Triumph: Black Life and Culture in the South since the Civil War* (Westport, Conn., 1976).

32. Mary Church Terrell, "The Justice of Woman Suffrage," *The Crisis* 4 (1912): 243–45.

33. Mary Church Terrell, "Club Work of Colored Women," *The Southern Workman* 30 (August 1901): 438; see also Terrell, "Woman Suffrage and the 15th Amendment," *The Crisis* 10 (1915): 191.

34. For Terrell's biography, see Giddings, *When and Where*, 20–22, 109–10; Dorothy Sterling, "Mary Church Terrell," in Barbara Sicherman and Carol Hurd Green, eds., *Notable American Women: The Modern Period* (Cambridge, Mass., 1980), 678–80; Dorothy Sterling, *Black Foremothers: Three Lives* (New York, 1979); Sharon Harley, "Mary Church Terrell," in John Hope Franklin and August Meier, eds., *Black Leaders of the Nineteenth Century* (Urbana, Ill., 1988). For Terrell's own tale, see Mary Church Terrell, *A Colored Woman in a White World* (Washington, 1968). Both Giddings and Sterling, in her longer portrait, claim that Terrell never devoted much actual time to motherhood even though she longed for it.

35. Terrell, *A Colored Woman*, 106–7.

36. Ibid., 108.

37. Giddings, *When and Where*, 17–18.

38. Terrell, *A Colored Woman*, 5.

39. For discussions of motherhood under slavery, see Deborah Gray White, *Ar'n't I a Woman? Female Slaves in the Plantation South* (New York, 1985), and Jacqueline Jones, " 'My Mother was Much of a Woman': Black Women, Work, and the Family Under Slavery," *Feminist Studies* 8 (1982): 235–69.

40. Mary Church Terrell, "The Duty of the National Association of Colored Women to the Race," *A.M.E. Church Review* 16 (1900): 340.

41. Mary Church Terrell, "President's First Address to the National Association of Colored Women, Nashville, Tenn., September 15, 1897," typescript, Terrell Papers, box 28, folder entitled "Speeches and Writings, 1891–1904," Library of Congress (LC).

42. Terrell, "President's First Address."

43. Ibid.

44. Ibid.

45. Here it appears that a class ranking all too often based on color reinforced the English language, which links darkness with evil.

46. Terrell, "President's First Address."

47. Ibid.; for this sense of connection, see, Terrell, "The Duty of the National Association of Colored Women," 347.

48. For an insightful analysis of this point, see Deborah Gray White, "Gender, Race, and Class and National Black Women's Organizations," Black History Month Talk, Howard University, 24 Feb. 1988; see also her "Fettered Sisterhood: Class and Classism in early Twentieth Century Black Women's History," paper delivered to the American Studies Association, Toronto, Canada, Nov. 1989.

49. See Sheila M. Rothman, *Woman's Proper Place: A History of Changing Ideals and Practices, 1870 to the Present* (New York, 1978), 103–6.

50. Mary Church Terrell, "Greetings from the National Association of Colored Women to the National Congress of Mothers," Terrell Papers, box 26, folder entitled "Third National Congress of Mothers, 1899," LC.

51. Ibid.

52. Ibid.

53. Terrell, "President's First Address."

54. Basically secular in their thinking, Terrell and Hunt Logan stood in contrast to the religious tone generally found among the club women.

55. Address by E.C. Morris, president of the Baptist State Convention of Arkansas, in *Minutes of the Second Mothers' Conference Held in Pine Bluff, Ark., September 8th, 9th and 10th, 1894* (Atlanta, 1894), 12, Terrell Papers, microfilm roll 17, frames 566–88, LC. There were nearly 500 of these clubs/schools at that time.

56. Ibid., 15, 41–42, 48.

57. Ibid., 25.

58. Ibid., 37.

59. Ibid.

60. Mary Church Terrell, "The Duty of the National Association of Colored Women to the Race," speech given at the Second Biennial Meeting, 14–16 Aug. 1899, Chicago; box 28, Terrell Papers, LC.

61. Mary Church Terrell, *The Progress of Colored Women* (New York, n.d.), in folder 149, box 102–5, Terrell Collection, Moorland-Spingarn Research Center.

62. Ibid.; for this concern with morality, see Gerda Lerner, *Black Women in White America* (New York, 1972), 163–71.

63. (No author), "National Association of Colored Women, Mss. Reports to 1899 Convention," in box 23, Terrell Papers, LC.

64. Ibid.

65. Ibid.

66. This definition of motherhood, however, varied from the dominant one that applauded mother care of children. Even white activist reformers who supported better conditions for working women preferred that mothers not work, but rather receive a mother's pension, if without a man, or be sup-

ported by a husband earning a family wage. For one example, see Florence Kelley, "Married Women in Industry," *Proceedings of the Academy of American Social and Political Science* (1910): 90–96. For further discussion see Sonya Michel, "The Limits of Maternalism: Policies toward American Wage-Earning Mothers during the Progressive Era," in this volume.

67. For the need of black women to work, see Elizabeth Pleck, "A Mother's Wages: Income Earning among Married Italian and Black Women, 1896–1911," in Nancy F. Cott and Elizabeth H. Pleck, eds., *A Heritage of Her Own: Toward a New Social History of American Women* (New York, 1979), 367–92.

68. Terrell, "The Duty of the NACW," *A.M.E. Church Review*, 347–48.

69. See Phyllis Palmer, "Housework and Domestic Labor: Racial and Technological Change," in Karen Sacks and Dorothy Remy, eds., *"My Troubles Are Going to Have Trouble with Me": Everyday Trials and Triumphs of Women Workers* (New Brunswick, N.J., 1984), 83–85, and Evelyn Brooks-Barnett, "Nannie Burroughs and the Education of Black Women," in Sharon Harley and Rosalyn Terborg-Penn, eds., *The Afro-American Woman: Struggles and Images* (Port Washington, N.Y., 1978), 97–108.

70. In contrast, W. E. B. Du Bois and Booker T. Washington posed their debate over black education in terms of an opposition between schooling and liberal arts. For the relation of the club women to their debate, see Giddings, *When and Where*, 102–8.

71. See Nannie Helen Burroughs, "The School of the 3 B's," 1938, box 309, folder entitled "National Trade and Professional School Brochures and Catalogues," Nannie Helen Burroughs Papers, LC.

72. Ibid.; (no author), *Making Their Mark—Results in the Lives of Graduates* (Washington, D.C., 1934), 14, box 309; National Association of Wage Earners Incorporated, "Constitution," box 308, folder entitled "National Association of Wage Earners," both in Burroughs Papers.

73. Davis, *Lifting*, passim; see also National Association of Colored Women, unpublished manuscript reports to 1899 convention, Terrell Papers, box 23, LC; Hutchinson, *Anna J. Cooper*, 85–129, for the work of club women, especially in Washington, D.C., and W.E. Burghardt Du Bois, ed. "Efforts for Social Betterment among Negro Americans," *Atlantic University Publications* 14 (1909): 47–64, 119–27; for southern work and the shift from philanthropy to social welfare, see Kathleen Berkeley, " 'Colored Ladies Also Contributed': Black Women's Activities from Benevolence to Social Welfare, 1866–1896," in Walter J. Fraser, Jr., Frank Saunders, Jr., and Jon Wakelyn, eds., *The Web of Southern Social Relations: Women, Family, and Education* (Athens, Ga., 1985), 181–203.

74. Lucy C. Laney, quoted in Neverdon-Morton, *Afro-American Women*, 5.

75. [Mrs.] Helen A. Cook, "The Work of the Woman's League, Washington, D.C.," in "Some Efforts of American Negroes for Their Own Social Betterment," *Atlanta University Publications* 3 (1898): 57–59.

76. Du Bois, "Efforts for Social Betterment," 60; see also 47–64, 119–27.

77 NACW, unpublished manuscript reports to 1899 Convention.

78. NACW, unpublished manuscript reports to 1897 Convention and 1899 Convention. For an exhaustive listing of club activities, especially as associated with southern black colleges, see Neverdon-Morton, *Afro-American Women*.

79. NACW, unpublished manuscript reports to 1899 Convention.

80. Du Bois, "Efforts for Social Betterment," 62–63.

81. For this incident, see Giddings, *When and Where*, 22–23. See also, Ida B. Wells, *Crusader for Justice: The Autobiography of Ida B. Wells*, ed. Alfreda M. Duster (Chicago, 1970).

82. Anna Julia Cooper before the colored clergy of the Protestant Episcopal church, in Anna J. Cooper, *A Voice from the South* (1892; rpt. New York, 1988), 31.

83. Elizabeth Anne Payne, *Reform, Labor, and Feminism: Margaret Dreier Robins and the Women's Trade Union League* (Urbana, Ill., 1988), 123. Of course, white women activists cannot be collapsed into an undifferentiated whole, but their differences became even more prevalent after suffrage. See William O'Neill, *Everyone Was Brave: The Rise and Fall of Feminism in America* (New York, 1969); Nancy Cott, "What's in a Name? The Limits of 'Social Feminism'; or, Expanding the Vocabulary of Women's History," *Journal of American History* 76 (1989): 809–29. The National Women's Trade Union League, discussed below, was a cross-class women's group, although privileged class "allies" dominated. That makes its use of motherhood all the more significant.

84. Fannia Cohn, quoted in Payne, *Reform, Labor, and Feminism*, 124. Payne explores the links between feminism and motherhood in the work of Margaret Dreier Robins and the National Women's Trade Union League. For the tension between difference and equal rights within feminism, see Cott, *Grounding*.

85. I have analyzed the NWTUL emblem in a different context in, *Art and Labor: Ruskin, Morris, and the Craftsman Ideal in America* (Philadelphia, 1986), 186–87; see also, Payne, *Reform, Labor and Feminism*, picture inserts, for an illustration of the emblem and "$acred Motherhood," and Payne, 126–28. For analysis of "$acred Motherhood," see my "Regulating Industrial Homework: The Triumph of 'Sacred Motherhood,'" *Journal of American History* 71 (1985): 750.

86. Frances Perkins, quoted in Payne, *Reform, Labor, and Feminism*, 134.

87. See Boris, "Reconstructing the 'Family'"; Linda Gordon, "Family Violence, Feminism and Social Control," *Feminist Studies* 12 (1986): 453–78; Gordon, "Child Abuse, Gender, and the Myth of Family Independence: Thoughts on the History of Family Violence and Its Social Control, 1880–1920," *New York University Review of Law and Social Change* 12 (1983–84): 523–37; and Molly Ladd-Taylor, "'My Work Came Out of Agony and Grief': Mothers and the Making of the Sheppard-Towner Act," in this volume.

88. For a good summary of these efforts, see Nancy Schrom Dye's introduction to Dye and Frankel, *Gender, Class, Race, and Reform*, 1–5; Seth Koven and

Sonya Michel, "Womanly Duties: Maternalist Politics and the Origins of Welfare States in France, Germany, Great Britain, and the United States, 1880–1920," *American Historical Review* 95 (1990): 1076–1108; Sara Evans, *Born for Liberty: A History of Women in America* (New York, 1989), 119–24; Muncy, *Creating A Female Dominion*; Wortman, "Domesticating the Nineteenth-Century City"; and Mary Ritter Beard, *Women's Work in Municipalities* (New York, 1915).

89. Linda Gordon, "Black and White Visions of Welfare: Women's Welfare Activism, 1890–1945," *Journal of American History* 78 (1991): 559–90, esp. 560. Gordon's work, which appeared after the original version of this article, parallels and extends my own thoughts. For evidence of state incapacity in the South, although not expressed in those terms, see C. Vann Woodward, *Origins of the New South* (Baton Rouge, La., 1951).

90. For that story, see Wanda Ann Hendricks, "The Politics of Race: Black Women in Illinois, 1890–1920" (Ph.D. diss., Purdue University, 1990).

91. For an empathetic relation, see Ladd-Taylor, in this volume; for a critical analysis, see Gwendolyn Mink, "The Lady and the Tramp: Gender, Race, and the Origins of the American Welfare State," in Linda Gordon, ed., *Women, the State, and Welfare* (Madison, Wis., 1990), 98–111.

92. On Americanization, see John F. McClymer, "Women as Americanizers, and as Americanized," paper presented at the Conference on Women in the Progressive Era, Washington, D.C., March 1988, 12–13, 15.

93. For the most insightful analysis of the WPP, see the work of Linda Schott, "Against Modernism: The Women's Peace Movement as Cultural Reform," paper delivered to the American Historical Association, December 1985, and Schott, "The Women's Peace Party and the Moral Basis of Women's Pacifism," *Frontiers* 8 (1985): 22–24. For an analysis of the slippery consequences of the appeal to female difference among contemporary women peace activists, see Micaela di Leonardo, "Morals, Mothers, and Militarism: Anti-Militarism and Feminist Theory," *Feminist Studies* 11 (1985): 599–617; see also, Linda Gordon, "The Peaceful Sex? On Feminism and the Peace Movement," *NWSA Journal* 2 (1990): 624–34.

94. 83 U.S. (16 Wall.) 130 (1872).

95. Ibid. at 141 (Bradley, J., concurring).

96. 208 U.S. 412 (1908).

97. For an analysis along these lines, see Sybil Lipschultz, "Social Feminism and Legal Discourse, 1908–1923," in Martha Albertson Fineman and Nancy Sweet Thomadsen, eds., *At the Boundaries of Law: Feminism and Legal Theory* (New York, 1991), 209–25.

98. 208 U.S. at 421–22. For the best exposition of *Muller* that situates it in a prior history of decisions, see Nancy Erickson, "*Muller v. Oregon* Reconsidered: The Origins of A Sex-Based Doctrine of Liberty of Contract," *Labor History* 30 (1989): 228–50. For a fuller discussion of gender and labor-standards legislation, see my "Quest for Labor Standards in the Era of Eleanor Roosevelt: The Case of Industrial Homework," *Wisconsin Women's*

Law Journal 2 (1986): 53–74. See also Susan Lehrer, *Origins of Protective Labor Legislation for Women, 1905–1925* (Albany, N.Y., 1987).

99. For an extension of this point, see Nancy Breen, "Shedding Light on Women's Work and Wages: Consequences of Protective Legislation," (Ph.D. diss., New School for Social Research, 1989).

100. On the problem of providing meaning to such terms, see Catherine A. MacKinnon, "Difference and Dominance," in *Feminism Unmodified: Discourses on Life and Law* (Cambridge, Mass., 1987), 32–45.

101. See, for example, LaFrances Rodgers-Rose, "Introduction: The Black Woman, A Historical Overview," in Rodgers-Rose, ed., *The Black Woman* (Beverly Hills, Calif., 1980), 16–17.

102. For this matter, see letter to Mrs. Simmons, president of the Consumers' League of New Jersey, from Mrs. Ida E. Brown, president of the New Jersey State Federation of Colored Women's Clubs, 6 May 1939, in Papers of the Consumers' League of New Jersey, Alexander Library, New Jersey Room Rutgers University, New Brunswick, N. J.; for immigrant mothers, see Eileen Boris, *Sweated Motherhood: The Politics of Industrial Homework in the United States* (New York, forthcoming 1994), chap. 6.

103. For a fine discussion of this point, see Aida Hurtado, "Relating to Privilege: Seduction and Rejection in the Subordination of White Women and Women of Color," *Signs* 14 (1989): 833–55.

104. MacKinnon, *Feminism Unmodified*, 32–33, 40.

105. For example, see Linda Gordon, *Heroes of Their Own Lives: The Politics and History of Family Violence* (New York, 1988). African-American women, however, were often denied benefits, as with mothers' pensions. See Joanne L. Goodwin, "An American Experiment in Paid Motherhood: The Implementation of Mothers' Pensions in early Twentieth Century Chicago," *Gender and History* 4 (1992): 323–42.

106. For more on this point, see Joan Williams, "Deconstructing Gender," *Michigan Law Review* 87 (1989): 87ff.

107. Gordon emphasizes this point in "Black and White Versions of Welfare," 580–85.

7

Catholicism, Feminism, and the Politics of the Family during the late Third Republic

Susan Pedersen

With the benefit of hindsight, we can see the First World War as something of a setback for European feminism, ushering in as it did conservative governments pledged to the restoration of domestic order and a resentful suspicion among soldiers that women had profited from the war. But feminists at the time may be forgiven for misreading the signs of reaction, for whatever its less tangible effects, the war also brought votes, work opportunities, and—albeit temporarily—social supports from the state to women in many belligerent countries.[1] These changes, and the unparalleled expansion of state capacities that accompanied them, also suggested new strategies for feminism in the postwar period. Many women began to argue that the governments that mobilized so efficiently for the war could tackle the problems of the peace with equal vigor; they promised to use their votes to ensure that the interests of women and children were not forgotten in this reconstruction. These women, identified in recent historical work by such various and ungainly titles as "new," social, maternalist, or "relational" feminists, often drew on established ideas of gender difference and roles, but rejected the conflation of maternity with either "private" life or economic dependence. They hoped to construct a new "maternalist" polity, in which the "service" of motherhood (as they called it) would itself become the basis for economic emancipation and political rights.[2]

Independent social supports for *all* mothers—"the endowment of motherhood"—can be seen as the ultimate vision of maternalist feminism.[3] Ironically, however, it was in France, where women remained disenfranchised until 1944, and not in Britain, Germany, or even the United States, that policies most closely resembling the endowment of motherhood were realized.[4] During the 1930s, a Catholic women's organization, the *Union féminine civique et sociale* (UFCS), devoted itself to a campaign for an unwaged mother's allowance; in 1938, they saw their efforts rewarded when the Radical government of Edouard Daladier incorporated an *allocation pour la mère au foyer* into the family allowance system. Henceforth, families receiving allowances for dependent children would receive an additional supplement for the unwaged mother.

How do we explain the introduction of this unique social policy? It would be tempting to see such benefits as a conscious challenge to mothers' economic dependence and to view the *Union féminine civique et sociale* as an exemplary "social feminist" organization.[5] Yet such an interpretation leaves several puzzles unexplained. The UFCS achieved its goal only by aligning itself with the cause of French pronatalism and denouncing married women's work; by contrast, the nonconfessional French feminist organizations, despite their long history of social-welfare work, greeted the allowance with ambivalence.[6] These tensions cannot be explained, as Naomi Black would have it, as another manifestation of the conflicting visions of "equity" and "social" feminism, especially since—as Karen Offen's work makes clear—virtually all the French feminist organizations critical of the UFCS must also be placed on the "social" end of this spectrum.[7] Only if we examine the religious and social obsessions of the Third Republic in its final decade can we trace how this allowance came to be seen not as a means of freeing mothers, but rather as a panacea for irreligion, unemployment, and *dénatalité*, and understand the role played by a group of devout Catholic women in this counterreformation.

Social Catholicism Confronts the Woman Question

The *Union féminine civique et sociale* was founded in March of 1925, one year before the Vatican's condemnation of the religious and protofascist *Action française*, and six years before the Papal Encyclical *Quadragesimo Anno* reaffirmed the Vatican's commitment to a Catholic vision of social justice in the modern world. Formed in part to ensure that women's suffrage, if granted, would be used to support Catholic aims, the UFCS became the most politically influential Catholic women's organization of the interwar years.[8] It had a membership of more than 10,000, the staunch support of the Catholic hierarchy, and, in the figure of Andrée Butillard, an articulate and well-placed leader.[9] Although active on a number of issues, the UFCS devoted itself throughout the 1930s to one main campaign: to "return" married working women to their vital social "mission" in the home.[10]

The UFCS saw itself, in essence, as the women's branch of the social Catholic movement—as an organization through which Catholics could respond not only to the challenge of industrialization and the rise of class politics, but also to what many saw as a revolution in women's roles and the rise of feminism. French social Catholics began meeting annually at the *Semaines Sociales* from the turn of the century to discuss the challenges posed by rapid social change and to refine their teachings on matters ranging from labor relations to the decline in the birthrate. Inspired by *Rerum Novarum*, Leo XIII's attempt to define an ideal of social justice opposed equally to bourgeois liberal individualism and to socialist doctrines of class struggle, social Catholics sought to adapt the teachings of the church to modern, industrial conditions. Drawing as well on a long French tradition of Catholic and paternalist social action, they built up a wide range of confessional institutions—mutualist and family associations, trade unions, and youth clubs—that, they hoped, would heal social divisions and reestablish society on a cooperative (if still hierarchical) basis.

No institution was more important for social Catholics than the family, which served as the model for the ways in which authority could be softened by love and "egoism" tempered by the need for mutual aid. And it was from the standpoint of the family that social Catholics began to elaborate their response to the rise of feminism and their own appeal to women. While Catholic thinkers did not swerve from their conviction that maternity was the fulfillment of women's nature, they insisted that this mission was honorable, worthy, and central to the task of moral regeneration. The providential nature of the gendered division of labor could be deduced by the unequal distribution of natural gifts between the sexes, they argued: after all, strength and reason had gone to men, delicacy, sensitivity, and devotion to women. This vision of unequal but complementary natures allowed Catholics to fashion a rhetoric of consolation for suffering motherhood, while also claiming that they, and not the growing nonconfessional feminist movement, offered women true fulfillment. In a classic statement, the Abbé Antoine argued in 1912:

> Radical feminism is profoundly flawed because it contradicts woman's true nature, her physiology, her psychology, her familial mission. Woman is the companion of man for an essential end: maternity. Everything that undermines maternity for woman is by nature anti-social. All feminist proposals must be judged in the light of this principle: no criterion is clearer or more far-reaching.
>
> True feminism, Christian feminism, should enable the woman to set up a home, and give her the possibility of staying there so she can raise and nurture her children; it thus advises woman against any work which will make her leave her home, any office which will forbid the girl to be a wife, the wife to be a mother. Thus understood, feminism has a great task to accomplish.[11]

The doctrine of "Christian feminism" was further elaborated in 1927, when social Catholics devoted their annual meeting to the problem of—as they put it—"woman." Several speakers at this conference moved beyond a recitation of biological difference to claim that "woman" was first and foremost a "person," with a spiritual worth and transcendent dignity equal to a man's. They were quick to point out that this spiritual equality did not undo the physical and intellectual inequalities which dictated that "woman" was still "wife and mother by nature."[12] Nevertheless, their emphasis on the "personhood" of women limited the degree of coercion allowable in the church's endorsement of childbearing, and opened up a sphere, however small, for independent action. As one speaker noted, although maternity may benefit society as a whole, the choice of marriage must be left to women alone, "because these individuals are persons, before being means."[13]

The UFCS adopted wholeheartedly this two-tiered doctrine of, on the one hand, the spiritual equality of the sexes and, on the other, the expression of their natural differences in complementary family roles. Although they recognized that women were freely entitled to work (if unmarried) or to contract marriage, they were convinced that woman's nature was "made" for motherhood, broadly defined as all housework, child rearing, and emotional nurturance. Andrée Butillard effectively summarized their argument in 1929 when she wrote that, while a man and a woman had the same "nature"—and by this she meant spiritual nature—they nevertheless had different "manners." "The woman" was intuitive, sensitive, and "less at ease with pure reason"; "legitimate feminism consists of seizing hold of and enhancing these marvelous natural gifts."[14] The UFCS devoted itself to doing just that.

At first glance, the preoccupations of the UFCS seem to fit within the broad church of French feminism in the late nineteenth and early twentieth centuries. Many women active in the nonparty and nonconfessional organizations of the suffrage movement also employed a rhetoric stressing sexual difference and complementarity. Rather than admitting any intention to adopt masculine attributes or invade "men's sphere," they argued that "women's sphere" was equally essential to the national good and hence equally deserving of public recognition. In part their rhetoric was strategic, reflecting their concern to reconcile their goals with the struggle against depopulation, degeneration, and social fragmentation that absorbed both Radical and conservative politicians during the early twentieth century. Bearing this rhetoric into the interwar period, Cécile Brunschvicg and her *Union française pour le suffrage des femmes* argued that it was in order better to fulfill their maternal duties that women sought political emancipation.[15]

Nevertheless, if we look closely at the uses to which maternalist rhetoric was put by the two groups, we find clear differences between them. Although both groups stressed the pleasures and pains of motherhood, the UFCS's eulogy of maternal devotion shaded into a more problematic identification of self-sacrifice as an essential feminine attribute. Rhetorically asking herself whether family duties brought fulfillment to "woman" rather than "immolation," Eve Baudouin, the editor of the UFCS's monthly newspaper, did not flinch from concluding that self-abnegation was reward enough for one intended by nature "to give herself with a generosity which finds its own exercise a recompense."[16] And the doctrine of fulfillment in sacrifice could easily be pushed further, to declare that all constraints upon women were freely— indeed happily—chosen by the women themselves. Vérine, a Catholic novelist who collaborated closely with UFCS, held that

> [t]he wife, the mother is a "person," but a person who only finds her real identity [*personnalité*] in the most total and complete

self-forgetfulness. . . . It is not law that has made us slaves . . . , it's Love. To love is to become freely the captive of those one loves. The woman whose happiness isn't absolutely conditional on that of her husband and children, the one who resembles Ibsen's Nora or Mme de Noaille's Sabine; the one who says to herself "I belong to myself" and not "I belong to them," that one is not worthy of being a woman and a mother. . . . Woman is not made by man, but she is made for man, for the child, for the home.[17]

This prescriptive rhetoric of an essential nature common to all women would seem to deprive individual women of freedom of action, but such, in fact, was not the UFCS's intention. Despite their avowed preference for a home-centered role, the UFCS staunchly argued that women must "choose" such a role. This does not mean, however, that they felt that each individual woman could best judge her own interest, still less that motherhood could be combined with waged work in a rich and socially useful life. The UFCS's idea of choice was Christian, not liberal: choices were not equal; one was right and one was wrong. As a being endowed with free will, a woman must herself "choose" her destiny, but the UFCS only saw one pattern of motherhood as in keeping with the will of God; any other free choice, clearly, was pathological and sinful. Butillard reserved her harshest criticism for those who, *given a choice*, nevertheless avoided their maternal duties. At a 1937 conference, she stated: "If, married and a mother, [the woman] freely prefers the exercise of a profession to the accomplishment of her providential mission, she will simply have run away from the duties of her station."[18]

Separate spheres, then, were the providential expression of divinely ordained natural difference, while individual choice was less a right than a mechanism allowing one to distinguish the just from the unjust. These are precepts deeply rooted in religious teachings and culture, but in their organic analogies, and their preference for duties not rights, they reveal a kinship with corporatist and antiindividualist thought. Indeed, it was this broader political affinity which further separated the UFCS from a feminist movement historically identified with secular and republican values. Andrée Butillard recognized this fundamental schism when, in an article entitled "Two Philosophies," she condemned "individualist" thought generally—and Kant, Rousseau, the

Renaissance, the Reformation, eighteenth-century *philosophes*, and the secular feminists in particular—for their mistaken idea that the individual was an end in him- or herself. On the contrary, she said, the individual was incomplete; a social being, "he only finds in association the possibility of being fully himself: family first, . . . then various associations."[19] Individual rights were secondary, since the family, the providential union of complementary beings for human perpetuation, was more than the sum of its parts, its collective right greater than the individual right of each member.[20]

This vision of the family as a harmonious arena untainted by the individual and contractual relations of a de-Christianized public sphere allowed Catholic women to articulate a powerful critique of the indignities suffered by women workers, but left them unable to imagine that the family itself could be a site of conflict. Unlike those feminists who insisted that women's conditions within the home—and indeed their very relations with their husbands—were legitimate matters for public concern, the UFCS identified the home as a bulwark against social disintegration, and was willing to countenance very little state interference in familial relations. Deeply opposed to divorce, the UFCS could only enjoin renewed self-sacrifice on those women whose husbands lacked respect for their labor: [M]others can help to improve this masculine mentality above all by the scrupulous performance of their job, which will, one day or another, force esteem."[21]

To their credit, the UFCS worked hard to hasten that day of grace. Clearly, for a Catholic women's group, the task at hand was to revive both a sense of Christian duty and the moral economy to support it—or, specifically, both to revalorize motherhood and to institute an economic system which would allow women to stay in their homes. Toward the first aim, the UFCS organized home-economics courses and a league for working-class housewives; toward the second, they worked to win special benefits for families with unwaged wives. At all times, they looked to the church for guidance and approbation, insisting, in Butillard's words, on their "absolute subordination to the directives of the Holy See."[22] Yet their decision to campaign to recast existing wage and welfare policies in the interests of unwaged mothers forced them to hunt for allies and arguments in a secular world where claims to orthodoxy made little impact. Having decided their goal, they were willing to use virtually any argument—economic, biological, pronatalist, or moral—against married women's work. In late 1932, the UFCS explained to the Catholic *Chronique Sociale de France* how to campaign against married women's work:

> An argument that one can make even in non-Christian circles is that the work of mothers is against nature. The woman who sets up a home has ipso facto duties and rights and, among these rights, that of staying in the home to build it up, develop it, enliven it. It is natural law which grants her this right, which civil law only makes explicit.
>
> The disorganization of the home—conjugal tie strained, *dénatalité*, inadequate education of children—are other arguments to exploit. Insist also on the professional and national interest of this reform. It is in the interest of industry [*la profession*] to do without the labor of mothers. The country will recover, in tomorrow's generation, a more abundant labor force which will allow the replacement at work of all the women who were obliged to work because of the war.[23]

This strategy was successful, but it made for strange bedfellows, as we shall see when we look at the reception and progress of the UFCS's campaign.

The Campaign for the Unwaged Mother's Allowance

Soon after its founding, the UFCS set out to discover why working-class women had renounced a home-centered role. Their inquiries among married women workers found, unremarkably, that these women worked because of economic need. Interestingly, the UFCS interpreted this data to mean that women would *prefer* to remain at home, were they economically able to do so. In 1931, then, the group formed a *Comité du retour des mères au foyer,* and began an almost ten-year campaign to alter the welfare and wage structure to permit (and even encourage) working-class wives to remain in the home.[24] As the name of their campaign committee implies, the "return" of women to the home was from the beginning the primary goal; the endorsement of economic incentives for unwaged mothers purely strategic. Many French industries and public services paid allowances for dependent children; surely, thought the UFCS, such allowances could be reworked to favor families with unwaged mothers. But would or could industry and government agree? And how malleable was the family-allowance system?

The French institution of family allowances was one of the success stories of social intervention in the interwar period. Although the introduction of social insurance in France lagged twenty years behind Britain and forty years behind Germany, in the case of family allowances business interests complemented the pronatalist concerns of politicians, facilitating the development of a hybrid system able to bypass the usual constraints on government finance. The state paid allowances for dependent children to civil servants, and in 1923 introduced special benefits for large families, but the more significant developments happened in private industry. During and immediately after the First World War, employers set up industry-based *"caisses de compensation,"* or equalization funds, which levied a contribution on all affiliated companies in proportion to the size of their work force and then paid out children's allowances to all workers in these firms. Affiliation was, of course, optional, but the employers' organizations put pressure on individual companies, and the larger firms in highly organized sectors like textiles and engineering usually complied. By 1930, over 32,000 companies were affiliated to 232 funds, which covered almost two million workers for family allowances.[25]

French social Catholics welcomed family allowances as a means of adjusting the liberal economic order to comply with the Catholic ideal of a family wage, but in fact this rapid development owed little to Christian sentiment except a philanthropic veneer.[26] Rather, the industrialists who joined together to pay family allowances had two interests: to stabilize wages and the work force in the inflationary early twenties, and to keep the state from interfering—in an excess of pronatalist zeal—in their affairs. The most egregious of the funds used family allowances as strikebreaking weapons, cutting off allowances for a month for any unexcused absences; more commonly, funds simply instituted a qualification period for the allowances, thus establishing a disincentive to worker mobility. Employers also found that family allowances were far cheaper than across-the-board wage rises, and the more farsighted consortia extended such benefits in the hopes of containing wage claims. In time, claimed the director of the Central Committee on Family Allowances, employers could hope to pay "a wage corresponding to the needs of a single person, but adjusted by allowances for fathers of families."[27]

Although they did not achieve all that employers hoped, family allowances did bring about a decisive change in the wage form. By distributing a portion of a wage bill formerly destined for all workers only to those with dependent children, employers in effect established a mechanism outside the bounds of the state for redistributing income from the childless to those with children. Not only did such benefits undercut workers' demands for a costly male "family wage," but they aroused the enthusiasm of the many politicians concerned about the steady decline in the French birthrate. In 1929, the Poincaré government responded to growing political pressure by submitting legislation requiring all employers affiliate to a fund; business consent was purchased by government promises to leave administration in the employers' hands. This bill became law in 1932, and was applied gradually to various industries throughout the 1930s.

The legal extension of family allowances recognized the claim of families with dependent children on society as a whole. Such allowances did little, however, to meet Catholic demands that the economy be reworked to favor not merely families with dependent children, but also families with a particular division of labor—or, more particularly, with a male wage earner and an unwaged wife. But did this mean that such a gender-based family policy was impossible? The UFCS felt it was not, and when they began their campaign in 1931 they issued their first appeal to the industrialists responsible for managing the allowance system. The employment of married women, they claimed, led to juvenile delinquency, a falling birthrate, and marital disunion; employers concerned with social well-being were urged to pay higher family allowances to men whose wives were unwaged.[28] Over some seven years, a series of talks, articles, books, and two international conferences laid responsibility for virtually every social ill at the feet of married women's work, and looked to special family allowances for families with unwaged wives as a means of "returning" women to the home.[29]

The UFCS's early appeal to industrialists won a few converts, most notably the Catholic textile manufacturer Philippe Leclercq, who established a special fund in the northern textile towns of Roubaix and Tourcoing to pay higher family allowances to households with unwaged mothers.[30] On the whole, however, the businessmen in charge of the family-allowance funds resisted UFCS propaganda. Only mildly pronatalist and largely secular, businessmen failed to see the necessity of costly allowances for *all* unwaged mothers; employers dependent on women workers also insisted that mothers could indeed reconcile waged work and home duties, and introduced factory-based home-economics courses to teach them to do so.[31] The government, incapable of financing mothers' allowances itself, and grateful for the social work undertaken by the funds, was reluctant to intervene. Only the coincidence of two factors—a spreading panic over the declining birthrate and economic depression—convinced political men of the importance of compensating families for nonwaged wives.

Fears about the military and economic dangers of a declining birthrate had been widespread in France from the end of the nineteenth century, but during the 1930s the rise of National Socialism in Germany and the fall in the birthrate below the level necessary to replenish the population convinced political men across party lines that something must be done. They turned for advice to the *Alliance nationale pour l'accroissement de la population française,* and to the semigovernmental *Conseil supérieur de la natalité,* both of which included many prominent politicians and nationalists.[32] These "official" pronatalists, best exemplified in the figure of Fernand Boverat, the Alliance's general secretary and the author of many of the reports of both groups, called for a tightening of family ties, and a refashioning of the political, economic, and moral bases of French society to favor families with dependent children. Since reproduction was an urgent national need, pronatalists argued, the fertile couple, rather than the individual man, should be considered the basic political unit; thus, welfare benefits and political rights (including extra votes) should flow from the performance of the "national service" of producing children. Their view of women was unrelievedly functionalist: the childless wife, according to Boverat, "lives parasitically on society," enjoying "the pleasures of married life without taking on its normal burdens."[33] Yet if the Alliance saw women as only so many walking wombs, they saw men as only so many soldier/progenitors: childless men were also viciously attacked by Boverat, who urged mothers to institute a campaign of public humiliation against them.[34] Their paramount concern for reproduction led them to reject the patriarchalism of their usual allies— the Catholic associations of fathers of families—and to argue that "producing" mothers, like fathers, deserved recognition.

The UFCS found in the pronatalist movement its most powerful ally. The Alliance began covering the women's campaign in February of 1932, and when Andrée Butillard argued at a conference later that year that the waged work of mothers was a major cause of *dénatalité*, the intrigued *Conseil supérieur de la natalité* (CSN) deputized one of its members (Mms Raymonde Grégoire, mother of ten) to study the question.[35] Following her report, the Council predictably concluded that mothers' waged work did indeed lower the birthrate, raise infant mortality, and destroy women's health; higher family allowances for unwaged wives were an appropriate solution.[36] By 1933, Boverat and several other prominent pronatalist leaders had joined the UFCS's national campaign committee, and from that date their organizations took as axiomatic the pronatalist desirability of "returning" women to the home. The obsessive Boverat spent the years between 1934 and 1936 working out a plan to use the family-allowance system to redistribute income on a massive scale not only between the childless and those with children, but also between families with waged and unwaged wives. By June of 1936, a housewives' allowance was part of the legislative program of the *Conseil supérieur*.[37]

The conversion of the pronatalists was the first condition of the UFCS's success; the second was the depression-era hostility to married women's work. Catholics, republicans, doctors, and social workers alike had long deplored the fact that it was more common in France than in many other countries for working women to remain in the labor force after marriage, a pattern due in part to the importance of agriculture, handicrafts, and small businesses in the French economy. At the onset of the depression in 1931, then, fully 44.3% of married women in France, compared with a mere 10% in Britain, were registered by the census as "employed." Most of these women workers were not in manufacturing industry, and French unemployment in the 1930s was a good deal lower than that of most other European countries—officially running around 300,000 throughout 1933—but the backlash against married women's work was severe. Few went so far as to argue for a simple prohibition of married women's work but many were willing to accuse working women of a "taste for luxury" and to envision a range of measures with which to whittle away their employment rights. Although the UFCS itself opposed any legal prohibition of married women's work, some of its allies were less scrupulous. Fellow social Catholics argued that the government should seize on the depression—"an occasion that one shouldn't let slip by"—to begin excluding not only married women but *all* women from work that was "incompatible with their sex, their strength, their special aptitudes or their dignity."[38]

The feminist movement responded to the pronatalist and social-Catholic convergence by mobilizing in defense of married women's work, but to cite their activity is not to say that it was equally effective: feminists lived through the 1930s badly on the defensive. Having always insisted on their own concern about the demographic situation and the health of the family, any coolness toward the UFCS's campaign could expose them to charges of bad faith. In fact, as early as 1933 the UFCS damned the secular feminists for their silence on the question of the mother's "right" to stay home;[39] pronatalists, more bluntly, charged them with hypocrisy. In 1929, Paul Haury, editor of the Alliance's journal, had congratulated French feminists for their profamily stance; by 1934, he had changed his mind. "Statistics show that social and political feminism is by no means a remedy for the decline of the family and the birthrate, quite the contrary," he wrote.[40]

Such opinions were impossible for feminists to tolerate, since they questioned the very compatibility of maternalism and women's rights—values which many feminists found inseparable. Cécile Brunschvicg retorted (truthfully) that feminists had always supported extending family allowances so as to allow mothers to give up waged work should they wish to do so, and the suffragist and feminist weekly, La Française covered the UFCS campaign sympathetically so long as the campaign emphasized married women's choice.[41] But feminists declined to say that women's work was pathological, unnatural, or incompatible with motherhood, and, as the defense of women's basic work rights absorbed more of their time, grew a bit short-tempered with the Catholics. In late 1935, when the UFCS and their pronatalist allies petitioned the International Labour Office in favor of a male family wage and financial incentives to return women to the home, La Française curtly remarked: "Let us hope that the leaders of the movement created to 'return woman to the home' . . . finally understand their duty to end a public opinion campaign which, badly understood, currently only serves to support the battle against women's freedom to work."[42] Having discovered the hard way that maternalist rhetoric was a double-edged sword, in the years immediately before the Second World War feminists talked less of women's work as an unhappy necessity and more of it as an inalienable right. Drawing attention to the fact that working women themselves emphatically rejected restrictions on their right to work, *La Française* became somewhat more sensitive to the fact that middle-class women, whether feminists or Catholics, had been too quick to speak on behalf of women well able to represent themselves. At the annual conference of the *Union française pour le suffrage des femmes* in 1935, Cécile Brunschvicg paid tribute to the socialist *Confédération générale du travail*, which was, as she recognized, a far more formidable ally, for working women than any feminist organization could be.[43]

No legal prohibition of women's work passed in interwar France. By the mid-1930s, however, welfare policies favoring families with unwaged wives were supported across the political spectrum as a more palatable means of combating both *dénatalité* and male unemployment. And the allure of legal intervention remained strong: in late 1934, a socialist deputy called on the government to give married women's jobs to unemployed men, and the men's unemployment allowance to the women.[44] A few months later, the UFCS suggested that the Ministry of Labor introduce a special allowance for a mother of a young child who voluntarily withdrew from the labor market to make room for an unemployed man.[45] The group also collaborated with Catholic deputies to draft legislation which would have replaced the first child's allowance with one for the unwaged mother, since, as they saw it, "when so many men search in vain for work, it is abnormal for women to be employed."[46] By the late 1930s, even many socialist and communist activists had forgotten much of their earlier critique of the pronatalist, militaristic state, and climbed aboard. Communists continued to try to distinguish themselves from "bourgeois" pronatalists by emphasizing the material rather than moral causes of population decline, but in fact their position was quite close to that of the *Alliance nationale*, as Boverat delightedly discovered when he called on Maurice Thorez in 1936.[47] Put simply, political men forgot their differences in their united concern to protect the Republic from a *grève des ventres* (reproductive strike).

Pronatalists also tried, as the UFCS had done, to bypass the legislative process, urging employers and government arbitrators to make mothers' allowances a part of the wage settlements negotiated in the wake of the strikes of 1936. In June of 1937, an unwaged mothers' allowance was established in the chemical industries of the Marne, and similar arbitrations followed.[48] Yet such initiatives had limited scope, since employers found the allowances costly and irrational, and resented interference in the operation of the family-allowance funds. Only ten or twenty percent of the 200,000 families covered by the largest Paris fund were in a situation where the mother had to work because of need, one of the fund's board members told the UCFS in 1937; must the fund then pay an allowance to *all* housewives in the hope of deterring these few?[49] By late 1938, the UFCS announced that some 300,000 families were receiving allowances for an unwaged mother as a result of private initiatives or arbitrations—not an insignificant number, but substantially less than the 1.6 million families in private industry now receiving allowances for children.[50] Clearly, further extension could only be won with government support.

This impasse was broken on 12 November 1938, when the Daladier government established by decree an *"allocation pour la mère au foyer"* equal to 10 percent (provisionally 5 percent) of a notional average wage.[51] The UFCS quickly credited their campaign for this victory; they had, after all, made representations to government ministries almost immediately before it was issued.[52] On closer examination, however, their claim to decisive influence weakens. The November decree was drafted and forced through over cabinet opposition by Alfred Sauvy, demographer, statistician, and *Alliance nationale* ally; its expressed aim was to encourage the birthrate.[53] In other words, insofar as UFCS pressure had been effective, it had been exercised through the medium of its pronatalist friends.

Yet to conclude that the UFCS was not directly able to determine policy is not to say they were unimportant. As an organization of women, the members of UFCS spoke with recognized authority on issues affecting their sex; by doing so, they contested the claim of the nonconfessional feminist organizations to represent women's interests. Disagreements over family policy during the 1930s occurred not only between women's organizations and political men, but also *between* women, who clashed over the meaning and purposes of allowances. These disagreements were significant, for by challenging the rhetorical linkage between maternalist benefits and women's emancipation at the heart of French feminism, the UFCS in effect made benefits for mothers palatable to political conservatives entirely uninterested in women's rights. Successful as this "illiberal maternalism" was, its victory came at a cost. The implications for women's freedoms become clearer when we examine more closely the quarrel between feminists and social-Catholic women in the closing years of the Third Republic.

Family Policy and Women's Freedom: Conversations between Women

At the heart of the quarrel lay the problem, naturally enough, of money. Reformers proposing to "endow" children—much less women—faced one unavoidable question: To whom should the money be paid? Ostensibly a matter of merely administrative interest, the question of payment opened up a virtual Pandora's box of legal and political problems. All rhetoric of indivisibility and reciprocity notwithstanding, "the family" rarely receives benefits or pay packets collectively; a particular person does. But to put money into the hands of any individual—mother, father, or social worker—is to make a decision about personal as well as collective rights. It offers officials a chance to favor some family members against others, and to alter, perhaps decisively, the distribution of power within the family itself.

Many feminists in Britain and America supported family allowances and mothers' pensions precisely because they recognized their potential to transform domestic relations.[54] Yet such questions had never preoccupied the industrialists and officials who had shaped the French family-allowance system in the early decades of the century. Family policies interested these men as a means of promoting industrial stability and possibly increasing the birthrate, not of improving the status of mothers. Problems of payment, like other administrative issues, had thus been solved in ad hoc fashion: while government-funded children's allowances were paid on principle to the legal head of household (usually the father), the policies of the privately controlled *caisses* varied. Some *caisses*, notably the huge *Caisse de compensation de la région parisienne*, paid all family benefits to the mother, hoping thereby to undercut men's demands for "family wages." Other industries, however, including the strongly paternalistic railroad companies, were hostile not only to payment to the wife but also to equal treatment of women workers, and resisted government pressure to extend children's allowances to their female work force.[55] Payment to the mother, in other words, developed when employers considered such a strategy advantageous; it was never accompanied by a rhetoric of women's rights. Indeed, whenever government committees or industrial organizations did invoke ideas of citizenship or rights, they urged that payments be given to the father, in view of his legal and moral standing as the *chef de famille*.[56]

With the campaign for the unwaged mothers' allowance, however, these questions of payment became an unavoidable topic of public discussion. Ironically, it was the pronatalists, rather than the UFCS, who spurred this debate, urging early on that not only the mothers' allowance but indeed all family benefits be paid by statute to the mother. Pronatalists were motivated above all by practical concerns: women, after all, took care of children, and would, they felt, be less likely to spend the money on drink. Probably the most outspoken advocate of payment to the mother was thus the ubiquitous Fernand Boverat, who also persuaded the *Conseil supérieur* to urge the government (without success) to pay the family allowances of unemployed men to their wives.[57]

Boverat's formula challenged neither family hierarchy nor the identification of allowances as the property of the family as a whole. Yet payments to mothers had other connotations, and ones less readily reconcilable with conservative social values. Not only had French socialists and trade unionists long been prone to claim that—in the words of a resolution passed by the *Confédération Générale du Travail* in 1929—"maternity should be recognized as a social function and paid for as such"; a generation of feminists had also refined arguments about the national value of maternity and the need for its public recognition.[58] In this alternative rhetoric, payment of mothers appeared as a measure of justice rather than expedience. And a few women went further, urging payment for mothers as a means of liberating women not only from excessive toil, but also from their husbands. One contributor to *La Française* argued in 1937 that since a mother fulfills a primary and essential role in society,

> [i]t is unjust, even iniquitous, to exploit her feelings and devotion, in order to keep her economically dependent on her husband, which is a sort of disguised slavery. It's the state, the society, that should grant the mother this family wage-supplement, and not through the medium of the father, but as a personal payment for her social role. This would only be the realization of true social justice.[59]

Such opinions remained controversial among the readers of *La Française*, since many feminists would not accept that marital relations were necessarily unequal simply because the wife had no independent income. Feminist activists and journalists did insist, however, that mothers were citizens performing socially useful work, and that they as individuals—and not only "the family" in which they were located—were entitled to greater recognition and rights.

It is in their response to these claims that the UFCS revealed their preferences most clearly. Although less than representative of feminist views, the above *La Française* article was repeatedly attacked by Butillard and others as a secular-feminist perversion of true teaching on women. Maternity was women's providential mission, not their profession, Catholic women retorted; to treat it as a job would turn women into the paid servants of either their husbands or the state.[60] The Housewives' League founded by the UFCS also expressed outrage at the equation of motherhood with a job:

> Come on! It's not to make money that a mother brings her children into the world and works at home from morning to evening and sometimes from evening to morning.
>
> It's to fulfill a sublime calling: the calling to give life; to create this wealth which no material wealth can equal.[61]

Housework was indeed valuable, claimed one UFCS militant, but it was wrong to try to assess and remunerate it. Founding a family involved sacrifice for both husband and wife, and attempting to weigh the respective rights of each would only lead to conflict and bitterness. Just as men worked to support the whole family group, so the mother's work benefited not the husband, but the family as a whole. The interests of individuals were inextricable.[62]

The battle of words between these nonconfessional feminist organizations and the UFCS gets to the heart of their respective concerns, and brings us back to their most fundamental theories. Essentially, the feminists' support both for married women's right to work and for improved state benefits for mothers turned on their belief that an *enforced* economic dependence of women on men would undermine women's status as citizens and, in many cases, would destroy marital harmony as well. In 1938, Lydie Morel put this view most uncompromisingly when she claimed that

> [f]ar from favoring a sound and peaceable family life, where the man and the woman are both called upon to make efforts

and concessions to get along, the economic dependence of the married woman encourages male tyranny and vices, and creates households where the spouses are tied not because they wish it but because the one who holds economic power enslaves the other.[63]

Maria Vérone, the prominent republican feminist, similarly believed that households with waged wives were happier than those in which the wife was dependent, since a man would have greater respect for a woman who remained with him out of love and not necessity.[64] Hidden behind such statements was the specter of marital discord, the fear that the woman without the capacity to earn would likewise have no recourse against marital violence or abuse.

The UFCS, by contrast, was preoccupied with questions of honor rather than power, and with family unity rather than individual right. They avoided any mention of marital conflict and evaded the very issue of payment until 1938. Indeed, as late as May of that year they asked the minister of the merchant marine to pay an additional allowance to *men* with unwaged wives.[65] Not until early 1939, when the UFCS's Campaign Committee met repeatedly to propose rules for the application of the 1938 decrees did the group argue for payment to the woman herself. Even at this stage they were careful not to claim that such payment was the mother's right, but rather said only that such a system would be more practical and would in no way harm the dignity of the father, recognized by law as the head of the household.[66]

In the battle for control of the meaning of family policy, there is no question but that the illiberal vision of the UFCS won out. Family and mothers' allowances became favorite topics of law theses throughout the 1930s, and were presented in these works in terms virtually indistinguishable from those of the UFCS—as a way of solving the national problems of unemployment and *dénatalité*, not of increasing women's choices or of granting a measure of economic independence to wives.[67] When the mother's allowance appeared in 1938, it did so only as part of a broader strategy of national renewal. Although the Family Code, which followed one year later, did stipulate that the mother's allowance (although not the more important children's allowances) be paid to the woman herself, only the presence of Fernand Boverat on the drafting *Haut Comité de la population* forced this concession.

And when the statutes were published only days after the Committee completed its work, some of these provisions had unaccountably vanished.[68] The minimal concessions ultimately granted were possible partly because the mother's allowance was *not* viewed as a threat to men's status as heads of households—a reasonable view, given the simultaneous introduction in the Family Code of harsh laws against abortion. Motherhood was to be "endowed," but women's choice to participate in this new state project was to be simultaneously curtailed.

We can find some indication of the reaction of some secular feminists to this new illiberal maternalism in their tentative opposition, during the last months of the Third Republic, to the very policies they had historically supported as measures of women's rights. A small number of socialist and communist women had from the beginning denounced the campaign for a mother's allowance as an attempt "to shut the woman back up in the narrow circle of the family, in the landscape of the husband's stewpot and the children's chamberpot"; "to wall her up in her sex."[69] Yet most feminist leaders had been more circumspect: not until the connection between family policies and the conservative campaigns against women's work and divorce became clear did some move away from older, "relational" arguments to insist that women were owed the same right to balance domestic and civic responsibilities that men enjoyed. The outbreak of war temporarily strengthened their hand, with the formidable Cécile Brunschvicg arguing in April of 1940 that the unwaged mother's allowance had—despite its brief existence—outlived its time. At a moment when the nation needed all possible workers in its war against Germany,

> it is unnecessary [*inutile*] and even scandalous that lazy women and those in ease receive a monthly allowance *because they don't have a job* and don't need to have one. The moment is ill-chosen for encouraging women to devote themselves only to the embellishment of their homes.[70]

Yet the defeat of the French in June of 1940 put an end to the brief moment in which women could argue that national needs called for not different but identical rights. Cécile Brunschvicg, at risk for her Jewishness rather than her feminism, spent most of the war years in hiding.[71]

With feminist critics silenced, conservatives and pronatalists brought their efforts to fruition during Vichy. Vichy family policy extended the 1938 and 1939 precedents increasing children's allowances and—to the distress of the UFCS—replacing the mother's allowance with a sizable special benefit for all families on a single wage.[72] At the same time, however, Vichy policy makers broke decisively with the remnants of Third Republic liberalism, ending the debate over women's work by forcing some married women out of work, and limiting women's choice to bear children by tightening marriage laws and repressing abortion and contraception ferociously. This combination of financial carrot and legal stick was accompanied by an outpouring of egregious propaganda, in which Vichy's *Commissariat général à la famille* and the redoubtable *Alliance nationale* outdid each other in inundating women with blunt tabulations of the state's financial incentives to procreation, romantic portraits of family life, gross denunciations of nonchildbearing women, and dubious medical counsels.[73] It was during Vichy that illiberal maternalism reached its apotheosis: women would be endowed but unfree.

The particular blend of social conservatism and pronatalist policies established during Vichy realized some of the UFCS's goals, but the group viewed these developments with a growing unease. The UFCS had always taken the moral high ground—they were going to return women to their beloved babies, from whom they had been wrenched away by an amoral economic order—and reserved their strongest criticism for those feminists and communists who, against all odds, persisted in defending the liberating potential of married women's work. In 1939, UFCS leaders seem to have realized for the first time that the economic and demographic arguments they had used so freely meant something quite different to secular pronatalists. Shocked by the coercive implications of the slogan *"faire naître"* [roughly, "make childbearing happen"], and at the request of numerous regional activists, Andrée Butillard attempted to define the organization's doctrine on *dénatalité*. "If *dénatalité* rages," she wrote, "it is because society is paganized"; religious renewal remained the ultimate goal.[74] Her discomfort with pronatalist functionalism led her not toward a liberal feminism but back to the church. In 1942, she reiterated her belief that only Catholic teaching could answer the woman question:

> Between a feminism freed from all moral constraints and the
> deformed conservatism which reduces woman to the role of

propagator of the human species, there is a just notion of the woman's personhood which determines her true place in society.

The social doctrine of the church frees woman in recalling both her basic nature equal to man's, and the personal inequalities which make of man and woman two complementary beings called upon to help each other in the roles determined by their different aptitudes.[75]

Such statements were courageous in the context of a regime very close to the "deformed conservatism" she deplored, but they signaled no change of view. At best, UFCS activists developed a new awareness of the dangers of their style of argumentation. Men and women were indeed complementary beings, the UFCS headquarters told its activists in 1943; however "avoid the phrase, 'woman is complementary to man' for the abuse that is made of it: the woman is a person, not a complement."[76] These critiques were muted, however, and both Butillard and the novelist Vérine served on Vichy's *Conseil supérieur de la famille*. Furthermore, having always argued from collective interest, the UFCS was ill-equipped theoretically to challenge policies which, in the interests of "the family," forced rather than "encouraged" women back into the home. Women's freedom, economic or otherwise, had never been the UFCS's primary goal. Individual rights of contract or employment appear as fundamental guarantors of liberty only within theories that recognize the possibility of conflict within the family itself. Social-Catholic doctrine did not; neither feminist criticism nor the Vichy years could force it to do so.

Conclusion

If European feminists between the wars agreed on anything, it was that an *enforced* economic dependence of women upon men was detrimental to women's equality, whether in the workplace, the state, or the home. Campaigns for equal opportunities in employment and for extended welfare rights for mothers both found their root in this understanding. During the 1920s and 1930s, the latter goal received the most attention, as "social feminists" like Eleanor Rathbone in Britain and Cécile Brunschvicg in France looked to state benefits for mothers and children to compensate for women's weak position in the labor market and to mitigate their vulnerability to men.

Yet the story presented above shows that benefits for mothers need not explicitly challenge fathers' power. Certainly, feminist concerns played no part in the introduction of the unwaged mother's allowance in France. To the contrary, benefits for mothers became possible only when economic and demographic crises coincided with the emergence of a women's campaign capable of aligning such policies with nationalist and pronatalist concerns and divorcing them from women's rights. The campaign's success thus came at the cost of collapsing the definition of women and mothers, stigmatizing feminists and wage-earning women, and paving the way for the more avowedly patriarchal policies of Vichy.

The *Union féminine civique et sociale* played a central role in making this outcome possible. The devout and courageous women who led the organization may have sought to enhance rather than restrict "woman's sphere," yet their conviction that both God and nature had destined "woman" for the home, and that the complementarity of the sexes rendered all conflict there trivial (if not impossible), drove them to develop arguments they could not contain and to contract alliances that overpowered them. The UFCS's religious allegiance was profound and by no means merely strategic: the organization sought to remake women's lives in light of Catholic doctrine, *and not vice versa*. Certainly the secular uses of their arguments surprised them, yet their own transparent orthodoxy protected them from self-recrimination. Having scorned political calculation, they saw the deformation of their ideals not as the consequence of their own political naiveté, but as renewed evidence of the perversions of a secular polity.

Despite its origins, the unwaged-mother's allowance not only survived but steadily lost its ability to coerce female behavior. To begin with, once recast as an allowance for families with dependent children living on a single wage, the allowance could benefit not only families with male earners and dependent wives, but equally divorced, single, or widowed parents—thus providing, ironically, something of a safety net for mothers seeking to survive without men. Yet an allowance that usually benefited unwaged mothers to the exclusion of those in the labor market was felt to be discriminatory. In the late seventies this and several other benefits were replaced with a special allowance for moderate-income families with at least three children or a child under three, which parents could use to replace lost earnings or defray child-care expenses, as they saw fit. The French welfare state today is remarkable for the generosity of its benefits for families with young children, but for the most part these benefits are not conditional on the mother's abstention from wage earning. In keeping with its pronatalist origins, French family policy targets children rather than mothers, in the hope of making child rearing less burdensome for both wage-earning and unwaged women. While the French welfare state is virtually nonredistributive across class lines, it is one of the most redistributive across family lines, effecting a substantial transfer of income from the childless to those with children within every social class. This strategy has not succeeded in raising the French birthrate above replacement level, but it has dramatically reduced the proportion of children in poverty, while leaving women with a degree of choice in their strategies for combining wage earning with motherhood.[77] French family policy may not be as "maternalist" as the nonconfessional feminist organizations of the interwar period would have wished, but nor is it as illiberal as both Catholics and pronatalists sought to make it.

Notes

For their comments on various versions of this essay, I wish to thank Gisela Bock, Anne Cova, Sarah Fishman, Laura Frader, Seth Koven, Karen Offen, and especially Thomas Ertman, who also helpfully insisted I finish it. I thank the *Union féminine civique et sociale* for permission to consult their records.

1. For these wartime developments, see Richard Wall and Jay Winter, eds., *The Upheaval of War: Family, Work and Welfare in Europe, 1914–1918* (Cambridge, 1988); I discuss the effects of wartime social spending on women's position in Britain in "Gender, Welfare and Citizenship in Britain during the Great War," *American Historical Review* 95, 4 (1990): 983–1006.

2. Arguments for the endowment of motherhood preceded the war, but the experience of war converted many feminists who had previously adhered to liberal ideas of the family's responsibility for self-support and limited state intervention. Karen Offen has recently defended the theory and achievements of "relational" feminism in "Defining Feminism: A Comparative Historical Approach," *Signs* 14 (1988): 119–257. Seth Koven and Sonya Michel discuss the tradition, achievements, and contradictions of maternalist feminism in "Womanly Duties: Maternalist Politics and the Origins of Welfare States in France, Germany, Great Britain, and the United States, 1880–1920," *American Historical Review* 95 (1990): 1076–1108; this article also reviews recent litera-

ture on the subject. Theda Skocpol traces the significant policy achievements of maternalism in America in *Protecting Soldiers and Mothers: The Politics of Social Provision in the United States, 1870s–1920s* (Cambridge, Mass., 1992).

3. I discuss the development of feminist campaigns for the endowment of motherhood in Britain in "The Failure of Feminism in the Making of the British Welfare State," *Radical History Review* 46 (1989): 86–110.

4. British widows' pensions and American mothers' pensions were available only to women unsupported by men. The French unwaged mother's allowance, by contrast, was paid to mothers with cohabiting and wage-earning husbands, and hence ran counter to the ideology of male breadwinning which underlay more limited measures.

5. For such a view, see Naomi Black, *Social Feminism* (Ithaca, N.Y., 1989).

6. This essay does not refer to the UFCS as "feminist" and should make its use of that term clear. By "feminist," I mean those persons and organizations who believe power to be unequally and unfairly distributed between the sexes; who believe this inequality to be, at least in part, a consequence of a history of gender antagonism and not only a by-product of other processes such as secularization or industrialization, and who are committed to changing those relations of power. Both "social feminist" and "egalitarian" organizations would fit this definition, but the UFCS, as is made clear below, would not. In this essay, the term "feminist" thus refers primarily to those nonconfessional women's organizations devoted to the achievement of women's suffrage and a range of social rights, and to those few Catholic organizations (for example, the St. Joan's Social and Political Alliance) that shared this goal. Although the UFCS had its own carefully thought-out beliefs concerning the duties and dignities of womanhood, the depth of the confessional divide within French politics meant that the UFCS was always identified (and identified itself) above all as a Catholic organization.

7. Black, *Social Feminism*. Offen stresses that, in a political climate obsessed with the specter of demographic decline and military vulnerability, virtually all feminist groups adopted a maternalist rhetoric, promising that women's familial role would be enhanced rather than undercut by an extension of political rights. See Karen Offen, "Body Politics: Women, Work and the Politics of Motherhood in France, 1920–1950" in Gisela Bock and Pat Thane, eds., *Maternity and Gender Politics: Women and the Rise of the European Welfare States, 1880s–1950* (London, 1991), 138–159.

8. The UFCS's ideals were reflected in the composition of its *Comité de patronage*, which included many prominent social Catholics—notably the law professor Eugène Duthoit, deputies Louis Duval-Arnould and Jean Lerolle, and Gaston Tessier, the general secretary of the *Confédération française des travailleurs chrétiens*. Jean Verdier, later cardinal of Paris, helped to found the group and drafted its doctrinal statement.

9. The UFCS had approximately 10,000 members in 1929, 13,000 in 1937, and 16,000 in 1942. The figure for 1929 is a police estimate quoted in Françoise Blum, Colette Chambelland, and Michel Dreyfus, "Mouvements des femmes (1919–1940)," *Vie Sociale* 11–12 (1984): 606; the 1937 figure is from a bro-

chure in the UFCS Folder at the Bibliothèque Marguerite Durand entitled "Union féminine civique et sociale," n.d. (probably 1937), 8; the 1942 figure is from [Andrée Butillard], *La Femme au service du pays* (Lyon and Paris, 1942), 82.

10. The most detailed account of the early years of the UFCS—and of its redoubtable leader—is found in Henri Rollet, *Andrée Butillard et le féminisme chrétien* (Paris, 1960). The organization's work is also discussed briefly in the recent work of Martine Martin, "Les femmes et le travail ménager en France entre les deux guerres," (Thèse du 3ème cycle, Université de Paris VII, 1984, and "Ménagère: Une profession? Les Dilemmes de l'entre-deux-guerres," *Le Mouvement Social* 140 (July–September 1987), 89–106. See also Black, *Social Feminism*.

11. M l'Abbé Antoine, "Les Affirmations de la théologie relatives à la société familiale," *Semaine sociale de France*, vol. 9 (Lyon, 1912), 49.

12. Eugène Duthoit, "La Famille. Donnée essentielle du problème de la Femme," *Semaine sociale*, 19 (1927), 49.

13. J. Vialatoux, "La Nature féminine et la signification du mouvement féministe," in ibid., 196–97.

14. Andrée Butillard, "Bon et mauvais féminisme," *La Femme dans la Vie Sociale*, March 1929.

15. On the arguments of prewar feminists, see especially, Karen Offen, "Depopulation, Nationalism, and Feminism in Fin-de-Siècle France," *American Historical Review* 89 (1984): 648–76; Stephen Hause with Anne R. Kenney, *Women's Suffrage and Social Politics in the French Third Republic* (Princeton, N.J., 1984). On interwar republican feminism, see especially, Anne Cova, "Cécile Brunschvicg (1877–1946) et la protection de la maternité," *Actes du 113e Congrès national des sociétés savantes: Colloque sur l'histoire de la sécurité sociale* (Paris, 1989), 75–104; Offen, "Body Politics."

16. Eve Baudouin, *La Mère au travail et le retour au foyer* (Paris, 1931), 117–18.

17. Vérine [Marguerite Lebrun], *La Femme et l'amour dans la société de demain* (Paris, 1925), 121. This and all other translations from the French are my own unless otherwise indicated.

18. UFCS, *La Mère au foyer, ouvrière de progrès humain. Documents d'études. Extraits du Congrès de juin 1937* (Paris, 1937), 18. The UFCS also subscribed to the belief that, by marrying, a woman took on "new and very serious responsibilities which she cannot properly fulfill if she works outside the home in a waged position." See the resolution of the National Union of Catholic Women's Leagues in the collection of documents from their 1933 conference. See also UFCS, *Le Travail industriel de la mère et le foyer ouvrier. Documents d'études. Extraits du Congrès international de juin 1933* (Paris, 1933), 185.

19. Andrée Butillard, "Deux philosophies. Pour la mère au foyer," *La Femme dans la Vie Sociale*, November 1933.

20. Andrée Butillard, "Désagregation de la famille par le travail de la mère au dehors," *La Femme dans la Vie Sociale*, November 1931.

21. Mme. Bruas [UFCS National Council], "L'Estime du mari pour la mère au foyer," in UFCS, *La Mère au foyer* (1937), 254.

22. [Butillard], *La Femme au service du pays*, 86.

23. F. van Goethem, "Enquête internationale sur le travail salarié de la femme mariée," *Chronique Sociale de France*, January 1933, 21–22.

24. Results of the UFCS's inquiry into the causes of married women's work can be found in the collection of documents from their 1933 conference, UFCS, *Le Travail industriel de la mère* (1933), 250. This investigation figured prominently in UFCS propaganda, but its results must be treated skeptically, since it was conducted among only 506 working mothers.

25. French lawyers at the time produced a large and tedious literature on the development of family allowances. More recent historical accounts from a variety of perspectives include: Susan Pedersen, *Family, Dependence, and the Origins of the Welfare State: Britain and France, 1914–1945* (Cambridge, forthcoming, 1993); Robert Talmy, *Histoire du mouvement familial en France, 1896–1939* (Paris, 1962); Dominique Ceccaldi, *Histoire des prestations familiales en France* (Paris, 1957).

26. In saying this, I am in fundamental disagreement with Antoine Prost, who has given French Catholicism much of the credit for the extraordinary success of French family policy. See Prost, "Catholic Conservatives, Population, and the Family in Twentieth Century France," in Michael S. Teitelbaum and Jay M. Winter, eds., *Population and Resources in Western Intellectual Traditions* (Cambridge, 1988), 147–64.

27. Georges Bonvoisin, "Rapport moral," Congrès national des allocations familiales, *Compte Rendu* 2 (1922): 71. For a discussion of the development of family allowances within the context of employers' labor strategies, see Pedersen, *Family, Dependence*, chap. 5, and Henri Hatzfeld, *Du paupérisme à la sécurité sociale* (Paris, 1971).

28. "Aux industriels," *La Femme dans la Vie sociale*, June 1931, and UFCS *Le Travail industriel de la mère* (1933), 189–220.

29. For coverage of the UFCS's campaign as a whole, see the detailed accounts in their paper, *Le Femme dans la Vie Sociale*, and the collection of documents from their two conferences: *Le Travail de La Mère* (1933), and *La Mère au foyer*, (1937). Eve Baudouin, editor of the UFCS's paper, also wrote a series of books and articles, most notably *La Mère au travail* and *Comment envisager le retour de la mère au foyer* (Paris, 1933).

30. The Leclercq initiative is described in UFCS, *La Mère au foyer* (1937), 143–48.

31. Paul Leclercq, the editor of *La Revue de la Famille*, a journal published by the central committee on family allowances and sent to many recipients of allowances, made this argument in an editorial discussing the UFCS's campaign. Leclercq, "A Notre Point de Vue: Le Père et la Mère au Foyer," *La Revue de la Famille*, July 1933, 3.

32. On the politics of the *Alliance nationale* in the interwar period, see especially Françoise Thébaud, "Le Mouvement nataliste dans la France de l'entre-deux-guerres: L'Alliance nationale pour l'accroissement de la population fran-

çaise," *Revue d'Histoire Moderne et Contemporaine* 32 (April–June 1985): 276–301, and Thébaud, "Maternité et famille entre les deux guerres: Ideologies et politique familiale," in Rita Thalmann, ed., *Femmes et fascismes* (Paris, 1986), 85–97.

33. Fernand Boverat, "Un Peu de mépris, s'il vous plait," *Revue de L'Alliance Nationale*, January 1933, 9.

34. Fernand Boverat, "Femmes de France, Secondez-nous," *Revue de l'Alliance Nationale*, September 1923, 284; see also the argument by Paul Haury, editor of the *Revue*, that fathering children was a citizenship duty comparable to military service. Haury, "Votre Bonheur, Jeunes Filles," *Revue de l'Alliance Nationale*, September 1934, 270–71.

35. Andrée Butillard et al., *Le Travail de la mère hors de son foyer et sa répercussion sur la natalité. Commission catholique du 14e Congrès de la natalité . . .* (Paris, 1933).

36. Conseil supérieur de la natalité, *Communications*, (1934), no. 3, minutes of the permanent section for 7 November 1932, 19 December 1932, and 16 January 1933.

37. The members of the UFCS's campaign committee are found in *La Femme dans la Vie Sociale*, December 1933. For the place of the housewife's allowance within the CSN's program, see CSN, *Procès Verbaux* (1936), no. 5, 29th session (28 June 1936), 3–8.

38. This argument was made by Joseph Danel, professor at the Catholic University of Lille. See, Danel "Le Travail des mères hors du foyer," in Butillard et al., *Le Travail de la mère*, 53. Louis Blain, an important Catholic trade unionist and a member of the UFCS's campaign committee in the Nord made similar arguments; see, "Réunion du Comité du Nord pour le retour de la mère au foyer," *La Femme dans la Vie Sociale*, September–October 1932. Married women's labor-force participation rates are given in T. Deldycke, H. Gelders and J.-M. Limbor, *La Population active et sa structure* (Brussels, 1968).

39. Andrée Butillard, "Chronique de l'Action," *La Femme dans la Vie Sociale*, January–February 1933.

40. Haury, "Votre Bonheur, juenes filles," 273; compare his earlier article, "Le Féminisme français," *Revue de l'Alliance Nationale*, March 1929, 69–73.

41. Cécile Brunschvicg, "Le Travail industriel de la mère et le foyer ouvrier," *La Française*, 24 June 1933, and "Le Congrès national de l'U.F.S.F.," *La Française*, 10 June 1933.

42. "Le Droit de la femme au travail," *La Française*, 14 December 1935; the text of the UFCS declaration to the ILO is in a folder at the Bibliothèque Nationale (B.N.), 4 Wz 5743.

43. See Cécile Brunschvicg's tribute to the CGT in: S.C., "Le Congrès national de l'U.F.S.F. [Union française pour le suffrage des femmes]. Deuxième journee," *La Française*, 23 March 1935. The feminist mobilization in defense of women's work rights was thoroughly covered in *La Française*; see also Evelyn Sullerot, "Condition de la femme," in Alfred Sauvy, *Histoire économique de la France entre les deux guerres*, vol. 3 (Paris, 1984).

44. Maria Vérone, "Femmes, defendez-vous!" *L'Oeuvre*, 14 December 1934.

45. "Une Double Démarche au Ministère du travail," *La Femme dans la Vie Sociale*, April 1935.

46. *Journal Officiel* (hereafter *J.O.*), *Documents parlementaires*, Chambre (1935), annexe no. 5193, 777; for the UFCS's role see UFCS, *La Mère au foyer*, 1937, 302–3, and *Revue de l'Alliance Nationale*, February 1936. The constitution of a new Assembly rendered this proposition defunct, but similar proposals were submitted to the new Chamber.

47. Andrée Boverat, "Une Conversation avec Maurice Thorez," *Revue de l'Alliance National*, June 1936, 173–74. The Communist party adopted a policy aimed at ridding the country of the "scourge of *dénatalité*" at its 1937 conference; see "Sauver la famille!" *Cahiers du Bolchévisme*, 20 February 1937, 243, and also, G. Levy, "Pour une politique de protection de la famille et de l'enfance," *Cahiers du Bolchévisme*, March 1939, 362–73. François Delpha shows how the Communist party's rapprochement with the pronatalists was accompanied by a "spectacular" shift in its portrayals of women in party propaganda; coverage of women in innovative economic and political roles gave way to coverage of such conventional "feminine" concerns as recipes, beauty tips, and so forth. François Delpha with Jean-Gabriel Foucaud, "Les Communistes français et la sexualité 1932–1938," *Le Mouvement Social* 91 (1975): 121–52.

48. Marie de Tailhandier, "L'Action pour la mère au foyer," *La Femme dans la Vie Sociale*, June 1937, and UFCS, *La Mère au foyer*, 1937, 310–11, 319–22.

49. Intervention by Partiot of the Caisse de compensation de la Région parisienne, in UFCS, *La Mère au foyer*, 1937, 141–42. See also Gustave Maignan, "Nature et portée des mésures prises en faveur du maintien de la mère au foyer," in Congrès national des allocations familiales, *Compte Rendu* 38 (1938): 39–49.

50. "La Préparation des décret-lois et l'action de l'UFCS," *La Femme dans la Vie Sociale*, December 1938; statistics on total allowances are compiled from records in the Archives nationales, F22 1513.

51. *J.O.*, *Lois et décrets*, 15 November 1938; the decree governing its application is in *J.O.*, *Lois et décrets*, 2 April 1938.

52. "La Préparation des décret-lois," *La Femme dans la Vie sociale*, December 1938; also the UFCS reports of letters and deputations in *La Femme dans la Vie Sociale*, January 1938, and June 1938.

53. Sauvy notes that the 12 November decree was intended only as a decoy; the Ministry of Finance tried to block its promulgation. See Sauvy, *Histoire économique*, vol. 1, 350ff.

54. For the British campaigns, see Pedersen, "Failure of Feminism"; for campaigns for mothers' pensions in the United States, see Skocpol, *Protecting Soldiers and Mothers*, chap. 8.

55. Documents concerning the administration of family allowances by the railroad companies reveal that they repeatedly turned down appeals from their female employees for equal access to family allowances throughout the 1930s, on the grounds that the wife was not the legal guardian of the children and thus was not entitled to allowances, even if the husband worked in a firm

which did not pay allowances. Pressure by the Ministry of Public Works was relatively ineffective in forcing the companies to change their policy, despite the fact that women civil servants were entitled to allowances. See A.N. F14 14947.

56. In 1921, for example, when the Chamber's Social Insurance Commission proposed paying new government allowances for large families to the mother rather than the father, enraged protests from government ministers and deputies forced them to back down. *J.O.*, Chambre, *Débats*, 10 March 1921, 1185–93, and 22 March 1921, 1362.

57. CSN, *Procès Verbaux* (1936), no. 5, 29th session (28 June 1936), 8, 15.

58. CGT, Congrès, *Compte Rendu* 20 (1929): 266; a similar resolution by the Conférence nationale des femmes socialistes is quoted in Suzanne Buisson, *Les Répercussions du travail féminin* (Paris, 1934), 24. For one argument in favor of payment of motherhood, see M. C., "Les Droits de la femme," *La Française*, 11 July 1936.

59. M.C., "Les Menagères et les lois nouvelles," *La Française*, 9 October 1937. See also her earlier article, "Les Droits de la femme."

60. For explicit attacks on this article, see: G. Robinet-Marcy, "L'Allocation en faveur de la mère au foyer. Les Reactions cégétistes et féministes," *La Femme dans la Vie Sociale*, March 1939; Andrée Butillard, "Regard sur notre travail social," *La Femme dans la Vie Sociale*, May 1938; Butillard, *La Femme au service du pays*, 36. For a feminist response, see "Le Droit au travail de la femme mariée II," *La Française*, 5 March 1938.

61. Ligue de la mère au foyer, *La Mère au foyer* (Paris, [1941]), 48.

62. Anne-Marie Louis Couvreur, "Valeur économique du travail ménager," *La Femme dans la Vie Sociale*, June 1939.

63. Lydie Morel, *Le Droit au travail de la femme mariée* (Geneva, 1937), 30.

64. Maria Vérone, "Le Travail de la femme mariée," *L'Oeuvre*, 24 October 1931.

65. "Une Démarche de l'Union féminine auprès de M. le Ministre de la Marine marchande . . .," *La Femme dans la Vie Sociale*, June 1938.

66. "Action pour la mère au foyer," *La Femme dans la Vie Sociale*, February 1939.

67. Two good examples are Mathilde Decouvelaere, *Le Travail industriel des femmes mariées*, Thèse, Université de Lille, Faculté de Droit (Paris, 1934), and Magdeleine Caunes, *Des Mesures juridiques propres à faciliter la présence de la mère au foyer ouvrier*, Thèse, Université de Paris, Faculté de droit, (Paris, 1938).

68. *J.O.*, Lois et décrets, 30 July 1939; Fernand Boverat, "Le Décret-loi du 29 July 1939," *Revue de l'Alliance Nationale*, August 1939, 253–54. It is important to note that although the basic children's allowances could be paid to either the father or the mother, many *caisses* did continue to pay to the mother. In such cases, children's allowances did far more than the unwaged mother's allowance to transfer income directly to women, since while the Family Code set the *allocation pour la mère au foyer* at 10 percent of a notional average wage, the children's allowances for a family of four amounted to 50 percent

of that wage. For a thorough discussion of the relative importance of various family benefits, see Pedersen, *Family Dependence*, esp. chap. 7.

69. The quotes are from Jeanne Rougé, "Le Retour de la femme au foyer," *Cahiers du Bolchévisme*, 1 March 1933, 296–297, and Buisson, *Les Repércussions du travail féminin*, 22. See also the dissenting comment by Marie Lenoël of the St. Joan's Social and Political Alliance at the UFCS's 1933 congress, *Le Travail industriel de la mère*, 182–83.

70. Cécile Brunschvicg, "Pourquoi conserver en temps de guerre l'allocation de la mère au foyer?" *La Française*, April 1940; see also Andrée Jack, "Le Code de la famille," *La Française*, February 1940.

71. On Brunschvicg's later life, see Cova, "Cécile Brunschvicg," 102–3.

72. For these later developments, see Jeanne Cann, *Les Allocations familiales, l'allocation de la mère au foyer et l'allocation de salaire unique dans le commerce et l'industrie*, Thèse, Université de Rennes, Faculté de droit, (Loudeac, France, 1944).

73. There is a good collection of Vichy propaganda toward women in SAN 7545, 7546, and 7548 at the Ministère du travail, Paris. This includes a rather astonishing leaflet by the *Alliance nationale* reviving the eighteenth-century idea that sperm is necessary to women's health. See Alliance nationale, "Les Dangers des practiques anticonceptionnelles" 1944, in SAN 7545. For a general account of Vichy policy toward women, see Michèle Bordeaux, "Femmes hors d'etat français, 1940–1944," in Thalmann, *Femmes et fascismes*, 135–55.

74. Andrée Butillard, "Problème de la natalité," *La Femme dans la Vie Sociale*, June 1939.

75. [Butillard], *La Femme au service du pays*, 11.

76. B.N. 4Wz 5743, "Canevas de formation sociale et civique, 1943–44," typescript.

77. For a summary of recent trends in French family policy, see Jean-Claude Chesnais, "La Politique de la population française depuis 1914," in *Histoire de la Population Française*, vol. 4 (Paris, 1988), 188–231; Rémi Lenoir, "Family Policy in France since 1938," in John S. Ambler, ed., *The French Welfare State: Surviving Social and Ideological Change* (New York, 1991), 144–86; Colin Birks, "Social Welfare Provision in France," in Roslyn Ford and Mono Chakrabarti, eds., *Welfare Abroad: An Introduction to Welfare Provision in Seven Countries* (Edinburgh, 1987), 66–98. The nonredistributive character of the French welfare state is stressed in terms of class by Jean-Pierre Jallade, "Redistribution in the Welfare State: An Assessment of the French Performance," in Jallade, ed., *The Crisis of Redistribution in European Welfare States* (Stoke-on-Trent, 1988), 221–53; the success of redistribution across family lines is emphasized by Alfred J. Kahn and Sheila B. Kamerman, *Income Transfers for Families with Children: An Eight Country Study* (Philadelphia, 1983). This literature is summarized and evaluated in Pedersen, *Family, Dependence*, introduction.

8

The Limits of Maternalism: Policies Toward American Wage-Earning Mothers During the Progressive Era

Sonya Michel

In each of the societies examined in this volume, one concept lay at the heart of maternalism: the importance of motherhood.[1] Indeed, the secret of maternalist reformers' political success lay in the fact that while they were extending their own sphere of influence and attempting to gain social entitlements, they were also affirming women's traditional role as mothers. Not surprisingly, they met the most resistance when they attempted to challenge gender conventions.[2] Therefore, whether deliberately or by default, the way reformers conceptualized women and motherhood usually reflected the deep-seated and long-held values of their own societies and particular cultures.

As the foregoing essays have shown, visions of motherhood and of maternal roles could vary greatly over time and place and according to the social and political locations of activists and reformers. These visions were crucial, for they determined the types of policies and programs maternalist reformers sought to establish, which, in turn, produced the options and resources available to client mothers and their children. A key element was the relationship between mothers and paid employment. Whether or not reformers sought policies that accepted mothers' labor-force participation affected mothers' ability to support themselves and their families, as well as the status of all women as workers. Hence waged labor for mothers was a decisive fault line in social-policy debates.

Maternalist positions on this issue varied from one society to the next. In France, for example, it had long been assumed that mothers would also be workers.[3] Charitable crèches, established as early as the eighteenth century, were taken over by the state in the 1830s.[4] In such a climate, maternalist reformers were able to push through maternity-leave and health-care measures designed to improve women's childbearing outcomes while protecting their status in the workplace. Female reformers were aided in their efforts by male pronatalists who realized that their only hope for increasing the French population was to ease women's double burden and support them as *both* mothers and workers.[5]

American values surrounding women and motherhood contrasted sharply with those of France. In nineteenth-century America, the maternal role was exalted to the exclusion of all other occupations for women. Many mothers worked in family enterprises or for wages, but the significance of their contributions to household economies—and thus the work itself—faded in a discourse of domesticity which presented breadwinning as a role appropriate only for men.[6] Though the terms of the discourse changed over time, the ideology of a strict gender division of labor became entrenched in Victorian American culture. Around the turn of the century, it gained new momentum as the male-dominated labor movement began to struggle for a "family wage" sufficient to allow a man to support his household.[7]

Nineteenth-century women reformers not only subscribed to this ideology but reinforced it through their own self-justifications. By the early twentieth century, the realities of urban industrial society made it increasingly difficult to sustain a consistent opposition to the employment of poor and working-class mothers. Yet few activists—even those who identified themselves as feminists—seemed willing to challenge the ideology openly by endorsing work for mothers. Whether sincerely or as a matter of political expediency, these activists continued to pay lip service to the ideal of the mother in the home. And this had the effect of limiting the ways in which they conceived and fought for social policies for women and children.[8]

Reformers' views of motherhood and labor came to the fore in Progressive Era debates over how to deal with the problem of mothers who lacked the support of a male breadwinner. Preferring to keep families together rather than remove children to orphanages or foster care, as had become customary by the late nineteenth century, reformers focused on two alternative policies: child care and mothers' pensions.

Institutional care for children outside their homes, in the form of a handful of charitable day nurseries, had been available to poor families since the late eighteenth century, but it was not until the founding of the National Federation of Day Nurseries (NFDN) in 1898 that child care was proposed as a general approach to the problems of mothers who were compelled to work outside the home because they lacked the support of an adult male.

The idea of mothers' pensions—cash payments—was relatively newer, though it had nineteenth-century precedents in philanthropic relief to poor fatherless families and in the federal pensions paid to dependents of Union veterans or victims of the Civil War.[9] Initiated on a small scale by a handful of juvenile court judges as early as 1906, mothers' pensions gained momentum as a general policy at the 1909 White House Conference on the Care of Dependent Children, when President Roosevelt stated, "[T]he goal toward which we should strive is to help [the widowed] mother so that she can keep her own home and keep the child in it. . . ."[10]

Though reformers framed the issue of institutional child care in maternalist terms, the practice itself—more than any other social programs—caused them profound uneasiness. By providing a substitute for a mother's care of her children while she worked for wages, child care threatened to undermine the notion of motherhood as women's naturally ordained and most important role. Maternalist reformers' ambivalence was reflected in the halting and highly qualified manner in which they advocated for day nurseries and in their reluctance to seek governmental financing. Mothers' pensions, in contrast, affirmed reformers' basic convictions because they were specifically aimed at enabling women to remain at home to care for their own children. Advocates of this policy had no hesitation in taking up Roosevelt's charge and lobbying state governments for legislation, producing a response one contemporary referred to as "the wildfire spread" of mothers' pensions.[11]

The single conceptualization of motherhood that undergirded these two divergent policies had different implications for each one. It affected the way they were presented, the advocacy movements that grew up around them, and the manner in which they were administered. The precedents they established, both separately and as a "policy array," affected the relationship between American women and the emergent welfare state and, through a process that has been called "policy feedback," continue to shape governmental policies toward women.[12] A closer examination of the political careers of child care and mothers' pensions during the Progressive Era exposes the strengths and weaknesses of a political strategy based on the ideology of American maternalism, and the limits imposed by its condemnation of maternal employment.[13]

The Child-Care Movement

From the founding of the first child-care institutions, supporters carefully specified the circumstances under which they believed a mother was justified in placing her children in a day nursery: when, due to death, desertion, illness, drunkenness, disability, unemployment, or incarceration, she lacked a male breadwinner and had to seek paid employment in order to support her children. Though nurseries accepted children precisely so that their mothers could take jobs outside the home, advocates were at pains to avoid giving the appearance that they intended to supplant permanently the "natural" male breadwinner with a female one, or in any way condoned permanent wage work outside the home for married women or women with children. Advocates remained guarded on this issue even as they updated their arguments to address external criticisms and shaped their self-presentation to conform to the shifting contours of philanthropic and child-welfare discourse. For the first few decades of their existence, day nurseries presented themselves simply as charitable stopgaps for families in crisis. With the founding of the NFDN, the rhetoric shifted to emphasize the health and educational benefits that poor and immigrant populations, both children and mothers, might derive from day nurseries. In the late 1910s and 1920s it shifted again, following the general trend in social work to stress the therapeutic potential of child care for families in all social groups.

Each rationale obscured the basic fact that nurseries were caring for children so that their mothers could work. Charity, welfare, Americanization, "family adjustment"—all of these were presented as higher goals that either legitimized or canceled out the negative implications of the service itself. Though maternal employment was an unavoidable component of the day nursery's operation—indeed, its raison d'être—it was treated as ancillary and barely tolerated. Nursery leaders sometimes acknowledged the heavy burdens of working mothers, but never to the extent of trying to help them gain higher wages or improve their working conditions. For this would have violated the leaders' sense of order, their belief that in an ideal world, *no* mother would be compelled to work outside the home.

The Day Nursery as Charity

The origins of day nurseries in the U.S. are somewhat hazy, with several institutions claiming the distinction of being the first.[14] My research indicates that as early as 1795 a group of Quaker women set up a child-care facility as an adjunct to their workroom for poor widows at the House of Industry in Philadelphia. Having first offered the widows "outdoor relief" in the form of spinning work, the philanthropists observed that the women's industry was hampered by "the smallness of their rooms, want of fuel, and embarrassment of their children."[15] They thus decided to bring the women under one room, where they could be fed, warmed, and supervised more economically and efficiently while earning their keep at spinning—and where their children could be cared for separately.[16] By mid-century several more nurseries had been founded in Philadelphia and they also appeared in New York City, Troy, New York, and Chicago. Only one of the Philadelphia nurseries followed the House of Industry's model of workroom cum nursery; the others were freestanding. Some acknowledged French crèches as their inspiration.

Though located in far-flung parts of the nation and seldom in contact with one another, these nurseries and the dozens more that were set up over the next few decades shared a remarkably uniform conception of their purpose and goals. They sought to enable poor women with children to work and thus prevent them from becoming dependent upon charity or public welfare, or, even worse, turning to prostitution. The Philadelphia Home for Little Wanderers expressed its mission melodramatically:

> What can a mother do with a young babe or child unable to take care of itself? She cannot go to work and take it with her, as few persons would employ one with such an encumbrance,

and she has no one to leave it with and be assured of its safety. What a relief to her mind and benefit to her and the child, to be permitted to bring it to our nursery and have it cared for during the day while she goes out to work. In this way a larger proportion of these classes are saved from crime by relieving them in a time of deep distress, than any other. Hunger, like "necessity," knows no law. It will find ways of relief honestly or otherwise. . . . [B]ut for the help . . . which we have rendered, many mothers with families [would] have gone to the almshouse, or done worse. We have saved them from this, and from the mortification or disgrace of being cared for by the commonwealth.[17]

It is notable that while the day nurseries considered it part of their mission to save women from prostitution, most would have nothing to do with those who had already "fallen"; they usually refused admission to any child whose legitimacy could not be proven.

Some institutions, such as the Margaret Etter Crèche in Chicago, helped women find employment; some, like the West Side Day Nursery in New York City, trained mothers for domestic service or the needle trades; others, such as Philadelphia's Day Nursery for Children, restricted admissions to the children of women who already had work.[18] But the day nurseries' endorsement of maternal employment was always conditional: it was acceptable only when a mother was in crisis—on the brink of, or in, poverty. Just after the Panic of 1873, for example, the Day Nursery of Philadelphia intoned, "In these times of unusual scarcity of employment for men, it necessarily devolves upon the women to do what they can in support of their families."[19] In other words, in *normal* times and in *normal* poor and working-class families, the role of breadwinner belonged to the man.

Indeed, nursery managers expressed concern that by admitting children from a family where the father was present but incapacitated (often—or so they suspected—because of drink), they were simply encouraging him in habits of indolence.[20] They were also wary of enabling mothers to shirk their duties by seeking work outside the home when they were not financially strapped but simply indulging a taste for luxuries. As Nathaniel Rosenau of the Fitch Crèche in Buffalo put it, "I do not believe that a day nursery should, under any circumstances, relieve parents from their proper social responsibilities."[21] To guard against improper use of a nursery's services, day-nursery managers insisted that each family be carefully investigated before admitting their children, using nursery matrons, friendly visitors, or, later, professional social workers for the purpose.

Like other nineteenth-century philanthropists, nursery advocates feared that charity could lead to "pauperization," but they insisted that their institutions allowed the poor to help themselves, rather than becoming dependent. Moreover, they argued, nurseries, like well-run orphanages, could prevent future generations from becoming pauperized by training them properly at the outset.[22] In addition, nurseries offered one benefit that was uniquely theirs, and uniquely maternalist: they allowed distressed families to stay together.[23] As the custom of offering "outdoor relief" came into increasing disfavor among American philanthropists, the poor mother faced with the double burden of wage earning and child rearing had few alternatives. She could leave her children at home by themselves or in the care of a "little mother"—an older sibling kept out of school for the purpose—or pay a neighbor to look after them. Or she could place her children in an orphanage or some other boarding institution, which, if she paid their board on a regular basis, would allow her to retain custody. If she fell behind in her payments, she might be compelled to surrender them for adoption or indenture.[24] The day nursery offered such a woman the chance to work *and* fulfill her parental responsibilities, thus keeping her children with her.[25]

Such reasoning allowed the advocates of day nurseries to remain consistent in their commitment to maternalist values, for they were able to present the poor mother's temporary employment as a duty to her children and a means of preserving the integrity of her home and family. In essence, these female reformers were defining and accepting a class difference in how the maternal role was to be fulfilled. But their values prevented them from allowing the day nursery to develop beyond a charity that provided short-term, stopgap solutions in family emergencies; they had no intention of using their institutions to encourage long-term maternal employment, even for poor and working-class women.

The Day Nursery as School and Clinic

In the 1890s the need for child care increased, as industrial accidents, dramatic business cycles, immigration, and the disruptions of urban domestic life sent more mothers into the work force.[26] Child-care philanthropists realized that the small number of existing day nurseries, most of them locally organized and supported, could not meet the growing demand for services. To add force to their appeals for funds to expand the scope of their charity, they defined a new function for the day nursery: in addition to relieving families in crisis it would also help to Americanize the growing population of immigrant children.

The Chicago World's Columbian Exposition of 1893 offered American women the opportunity to present their benevolent activities to a broader public. A group of New York philanthropists decided to set up a Model Day Nursery that could demonstrate the most up-to-date, "approved methods of rearing children from infancy on. . . ."[27] The popular image of charitable nurseries was one of dreary, highly regimented institutions, reeking of carbolic disinfectants and overcooked vegetables, crowded with pale, bored, and listless children. The Model Day Nursery, with its spacious, well-equipped rooms, cheerful caretakers, and carefully planned educational activities, was deliberately designed to counter such an impression. The nursery charged fairgoing parents a fee of twenty-five cents to leave their children for the entire day (a sum that was five times the average charge in a charitable day nursery) and invited the general public to observe "the gambols of the little ones" through special windows at the front of the exhibit.[28]

Josephine Jewell (Mrs. Arthur) Dodge, the moving force behind the exhibit, was not satisfied with merely providing a service to mothers "enjoying the wonders of the Exposition" or staging amusing tableaux vivants of childhood innocence. Rather, she hoped to "inspire thousands of philanthropic women with time and money at their disposal to establish in their own cities and towns similar nurseries where poor women obliged to labor for the support of their families may leave their little ones in safety."[29] After their triumph in Chicago, Dodge and her associates decided to launch a national child-care movement, setting up the Association of Day Nurseries of New York City in 1895 and the National Federation of Day Nurseries in 1898 (Dodge served as president of both).[30] While offering advice and encouragement to would-be nursery founders and working to improve conditions in existing institutions, these organizations continued to present the day nursery as a worthy and useful charity.

During more than twenty years in office, Dodge stamped the organization with her conservative brand of maternalism.[31] Married to a founder of the New York Charity Organization Society, Dodge herself had started two day nurseries in New York City and was expert at operating in the world of philanthropy. She considered this type of activity entirely appropriate to her sex and class, but strongly believed that women should remain aloof from politics, lest their credibility and moral authority as reformers become tainted or their energies diverted. Putting organizational power behind her convictions, in 1911 she founded the National Association Opposed to Woman Suffrage, over which she presided for six years. From this platform she asserted that "[r]eform work, welfare work . . . are not the sole end of government. . . . [G]overnment is not reform legislation. In the last analysis government is concerned with the protection of persons and property."[32] The implication was that social reform and welfare should remain in the civic sector. Dodge's desire to keep social welfare out of government hands was nurtured by her ongoing association with the Charity Organization Society, which generally regarded official government efforts at providing charity as irresponsible, when not actually corrupt.[33]

Dodge's opposition to state responsibility for social welfare helps to explain why the NFDN never made a concerted effort to win government funding for child-care programs. At first she seemed to support such a course; at the NFDN conference of 1905, she referred favorably to the municipally sponsored crèches in France and Russia: "Is the American public less keen to recognize the value of this work than the municipalities of Paris and St. Petersburg—both giving sanction and large concessions of money? Up to the present time, there has been no public financial recognition of the importance of day nurseries [in the U.S.]."[34] Other reformers also advised NFDN to seek public funding for nurseries. At the 1912 conference, infant-mortality expert Edward Bunnell Phelps called on the nursery movement to expand its services and suggested that it could win government support by taking its cue from successful campaigns for workmen's compensation and municipal milk stations.[35] Yet the reports of both the national organization and its local chapters during the Progressive Era give no indication of any efforts to lobby for public funding at the municipal, state, or federal level.[36]

NFDN leaders did, however, enlist the government's help in regulation as part of its effort to upgrade the status of day nurseries and transform them into a modern form of philanthropy. As a first step, the organization drew up specifications for member nurseries, threatening to withhold membership from any nursery that failed to meet them. This threat was not particularly compelling, however, in part because expulsion of its members would have weakened the fledgling organization, and in part because many of the nurseries the NFDN sought to regulate did not, for one reason or another (usually lack of funds), belong in the first place.[37] Recognizing their own lack of authority, local chapters lobbied municipal and state governments to pass legislation regulating nurseries, with early successes in New York City, Chicago and Richmond, and statewide in California.[38] Agencies of health, charity, or public education were usually designated to carry out inspections and enforce the laws.

At the same time, the NFDN also tried to raise standards by educating the philanthropists and practitioners involved in day-nursery work through frequent local, regional, and national conferences. Organization leaders believed that they had much to gain by aligning nurseries more closely with the "most progressive" forms of child welfare, health, and education. The kindergarten movement, for example, also had its roots in charity, but by the late nineteenth century had gained widespread popular acceptance and attracted parents of all classes seeking the benefits of education for their young children. Hoping that some of this favorable opinion might rub off on day nurseries, Josephine Dodge asserted in 1897, "As kindergarten training has appealed to the public's intelligence, it has been included in the nursery regime."[39]

She was, in fact, exaggerating. Though the NFDN devoted many conference sessions to the methods of Froebel and later Montessori and progressive nursery education, few late-nineteenth-century nurseries offered full-fledged educational programs, and those that did not were slow to absorb the principles of early-childhood pedagogy.[40] Many board members resisted the new methods because they believed that what was appropriate for working-class children, particularly those from immigrant families, was not imaginative play but didactic lessons in patriotism and American middle-class customs and manners. At one Philadelphia day nursery, for example, "[c]hildren . . . learned to associate American flags and patriotic songs with cleanliness, order, thrift, and adherence to rules."[41] Nurseries with more progressive-minded boards and managers found that trained kindergarten and nursery-school teachers were hard to come by and commanded salaries far higher than those of the low-skilled nursery maids who constituted the bulk of their staffs.[42] Nurseries that could not set up educational programs on their own premises often sent other preschool charges to nearby kindergartens (sometimes located in the same settlement house) for part of the day, but this left younger children with little relief from what was very likely an arid and monotonous routine.[43] In 1906 Dodge felt compelled to admit:

> The kindergartens of our nurseries . . . are not what they should be. . . . One can hardly expect the best of trained kindergartners to devote their time where conditions are impossible to control, and all our best workers are obliged to adapt their methods to the irregular attendance of the pupils.[44]

Though nursery managers found it difficult to undertake a wholesale restructuring of their programs for educational purposes, they did manage to incorporate the protocols of the advancing child-health movement.[45] NFDN standards required a physician's examination before admission and regular monthly exams thereafter (local physicians usually volunteered their services); in addition, each child was subjected to a daily inspection by the nursery matron. Physicians' warnings about the transmission of germs only reinforced the nurseries' long-held concern with cleanliness. In most nurseries, children were stripped upon arrival, bathed, and dressed in nursery clothing, while their own ragged garments hung in specially designed ventilated closets, to be donned again only upon departure. The NFDN stipulated that each child be given her own towel, toothbrush, and eating utensils, and prescribed a specific "dietary," with copious amounts of "fresh, pure milk," for the children's meals. Nurseries also enlisted mothers' cooperation in keeping children robust and free from disease by offering classes or clubs where they could learn how to practice proper hygiene and nutrition at home.[46] Nurseries in

Chicago and Boston pioneered in setting up cooperative programs with district nurses who went into the homes of nursery families to reinforce health advice, identify medical problems, and trace paths of contagion. Nurses also referred needy families to nurseries when they felt it was appropriate.[47]

Finally, NFDN leaders struggled to gain legitimacy in the field of child welfare. The day nurseries' greatest strength lay in their ability to keep families intact, a goal that was very much in keeping with progressives' growing repudiation of the practice of institutionalizing children.[48] In 1902, eight New York Charity Organization Society districts requested the establishment of day nurseries, and at the 1905 NFDN conference, Dodge proudly noted that Josephine Shaw Lowell, founder of the New York COS had testified that day nurseries served the state "in keeping children out of the institutions by providing a day home."[49] At the same conference, Edward T. Devine, executive secretary of New York COS, paid tribute "to the breadth of view and the thoroughness of the leaders in the Day Nursery movement[,] to the absence of amateurishness, and to the genuine need for the service which you perform."[50]

Despite Devine's flattering remarks, Dodge was well aware that she and her colleagues in the NFDN lacked the professional training and status that were becoming de rigueur in welfare work. When the organization was invited to hold a session at the 1906 Conference of Charities and Corrections, Dodge admitted deferentially that the NFDN appeared "for the first time among a body of experts, and as comprising perhaps the largest body of amateurs who have ever attempted an extensive work." She appealed for "advice, interest and co-operation from all educational and philanthropic bodies. . . ."[51]

Yet the organization seemed to cherish its amateur status. Its commitment to traditional notions of the virtues of private charity made it ambivalent toward the need for professionalization. National meetings were dominated by upper-class lay board members, while the matrons and staff members who actually ran the nurseries had little voice in setting policy. Socially prominent NFDN women were no doubt genuinely interested in improving day nurseries, but it was also true, as Anne Firor Scott notes, that "women's clubs were sometimes a road to social status." This may have prevented movement leaders from accepting matrons and superintendents, who generally came from lower-middle-class or working-class backgrounds, as equals in the cause of child care.[52] With obvious pride, Dodge claimed that by 1914 college girls and educated women were coming to regard the position of day-nursery matron or superintendent to be "just as much a calling and goal to work for as the Settlement or other social work,"[53] but there is little evidence that the class composition of nursery staffs actually changed. At the same time, neither matrons nor other nursery workers made any effort to break away from the NFDN to form their own organization, as did social workers, early-childhood educators, and other groups of women involved in public service during this period.[54] Such a move would have lent these staff members a professional identity and a degree of authority that they—and child care as a field—otherwise lacked.

Thus the NFDN continued to operate as a philanthropic and advocacy, rather than a professional, organization. Its leaders tended to look outside of their own movement for guidance and legitimation, often developing policy in response to external critiques, rather than listening to the voices of those who had daily direct contact with day-nursery clients and thus knew them best—the matrons and nursery staff workers. Had they done so, day-nursery policy might have taken a different direction, for, as historian Anne Durst has argued, staff members did not always see eye to eye with the leadership, particularly around issues such as maternal employment. Durst found that nursery personnel were more sympathetic and less judgmental toward their clients, and generally regarded nurseries as a service for which there was an ongoing need among low-income families.[55] Because of such attitudes, and also probably because of a lack of time, matrons were not always as scrupulous in carrying out home visits and screening applicants as nursery leaders expected them to be. But they stopped short of challenging official policy.

Nursery leaders emphasized the need for investigating clients as a defense against accusations that they were dispensing charity indiscriminately. For example, several years after he had publicly praised the work of the NFDN, Edward Devine wrote, "It has already become reasonably clear that indiscriminate aid in the form of care for children in day nurseries is nearly as objectionable as any other form of indiscriminate relief."[56] As the child-welfare movement gained prominence, day-nursery leaders became highly sensitive to such criticisms. In the mid-1910s, the NFDN began advising member nurseries to assign someone other than the matron the task of visiting families—possibly a trained nurse. But the changing scope of social work demanded an even greater degree of professional specialization. At the 1916 NFDN conference, one member lamented that the "nurseries . . . lagged behind [the] movement to advance the national wealth through scientific study and through conservation of its child life. We still follow . . . old methods and hold up old aims."[57]

The Politics of Child Care

As the sole national organization devoted wholly to the cause of child care, the NFDN's views dominated discourse in the field over many decades, blocking out other, more progressive, perspectives. Leading female African-American philanthropists, for example, took a very different view of the function of day nurseries. Though they, too, expressed maternalist values, they also accepted maternal employment as a fact of life, and simply wanted to free working mothers from anxiety by keeping their children safe.[58] From the 1890s on, local affiliates of the National Association of Colored Women (NACW) established numerous urban day nurseries for African-American children.[59] There is no evidence, however, that the NACW and the NFDW ever exchanged views on day nurseries, much less that the NFDN altered its staunch maternalist convictions in response to the NACW's position.

From neither within nor without, then, did the NFDN feel serious pressure to reconsider its views and move toward normalizing its conception of maternal employment and the purpose of the day nursery. By remaining steadfastly traditional, however, the organization—and the child-care movement—began to lose ground. Despite efforts to expand and modernize day nurseries, the NFDN's ambivalence about its own aims, its reluctance to professionalize, and its mixed success in bringing nursery practices up to the levels demanded by experts in other fields combined to undermine the cause of child care. Weakened, the movement was hard put to counter objections to day nurseries, particularly when they came from one-time allies.

No less a figure than Jane Addams was one friend who changed her mind about child care. During the early days of Hull House, Addams had endorsed the establishment of a day nursery in response to the obvious needs of neighborhood women, whose children, left alone while they worked, frequently came to harm. But in 1905 she confided to a group of female philanthropists:

> The day nursery is a "double-edged implement" for doing good, which may also do a little harm. . . . The conduct of day nurseries is full of little temptations to blunder with human life. How far the wife can be both wife and mother and supporter of the family raises the question of whether the day nursery should tempt her to attempt the impossible. . . . The earnings of working women are very small at the best. . . . [And what of] the careers of children after leaving day nurseries[?] One . . . investigation made in Chicago has disclosed results which are neither encouraging nor reassuring.[60]

Addams was led to take this position by her experience with the working mothers she had encountered. In *Twenty Years at Hull House* she recounted the tragic tale of "Goosie," a small boy who frequently came to the nursery covered with down from the feather-brush factory where his mother worked. One windy day, as his mother was hanging out her laundry on the roof of their tenement, Goosie was blown off and fell to his death. As Addams tells it,

> After the funeral, as the poor mother sat in the nursery postponing the moment when she must go back to her empty rooms, I asked her . . . if there was anything more we could do for her. The overworked, sorrow-stricken woman looked up and replied, "If you could give me my wages for tomorrow, I would not go to work in the factory at all. I would like to stay at home all day and hold the baby. Goosie was always asking me to take him and I never had any time." This statement revealed the condition of many nursery mothers who are obliged to forego the joys and solaces which belong to even the most poverty-stricken. The long hours of factory labor necessary for earning the support of a child leave no time for the tender care and caressing which may enrich the life of the most piteous baby.[61]

To Addams and other leaders in the field of maternal and child welfare, child care no longer presented a viable general solution for the problems of poor women. Many, in fact, believed that it simply created more problems. It was not only day nurseries, but the plight of working mothers—their low wages, their poor health and exhaustion due to overwork—and the poor quality of their families' lives that led to dissatisfaction with day nurseries and the search for an alternative.

The Movement for Mothers' Pensions

With regard to policies toward wage-earning mothers, the Progressive Era proved to be an important "switch point." As the day-nursery movement stagnated, the idea of mothers' pensions rapidly moved into position as the predominant paradigm in the field of child welfare.[62] The fortunes of the two policies were not unrelated, for criticism of the child-care system often turned into approval for mothers' pensions.

One of the earliest critics to make this connection was Julia Lathrop, a reformer who later became the first chief of the U.S. Children's Bureau. At the 1905 NFDN conference, Lathrop, then a resident of Hull House, echoed Jane Addams' sentiments regarding child care and working mothers:

> The fact is that the working mother is the most melancholy figure in the working world, not alone because she is unskilled, ill-paid and harassed by . . . unspeakable anxieties . . . but because the records of the world show that her children recruit the ranks of youthful delinquents and later of adult criminals.[63]

Citing Australia, Germany, and Switzerland as examples, Lathrop recommended the adoption of mothers' or widows' pensions.

At the same conference, Dr. Lee R. Frankel of United Hebrew Charities expressed similar concerns about maternal employment:

> Why is it necessary for the mothers to work? It is a very unfortunate thing that under modern industrial and economic conditions it may be impossible for a man to earn enough to properly support his family, and it is most deplorable that as a result it becomes necessary for the mother to go out into the world and work for those lives entrusted to her care.

For families with male breadwinners present, institution of the family wage was the obvious solution; if the male breadwinner had died, Frankel's alternative was the same as Lathrop's: "a system of pensions that shall give a widow the chance to rear her own children."[64]

Though Lathrop cited European models for mothers' pensions, such measures were not in fact entirely foreign to the U.S. Payments to destitute mothers, whether in cash or in kind, had long been a practice in American social provision, both public and private. In some cities, relief was provided by maternalist associations formed expressly for that purpose as early as the antebellum period. In other cities and in rural areas, public outdoor relief was sometimes available. The widows of Civil War veterans also received pensions, usually more generous than the payments allotted from other sources.[65] All of these payments were intended to substitute for the earnings of the absent male breadwinner, on the assumption that a woman alone could not support a household.

Military pensions had been modified and expanded several times during and after the Civil War, largely to avert what historian Megan McClintock has labeled a "crisis of domesticity."[66] Pensions were initially offered to the soldiers themselves as an inducement to enlist; the extension to dependents was precipitated by widespread concern for civilians who became the "innocent victims" of war. While soldiers and their dependents were *entitled* to pensions by law, in practice, they did not receive the funds without question. Female pension recipients in particular soon fell under the same type of suspicion that was directed toward charity recipients in the nineteenth century.[67] According to McClintock, "Over time, protecting the home from outside threats evolved into supervision of the family and the behavior of individual family members. Marital status, dependency, and morality were used to identify worthy recipients of government assistance."[68] Employing tests similar to those used by private charity workers, pension administrators sought to uncover fraudulent claims and discourage widows from cohabiting with men while retaining their pensions.[69]

Toward the end of the nineteenth century, nonmilitary payments to poor women, whether from public or private charitable sources, came under increasing criticism from groups like the Charity Organization Society for their propensity to "pauperize" recipients.[70] Charity official Lee Frankel, for one, denied this charge:

> We have demonstrated that we can take care of widows and their children without pauperizing them. We have instances

where women have been carried on our books for ten or twelve years, and we have invariably found that their self-respect has been preserved—even the children may not know that the mother receives a pension.[71]

In any case, both public and private relief (though not federal pensions) tended to be sporadic and inadequate; as a result, poor female-headed families, particularly those of widows, were regularly broken up, with children being sent off to orphanages, indentured situations, or, later, foster homes, so that the mothers could work and support themselves.

This was the cycle that advocates of mothers' pensions helped to break. Over and over again, reformers lamented the folly of removing children from "worthy" mothers simply on account of poverty. President Theodore Roosevelt told representatives at the 1909 Conference on the Care of Dependent Children, "Surely . . . the goal toward which we should strive is to help the mother, so that she can keep her own home and keep the child in it; that is the best thing possible to be done for the child."[72]

The popular press also dwelled on the pathos of separating mothers and children. Typical was a 1913 article from *The Outlook* describing a court scene in which the judge had just ordered a family to be broken up:

> One of the children was a boy seven years old and the other a girl four years old. The mother begged to be allowed to keep them. The little boy threw himself into her arms, sobbing, "Oh, mamma, I can't leave you." But it was of no use. The mother was too poor to care for the children properly. So the law tore them apart.[73]

Judges themselves were hardly inured to the emotional pain they were compelled to inflict. Referring to "the tragic separation between mothers and children," Judge Merritt W. Pinckney of the Chicago juvenile court admitted, "Words cannot begin to draw the child's fear and the mother's agony, the collapse of all things strong and holy at such a time."[74]

Family breakup also came under fire because it usually led to some form of institutionalization for children. According to reformer Mary Conyngton, "Even a very poor home offers a better chance for [a child's] development than an excellent institution."[75]

Dissatisfaction with the regimentation, inefficiency, and corruption of institutions led some child-welfare experts to support foster homes for dependent children. But neither foster homes nor institutions made sense economically. It was far cheaper—half as much, by some estimates—to pay women for keeping their own children at home.

Campaign by Coalition

Most historians mark the 1909 White House Conference as the moment when a full-fledged campaign for mothers' pensions was launched. Roosevelt left open the question of how pensions should be funded and administered: "How the relief shall come, public, private, or by a mixture of both, in what way, you are competent to say and I am not."[76] It was generally agreed, however, that the resources of private charity were inadequate, so supporters quickly moved in the direction of *public* funding. As for administration, that evolved on an ad hoc basis that drew on both public and private resources.

Unlike the day-nursery movement, which was virtually paralyzed under the leadership of the NFDN, the mothers' pension campaign was run by multiple organizations working in coalition.[77] Though the National Congress of Mothers (NCM) and the General Federation of Women's Clubs (GFWC) took the lead, a number of other groups were involved, including the National Consumers' League and the Women's Christian Temperance Union. Labor organizations also lent limited support. Endorsements from juvenile-court Judges Pinckney, Ben Lindsey of Denver, and E. E. Porterfield of Kansas City and Progressive politicians, including Roosevelt, Robert LaFollette, and Louis Brandeis, added momentum.[78] The linkage between the media campaign, waged especially effectively by William Hard in the pages of a popular women's magazine, *The Delineator,* and the sophisticated and highly efficient political methods of the women's organizations was what ultimately produced numerous legislative successes.[79]

From the outset, the reformers' aim was to establish pensions at the state, rather than the federal, level. There were probably several reasons for this. Civil War pensions had established a precedent for federal provision, but by the late nineteenth century, the pension bureaucracy had become notoriously corrupt, and pension advocates no doubt wanted to avoid any association with it.[80] Moreover, all other welfare measures and programs in place at the time, including the system of family dispersion that mothers' pensions were intended to supplant, were organized and administered primarily by municipal, county, and state authorities. By the time the campaign got fully under way, two states had already tested the waters for mothers' pensions: New York, where in 1898 the legislature passed a bill (vetoed by the governor) that would have paid widowed mothers the equivalent of what it cost to keep their children in institutions, and California, where by 1906 several counties were already providing aid to children in their own homes.[81]

Another important reason for the state-by-state strategy was the fact that the maternalist politicians who spearheaded the campaign were most comfortable working at that level. Though national in scope, the NCM and GFWC were both structured along state lines and relied, in this presuffrage period, on spheres of influence in municipal and state politics to exert their greatest pressure.[82] Nevertheless, by mobilizing affiliates in nearly every state, they were able to coordinate their efforts to create a "domino effect" that resulted in the rapid passage of legislation in state after state.[83]

In addition to evoking the tragedy of family breakup and registering their opposition to institutionalizing children, each of the groups involved in the coalition mustered a specific set of arguments in favor of the mothers' pensions. Those of the two leading organizations were characteristically maternalist in tone. The NCM, for example, found mothers' pensions, in Theda Skocpol's terms, "ideologically comfortable"—a logical extension of their emphasis on "the special importance of mother-love for the proper nurture of children."[84] NCM spokeswomen repeatedly linked motherhood to the greater good of society and to advances in social reform. In a 1914 address, Mrs. Frederic Schoff, president of the National Congress of Mothers and Parent-Teacher Associations (as the organization came to be known), called upon mothers to

> build a bridge upon which struggling humanity may safely cross into a new land, leaving forever the old, with its unending reformatory movements, its shattered homes; and the keystone

of that bridge will be maternal love, while in that fair domain the splendid edifice of the new civilization will bear the cornerstone of home.[85]

The GFWC's support for mothers' pensions had two distinct, yet mutually reinforcing, purposes: to alleviate the plight of women without breadwinners, and to augment the organization's own power. GFWC members acknowledged that women's political influence was linked to their moral authority as women and especially as mothers, but they also knew that the status of motherhood was not in itself guaranteed. In 1912, the organization resolved that "there should be a progressive legislative policy for the greater honor and greater stability of home life," including measures to deal "with the great and growing evils of non-support and desertion of children by their fathers." The resolution went on: "We believe that the function of motherhood should bring to a woman increased security rather than increased insecurity and that the [mothers' pension], in safeguarding motherhood, safeguards the race."[86] By emphasizing the social importance of motherhood, GFWC members were enhancing their own status and what they stood for *as public actors*. At the same time, however, by calling for state support for motherhood, these middle-class clubwomen were expressing concern about the security of all women—including themselves. Since dependency on male breadwinners was precarious even for them, they too might one day be compelled to seek outside aid.

It was perhaps this fear, in conjunction with their belief in the importance of motherhood, that led clubwomen to seek a rationale for mothers' pensions that would clearly distinguish them from the charity payments of the past. Denying opponents' charges that the pensions were simply another form of relief (and thus pauperizing), they contended that it was a form of salary or wages for the *work* of motherhood. Mary Wood told the 1912 biennial GFWC convention that pensions "would relieve the stigma of pauperism—felt under existing Charity relief. . . . The woman who produced citizens and soldiers should be placed in a class with the disabled solider, during the period she is unable to earn for herself and children."[87]

Progressive reformer William Hard also argued for mothers' pensions on the grounds that motherhood had a civic value, though he did not specifically compare it to military service. Hard

pointed approvingly to the British conceptualization of social provision, especially the formulations of New Liberal sociologist L. T.
Hobhouse, who wrote, "We no longer consider it desirable to drive
the mother out to her charing [*sic*] work if we possibly can, *nor
do we consider her degraded by receiving public money. We cease,
in fact, to regard the public money as a dole; we treat it as a payment
for a civic service....*"[88] Hard also believed that a pensioned mother
should be seen not as a dependent of the state (as pension critics
would have it) but as

> an independent citizen kept from self-support only by the pres-
> ence of future citizens at her knees and requiring, in order that
> as she fulfills her instinctive duty to them she may also fulfill
> her indirect civic duty to the state, the means of support really
> for them and only incidentally for herself.[89]

Motherhood as Service

Several recent studies of the mothers' pension movement have
claimed that motherhood-as-service arguments such as those
made by Hard and, to a certain extent, by the GFWC, succeeded
in transforming the relationship between motherhood and the
state and raising mothers' pensions above the level of relief.[90]
According to sociologist Ann Shola Orloff, pensions

> reflected a new liberal view of the necessity of modern social
> programs to replace poor relief because of a new understanding
> of industrial society, which implicitly if not explicitly recog-
> nized "equality in difference" for men and women in a notion
> of socially-valuable labor as the basis for entitlement.[91]

This meant that, at least in the eyes of their architects, mothers'
pensions were regarded as the equivalent of Civil War pensions
or work-related legislation such as workers' compensation, which,
though not gender-specific, was another important form of state
provision available to men.

On these grounds, Orloff challenges political scientist Barbara
Nelson and other scholars who argue that, from the moment of
conception, differences between mothers' pensions and workmen's compensation constituted the basis for a "two-channel,"

gendered welfare state.[92] Rather, according to Orloff, it was developments in the funding and administration of mothers' pensions that led to the discriminatory practices that persistently mark American social provision for women and children. Thus she seeks to separate the intentions of policy makers from the programs and policies themselves.

Orloff and the others who share her views are not mistaken in identifying a transformative potential in mothers' pensions. However, it is difficult to separate intentions from practice, in part because many of the flaws in the policy appear to have been inherent from the outset. For one, the notion of service to the state could be misconstrued to the detriment of pension recipients. To many reformers, the value of motherhood was strictly instrumental: the community needed mothers to prevent social problems.[93] Juvenile-court judges in particular regarded maternal absence due to employment as a direct cause of juvenile delinquency; they wanted to keep mothers at home. Thus the aim of pensions was not to underwrite mothers fulfilling their responsibilities as they saw fit, but to mobilize them as agents of the state, following a preestablished agenda. This, in turn, gave the state an opening to supervise pensioned mothers and ensure that they were performing their duties as prescribed.

The rhetoric of the leading organizations in the mothers' pension coalition also undercut the radical potential of pensions by presenting the state not as the *beneficiary* of women's work as mothers but as the *benefactor* that would enable women to preserve their maternal roles. In 1911 the NCM resolved

> that families should, if possible, be held together. That the mother is the best caretaker for her children. That when necessary to prevent the breaking up of the home the State should provide a certain sum for the support of the children instead of taking them from her and placing them elsewhere at the expense of the state. . . .[94]

This resolution positioned the NCM (and, by implication, potential pension recipients) as supplicants to the state. Perhaps operating on the principle that flattery is the best strategy, one member urged her fellows to intensify their lobbying efforts on the assumption that

[t]he state is a parent, and as a wise and gentle and kind and loving parent should beam down upon each child alike. At the knee of this great, just, loving mother or father, no child should beg in vain. . . . From the fountain head—*the state*—all benefits should issue. . . .[95]

While leaving open the question of the *gender* of the state, such rhetoric portrayed pensioned mothers not as the partners of an egalitarian state but as dependents upon its largesse.

On the whole, popular support for mothers' pensions was not based on a conceptualization of motherhood as service to the state that entitled women to compensation. Rather, it drew on a combination of hardheaded economic pragmatism and sentimental encomiums to motherhood. In this sense, the rhetoric reinforced a conventional view of gender roles while also granting blanket permission to legislators to keep the costs of mothers' pension programs as low as possible, in the name of greater economy.

The Politics of Implementation

The radical potential of mothers' pensions was further eroded through the process of implementation. Initially, pension legislation in most states was enabling but not mandatory; funding levels, usually left up to municipalities or counties, were seldom adequate to cover all potential recipients. So choices had to be made. The rhetoric of the mothers' pension campaign implicitly offered an image of the "ideal recipient": a worthy woman who had been widowed or otherwise deprived of the support of a male breadwinner through no fault of her own; virtuous, hardworking, self-sacrificing, devoted to her children; without resources and therefore dependent upon the state. For many this image no doubt brought to mind white, native-born middle-class women, much like those who were advocating for pensions. In practice, however, many applicants for pensions came from very different class, ethnic, and racial backgrounds and did not readily conform to the norms and styles of motherhood inherent in the ideal. If they did not appear to be amenable to change or willing to learn, they would be denied pensions. Historian Joanne Goodwin has found that in the early days of mothers' pension administration in Chicago, many women were rejected on moral grounds or for lack of cooperation with the authorities, but even more were denied because they appeared to be *too* self-sufficient; that is, they were deemed to be "adequate earners" and thus not in need of pensions.[96] Either way, they fell short of the ideal.

Problems also arose in the constitution of pension bureaucracies. After passing legislation, each state had to scramble to set up its own administrative apparatus. In some, authority was granted to juvenile courts; in others, entirely new agencies had to be formed, some at the county and local level.[97] Most states required a thorough investigation of each applicant before a final decision was made. This task was usually assigned to a charity worker who had experience in making home visits;[98] the findings were then reported to the pension-granting authority.[99]

Eligibility boards were made up of welfare officials, male business leaders, and prominent women who were familiar with welfare issues.[100] Reformers who supported mothers' pensions as a means for equalizing women's status seldom ended up in positions of power. In Chicago, for example, leading progressive reformers such as Julia Lathrop, Sophonisba Breckinridge, and Edith Abbott, who had been central to the formulation and passage of pension legislation, suddenly found themselves boxed out, helpless to influence administration. Workers from private charity agencies moved in, establishing harsh investigative routines and protocols of constant surveillance. Instead of replacing poor relief with a nonstigmatizing policy, Abbott complained that "the courts and influence of private agencies had subverted that goal and made it relief once again."[101]

Political scientist Libba Gaje Moore argues that such practices came to constitute a kind of "subpolicy" that allowed local prejudices and values to dictate who would receive pensions.[102] African-American mothers were systematically excluded from receiving benefits, though more of them headed families than white women. A 1931 study found that only three percent of pension recipients nationwide were black, with even lower proportions in southern states.[103] Many foreign-born women failed to meet residency requirements; others were taken onto the rolls but then closely supervised.[104] For all women, gaining initial approval was no guarantee of security; a mother could be dropped from the pension rolls at any time if authorities deemed that she was no longer "fit." Moreover, the laws themselves were highly mutable; the categories of eligibility could change, or levels of funding could drop, leaving large groups of mothers without resources. As Moore notes, "The poor . . . had no contractual rights to relief, only limited statutory claims. . . ."[105]

Aware that such practices undermined the spirit of mothers' pensions, at least as they had been initially envisioned, welfare advocate Sophie Loeb offered impassioned testimony before a U.S. Senate committee considering a mothers' pension bill for the District of Columbia in 1926. Loeb, then president of the Child Welfare Committee of America, had helped formulate pension legislation for New York State and studied pension and social-insurance policies from across the U.S. and Europe. She claimed that in the early days, when pensions were administered by the public-welfare agency in New York City, "the best mothers . . . refused to come to us. The very mothers that we were anxious to reach, good mothers, that would rather put their children in institutions if they had to than accept from the Board of Charity."[106] Eventually, New York State had to amend its law and set up an independent agency to administer pensions. Loeb urged the Senate not to repeat New York's mistake, noting that when a pension is delivered discreetly and without stigma,

> [i]t is a civic function, and it creates that spirit in that family that the local community is getting behind that mother and giving her the help of her own home to bring up her own children. . . . We are trying to make it possible for these people to wear the same badge of honor as the mother in Denmark [who receives respect as well as a generous pension]; that she is not coming as a beggar, but she is coming as one like a great soldier who is trying to bring up her children in the best way she can.[107]

As Loeb's testimony revealed, entrenched welfare practices tended to drag mothers' pensions into a quagmire of charity. Rather than constituting a break with the stigmatization and moralism that had characterized the nineteenth-century treatment of indigent mothers, the new policy tended to perpetuate them. The application process, with its invasive questioning and embarrassing investigations, was hardly calculated to enhance the dignity of applicants.[108] Ongoing supervision and changeable laws produced feelings of uncertainty rather than entitlement and pride in recipient mothers. Loeb, along with other visionary reformers, had looked to mothers' pensions as a means of elevating the status of poor women and gaining for *all mothers* the recognition and gratitude of the state. But their hopes were harshly and utterly dashed by the actual administration of the policy.

Child Care or Mothers' Pensions?

For a time it appeared that the advent of mothers' and widows' pensions in state after state throughout the 1910s might in fact eliminate the need for day nurseries altogether.[109] After all, the stated purpose of the legislation was to allow mothers who lacked a male breadwinner to forego paid employment so that they could remain at home with their children. In practice, however, pensions did not have that effect. A sizable proportion of poor and low-income mothers derived no benefits from pensions, either because they did not fit the criteria or because the pool of funds in their states was exhausted.[110] Many pension recipients continued working for wages because the amounts granted were too low to support their families.[111] In Pennsylvania, for example, a 1927 study found that the wages of mothers on pensions constituted twenty-one percent of their families' total income.[112] The same year, Sophie Loeb testified that in New York City 3,479 out of 8,640 pensioned widows held jobs outside the home because pension levels were inadequate. Many states nonetheless explicitly prohibited recipients from working.[113] Others advised them to seek only part-time work or, if their children were very small, take in industrial homework. Such restrictions and recommendations channeled women into the lowest-paid, least stable, and least desirable of jobs, when they were not barred from the labor market altogether.[114]

There was little consensus as to how pension rates should be calculated. Some states regarded payments as an allowance for children, on the more or less implicit assumption that the mother would somehow support herself.[115] Joanne Goodwin found that, in Illinois, legislators actually shifted their concept of the level of support from being the "amount necessary for proper care" to one that would provide only "partial support," with the remainder of a family's income coming from wage earning, including the mother's.[116] It was taken for granted that supplements were necessary, because women could not be expected to earn a "family wage." Few reformers questioned the concentration of women in low-paying occupations or challenged deeply entrenched gender-based wage differentials. Indeed, while pensions clearly eased the burden of those who received them, their very existence undercut possible claims for increasing women's wages on the grounds that they, too, had dependents to support. The right to a "family wage" remained a male prerogative.

Instead of discouraging the use of day nurseries, pensions had the opposite effect, for administrators tried to prohibit mothers from taking employment outside the home if their children were not properly supervised.[117] In 1916, the New York Association of Day Nurseries reported:

> The granting of pensions [in New York City] . . . has as yet made no perceptible difference in the nursery situation. Three hundred and eighty-four widows are now receiving a pension, but as far as we are able to learn, only three or four were nursery mothers. The larger appropriation that is expected in the near future will have no appreciable effect on the nurseries.[118]

On an ideological level, however, the establishment of mothers' pensions *did* have an appreciable effect on day nurseries. Both to the general public and to nursery advocates, the existence of an alternative policy once again threw into question the raison d'être of the entire day-nursery project. It was not sufficient for nursery advocates to point to the educational and health benefits offered by the nurseries, for these could be provided by the growing number of nursery schools, public kindergartens, clinics, and, in the 1920s, by the government itself through programs like Sheppard-Towner. The one function that remained unique to the day nursery was its work in child welfare, and it was this aspect, above all others, that nursery leaders began to stress. At the 1919 NFDN conference, one speaker spelled out the day nursery's special function:

> Like all progressive social agencies we have as an ideal our eventual elimination and a chance for every mother to stay in her home, but until the social evils which brought us into existence have been wiped out by more vigorous community pressure, we must still exist to protect children who might

otherwise be neglected or families who might still be disorganized.[119]

Increasingly, day nurseries defined their work as having to do with "family adjustment," which required some type of therapeutic approach.

Therapy, however, was not what mothers needed; maternal employment was not an "abnormal" condition, either psychologically or sociologically. Only a minority of married women were employed, but their numbers were rapidly increasing. From about 1900 to 1910, the percentage doubled (from approximately five percent to ten percent). In the 1910s, the rate dipped slightly, though the absolute number grew in proportion to the population increase, and after 1920, the rate resumed its steady upward trend. During these same decades, the birthrate declined sharply, but due to economic and social conditions, many wage-earning women were also the mothers of young children.[120] Nursery reformers noted that because there was a growing number of families in which both parents worked, and "[i]n all grades of society [more women were] entering business and professional life," the day nursery and nursery school had "come to stay,"[121] but they still stopped short of calling for nurseries to accommodate any and all two-earner families. Since casework, psychology, psychiatry, and child training were now seen as the core of the day-nursery program, they preferred to accept children who demonstrated psychological need.

The emphasis on the psychological transformed the day-nursery movement's sense of mission but did nothing to dislodge its underlying opposition to maternal employment. Along with mothers' pension advocates, nursery reformers continued to insist that women's maternal duties should be centered around child rearing in their own homes. They refused to support or even consider policies that might allow mothers to choose the combined role of wage earner and child rearer, even though mothers' pension laws, as implemented, compelled many mothers to seek paid employment, usually under conditions that were far from ideal. As day-nursery services continued to be offered on a limited, highly qualified basis, mothers' pensions became the dominant paradigm in maternalists' campaigns for social provision to poor and single mothers.

Only a few feminists recognized the danger of this position.

One was Charlotte Perkins Gilman, who argued that pensions commodified motherhood. "Motherhood is not an economic function," she wrote in *The Forerunner* in 1914; "it is physiologic and psychologic. It is not, or should not be, for sale or for hire."[122] Instead, the state should provide "baby gardens," which would be far more economical, as well as providing positive benefits for children. In keeping with her fundamental insistence on women's need for economic independence, Gilman argued that, in general, child care should be provided for mothers who want to work.[123] In her view, "[t]he care of children belongs to women," though not all were equally well-suited for the task.[124]

Another feminist and radical, Benita Locke, put her finger precisely on the gender implications of mothers' pensions in the first issue of Margaret Sanger's *The Woman Rebel*, also published in 1914:

> There is little doubt but that, if the pension scheme be adopted, it will restrict the freedom of the mother. It will also prohibit her from working outside the home, with the result that, as the benefits will not provide complete support, the sweated industries will be subsidized. . . . Prohibition of work for wages and enforced homekeeping are tyrannous extractions to place on the worker, and are some of the signs of that new slavery which an institutional state is endeavoring to impose. . . . Mothers pensions will create a capitalized interest in one kind of legislation. Let that interest find and join hands with public sentiment—and then will rally all the seekers of special privilege. The tide of pensions will grow.[125]

Locke's prophesies were remarkably accurate. Mothers' pensions ended up limiting mothers' options and channeling them into an unfavorable labor market. Moreover, buoyed by widespread public support for a traditional notion of motherhood, pensions gained a monopoly on state policy toward women. But once again, figures like Locke and even Gilman were too marginal to shift the course of public opinion.[126]

Mothers' pensions succeeded because they affirmed women's maternal role, whereas child care (had it ever been put on the public agenda) would have challenged it. The policy that received the imprimatur of government support was the one that upheld a traditional division of labor between women and men. Despite the stigma that attached to mothers' pensions and their successors, Aid to Dependent Children and Aid to Families with Dependent Children, the stinginess of funding, and the condescending and discriminatory manner in which they were administered, governmental payments to poor mothers eventually became a form of *entitlement*—for good or for ill, a social right of American women.[127] Publicly supported child care, however, has never achieved that status.[128]

The state's interpretation of motherhood conformed to the predominant maternalist conception in terms of its narrowness (i.e., mothers at home, not in the work force), but social provisions fell far short of the exalted status for women promised by the rhetoric of "sacred motherhood." Caught in the conjuncture of an inadequate pension program and a nonexistent public child-care system, mothers were denied full support for child rearing but also restricted in their ability to combine motherhood with wage earning.

Had the maternalist reformers who spearheaded the day nursery movement embraced a broader view of women, they might, with their organizational strength, have been able to push at the limits of public opinion and gain support for a panoply of policies that allowed mothers a range of options, including remaining at home with their children, adequately supported, or competing freely on the job market while their children received good care.[129] Given the gender segmentation of the American labor market during the 1910s and 1920s, women's job opportunities may not have been wide open at the outset. But the ready availability of child care (assuming it was well run and affordable) would have endowed them with a degree of security, as well as the possibility of pursuing more or less continuous employment which, in turn, would have situated them more favorably to struggle for better wages and working conditions. As it was, motherhood, whether actual or potential, was repeatedly used as a rationale for relegating women to the least skilled and lowest-paying positions.

The case of child care and mothers' pensions reveals both the strengths and the limitations of an ideology rooted in arguments about women's natural capacities as mothers. While maternalism empowered the early female philanthropists to establish day nurseries and the NFDN to improve them, maternalism also cast public child care as a peculiarly unstable enterprise with a self-divided and self-defeating sense of purpose. Similarly, it was maternalism that fueled the campaign for mothers' pensions, but also maternalism that contributed to the humiliating and punitive treatment of recipients. Ironically, after the turn of the century maternalist ideology itself began to weaken as parent education and other fields challenged the notion of maternal instinct and called for training and professionalization for those who dealt with children.[130] What became extracted and reified was the single trope of the woman as mother in the home, which continued to be reproduced not only by experts on children and the family, but also by policy makers seeking to restrict governmental services for women. It was the limited vision of women's rights and responsibilities, not the idea of child care as a public service to all, that became maternalism's legacy to the American welfare state.

Notes

My thanks to Eileen Boris, Vernon Burton, Mark Leff, Ann Shola Orloff, and Seth Koven for their very helpful comments on this essay.

1. I am using the term maternalism as defined in the introduction to this volume.

2. Conversely, when maternalist reformers sought to challenge traditional definitions or were seen to undermine them, they were less successful; see, for example, the response to attempts by Australian feminists to use motherhood as the basis for radical social entitlements for women in Marilyn Lake, "A Revolution in the Family: The Challenge and Contradictions of Maternal Citizenship in Australia," in this volume.

3. According to Jane Jenson, "In France, [female identity] included the possibility—and indeed at times the assumption—of the validity and importance of women's paid work, both for single and married women. . . . Legislation protecting both working women and mothers and infants . . . reflect[ed] a certain societal agreement that if women workers were not exactly the same as men, women *were* nonetheless workers." Jenson, "Representations of Gender: Policies to 'Protect' Women Workers and Infants in France and the United States before 1914," in Linda Gordon, ed., *Women, the State, and Welfare* (Madison, Wis., 1990), 153.

4. Gail Richardson and Elisabeth Marx, *A Welcome for Every Child*, report of the Child Care Study Panel of the French-American Foundation (New York, 1989), 20. According to Rachel Fuchs, the first crèches were not established in Paris until 1844; see *Abandoned Children: Foundlings and Child Welfare in Nineteenth-Century France* (Albany, N.Y., 1984), 100. The term "crèche" became common coin for child-care institutions in other societies, including the United States, during the nineteenth century.

5. See Alisa Klaus, *Every Child a Lion: The Origins of Infant Health Policy in the United States and France, 1890–1920* (Ithaca, N.Y., forthcoming), and "Depopulation and Race Suicide: Maternalism and Pronatalist Ideologies in

France and the United States," in this volume; Mary Lynn Stewart, *Women, Work, and the French State: Labour Protection and Social Patriarchy* (Kingston, Ont., 1989); and Jenson, "Representations of Gender."

6. Mary Ryan, *The Empire of the Mother: American Writing about Domesticity, 1830–1860* (New York, 1985), and Sylvia D. Hoffert, *Private Matters: American Attitudes toward Childbearing and Infant Nurture in the Urban North, 1800–1860* (Urbana, Ill., 1989). Depending on social class, paid employment was also seen as appropriate for older children and for young women prior to marriage. The views of African Americans were somewhat different in this regard. Immediately following Emancipation, many African-American families attempted to free women from the necessity of waged labor so that they could devote their full energies to their homes and children, but financial necessity due to persistent discrimination eventually led African-American wives and mothers into the paid labor force, where their participation rates were consistently higher than those of native-born whites and other ethnic groups. See Jacqueline Jones, *Labor of Love, Labor of Sorrow: Black Women, Work, and the Family from Slavery to the Present* (New York, 1985), 45–46, and Teresa L. Amott and Julie A. Matthaei, *Race, Gender and Work: A Multicultural Economic History of the United States* (Boston, 1991), 157, 166. Jones notes that whites, both northern and southern, tended to exempt black women from cultural prohibitions against maternal employment; they accused nonworking black mothers of the "evil of female loaferism." John William DeForest, *A Union Officer in the Reconstruction* (New Haven, 1948), 94; quoted in Jones, *Labor of Love*, 45.

7. On the family wage, see Alice Kessler-Harris, *A Woman's Wage: Historical Meanings and Social Consequences* (Lexington, Ky., 1990), chaps. 2 and 3, and Martha May, "Home Life: Progressive Social Reformers' Prescriptions for Social Stability, 1890–1920" (Ph.D. diss., State University of New York at Binghamton, 1984), chap. 3.

8. This line of analysis can begin to explain the paradox of American maternalism described in the introductory essay, namely: How was it that in the U.S., where maternalist organizations were strongest and maternalist reformers made the greatest headway into the federal government, gains for women were minimal, not only in degree but also *in kind?*

9. Megan McClintock, "Shoring Up the Family: Civil War Pensions and the Crisis of American Domesticity," paper delivered to the American Historical Association, Chicago, 1991. McClintock argues that the pensions were explicitly intended to obviate the need for maternal employment by replacing absent (male) breadwinners, thus preserving the traditional family structure.

10. Theodore Roosevelt, quoted in U.S. Congress, Senate, *Conference on Care of Dependent Children: Proceedings*, 60th Cong., 2d sess., 1909, S. Doc. 721, 36.

11. This phrase comes from the title of a 1915 popular magazine article, "Wildfire Spread of 'Widows' Pensions'—Its Start—Its Meaning—and Its Cost," *Everybody's Magazine* 32 (June 1915): 780–81; rpt. in Edna D. Bullock, comp., *Selected Articles on Mothers' Pensions* (White Plains, N.Y., 1915), 87–89.

12. The term "policy feedback" comes from Margaret Weir, Ann Shola Orloff, and Theda Skocpol, "Introduction: Understanding American Social Politics," in Weir, Orloff, and Skocpol, eds., *The Politics of Social Policy in the United States* (Princeton, N.J., 1988). It occurs when social policies, "[o]nce instituted . . . in turn reshape the organization of the state itself and affect the goals and alliances of social groups involved in ongoing political struggle" (25). Edward Berkowitz uses the term "bureaucratic genealogy" for a related phenomenon, "the programs and precedents that give rise to the subject under analysis," e.g., a particular program or issue; see Berkowitz, "History, Public Policy and Reality," *Journal of Social History* 18 (1984): 82.

13. This approach also suggests the utility of looking at policies in concatenation with one another, rather than in isolation; for, together, policies and institutions targeted on women created (or circumscribed) their range of life choices.

14. Amateur historians compiling histories for purposes of publicity and promotion have invented and perpetuated several myths of origin. Some chroniclers insist that the Troy Day Home Nursery, founded in 1856, was the first; others grant the distinction to the Nursery for the Children of Poor Women, founded in New York City in 1854. But the Philadelphia institution described below preceded *both* of these by decades.

15. Elizabeth Marshall, "An Account of Anna Parrish," n.d., holograph, Quaker Collection, Haverford College, 31.

16. For a detailed discussion of the operation and financing of this nursery, see Sonya Michel, "Constructing a System of Care: Wage-Earning Mothers, Benevolent Women, and the Nineteenth-Century American Day Nursery," paper delivered to the American Historical Association, New York, 1990.

17. (Philadelphia) Home for Little Wanderers, *The Little Wanderer* 1.4 (March 1868): 18.

18. John Visher, *Handbook of Charities*, 3d edition (Chicago, 1897), 94; Lillie Hamilton French, "While the Mother Works: A Look at the Day Nurseries of New York," *Century Illustrated Monthly* (December 1902): 174–86; [Philadelphia] Day Nursery for Children, *Fourth Annual Report* (1867), 6.

19. [Philadelphia] Day Nursery for Children, *Eleventh Annual Report* (1874), n.p.

20. Some nurseries categorically excluded families in which this was suspected; see, for example, Nathaniel S. Rosenau, "The Fitch Crèche and the Labor Bureau of the Charity Organization Society of Buffalo," *Thirteenth Annual Conference of Charities and Correction* (1886), 179. But others believed that through the nursery, the lazy or intemperate father might be reached and reformed; see M. H. Burgess, "Day Nursery Work," *Nineteenth Annual Conference of Charities and Correction* (1892), 424.

21. N. S. Rosenau, "Day Nurseries," *Twenty-First National Conference of Charities and Correction* (1894), 334.

22. As a rule, nurseries did not accept infants, but took children from around the ages of one to six or seven—whenever they could enter school.

23. Nurseries almost always restricted their services to poor families that had only one wage earner, usually the mother. Low-income *two*-parent families also depended on mothers' wages, but they were normally deemed ineligible for nursery services.

24. This was common practice across the country; for one city, see Priscilla Ferguson Clement, *Welfare and the Poor in the Nineteenth-Century City: Philadelphia, 1800–1854* (Rutherford, N.J., 1985), chap. 4.

25. Male philanthropists did not readily see the benefit of such arrangements. The founders of the Leila Day Nursery in New Haven, Connecticut, in 1885 met with opposition from town leaders who contended "that two orphan asylums and a county children's home were sufficient to meet the child care needs of the community." Margaret O'Brien Steinfels, *Who's Minding the Children? The History and Politics of Day Care in America* (New York, 1973), 49.

26. The rate of labor-force participation for married women rose from 3.3 percent in 1890 to about 5.5 percent in 1900, and 9 percent in 1920. See Alice Kessler–Harris, *Out to Work: A History of Wage-Earning Women in the United States* (New York, 1982), 109, 122, and Claudia Goldin, *Understanding the Gender Gap: An Economic History of American Women* (New York, 1990), chap. 5. Goldin points out that the rate for African-American women was ten times higher than for white women in 1890. The census figures on which these calculations are based did not indicate the presence or age of children in the households of working women, but it can be assumed that if both the percentage and absolute number of married working women rose, the number of working mothers must have risen as well. Moreover, these figures are probably misleadingly low due to the undercounting of self-employed, part-time or homeworking mothers.

27. "The Children's House," pamphlet held at the Chicago Historical Society.

28. Ibid.

29. Mrs. Arthur Dodge, quoted in ibid.

30. The Exposition, with its Congress of Representative Women and Women's and Children's Buildings, served as a focal point for existing national women's organizations and galvanized others to form. Along with the NFDN, the National Association of Colored Women, the National Council of Jewish Women, and the General Federation of Women's Clubs, among others, were also formed at this time. See Anne Firor Scott, "Women's Voluntary Associations: From Charity to Reform," in Kathleen D. McCarthy, ed., *Lady Bountiful Revisited: Women, Philanthropy, and Power* (New Brunswick, N.J., 1990), 43–44.

31. Her conservative maternalism had both class and gender components; that is, she insisted that women's primary role should be that of motherhood, defined as the care of children in the home; and she opposed governmental intervention to correct social problems, preferring to leave such matters in the hands of private charities run by the social elite.

32. Mrs. Arthur Dodge, "Woman Suffrage Opposed to Woman's Rights," *Annals of the American Academy of Political and Social Sciences* 14 (November

1914): 100. Dodge's views were close to those of another conservative maternalist and antisuffragist active during this period, Elizabeth Lowell Putnam of Boston. Putnam, whose area of concern was maternal and child health, organized clinics and also lobbied for pure-milk laws in her home state, but later opposed federally supported measures like the Sheppard-Towner Act and tried to bring down the Children's Bureau. See Sonya Michel and Robyn Rosen, "The Paradox of Maternalism: Elizabeth Lowell Putnam and the American Welfare State," *Gender & History* 4,3 (1992): 364–86. Dodge's view on suffrage paralleled those of Mary (Mrs. Humphry) Ward, who also combined child welfare and antisuffrage work; see Seth Koven, "Borderlands: Women, Voluntary Action, and Child Welfare in Britain, 1840 to 1914," in this volume.

33. COS officials criticized governmental methods of distributing relief for pauperizing recipients by failing to change their habits and thus perpetuating dependency; see Daniel Levine, *Poverty and Society: The Growth of the American Welfare State in International Comparison* (New Brunswick, N.J., 1988), 29–30.

34. Mrs. Arthur Dodge, quoted in Federation of Day Nurseries, *Report of the Conference* (1905), 11 (hereafter cited as FDN, *Report*).

35. Edward Bunnell Phelps, "Some Possibilities of New Life and Broader Usefulness for the Day Nursery Movement in This Country," FDN, *Report* (1912), 50–51; and Mrs. Arthur Dodge, "Address of the President of the Federation," FDN, *Report* (1914), 17.

36. Phelps noted that the city of Los Angeles had established a day nursery near a public school in an immigrant neighborhood, though this had been done not at the urging of the NFDN but at the behest of the Board of Education to prevent truancy on the part of girls compelled to stay at home and play "little mother" to younger siblings. See Phelps, "Some Possibilities," 50.

37. According to Margaret Steinfels, only one nursery was ever dropped from membership for noncompliance; Steinfels, *Who's Minding the Children*, 54.

38. See Mrs. Arthur M. Dodge, "Address of the President of the Federation" (1914), 24; Mrs. R. R. Bradford, "Standardization of Day Nurseries," FDN, *Report* (1916), 60; and "Report of the Philadelphia Association of Day Nurseries," FDN, *Report* (1916), 106.

39. Mrs. A. [Josephine] Dodge, "The Development of the Day Nursery," *The Outlook* 56 (1897): 62.

40. One exception was the network of day nurseries and charitable kindergartens founded in Boston by philanthropist Pauline Agassiz Shaw, beginning in 1878. See M. H. Burgess, "The Evolution of 'The Children's House,'" *Kindergarten Review* 12 (1901–2): 401. See also Sonya Michel, "The Challenge to Educate: Day Nurseries and Early Childhood Education in the Progressive Era," paper delivered at the History of Education Society, Chicago, 1989, 11–13.

41. Elizabeth Rose, "Americanizing the Family: Class, Gender, and Ethnicity in a Jewish Settlement House," paper delivered to the Eighth Berkshire Conference on the History of Women, New Brunswick, N.J., 1990, 9.

42. Training for nursery personnel was always a problem. Beginning in the late nineteenth century, the Fitch Crèche of Buffalo offered a training program for nursery maids, in which an attempt was made to "dignify labor," but nursery managers always complained about the difficulty in attracting "the higher type of girl" into day-nursery work. See comments by Miss Love of the Fitch Crèche, FDN, *Report* 1914, 9. For details on qualifications and wages for staff, see Anne Durst, "Day Nurseries and Wage-Earning Mothers in the United States, 1890–1930," (Ph.D. diss., University of Wisconsin-Madison, 1989), chap. 4.

43. For a more detailed discussion of this problem, see Michel, "Challenge to Educate."

44. Mrs. Arthur M. Dodge, "Address of the President of the Federation," FDN, *Report* (New York, 1906), 10.

45. The following discussion is based on data drawn from FDN *Reports* From 1916, 1919, 1922, 1925, and 1929. On the child-health movement, see Richard Meckel, *Save the Babies: American Public Health Reform and the Prevention of Infant Mortality, 1850–1929* (Baltimore, 1990).

46. See Meckel, *Save the Babies*, chap. 4, for a discussion of maternal education as part of the child-health movement.

47. Mrs. William Conger and Miss Ward, "District Nursing in Relation to Day Nurseries," FDN, *Report* (1905), 53–55.

48. See Michel B. Katz, *In the Shadow of the Poorhouse* (New York, 1986), 118–21.

49. Mrs. Arthur M. Dodge, "Recognition—Co-Operation," FDN, *Report* (1905), 10. At the same conference, the Rev. Harris E. Adriance, another New York COS official, also praised day nurseries for preserving families; see Adriance, "The Day Nursery as a Conserver of the Home," FDN, *Report* (1905), 18–21.

50. Edward T. Devine, "The Need of Co-Operation between Day Nurseries and Other Organizations," FDN, *Report* (1905), 17.

51. Dodge, "Address" (1906), 7.

52. Scott, "Women's Voluntary Associations," 48.

53. Comments by Dodge, FDN, *Report* (1914), 11.

54. See Roy Lubove, *The Professional Altruist: The Emergence of Social Work as a Career, 1880–1930* (Cambridge, Mass., 1965).

55. Durst, "Day Nurseries," esp. chap. 4.

56. Edward Devine, *The Principles of Relief* (New York, 1910), 339.

57. Bradford, "Standardization," 56.

58. See Rev. Joseph E. Smith, "The Care of Neglected Children," in *Social and Physical Condition of Negroes in Cities*, Atlanta University Publications 2 (Atlanta, 1897), 41–42. On racial differences among maternalists generally, see Eileen Boris, "The Power of Motherhood: Black and White Activist Women Redefine the 'Political,' " in this volume, and Linda Gordon, "Black and White Visions of Welfare: Women's Welfare Activism, 1890–1945," *Journal of American History* 78 (1991): 559–90.

59. This was especially true throughout the South, where there was a high concentration of black female-headed households in urban areas. See Orville Vernon Burton, "The Rise and Fall of Afro-American Town Life: Town and Country in Reconstructed Edgefield, South Carolina," in Burton and Robert C. McMath, Jr., eds., *Toward a New South? Studies in Post–Civil War Southern Communities* (Westport, Conn., 1982), 152–92.

60. Jane Addams, quoted in "The Day Nursery Discussed by Miss Addams," *Charities and the Commons* 15 (1905): 411. The "results" she had in mind were reports of encounters between these children and the police, sometimes leading to arrests for loitering, petty theft, and similar offenses.

61. Jane Addams, *Twenty Years at Hull-House* (1910; rpt. New York, 1960), 130–31.

62. In fact, day nurseries never achieved the level of popularity NFDN leaders had envisioned; in the social-welfare literature from about 1900–1920, the number of articles, conference addresses, and studies on day nurseries was far smaller than those concerning mothers' and widows' pensions. At the 1911 conference held in conjunction with the Chicago Child Welfare Exhibit, for example, day nurseries were not even mentioned, even though prominent activists involved with child care, such as Jane Addams and Julia Lathrop, participated. The National Federation of Day Nurseries was not represented. See Sophonisba P. Breckinridge, ed., *The Child in the City* (Chicago, 1912).

63. Julia C. Lathrop, "The Day Nursery Child and His Future," FDN, *Report* (1905), 30.

64. Lee R. Frankel, quoted in "National Conference on Day Nurseries: A Report," *Charities* 14 (1905): 777.

65. McClintock, "Shoring Up the Family," and Amy E. Holmes, " 'Such Is the Price We Pay': American Widows and the Civil War Pension System," in Maris Vinovskis, ed., *Toward a Social History of the American Civil War: Exploratory Essays* (New York, 1990), 171–95. Only the dependents of Union soldiers were eligible for federal benefits; after the war, some southern states passed pension legislation for Confederate veterans and their dependents.

66. McClintock, "Shoring Up the Family."

67. It should be noted that, because of widespread corruption in pension distribution, *all* pension recipients, including veterans themselves, were subject to scrutiny, but women alone were subjected to investigation concerning their sexual morality.

68. McClintock, "Shoring Up the Family," 8.

69. However troublesome the application process, pensions made a critical difference in the household economies of dependent families; see Holmes, " 'Such Is the Price.' "

70. See Katz, *In the Shadow*, chap. 3. According to the theory of "scientific charity" on which the Charity Organization operated, outdoor relief "pauperized" its recipients by undermining their will to work and become independent.

71. Lee Frankel, quoted in "Summary," FDN, *Report* (1905), 7.

72. Theodore Roosevelt, quoted in U.S. Senate, *Conference on Care of Dependent Children*, 36.

73. "The Needy Mother and the Neglected Child," *The Outlook* 104 (7 June 1913); rpt. in Bullock, *Selected Articles*, 25.

74. Merritt W. Pinckney, quoted in Frederic C. Howe and Marie Jenney Howe, "Pensioning the Widowed and the Fatherless," *Good Housekeeping* 57 (September 1913); rpt. in Bullock, *Selected Articles*, 119–20.

75. Mary Conyngton, *How to Help* (New York, 1909), 186; quoted in Leff, "Consensus for Reform," 398.

76. Theodore Roosevelt, quoted in U.S. Senate, *Conference on Care of Dependent Children*, 36.

77. For a detailed discussion of the different groups involved and the political differentiations among them, see Leff, "Consensus for Reform."

78. Ibid., 402–13.

79. See Theda Skocpol, *Protecting Soldiers and Mothers* (Cambridge, Mass., 1992), chap. 8. One exception to this pattern was Illinois, where individual reformers such as Julia Lathrop, Edith Abbott, and Sophonisba Breckinridge played key roles in formulating legislation, but where grass-roots women's organizations were less important; see Joanne Goodwin, "Gender, Politics, and Welfare Reform: Mothers' Pensions in Chicago, 1900–1930," (Ph.D. diss., University of Michigan, 1991), chap. 4 and 290.

80. One of the best discussions of the corruption of the system, largely due to political patronage, is Ann Shola Orloff, "The Political Origins of America's Belated Welfare State," in Weir, Orloff, and Skocpol, *The Politics of Social Policy*, 45–52.

81. Leff, "Consensus for Reform," 399. He also notes that Oklahoma and Michigan used public funds to pay "school scholarships" to the children of indigent widows.

82. In a certain sense, these organizations were only as good as their state connections allowed them to be. The GFWC had affiliates in all 48 states by 1912, while the NCM had branches in only 22 states by 1911 and 36 by 1919; see Skocpol, *Protecting Mothers and Soldiers*, chap. 8.

83. Skocpol, *Protecting Soldiers and Mothers*, 456–65. The establishment of the U.S. Children's Bureau in 1912 gave maternalists a beachhead in Washington, but its clout remained minimal for some time, and its early chiefs, Julia Lathrop and then Grace Abbott, continued to work through lines of power that traced down through state and local agencies and organizations. The Bureau worked with existing organizations and encouraged the creation of state-level bases where there were none; for example, according to Robyn Muncy, Lathrop saw to it that agencies of maternal and child health were established in as many states as possible, usually headed by someone *she* had handpicked and with whom she remained in constant contact. See Muncy, *Creating a Female Dominion in American Reform, 1890–1935* (New York, 1991), 100–101.

84. Skocpol, *Protecting Soldiers and Mothers*, 448.

85. Mrs. [Frederick] Schoff, "Laying Foundations of Race Betterment," *Third International Congress on the Welfare of the Child* (Washington, D.C., 1914), 9.

86. GFWC, *Official Report of the Eleventh Biennial Convention* (1912), 185; quoted in Skocpol, *Protecting Mothers and Soldiers*, 443.

87. Mary Wood, "The Legal Side of Industrial Betterment," GFWC, *Official Report of the Eleventh Biennial Convention*, 185; quoted in Skocpol, *Protecting Soldiers and Mothers*, 443. This claim that motherhood should be seen as the equivalent of solidering was made in the strongest and most explicit terms by Australian feminists struggling for an endowment of motherhood during the same period; for example, they compared the physical risks of childbirth with those of battle. See Lake, "A Revolution in the Family."

88. L. T. Hobhouse, quoted in William Hard, "The Moral Necessity of 'State Funds to Mothers,' " *Survey* 29 (1913): 773; Hard's italics. British and American policy movements sometimes influenced one another reciprocally; according to Jane Lewis, later in the decade British reformers pointed to the success of mothers' pension policies in the U.S. as an argument to extend them in their own country. See Lewis, "Models of Equality for Women: The Case of State Support for Children in Twentieth-Century Britain," in Gisela Bock and Pat Thane, eds., *Maternity and Gender Policies* (London, 1991), 73–92.

89. Hard, "Moral Necessity," 773.

90. Ann Shola Orloff, "Gender in Early U.S. Social Policy," *Journal of Policy History* 3 (1991): 249–81; Wendy Sarvasy, "Beyond the Difference versus Equality Policy Debates: Postsuffrage Feminism, Citizenship, and the Quest for a Feminist Welfare State," *Signs* 17 (1992): 329–62; and Molly Ladd-Taylor, "Mothers' Pensions: Payment for Childrearing or Charity for Children?" paper presented to the Conference on Women's History and Public Policy, Sarah Lawrence College, 1989.

91. Orloff, "Gender in Early U.S. Social Policy," 252.

92. Barbara Nelson, "The Origins of the Two-Channel Welfare State: Workmen's Compensation and Mothers' Aid," in Gordon, *Women, the State, and Welfare*, 123–51.

93. For example, Colorado's mothers' pension law, one of the earliest in the nation, stated, "This act shall be liberally construed for the protection of the child, the home, and the state, and in the interest of public morals, and for the prevention of poverty and crime"; quoted in Ben B. Lindsey, "The Mothers' Compensation Law of Colorado," *Survey* 29 (1913): 716.

94. "Resolutions Adopted by the Second International Congress on Child Welfare, National Congress of Mothers," *Child-Welfare Magazine* 5,10 (June 1911): 196; quoted in Skocpol, *Protecting Soldiers and Mothers*, 451–2.

95. Address on Mothers' Pensions before the Congress of Mothers at Washington, D.C., from *The Texas Motherhood Magazine*, quoted in Mary E. Richmond, "Motherhood and Pensions," in Bullock, *Selected Articles*, 64; italics in original.

96. Goodwin, "Gender, Politics, and Welfare Reform," 276. Between 1911 and 1927, 49 percent of applicants were denied on grounds of "economic sufficiency"; 8 percent for lack of cooperation; and 4 percent for lack of fitness or moral standards. The other 37 percent were deemed legally ineligible because of technicalities in the law concerning nativity, citizenship, and marital status (desertion was usually disqualified).

97. The various types of administrative structures are laid out in David, "Mothers' Pensions," 579–80.

98. Though the COS and other social-work organizations had initially opposed pensions, chiefly on the grounds that they, like other forms of "outdoor relief," pauperized recipients, they now rushed in to fill the administrative vacuum and put their own stamp on the policy through the use of casework. For charity workers' opposition, see articles by Mary E. Richmond, Frederic Almy, C. C. Carstens, and Edward T. Devine in Bullock, *Selected Articles*.

99. For a detailed description of the process in Chicago, see C. C. Carstens, "Public Pensions to Widows with Children," *Survey* 29 (1913); rpt. in Bullock, *Selected Articles*, 161–64. For other locales, see A. E. Sheffield, "Administration of the Mothers' Aid Law in Massachusetts," *Survey* 31 (1914): 644–45, and Gertrude Vaile, "Administering Mothers' Pensions in Denver," *Survey* 31 (1914): 673–5; both also in Bullock.

100. For example, in 1914, the board of Hamilton County, Ohio, included two businessmen, a vice-president of Associated Charities who was also a minister, a labor union officer and journalist, and two middle-class wives; see T. J. Edmonds and Maurice B. Hexter, "State Pensions to Mothers in Hamilton County, Ohio," *Survey* 32 (1914): 289–90; rpt. in Bullock, *Selected Articles*.

101. Joanne Goodwin paraphrasing Edith Abbott, "The Experimental Period of Widows' Pension Legislation," *Proceedings, National Conference of Social Work* (1917), 154–65, in Goodwin, "Gender, Politics, and Welfare Reform," 219.

102. See Libba Gaje Moore, "Mothers' Pensions: The Origins of the Relationship between Women and the Welfare State," (Ph.D. diss., University of Massachusetts-Amherst, 1986), 148.

103. Moore calculates that in 1931, "[a]bout half of the black families aided nationwide were from counties in Ohio and Pennsylvania"; "Mothers' Pensions," 158. Goodwin shows that in Chicago from 1910 to 1930, the proportion of Afro-American households receiving mothers' pensions was at least 1 percentage point, and usually 2, less than their proportion of the population; "Gender, Politics, and Welfare Reform," 253. See also Leff, "Consensus for Reform," 414.

104. Moore, "Mothers' Pensions," 156.

105. Ibid., 145. On the surface, mothers' pensions appeared to grant women more autonomy in raising their children than they were afforded by, for example, day nurseries, but because of the intense surveillance to which they were subjected, pension recipients were in fact quite limited.

106. "Statement of Miss Sophie Irene Loeb," before U.S. Senate, Subcommittee of the Committee on the District of Columbia, 11 January 1926, 10. My thanks to Caroline Waldron for drawing my attention to this document.

107. Ibid., 13–14.

108. In most states, the process was also time-consuming and drawn out, adding to the anxieties and desperation of the applicants; see Nelson, "Origins of the Two-Channel Welfare State."

109. See Skocpol, *Protecting Soldiers and Mothers,* chap. 8. By 1927, mothers' aid laws had been passed in all but two states.

110. Pennsylvania was one of these; see Emil Frankel, "Source of Income, Standards of Mothers' Work and of Children's Education in Families Aided by the Pennsylvania Mothers' Assistance Fund," *Proceedings of the National Conference of Social Work,* 54th Annual Session (1927), 523–57. The 1927 study showed that $4,000,000 was needed to fund all who were eligible, but that year the legislature appropriated only $2,750,000, which was still an increase of $1 million from the previous biennium (257).

111. Allotments were calculated on the basis of so much *per child;* there was no funding for the support of the mother per se; see Davis, "Mothers' Pensions," 578–79; see also Moore, "Mothers' Pensions," 174–79. Moore calculates that in 1918, the minimum cost of living for a mother and three children was $1000 per year, or $83 per month; yet the maximum grant in all states fell short of that, ranging from as low as $20 to only as high as $60 or $70. Pensions for Civil War veterans' dependents, by contrast, had been relatively generous. See McClintock, "Shoring Up the Family," and Holmes, " 'Such Is the Price.' "

112. Frankel, "Source of Income," 256.

113. In the 1910s, these included Idaho, Illinois, Missouri, New Hampshire, Ohio, South Dakota, and Utah; see May, "Home Life," 257.

114. Moore, "Mothers' Pensions," 182–83. Most states also prohibited women from keeping boarders, a time-honored wage-earning strategy, particularly among immigrant women, but one that supervisors frowned upon as immoral.

115. Rather, they were calculated as an allowance *for children,* on the more or less implicit assumption that the mother would somehow support herself. This reasoning stems from the fact that one of the original arguments for mothers' and widows' pensions was that they would cost the same as, or less than, the state was paying to keep children in institutions. See Mary E. Shinnick, "Pensioning of Widows," *Second National Conference of Catholic Charities* (1912), 122–26, and David F. Tilley, "Review of the Legislation Relating to Mothers' Pensions," *Third National Conference of Catholic Charities* (1914), 129–40. See also Bullock, *Selected Articles.*

116. Goodwin, "Gender, Politics, and Welfare Reform," 204–5.

117. Ibid., 254. In general, mothers' pensions brought with them increased surveillance of poor families, including closer regulation of the types of work mothers were allowed to take.

118. "Report of the New York Association," FDN, *Report* (1916), 98.

119. Grace Caldwell, "Standards of Admission to Day Nurseries," FDN, *Report* (1919), 54.

120. See Susan Householder Van Horn, *Women, Work, and Fertility, 1900–1986* (New York, 1988), 6, and Claudia Goldin, *Understanding the Gender Gap*, chaps. 2 and 5.

121. Eva Whiting White, "Day Nurseries in the Child Welfare Program," *Day Nursery Bulletin* 6, 9 (July 1930): 3. White was president of the Women's Educational and Industrial Union.

122. Charlotte Perkins Gilman, "Pensions for 'Mothers' and 'Widows,' " *The Forerunner* 5 (January 1914): 7.

123. See Ann J. Lane, *To Herland and Beyond: The Life and Work of Charlotte Perkins Gilman* (New York, 1990), chap. 9.

124. Lane, *To Herland*, 262.

125. Benita Locke, "Mothers' Pensions: The Latest Capitalist Trap," *The Woman Rebel* 1,1 (March 1914): 4–5.

126. Nor was an alternative forthcoming from the maternalists' sworn enemy, the National Women's party (NWP). The party repeatedly expressed its support for the inalienable right of women—both married and single—to work, and claimed that women took paid employment not for frivolous reasons but out of necessity. They seemed reluctant, however, to explore fully the social implications that arose when mothers exercised such a right, or to take the logical next step of calling for universal child care to support it. Instead, at least some NWP members seemed to share the NADN's restricted position on employment for mothers of young children. Mrs. Harvey Wiley, chairman of the Homemaker's Council of the Woman's party, wrote in *Equal Rights* in 1923, "In my opinion women with young children should stay at home, unless they are compelled to go out and earn money. . . . Personally I do not believe in the combination of a career with the rearing of young children unless stern necessity compels the mother not only to make her contribution of service to the home but also to supply the money with which to create it." Wiley, "The Work of the Woman's Party," *Equal Rights* 1,3 (3 March 1923): 21. Wiley and other NWP members came out squarely in support of mothers' pensions and also called for a more universal "endowment of motherhood," echoing the demands of many British feminists. (On the British movement, see Lewis, "Models of Equality.")

127. For an expression of this sense of entitlement, see the Congressional testimony of Beulah Sanders, vice-chairman of the National Welfare Rights Organization and chair of the New York Citywide Coordinating Committee of Welfare Groups; U.S. Congress, Joint Economic Committee, *Hearings on Income Maintenance Programs, June 1968*, vol. 1 (Washington, D.C., 1968), 66–71. My thanks to Ben Donovan for bringing this document to my attention.

128. See Nancy Fraser, "Struggle over Needs: Outline of a Socialist-Feminist Critical Theory of Late-Capitalist Political Culture," in Gordon, ed., *Women, the State, and Welfare*, esp. 221.

129. Compare the American maternalists' views with those of the Australian feminists described by Lake in "Revolution in the Family."

130. See Kathryn Kish Sklar, "The Historical Foundations of Women's Power in the Creation of the American Welfare State, 1830–1930," in this volume.

9

"My Work Came Out of Agony and Grief": Mothers and the Making of the Sheppard-Towner Act

Molly Ladd-Taylor

Several months after the 1921 Sheppard-Towner Maternity and Infancy Protection Act was passed, an Alabama mother wrote the federal Children's Bureau to inquire if the stories about the bill's provisions were true. "If so I sure am glad," she wrote. "I do hope it will help us Poor Country people who need help. We live on a farm and have very hard work to do. I am 27 yrs. old and have Five Little one's to Care for besides my husband an[d] his Father."[1] Many other working-class and farm mothers wrote similar letters asking the government for help with child care and expressing hope that the "maternity bill" would improve their health and make their work easier. Indeed, the Sheppard-Towner Act was the product of an unusual alliance between grass-roots mothers, club women, and Children's Bureau officials. Children's Bureau chief Julia Lathrop learned from her correspondence and personal contacts with poor women about their ill health and suffering, and she designed the Maternity and Infancy Act, which provided education for pregnant women and new mothers, with their needs and requests in mind. Grass-roots mothers thus played an important if indirect role in the creation of one of the earliest United States social-welfare measures.

Scholars of women's role in the formation of American maternal-and child-welfare policy have stressed the interaction between

---

This essay is adapted from chapter 6 of *Mother-Work: Women, Child Welfare, and the State, 1890–1930* (Urbana: University of Illinois Press, in press), © 1994 by the Board of Trustees of the University of Illinois Press.

women's voluntary associations and female reformers in government.[2] However, we know less about the part women clients
played in policy formation. The extensive correspondence
between grass-roots mothers and the federal Children's Bureau
staff makes the Sheppard-Towner Act a promising starting point
for investigation. The Children's Bureau correspondence shows
that public maternal- and child-health services were not simply
imposed by middle-class maternalists on an unwilling (or even
willing) population. Sheppard-Towner grew partly out of what
one historian called a "powerful if unsteady pressure" from poor
and working-class women who struggled with the arduous work
of reproduction and caregiving and sought more control over their
health and working lives.[3]

The first "women's" legislation to pass after women won the
vote, the Sheppard-Towner Act provided federal matching grants
to the states for information and instruction on nutrition and
hygiene, prenatal and child-health clinics, and visiting nurses for
pregnant women and new mothers. The bill, written by Children's
Bureau chief Julia Lathrop and sponsored by Texas senator Morris Sheppard and Iowa congressman Horace Towner, was modeled on the 1914 Smith-Lever Act, which provided federal
matching funds for agricultural extension programs. A modest
bill that provided only education but not material assistance or
medical care, Sheppard-Towner passed Congress by a wide margin and was signed into law by President Warren G. Harding
on 23 November 1921. Despite its narrow provisions, Sheppard-
Towner was vigorously opposed by a coalition of medical associations and right-wing organizations, who claimed it was a commu-
nist-inspired step toward state medicine that threatened the home
and violated the principle of states' rights. The anti–Sheppard-
Towner coalition gained strength over the course of the 1920s,
and in 1926, when the bill was to be renewed, it forced supporters
to accept a compromise that extended funding for two years, but
then repealed the law itself in 1929, thus ensuring that all federal
appropriations for maternal and infant care would cease.[4]

The 1921 enactment of the Sheppard-Towner Act was the culmi-
nation of long-standing efforts to get the government to take
responsibility for child welfare. Club women, settlement residents,
and public-health workers had engaged in infant-welfare work
since the 1880s, organizing infant and prenatal clinics, distributing pure milk to needy children, and running educational pro-

grams for mothers. In 1908, New York City established the Bureau of Child Hygiene of the New York Department of Health, the nation's first tax-supported child-health agency. By 1923, forty-eight states had bureaus of child hygiene, all but three of them headed by women. The activities of state child-health agencies were modeled on the prenatal and maternal-education programs pioneered by voluntary organizations such as the Boston Women's Municipal League; they, in turn, served as the model for the 1921 Sheppard-Towner Act.[5]

Although the Sheppard-Towner Act was the product of the mainstream Progressive Era maternalist movement, it was in many ways unique among maternalist reforms. Like many female reformers, Sheppard-Towner supporters accepted and reinforced the idea that women were primarily responsible for children's welfare, and promoted a narrow view of homelife that often conflicted with working-class values. Yet unlike other efforts to protect motherhood (such as mothers' pensions and protective labor legislation), the Sheppard-Towner Act was conceived as an entitlement for all women, not just the poor. The maternity act was also unusual in that some of the women who campaigned for the bill became "clients" of Sheppard-Towner programs. Although the bill was intended primarily for those who did not have access to private physicians, Sheppard-Towner "clients" included middle-class women who read the best-selling Children's Bureau publication *Infant Care* and attended lectures on child health as well as impoverished women who were visited by public-health nurses at home. Clients probably influenced the development of all welfare programs, but they played an especially large role in the campaign for the Sheppard-Towner Act, sometimes writing letters to the government or joining committees to secure the bill's passage. In contrast to other welfare programs, the implementation as well as enactment of the Maternity and Infancy Act depended as much on the voluntary activities of individual and organized women as on the work of professionals.[6]

Sheppard-Towner was a priority of women activists both because maternalists assumed that child welfare was women's responsibility and because so many women had been personally touched by the dangers of childbirth and infant death. In 1915, approximately six women and one hundred infants died for every 1,000 live births in the U.S. birth-registration area. Deaths were even greater outside the registration area, and mortality was twice as high among people of color. Nationally, eleven African-American women and 181 black infants died for every 1,000 live births.[7] Few were untouched by the suffering; one historian estimated that one woman in thirty might be expected to die from childbirth-related causes over the course of her fertile years.[8] Children's Bureau chief Julia Lathrop, who was named for an aunt who had died as a child, had a grandmother who died in childbirth.[9] National Consumers' League director Florence Kelley, a leading child-welfare reformer, was one of eight children, all but three of whom died in infancy and early childhood.[10] Jane Addams, the eighth of nine children, was just two years old when her mother and a new baby died from complications of childbirth. Three other Addams children had already died, two of them before their first birthdays.[11] Physician Dorothy Reed Mendenhall, one of the few married women on the Children's Bureau staff, lost two children before they were four years old and suffered permanent injury as a result of bad obstetrics. Her grandmother too had died in childbirth. "Undoubtedly," Mendenhall later reflected, "the tragic death of my first child . . . was the dominant factor in my interest in the chief function of women, 'the bearing and rearing of children.' Most of my work came out of my agony and grief. . . . *A mother never forgets*."[12]

Sheppard-Towner proponents turned women's private suffering to political advantage. In eloquent testimony in congressional hearings, Florence Kelley charged that the large number of preventable deaths betrayed the low value society placed on women's and children's lives. She insisted that women deeply resented the fact that congressmen claimed that government could not afford to provide health care for women and children, even though they legislated salary and pension increases for postal employees and veterans. "No woman in the United States would begrudge those increases of salaries," she said angrily, "but when we are told that this country is so poor and this Congress so harassed by things of greater importance than the deaths of a quarter of a million of children a year . . . we say to ourselves, 'Surely we are not to take this seriously? . . . Why does Congress wish women and children to die?' "[13]

The most important organization in the maternal- and infant-health movement in the 1910s and 1920s was the U.S. Children's Bureau, established in 1912 as a division of the Department of Commerce and Labor. Originally the idea of Kelley, a longtime settlement resident, and Lillian Wald, nurse and founder of New York's Henry Street Settlement, the federal Children's Bureau was brought into existence by a coalition of settlement-house residents, club women and child-welfare reformers. Its first two directors were former Hull House residents Julia Lathrop (from 1912 to 1921) and Grace Abbott (from 1921 to 1934). As the first federal agency headed and staffed primarily by women, the Children's Bureau operated as women's branch of the federal government in the 1910s and 1920s. It built on the work of voluntary women's organizations, but invested them with new legitimacy and coordinated their disparate activities into an effective nationwide campaign for maternal- and child-welfare reform.[14]

The Children's Bureau was both the product of women's welfare activism and an inspiration for it, although the agency's small budget and limited mandate suggest the Congress initially intended it to be merely symbolic. Limited by law to research and educational activities, the Bureau began with an appropriation of only $25,640 and a small staff of fifteen—fewer resources than many private child-welfare organizations had at the time. However, Children's Bureau chief Julia Lathrop successfully overcame the problem of limited resources by using her close ties to women's clubs, social settlements, and labor and civic groups to build grassroots support for the federal agency. Convinced, like other Progressive reformers, that education and research could lead to social change, she designed a baby-saving campaign comprised of the popular pamphlets *Infant Care* and *Prenatal Care*, a birth-registration drive, and investigations into infant mortality that she hoped would build public support for the federal agency. It did. In 1914, Lathrop successfully mobilized club women, the press, and her reform network to pressure politicians to increase Children's Bureau funding. After a difficult fight, the Bureau won an appropriation of $139,000, over five times greater than that of the previous year.[15]

The influence of settlement-house ideology is evident in the style of the Children's Bureau and in the design of the Sheppard-Towner Act. Like most settlement workers, Lathrop and her staff used maternalist rhetoric to justify women's involvement in the political arena and federal involvement in child welfare. Although they consciously sought to expand employment opportunities for educated women, the Children's Bureau staff did not challenge the assumption that women were primarily responsible for children's welfare. Despite choosing career over marriage and family in their own lives, Lathrop and her colleagues assumed that most women would marry, have children, and remain at home.[16]

The Children's Bureau staff also held the social-settlement belief in the reciprocal dependence of the social classes. Convinced, like Hull House founder Jane Addams, that social conflicts could be resolved by building personal relationships across classes and cultures, Lathrop kept the Children's Bureau in close touch with its constituency. Whether giving child-health demonstrations or conducting investigations into infant mortality, staff members in the field depended on the cooperation of local women's clubs and individual mothers. That only two of 1,553 mothers visited during an investigation of infant mortality in Johnstown, Pennsylvania, refused to be interviewed by Bureau agents is a testament both to the sensitivity of the Bureau staff and to mothers' desire for government involvement with child health.[17] But the federal Bureau's biggest success at building cross-class alliances occurred through the mail. The agency received hundreds of letters each month, and staff members responded personally to every one. The Bureau's unusually close interaction with grass-roots women benefited its employees as well as its supporters and clients. Club women felt part of a national baby-saving movement with a leadership responsive to their concerns. Poor mothers received needed information and, occasionally, money, clothes, and nursing care paid for out of their own pockets by the Bureau staff or donated by Children's Bureau contacts.

Equally important, the Bureau staff found meaningful work and got an education about the poverty and ill health of many American mothers. Lathrop, for example, was deeply moved by the strength of a Wyoming mother expecting her third child who lived 65 miles from a doctor and was "filled with perfect horror at the prospects ahead." The two women had a lengthy correspondence, and Lathrop make a personal contribution to the mother's layette and sent a public-health doctor to visit. Appealing to wealthy friends, she raised $157.61 for hospital and medical fees and for the woman's room and board in town.[18]

Lathrop's 1916 correspondence with an Idaho mother exemplifies her effort to build a bond with her constituents. Pregnant with her fifth child, Mrs. M. R. lived twenty-five miles from a doctor, was burdened by overwork and poverty, and feared she would die. "Talk about better babys," she wrote bitterly, "when a mother must be like some cow or mare when a babys come. If she lives, all wright, and if not, Just the same." Lathrop wrote back with a "great deal of sympathy" and expressed her hope that some day "our country will be so organized that there will be a doctor and nurse stationed . . . so that no one can be twenty-five miles from a physician." Enclosing the Bureau's infant-care bulletins, Lathrop explained that their author was herself the mother of five. "They were all very young when she was left a widow and had to begin to earn a living for them and for herself. That took courage, and I can see plainly that your life requires great courage too." Most women responded warmly to such encouraging words; one young woman wrote a staff physician that "words cannot express what I feel for you in my heart. I can only write that I thank you infinitely for your kindness towards helping me with my baby."[19]

In the context of today's despised welfare system, it seems remarkable that many working-class and farm mothers viewed Children's Bureau officials more as benevolent distant aunts than as intrusive federal bureaucrats. Bureau files contain many letters from women who felt they had benefited from their interaction with Bureau agents and from the attention of the Bureau's local supporters. In one case, a pregnant mother of three from Chicago wrote a nasty letter to the Children's Bureau, explaining bitterly that she was abused by her husband and that local charities refused to help her. Yet after Lathrop wrote her a sympathetic letter and sent Alice Hamilton of Hull House to visit, the woman wrote back to apologize for the tone of her earlier letter. Hamilton was so supportive, she wrote, "so different from the other people I have met."[20] Perhaps because their contact with the Bureau was indirect (through the mail) and sporadic (personal attention came from an occasional visitor, rather than a caseworker)—and perhaps because Bureau officials could give small amounts of money or clothes but could not withdraw material assistance—poor women felt they only gained from contact with the federal agency.

Federal involvement in maternal and infant welfare gave legitimacy to women's concerns about their health, raised their expectations for care, and inspired some of them into activism. "It seems strange that conditions . . . year after year . . . have been perfectly needless," the Wyoming woman wrote to Lathrop "It is only necessary to make the people realize that their conditions are not normal." Like many other Children's Bureau correspondents, she volunteered to help the agency "in any way." Although the records do not reveal whether individual letter writers became welfare activists, it is clear that baby saving became a grass-roots movement of enormous proportion. In 1918, the second year of World War I, eleven million women participated in the Children's Bureau baby-saving campaign. The same year, Jeannette Rankin of Montana, the nation's first congresswoman, introduced the maternity bill into Congress.[21]

After the suffrage victory in 1920, women's organizations across the country made the passage of the Maternity and Infancy Act (then sponsored by Senator Sheppard and Congressman Towner) their top priority. The National Congress of Mothers and Parent-Teacher Associations, the League of Women Voters, the General Federation of Women's Clubs, the Women's Trade Union League, the National Consumers' League, the National Council of Jewish Women, the Woman's Christian Temperance Union, the Daughters of the American Revolution, and the Business and Professional Women's Clubs were among the organizations supporting the bill. Coordinating their efforts through the newly formed Women's Joint Congressional Committee, they reputedly formed "one of the strongest lobbies that has ever been seen in Washington." Thousands of individual women also participated in the campaign. So many sent their congressmen petitions and letters urging passage of the bill that one senator's secretary remarked, "I think every woman in my state has written to the Senator."[22]

The well-organized women's lobby, combined with politicians' fears of provoking the wrath of newly enfranchised women voters, led to an easy victory, and the Sheppard-Towner Act passed the Senate by 63 to 7 and the House of Representatives by 279 to 39. Yet support for the bill was soft. "On a secret ballot I don't think it would have got 50 votes," observed Alice Robertson, the only woman in Congress and a staunch opponent of Sheppard-Towner. "Nineteen men who voted for it—so one of them told me—were cursing it and themselves at once in the cloak room."[23]

Although it was an important victory for maternalists, Sheppard-Towner represented a compromise with those who feared the growing power of the federal government (and of the women in it). The final version of the maternity bill was considerably weaker than the bill introduced in 1918 by Jeannette Rankin and Senator Joseph Robinson. The Rankin-Robinson bill specifically targeted rural areas, where mortality was thought highest, and it provided for "medical and nursing care at home or at a hospital when necessary," as well as instruction in hygiene. By contrast, Sheppard-Towner provided no hospital or medical care, forbade outright financial aid, reduced the Children's Bureau's authority over administration, and sharply cut appropriations. Unlike the Rankin-Robinson bill, which invested administrative authority in the Children's Bureau, Sheppard-Towner kept responsibility for the bill's daily administration with the Children's Bureau, but transferred ultimate authority to a newly created Federal Board of Maternity and Infant Hygiene, composed of the Children's Bureau chief, the surgeon general of the Public Health Service, and the U.S. Commissioner of Education. Furthermore, although the original Sheppard-Towner bill requested an appropriation of $4,000,000, the version that passed allocated only $1,480,000 for fiscal year 1921–22 and $1,240,000 for the next five years. No more than $50,000 was given to the U.S. Children's Bureau for administrative expenses; $5,000 went to each state outright and an additional $5,000 to states that provided matching funds. Most damaging, Congress appropriated funds for only five years, requiring the bill to be renewed in 1927.[24]

Although the Sheppard-Towner Act was mainly educational, the Children's Bureau learned in its early years that educational programs could be turned to advantage. A bill that did not provide material assistance and medical care could not entirely protect infant health, but Sheppard-Towner educational programs had an important political advantage: public education had already been established as a right available without loss of dignity or self-respect to people of all classes. Moreover, although government-sponsored instruction could be intrusive, Sheppard-Towner educational programs were not compulsory, at least for mothers. Clients were free to accept or ignore the experts' advice and to raise their children as they wished. Many women lacked vital information about reproduction and desperately wanted education that would give them more control of their bodies. Furthermore, Sheppard-Towner agents in the field performed preventive health examinations, assisted women during childbirth, and worked with the Red Cross and local women's groups to provide much-needed clothing and furniture to impoverished families. In the actual implementation of the bill, the line between health education, nursing care, and even material assistance was often blurred.

Like its educational provisions, Sheppard-Towner's concessions to states' rights proponents had both positive and negative effects. The bill gave states wide discretion in the development of maternity and infancy programs. Each state had to pass special enabling legislation and provide a plan for implementing the program before it could receive funds. This meant that Sheppard-Towner (like other American welfare programs) was marked by great local variation in funding and support. While the bill's decentralized administration had the advantage of allowing communities to devise programs that suited their needs, it also made maternity work vulnerable to political opposition and incompetent administration. Local politics, the personnel in the state bureaus of child health, attitudes of local physicians and civic leaders, and the state's climate and geography (such as snow, mountains, floods, and poor roads) determined the success or failure of Sheppard-Towner in each state.[25]

Most states responded quickly and enthusiastically to the Sheppard-Towner Act. Forty-one states passed enabling legislation in 1922, and eventually only three (Massachusetts, Connecticut, and Illinois) refused to do so. Almost every state used Sheppard-Towner funds to hold health conferences, make home visits, promote birth registration, and distribute literature, especially *Infant Care* and *Prenatal Care*. A number of states also organized training programs for midwives, conducted campaigns to immunize children against diptheria and smallpox, and promoted the use of silver nitrate to prevent blindness in infants. By 1929, the bill's last year of operation, the Children's Bureau estimated that Sheppard-Towner workers had held 183,252 prenatal and child-health conferences and helped establish 2,978 permanent health clinics. Public-health nurses visited 3,131,996 homes between 1923 and 1929 and distributed 22,030,489 pieces of literature in the last five years of the act. According to the Children's Bureau, Sheppard-Towner reached more 4,000,000 babies and 700,000 expectant mothers in its last four years alone.[26]

The most successful state programs used Sheppard-Towner funds both to provide services and to build a strong grass-roots campaign for maternal and child welfare. Literature distribution is a case in point. When mothers shared the pamphlets *Infant Care* and *Prenatal Care* with friends and relatives, they both passed on much-needed information and created a wider demand for health care. Similarly, child-health conferences provided useful services while building community support for public health care. The conferences could be social as well as educational events in rural areas; some communities closed schools, businesses, and stores so that everyone could attend. Families came for the films, refreshments, prizes, and festive atmosphere of the clinics, as well as for physical exams and child-rearing advice. Although attendance was likely to be small at a poorly organized clinic, conferences actively supported by local club women, civic leaders, and physicians were generally well attended. In 1924 over 200 women attended a meeting in a remote county in Mississippi. Some mothers rode horseback or walked several miles with small children to attend the conferences in one-room schoolhouses or local churches.[27]

In states where difficult terrain, inclement weather, lack of roads, or a busy harvest season made it difficult to get a crowd to clinics, nurses spent most of their time on home visits. They showed mothers how to prepare safe modified milk or get the house ready for childbirth, helped with delivery, and even treated sick children. After a New Mexico nurse taught a mother how to keep milk cool, clean, and free from flies, a fourteen-month-old boy weighing less than nine pounds began to gain weight. The same nurse also dispensed medicine which cured an eye infection and saved the sight of the woman's other child, a three-month-old baby who weighed only five pounds.[28]

In implementing the Sheppard-Towner Act, the federal Children's Bureau made a serious effort to reduce infant and maternal mortality among all racial and ethnic groups. Although most Sheppard-Towner workers were white, the Bureau employed African-American physician Ionia Whipper and a few black nurses to work in African-American communities; it also hired a few Spanish-speaking nurses to work among Mexicans and American Indians to work on reservations. However, Sheppard-Towner was premised on ideas about science and medicine that were rooted in the cultural beliefs of the Anglo-American middle class. In an attempt to save lives and provide up-to-date medical care to women of color, Bureau officials tried to suppress what they considered superstition and the dangerous healing practices of immigrants and African Americans, and to replace them with modern science and medicine. They assumed that educating ethnic women about new scientific thinking on child care would convince them that infant deaths were preventable and lead them to demand further health and welfare services.

Their secular faith in science and medicine sometimes put a wedge between Sheppard-Towner nurses and their patients. For example, prenatal examinations challenged traditional religious beliefs about feminine modesty and maternal suffering, and sometimes provoked opposition from the community. In Florida, six white women left a meeting of twenty after the nurse began to talk about prenatal care. "The Lord gives and the Lord takes and we have no business talking of such things," they reportedly said. Yet evidence from the Children's Bureau records suggests that many expectant mothers did want to be examined. "We find there is a great demand for examination on the part of women who are suffering from lack of care at previous childbirths," reported a North Dakota official. However, some women felt undeserving because their families considered prenatal care to be an unnecessary indulgence. Those embarrassed to seek help for themselves sometimes borrowed neighbors' children so that they could justify going to the clinics. Others fought with their families for their right to prenatal care, slowly changing social attitudes.[29]

Poor women were often grateful for health care, but they rarely abandoned traditional practices, such as employing midwives and having female friends and relatives present during childbirth. Most women combined old and new methods of child care and delivery, and rejected the efforts of Sheppard-Towner agents to replace traditional healing with modern medicine. In New Mexico, for example, the family of a woman who had been in labor for six days refused to relinquish the midwife's services, even though the doctor refused to help if she were there. Similarly, a Sheppard-Towner nurse in Montana reported with annoyance that a Native American family barred whites from intervening in a case they considered the domain of the traditional healer.[30]

Although Sheppard-Towner agents imposed their ideas about modern science and medicine on their clients, poor mothers were not passive victims of middle-class efforts to control their childbirth and child-rearing practices. They were free to accept or refuse government assistance, and, for the most part, they were enthusiastic about Sheppard-Towner services. For midwives, however, Sheppard-Towner programs were compulsory. Despite insisting that care given by trained midwives was just as good as medical care, Children's Bureau officials reproved what they considered the superstitious and unhygienic practices of African-American and immigrant midwives. They blamed untrained birth attendants for the high infant- and maternal-mortality rates in their communities, and concluded that lives could be saved by educating midwives and stopping the oldest and most "dangerous" of them from practicing.

In the thirty-one states that established midwife training programs, efforts to license and regulate midwives—most of whom were women of color—depended on the legal authority of Sheppard-Towner agents. Anglo-American nurses who were unfamiliar with local customs had the power to grant or withhold licenses, and thus to threaten the livelihood of local midwives. They did not hesitate to take advantage of what they considered midwives' "very wholesome fear" of license-granting agencies.

Understandably, many midwives were distrustful of the nurses and resented the government's intrusion into their practices; Sheppard-Towner agents in New Mexico reported difficulty locating Hispanic midwives who often hid out in the hills until the nurse left the county. As a result of Sheppard-Towner programs, the number of midwives dropped from over 6,000 to 4,339 in Virginia and from 4,209 to 3,040 in Mississippi. Some birth attendants were probably driven underground, continuing to practice but living in fear of prosecution, but others undoubtedly left the work out of fear or because of the reduced demand for their services.[31]

While many midwives resisted government efforts at instruction, there is evidence that others welcomed the training programs. Perhaps they saw midwife classes as a recognition of their work, a way to save lives and make their jobs easier, or a way to facilitate the nearly impossible task of collecting fees. Perhaps they found the classes entertaining and enjoyed the opportunity to win prizes, have their pictures taken, and drink Coca-Cola. Like the mothers who used Sheppard-Towner services, midwives turned government programs to their advantage and welcomed certain features of modern medicine. Anxious to save lives and improve health, they abandoned some traditional remedies and combined other practices with medical procedures they considered useful. As a result of Sheppard-Towner classes, a growing proportion of midwives paid attention to prenatal care, followed sanitary procedures such as substituting newspaper pads for old quilts during childbirth, and called doctors during difficult deliveries. But they also continued to use herbal treatments, favor traditional birth positions, and maintain certain rituals, such as placing a knife under the bed to "cut the pain" and burying the placenta.[32]

Although the Children's Bureau staff's cultural bias against traditional healing probably impeded maternity and infancy work in communities of color, the administrative structure of the Sheppard-Towner Act did so even more. Despite the Children's Bureau's efforts to extend health services to all sectors of the population, the bill's decentralized administration permitted states to provide inferior services to people of color. For example, although Native American infants in Montana were 2.7 times more likely to die than whites, the state did not have a full-time nurse on the reservations. Similarly, even though death rates were significantly higher among blacks, the Georgia State Board of Health hired an inexperienced nurse to work with African-American midwives because it considered the salary demanded by an experienced nurse "too much for any negro." The Children's Bureau staff, perhaps unwilling to jeopardize support for the Sheppard-Towner Act among white voters and politicians, did not comment.[33]

The Children's Bureau made a number of compromises in the process of lobbying for and administering the Sheppard-Towner Act. These concessions weakened the bill's impact, especially in communities of color, and contributed to its ultimate defeat. For example, although most members of the Children's Bureau's reform network believed that universally available medical and nursing care was a "minimum standard" for child welfare, they supported a bill that provided no medical care and gave the Children's Bureau little real control over Sheppard-Towner administration in the hopes that it would be more acceptable to medical and right-wing organizations. However, the passage of the Sheppard-Towner Act changed the role of the Children's Bureau from that of leader of a campaign to get the government to assume responsibility for child welfare into that of an administrator and defender of an existing—and inadequate—program. Bureau officials were caught between their roles as reform-minded "outsiders" who had little power in government and pragmatic "insiders" who could not afford to jeopardize the status quo if they were to mollify their opponents, defend their own positions in government, and protect the welfare programs for which they had fought so hard.[34]

Children's Bureau officials made a number of concessions to

the medical opponents of the Sheppard-Towner Act. In an attempt to quell doctors' fears that public-health services would threaten their incomes and control over the health-care system, they distinguished between the preventive public-health education Sheppard-Towner provided and private medical care. Physicians treated sick children, the Bureau argued, but infant-welfare clinics were educational and were geared toward the healthy child. In some states, Sheppard-Towner workers even refused to examine children who did not have permission from their doctors (if they had one).[35] Yet although many individual physicians supported the maternity bill, the Children's Bureau's efforts to appease doctors had little effect on the medical establishment. The American Medical Association questioned the expertise of the "lay" women of the Children's Bureau, insisting that maternity and infancy programs should be administered by the medically run Public Health Service, rather than by the female social workers (or female physicians) at the Children's Bureau. By improving obstetric training in medical schools and convincing doctors to incorporate the preventive health examinations popularized by the Sheppard-Towner Act into private medical practice, the AMA undercut the Children's Bureau's authority in child health.[36]

The time and energy of federal and state administrators were drained by fighting the persistent and increasingly influential opposition to the bill. On the national level, the energy of Children's Bureau staff members was diverted from helping state administrators implement maternity and infancy programs to fighting the two legal challenges to the bill's constitutionality and working to renew appropriations in 1926. In addition, since the law required each state to pass enabling legislation and renew funding in order to receive federal grants, there were also constant political battles in the states. Just two years after the Sheppard-Towner administrator in Oklahoma complained that she had "wasted" three months fighting proposed legislation to get rid of her agency, she had to fight a new Health Commissioner's efforts to stop distributing prenatal literature—the most successful part of the state's Sheppard-Towner program.[37]

In Nevada, one of two or three states which Grace Abbott felt was "not making some real headway," the poor administrative skills of the director were compounded by physicians' objections to the fact that the agency that administered the Sheppard-Towner Act was not directed by a doctor. As a result, the state's Sheppard-

Towner programs languished. A nurse in one of the richest counties in the state had no supplies except for scales; a nurse in another county had only three cases in one year. Discouraged by the ineffective services, some women activists lost the enthusiasm needed to sustain them during the difficult battles for renewal. "I am so thoroughly disgusted with the situation that I feel that I cannot waste any more time in trying to do something . . . so long as the present people are in charge," complained the president of the Nevada League of Women Voters.[38]

Despite its ineffectiveness in some areas, the Sheppard-Towner Act had a significant impact on the health of women and children across the country. By 1929, its last year of operation, the Children's Bureau estimated that almost one-half of all babies born in that year had been affected by its advice. According to the Bureau, infant deaths dropped from 76 to 69 per 1,000 live births between 1921, and 1928. Deaths due to gastrointestinal disease, most easily by educational programs, declined by 47 percent. However, among babies of color, mortality remained high. When Sheppard-Towner began in 1921, 108 babies of color died for every 1,000 live births; by 1928, the infant death rate had fallen only slightly, to 106 (compared to 64 for whites). The 1921 statistics were probably artificially low since several states with high African-American death rates had not yet joined the birth-registration area. Moreover, most rural people of color were so poor and conditions in their communities so dire, that the meager resources of the Sheppard-Towner Act were unable to make much of a dent in improving their health. The decentralized administration of the Sheppard-Towner Act and the Children's Bureau's cultural bias against traditional healing probably also lessened the effectiveness of maternity and infancy work among racial minorities.[39]

White farm women appear to have been the chief beneficiaries of Sheppard-Towner programs. Although Children's Bureau statistics actually showed a slightly higher infant-mortality rate in cities than in the country (possibly because birth registration often lagged behind there), Sheppard-Towner targeted rural areas. This is partly because health agencies had already been established in a number of cities; it is also no doubt because Julia Lathrop and her staff had been influenced by their correspondence and personal contacts with white farm women, who were the main audience for *Infant Care* and *Prenatal Care* and thus the principal clients of the Children's Bureau. Targeting the country was astute not only because white farm women already shared the Bureau's cultural values regarding family life, science, and medicine, but also because there was less danger of conflict with the medical profession, since the specialists who dominated the AMA had less influence in rural areas.[40]

Women's enthusiasm for Sheppard-Towner services is documented in the letters they wrote to the federal and state children's bureaus. A West Virginia mother of twins wrote to her state child-health department, "I trust you'll find by many letters that your work is doing much and will continue it. There are many who do not Pay attention But It Is a great Benefit to those that do." A Georgia woman agreed, "I don't see how we poor mothers could do without them [prenatal clinics]. . . . I am the mother of 14 children, and I never was cared for till I begin going to the good will center clinic. . . . We are so glad the day has come when we have someone to care for our babies when they get sick."[41]

Yet neither evidence of Sheppard-Towner's accomplishments nor of women's support for the measure could ensure its renewal in the conservative 1920s. The 1924 elections brought into power a Congress more concerned with cutting taxes than with providing for social welfare, and a president who was an ally of big business and critic of a strong federal government. Also, politicians who supported the Sheppard-Towner Act in 1921 because of its sentimental appeal to motherhood and their fear of the unknown female vote knew by the end of the 1920s that women did not vote as a bloc and that they had nothing to fear. Consequently, when the Children's Bureau tried to extend Sheppard-Towner appropriations, which were to expire in June 1927, the American Medical Association and the right-wing Sentinels of the Republic and Woman Patriots moved to defeat the bill itself. Using basically the same arguments as they had in 1921, opponents described Sheppard-Towner as an "entering wedge" to socialism and an attack on the sanctity of the family and denounced Lathrop, Abbott, and Kelley as Bolsheviks. These allegations, which had little pull in 1921, won some converts by mid-decade. For example, the Daughters of the American Revolution, which warmly supported the maternity act in 1921, became a staunch opponent in 1926.[42]

The bill to renew Sheppard-Towner passed the House easily by a vote of 218 to 44, but right-wing senators blocked it in the Senate for eight months. They forced the Children's Bureau to agree to a compromise measure that extended appropriations for two years until 1929, and then automatically repealed the law itself. Between 1928 and 1932, fourteen bills that would reverse the repeal of the Sheppard-Towner Act were introduced in Congress. All of them failed. The Children's Bureau itself opposed many of the renewal bills because they transferred responsibility for overseeing maternity and infancy work to the Public Health Service.[43] Although some states continued maternity and infancy aid after 1929, the financial constraints of the Depression forced deep cuts, making health care once again unavailable to women who lived in remote areas or who could not afford private physicians—the women who benefited most from the Maternity and Infancy Act.

Federal funds for maternity and infancy protection were restored under Title V of the 1935 Social Security Act. Yet unlike Sheppard-Towner, which was conceived as a "community service to all classes," the child-health provisions of the Social Security Act were needs-based, and benefits were limited to the poor. Distinguished from "entitlement" programs like Social Security old-age insurance, which mainly benefit men, public maternal- and child-health services were (and are) stigmatized as charity and cut off from mainstream political support.[44]

In many ways, the Sheppard-Towner Act was a victim of its own success. The maternity act prodded physicians to incorporate preventive health services into private medical practice, and it reduced mortality among white infants. As a result, it made publicly funded maternal- and child-health care appear less necessary to white middle-class voters. Furthermore, once child-welfare policy entered the political mainstream, women lost control over its direction. Although individual women continued to play important roles in the development and administration of child-health services, by the 1930s male physicians and bureaucrats had come to dominate child-health policy. It is ironic that Sheppard-Towner mobilized thousands of women activists to help with maternity and infancy work, but set up a public-health bureaucracy that eventually supplanted them.[45]

The Sheppard-Towner Act was the product of a unique historical moment, for the political possibilities of maternalism and the material interests of grass-roots mothers converged in the immediate aftermath of the suffrage victory. Women in government, club women, and working-class and farm mothers agreed on the urgency of improving maternal and child health and pressed the government for reform. Yet the threads that (however tenuously) bound women together in the baby-saving campaign unraveled in the mid-1920s. Middle-class women benefited disproportionately from improvements in health care, employment opportunities in welfare programs, and the right to vote. As relatively privileged women made strides toward equality in the public sphere, motherhood became less central to their political identity. However, for poor and working-class women, who still shoulder the burden of child welfare in a period of economic recession and constricting government support, motherhood remains a dominant political concern.

Notes

1. Mrs. L. W., Alabama, 13 March 1922, rpt. in Molly Ladd-Taylor, *Raising a Baby the Government Way: Mothers' Letters to the Children's Bureau, 1915–1932* (New Brunswick, N.J., 1986), 193.

2. See, for example, Seth Koven and Sonya Michel, "Womanly Duties: Maternalist Politics and the Origins of Welfare States in France, Germany, Great Britain, and the United States, 1880–1920," *American Historical Review* 95 (1990): 1076–1108, as well as the introduction to this volume; Theda Skocpol, *Protecting Soldiers and Mothers: The Politics of Social Provision in the United States, 1870s–1920s* (Cambridge, Mass., 1992).

3. Linda Gordon, "Family Violence, Feminism, and Social Control," *Feminist Studies* 12 (1986): 453–78. See also her *Heroes of Their Own Lives: The Politics and History of Family Violence* (New York, 1988).

4. On the Sheppard-Towner Act, see J. Stanley Lemons, *The Woman Citizen: Social Feminism in the 1920s* (Urbana, Ill. 1975), 153–80; Sheila Rothman, *Woman's Proper Place: A History of Changing Ideals and Practices, 1870 to the Present* (New York, 1978); Robyn L. Muncy, *Creating a Female Dominion in American Reform, 1890–1935* (New York, 1990), 93–123: and Lela B. Costin, *Two Sisters for Social Justice* (Urbana, Ill., 1983), 125–50. The opposing coalition also included conservative maternalists; see Sonya Michel and Robyn Rosen, "The Paradox of Maternalism: Elizabeth Lowell Putnam and the American Welfare State," *Gender & History* 4 (1992): 364–86.

5. S. Josephine Baker, *Fighting for Life* (New York, 1939), 135, 201, and Lemons, *The Woman Citizen*, 166. Early efforts to combat infant mortality are discussed in Richard A. Meckel, *Save the Babies: American Public Health Reform and the Prevention of Infant Mortality* (Baltimore, 1990). Ironically, Elizabeth Lowell Putnam was a founder of the Boston organization; see Michel and Rosen "Paradox of Maternalism."

6. In 1929, Sheppard-Towner had 1,054 paid employees, and at least 7,339 volunteer workers. U.S. Children's Bureau, *The Promotion of the Welfare and*

Hygiene of Maternity and Infancy for the Fiscal Year Ending June 30, 1929, publication no. 203 (Washington, D.C., 1931), 6.

7. U.S. Bureau of the Census, *Historical Statistics of the United States, Colonial Times to 1970*, pt. 1 (Washington, D.C., 1975), 57; U.S. Children's Bureau, *Maternal Mortality*, publication no. 158 (Washington, D.C., 1926), 37.

8. Judith Walzer Leavitt, *Brought to Bed: Childbearing in America, 1750–1950* (New York, 1986), 25.

9. Jane Addams, *My Friend, Julia Lathrop* (New York, 1935), 4.

10. Edward T. James, Janet Wilson James, and Paul S. Boyer, eds., *Notable American Women* (Cambridge, Mass., 1971), 2:316.

11. Allen F. Davis, *American Heroine: The Life and Legend of Jane Addams* (New York, 1973), 5.

12. Dorothy Reed Mendenhall, typescript autobiography, folder J, 19–20, Dorothy Reed Mendenhall Papers, Sophia Smith Collection, Smith College.

13. Florence Kelley, quoted in House Committee on Interstate and Foreign Commerce, *Public Protection of Maternity and Infancy, Hearings on H.R. 10925*, 66th Congress, 3rd Session, 21 December 1920, 28.

14. On the early years of the Children's Bureau, see Molly Ladd-Taylor, "Hull House Goes to Washington: Women and the Children's Bureau," in Noralee Frankel and Nancy S. Dye, eds., *Gender, Class, Race and Reform in the Progressive Era*, (Lexington, Ky., 1991), and Muncy, *Creating a Female Dominion*, 38–65.

15. Nancy Pottishman Weiss, "Save the Children: A History of the Children's Bureau, 1903–1918" (Ph.D. diss., University of California at Los Angeles, 1974), 179–85, and Jacqueline K. Parker and Edward M. Carpenter, "Julia Lathrop and the Children's Bureau: The Emergence of an Institution," *Social Service Review* 55 (1981): 60–76.

16. See Molly Ladd-Taylor, *Mother-Work: Women, Child Welfare, and the State, 1890–1930* (forthcoming, Urbana, Ill., 1993.), chap. 4.

17. Weiss, "Save the Children," 191.

18. Mrs. A. P., Wyoming, 19 October 1916 and 21 November 1916, rpt. in Ladd-Taylor, *Raising a Baby*, 49–51, and Julia Lathrop to Mrs. W. F. Dummer, 16 June 1917, Grace and Edith Abbott Papers, Regenstein Library, University of Chicago.

19. Mrs. M. R., Idaho, 4 January 1916; Lathrop to Mrs. M. R.; and Mrs. F. D., Quebec, 18 December 1921, rpt. in Ladd-Taylor, *Raising a Baby*, 133–34, 111.

20. Mrs. H. B., Illinois, 28 February and 20 March 1916, rpt. in Ladd-Taylor, *Raising a Baby*, 148–53.

21. Mrs. A. P., Wyoming, 21 November 1916, rpt. in Ladd-Taylor, *Raising a Baby*, 51, and Grace Abbott, "Ten Years' Work for Children," *North American Review* 218 (August 1923): 189–200.

22. Quotations in Lemons, *Woman Citizen*, 166, 155.

23. Alice Robertson to Elizabeth Lowell Putnam, 21 November 1921, folder 300, Elizabeth Lowell Putnam Papers, Arthur and Elizabeth Schlesinger Library on the History of Women in America, Radcliffe College.

24. Joan E. Mulligan, "Pregnant Americans, 1918–1947: Some Public Policy Notes on Rural and Military Wives," *Women and Health* 5 (Winter 1980): 23–38, and Louis J. Covotsos, "Child Welfare and Social Progress: A History of the United States Children's Bureau, 1912–1935" (Ph.D. diss., University of Chicago, 1976).

25. The following analysis is based on the administrative records of the Sheppard-Towner Act in the Children's Bureau Records, Correspondence and Reports Relating to Surveys and Programs, 1917–1954, National Archives (hereafter cited as C&R, CB).

26. Children's Bureau, *Promotion of the Welfare . . . 1929*, 27.

27. "Semi-Annual Report: Narrative Report of Activities," [Arkansas]," 1 July 1924 to 1 January 1925, file 11–5–8, C&R, CB, and "Narrative and Statistical Report," [Mississippi], March 1924, file 11–26–1, Children's Bureau Records, Central Files, 1914–1940, National Archives (hereafter cited as CF, CB).

28. Dorothy Anderson to G. S. Luckett, 6 October 1926, file 11–33–8, CF, CB. See also Sandra Schackel, *Social Housekeepers: Women Shaping Public Policy in New Mexico, 1920–1940* (Albuquerque, 1992).

29. Division of Maternity and Infancy Hygiene, Bureau of Child Welfare, Florida State Board of Health, "Biennial Report," 1 July 1922 to 31 December 1922, file 11–11–8, C&R, CB; "Semi-Annual Report of Maternity and Infancy Work [North Dakota]," 1 January to 30 June 1923, file 11–36–8, C&R, CB; and "Conference of Directors of State Divisions Administering the Federal Maternity and Infancy Act held under the Auspices of the Children's Bureau," 19–21 September 1923, file 11–0, C&R, CB, 39.

30. Dorothy Anderson to G. S. Luckett, 6 October 1926, file 11–33–8, CF, CB, and Child Welfare Division, Montana State Board of Health, "Narrative Report of Activities," 1 July to 31 December 1924, file 11–28–8, C&R, CB. Schackel, however, documents many instances in which Anglo nurses showed great sensitivity toward Hispanic and Native American patients in New Mexico; see *Social Housekeepers*, chaps. 2 and 3.

31. "Report of Work Done under the Maternity and Infancy Act in the State of New Mexico," 1 July 1925 to 30 June 1926, file 11–33–8, C&R, CB; U.S. Children's Bureau, *The Promotion of the Welfare and Hygiene of Maternity and Infancy for the Year Ending June 30, 1924*, publication no. 146 (Washington, D.C., 1925), 13; "Report of Work Done under the Federal Maternity and Infancy Act in the State of Mississippi," 1 July 1928 to 30 June 1929," file 11–26–8, C&R, CB; and "Report of Work Done under the Federal Maternity and Infancy Act in the State of Virginia," 1 July 1928 to 30 June 1929, file 11–50–8, C&R, CB.

32. Molly Ladd-Taylor, " 'Grannies' and 'Spinsters': Midwife Training under the Sheppard-Towner Act," *Journal of Social History* 22 (1988): 255–75.

33. "Report of Work Done under Federal Maternity and Infancy Act in the State of Montana," 1 July 1926 to 30 June 1927, file 11–28–8, C&R, CB; [Georgia]

Division of Child Hygiene, "Annual Report," 1925, file 11–12–8, C&R, CB; and Clark Goreman, Georgia Committee on Interracial Cooperation, to Blanche Haines, 8 July 1926, file 11–12–2, CF, CB.

34. Judith Sealander, *As Minority Becomes Majority: Federal Reaction to the Phenomenon of Women in the Work Force, 1920–1963* (Westport, Conn., 1983), 3–11, notes a similar phenomenon in the Women's Bureau.

35. "Conference of Directors of State Divisions Administering the Federal Maternal and Infancy Act," 19–21 September 1923, file 11–0, C&R, CB, 24.

36. Rothman, *Woman's Proper Place*, 142–53. On the conflict between male physicians and female professionals, see Muncy, *Creating a Female Dominion*, 135–50.

37. "Narrative Report of the Bureau of Maternity and Infancy, State Department of Public Health, State of Oklahoma," 1 January 1925 to 1 July 1925, file 11–38–8, CF, CB, and Lucile Blachly to Blanche Haines, 1 July 1927, file 11–38–1, CF, CB.

38. Grace Abbott to Lillie M. Barbour, 13 July 1925, file 11–30 –1, CF, CB; Marie Phelan to Florence Kraker, 30 October 1924, file 11–30–1, CF, CB; Marie Phelan to Blanche Haines, 15–20 June 1925, file 11–30–1, CF, CB; Lillie Barbour to Grace Abbott, 2 July 1925, file 11–30–1, CF, CB; Mrs. J. B. Clinedinst to Grace Abbott, 2 January 1928, file 11–30–8, CF, CB.

39. The white infant-mortality rate was 72 in 1921. Children's Bureau, *Promotion of the Welfare . . . 1929*, 27–37, 132.

40. In 1921, 78 city infants under one year old died for every 1,000 live births, while 74 infants died in rural areas. By 1928, the infant-mortality rate had declined to 69 in the cities and 68 in rural areas. Children's Bureau, *Promotion of the Welfare . . . 1929*, 31.

41. West Virginia Division of Child Hygiene and Public Health Nursing, "Extracts from Statements of Mothers Who Took Motherhood Correspondence Course," enclosed in Katharine Lenroot to Julia Lathrop, 23 September 1926, file 11–0, CF, CB. "Letters of Georgia Women Attending Prenatal Clinic," enclosed in Joe Bowdoin to Dorothy Kirchwey Brown, 30 April 1929, box 2, folder 39, Dorothy Kirchwey Brown Papers, Schlesinger Library.

42. Lemons, *Woman Citizen*, 171–75; Michel and Rosen, "Paradox of Maternalism."

43. Joseph Chepaitis, "The First Federal Social Welfare Measure: The Sheppard-Towner Maternity and Infancy Act, 1918–1932" (Ph.D. diss., Georgetown University, 1968), 278.

44. Costin, *Two Sisters for Social Justice*, 221–26. On the two-tier welfare system, see Barbara J. Nelson, "The Origins of the Two-Channel Welfare State: Workmen's Compensation and Mothers' Aid," in Linda Gordon, ed., *Women, the State, and Welfare* (Madison, Wis., 1990), 123–51.

45. My interpretation here complements Estelle Freedman's pioneering "Separatism as Strategy: Female Institution Building and American Feminism, 1870–1930," *Feminist Studies* 5 (1979): 512–29. For a somewhat different view, see Susan Ware, *Beyond Suffrage: Women in the New Deal* (Cambridge, Mass., 1982).

10

Women in the British Labour Party and the Construction of State Welfare, 1906–1939

Pat Thane

Introduction

British women played an active public role in politics and voluntary organizations in the later nineteenth century and throughout
the interwar years. Far more so than has been appreciated. The
structure of the British state provided—limited—space for these
activities as did the major political parties. This state has been
described as a "minimal," "nightwatchman," or "weak" state. This
is seriously to misunderstand it. It was characterized by a small,
but strong and flexible, core firmly directing the key activities of
state and supervising the delegation of functions defined as less
essential to local authorities and voluntary organizations. It was
at the latter level that women could wield the most influence.

The salience of parties in British politics attracted women to
them. Very many women were attracted either by the hope of
using them as vehicles to advance women's position in society, or
to advance levels of social-welfare provision, or often both. The
experience of the reality of poverty which many middle- and
upper-class women acquired through philanthropic work drew
many of them to the belief that only the state had the resources
adequate to relieve it; and parties were the channels through
which the state could be brought to acknowledge that obligation.
At the same time, both the state and the parties were most
receptive to women when they confined their political activities
to the caring sphere of social politics and to activity at the local

and the voluntary levels. This conjuncture enabled women to influence the shaping of the British "welfare state."

This essay seeks to substantiate this interpretation by taking the example of the aims, visions, and actions of women in a political party which achieved real power in the period under scrutiny. It aims to begin the work of assessing their role in the making of the welfare state in the context of the political and ideological structures within which they had to work.

Origins and Composition of the Labour Women's Organizations

The British Labour party was responsible for the legislation which collectively constructed a "welfare state" following the Second World War. This legislation built upon wartime and prewar proposals and experiments. Many of these originated in the ideas and actions of women, including female members of the Labour party. Women were a majority of voters in the general election of 1945 which brought Labor its first ever outright, landslide victory and a majority of the women who cast their votes voted Labour.[1]

Female support for the party was institutionalized from the time of its foundation in 1906, even though women did not obtain the vote in general elections until 1918 (and then only at the age of 30). In 1906, the Women's Labour League (WLL) was founded to support the party.[2] From 1918 women were integrated into the party structure and organized in Women's Sections (WS) of party branches. They formed a semiindependent female network within a mixed-sex party.

British women, like British working men, were politically active before they obtained the national vote.[3] Indeed the development of powerful women's organizations attached to the major political parties was an important feature of British politics at an earlier stage than in other leading states. Quasi-independent women's organizations grew in the Liberal party from 1887. They had a total membership of 69,933 in 1898, 115,097 by 1914. The mixed-sex Primrose League, a support organization for the Conservative party formed in 1883 "must have included hundreds of thousands of women."[4] Women made up 43 percent of Fabian Society membership in 1913.[5] In contrast, women were barred from joining political organizations in Wilhelmine Germany and in pre-1914

France. In the U.S. women's divisions of state and national parties did not appear until 1920.[6] Women's experience of activism in male-dominated parties increased frustration at the limits placed on them in public life and helped propel many toward one form or another of feminism. These party organizations drew many women into feminism rather than diverting them from it.[7] The definition of feminism used in this paper is broad enough to include any women or group who placed prominently on their agenda the advancement of women's relative position in any respect.

In Britain, women's participation in political parties was part of a movement to advance women which was very broadly based in terms of social composition, aims, and activities. It included large numbers of women from all classes, regions, and levels of education: in trade unionism, in the professions, in the home; and women active in a range of campaigns (for higher education for women, for temperance, against the Contagious Diseases Acts and much else) of which the suffrage movements (militant and nonmilitant) were sometimes, though not necessarily, a part.

In the political organizations women were not mere acolytes of men. Women played an important and acknowledged organizational role in the Conservative, Liberal, and Labour parties.[8] Party was central to British policy making and public administration. From the 1880s the major political parties were increasingly ideologically and sociologically distinct. They were nationally organized and effective channels for political action. At least until 1914 interest groups could more readily achieve their aims by acting within parties or by putting pressure upon them, rather than through influencing the bureaucracy.

The Labour party was male-dominated in the sense that, even after 1918, the leadership and members of Parliament (MPs) were overwhelmingly male and decision making at the annual conference was dominated by male-controlled trade unions. Yet in the interwar years women were a majority of individual members of the party[9] and in some branches constituted a very high proportion. The size of the female membership reached 250 to 300,000 in the interwar years and rose still higher after 1945.

They included women from a cross section of occupations, paid and unpaid: housewives, manual workers, women employed professionally or voluntarily in a range of social services (e.g., doctors, nurses, teachers, health visitors, housing managers) as well as recipients of welfare services (including many from unemployed households during the depression). They came from all regions.[10] They were conscious and proud of their mix. They drew on the wide range of experiences and expertise in their ranks in seeking to assess, analyze, and propose remedies for social problems. Labour women brought their own direct experiences to bear on policy making from a variety of perspectives. As the ex-shopgirl Margaret Bondfield[11] explained in her chairman's (this was the term always used) address to the 1909 conference, the Womens Labour League "provided a common platform, a uniting ground for the women who were free to study, to plan, to execute, and the house-mothers, wives of trade unionists and wage-earning women who brought their practical experience of life's difficulties." Probably a majority of members identified themselves as primarily workers in the home, indeed they often described themselves as "the housewives trade union."

The WLL and later the WS cut across classes, though clearly a majority of the membership throughout the period came from working-class backgrounds. The middle-class origins of some of its prominent figures have obscured this fact; and Christine Collette rightly emphasizes how problematic it is simply to ascribe "middle-class" status (with the assumption that we know what this implies) to women who, whatever their social origins, devoted their adult lives to the attainment of socialism, to advancing the cause of the working class, and who often married men of working-class origins. Furthermore, middle-class origins or life-styles did not necessarily indicate incapacity to understand the lives of poor women.[12]

Nor did working-class members come only from a secure "labor-aristocratic" upper stratum of the working class. In general such conceptions of strict stratification in the British working class are at odds with the evidence.[13] Furthermore, female labor organizations appear to have sought more vigorously and effectively than male ones to bring together members of all sections of the working class. For example, the Women's Cooperative Guild (WCG), the largest such organization, founded in 1883,[14] came into conflict with male cooperators over its determination to bring the benefits of cooperative retailing to all working-class women, especially the poorest women, who most needed it.[15] Other factors may also have contributed to Labour women's greater sensitivity to inter- as well as intraclass solidarity. The competitive work environment encouraged sectionalism among working-class males as well as antagonism between classes, both of which were weaker influences upon female lives. Finally, middle- and upper-class women were more likely than their male counterparts to be drawn into Labour politics (as they and others were to feminism) through direct contact with poorer women in the course of voluntary work. For many, these face-to-face encounters fostered deep respect for laboring women and determination to diminish their deprivation.[16]

Women living in conditions of severe permanent poverty were less likely to be Labour activists than women from more economically secure backgrounds; the exhausting drudgery of their lives left them no time for politics. The women's sections saw as their central purpose to remedy the debilitating realities of laboring women's lives in terms acceptable and empowering to them. They sought as the basis for action to establish the real needs and hopes of poor women by drawing them into the organization. Many of the members could do so the more easily precisely because the barriers between the "labor aristocracy" and the rest of the working class, between "rough" and "respectable," secure workers and "residuum," were less clear-cut than is sometimes thought. A very high proportion of the British working class, including the most skilled, at some point in their lives, many of them repeatedly, suffered severe poverty due to unemployment, sickness, a strike, the seasonality of work, the death of a partner, or other regular hazards. Few manual workers had protection (friendly benefits, insurance) against these episodic life crises before 1914 and very many still did not by 1940. Women were especially vulnerable to all such hazards.[17] As a League publication put it in March 1911, "The readers of this paper know only too well that unemployment and underemployment play a part in the lives of almost all wage-earners. Even among skilled workers there is always a small percentage out of work."[18] Many members who lacked direct experience of poverty acquired it through voluntary work or support of strikers' families in some of the prolonged strikes of the period.[19]

The Ideas of the Labour Women

The WLL had its origins in the first-wave women's movement.[20] The members had a well-defined world view which incorporated into a coherent whole conceptions of gender roles and the inter-section of these roles with the construction and outcomes of state policy. Labour women had a clear vision about how both should be changed. They had no illusions that they would benefit from significant male support and WLL women were committed to women's potential as agents of change through use of their grow-ing citizenship rights. They also were committed to the potential role of state-welfare policy and administration in relation to other agencies (notably the labor market) in maximizing the "welfare" of the population as a whole and the relative welfare of women. These ideas were, of course, debated and contested among the women and between men and women in the party and were most fully developed in the interwar years. What follows is a summary of the mainstream view as expressed in their publications and at their conferences.

WLL women assumed that most women would follow and aspire to a primarily domestic role and that, in principle, this was desirable, at least while children were young. But they recognized that not all women would make this choice and emphasized strongly that both domesticity and activity in the paid labor mar-ket were acceptable goals for women provided that either was freely chosen rather than, in the former case, imposed by male authority or, in the latter, by poverty. The working-class Scots-woman Mary Sutherland, who was at the time editor of the organi-zation's monthly journal, *Labour Woman*, and chief woman officer of the party, merely echoed years of previous commentary when she asserted in February 1944 that

> [T]he right of a married woman to earn outside the home must be insisted on; and equally her right not to be forced to work outside the home through economic necessity if she wants to make home and children her work (in the past outside employ-ment for married working women has meant the burden of two full-time jobs instead of one).[21]

Indeed, a central aim of the organization was to make those "rights" the reality they normally were not. The WLL supported strategies for promoting economic independence for women who chose or needed it by encouraging female trade unionism, and by demanding legislative improvements in female pay and working conditions. They also called for improved social services, such as day nurseries, to provide support and greater freedom for *all* working mothers, including those who chose to make home and family their work. Their consistent demand (strongest in the 1930s) was not simply for "equal pay," which, it was rightly pointed out, could be restricted to the few areas of precisely equal work between men and women, but for *comparable* pay, so that women's wage rates in all occupations, especially those defined as exclusively female, which were especially low-paid, should be raised to equivalent levels with those of men.[22]

They protested strongly against the "marriage bar" which existed in many occupations, including manual ones, as an unjustifiable restriction of women's freedom to work.[23] They pressed for higher pay and status for nurses and encouraged women to enter new sectors of the social-service professions such as housing management. They sought to fight the danger that such women,

> like women workers in many branches of industry, will be looked upon as a reserve of relatively unskilled and badly paid labour, instead of being enabled to secure a place for themselves as highly skilled officials occupying posts of status and authority at appropriate rates of remuneration.[24]

However, WLL women did not believe that activity in the labor market was the only or best route to social status and influence. They argued that women could effectively achieve personal dignity and public influence from their home base and should be given time and encouragement to do so. The woman who took her domestic role as her primary work did not necessarily become submerged in the home and cut off from public affairs, as many of the Labour women themselves demonstrated. WLL women urged women workers in the home to contribute their important perspective to public debate.

They insisted that work in the home was in no way different—except in often being harder and the hours longer—from work in the formal labor market and was certainly as vital to the economy as a whole.[25] They were impressively careful in their use of language to avoid the equation of "work" with paid work in the formal labor market. Marion Phillips (the first chief woman officer) told women voters in 1920, "The Labour Party is the party of the workers and so it realizes the needs of women, for who are workers to such an extent as they? We need shorter hours in the workshop and the factory but still more do we need shorter hours and less anxiety for the woman in the home."[26] These aspirations led to important campaigns, especially during both wars, for better-designed, low-cost housing. This was, in part, intended to allow the homeworker free time to use for herself rather than for her family. The purpose of welfare policies in the eyes of the Labour women was not only material improvement but the freeing and empowerment of women and improvement in the *quality* of life. The editorial in *Labour Woman* in September 1922 asserted:

> As soon as married working women organize themselves strongly and make use of their political power in local and national elections, so soon will they be able to make such improvement in housing and the care of houses as will reduce their labour and give them a chance for more fruitful leisure.... They must raise themselves out of the overwork and drudgery of their lives and insist on conditions which give them opportunities for
>
> FREEDOM
> HEALTH
> REASONABLE LEISURE
> and USEFUL PUBLIC SERVICE[27]

Once they had the vote, women had to be assisted to use it. The aim of the Labour women from the beginning was to help women to use their growing civil rights by seeking election, co-option, or appointment to the growing number of public bodies open to some of them even before 1918. Another important and unusual feature of the British situation was the significant number of women who could vote and hold office at the local level from the mid-nineteenth century.[28] By 1913 women could vote for and be elected to county, borough, urban and rural-district, and parish councils, and to the boards of the poor-law guardians (but not all women, or indeed the same women for all of these authorities!). They could be appointed to local education, library, distress (relief of unemployment), midwifery, national-insurance, old-age-pensions, school-care, and labor-exchange committees and to trade boards for settling wages in low-paid, mainly female, "sweated" occupations. In 1914–15 there were 1,546 women elected as poor law guardians, 200 rural-district councillors, 48 municipal and county councillors, and 679 appointed to school boards. In 1902, women protested the abolition of separately elected boards of education, on which they had long been active and effective since their formation in 1870. This led the government hastily to enact that each of the successor bodies, the education committees of local councils, should include at least two women. Such involvement indeed made deprivation of the national vote even more absurd. By 1919–20 the numbers rose to 2,039 Poor Law Guardians and 320 municipal and country councillors.[29] The range of elected and appointed offices open to women grew after 1918. From 1919 on they could be appointed to the bench of magistrates; 61 of the first female magistrates were Labour women.[30] In no other major state in Europe or the United States did women have a comparable institutional role at such an early date.[31] While the power it gave them certainly should not be overestimated, it has not yet been fully explored.

Leaders of the Labour women also encouraged them to observe closely the administration of local services, to ensure that the obligations of local authorities were carried out and that permissive legislation was implemented to the maximum. They believed in and sought to practice participatory democracy. *Labour Woman* assisted them with briefing articles on new legislation and major policy areas and the WS offered political and administrative education through pamphlets, lectures, summer schools (attended by hundreds of women annually), and classes on public speaking. Margaret MacDonald told the 1907 conference how "at their meetings many women had shown powers of organizing and speaking which they had not shown when attending meetings where men took part and they were able to express their opinions as women on matters of which they had special knowledge."[32]

Underlying both their policy recommendations and the role of individual members who attained official or professional positions was the belief that the recipients of welfare should not be treated as passive or "patronized." They resolved in 1925 that "it was not a question of superior people trying to go in and teach the mother her job, she had the right to every kind of knowledge and the working mothers were asking for teaching on all the subjects which affected them in the life of their children."[33] Social legislation should be designed to reinforce this "right." An article in *Labour Woman* encouraging women to train in the new profession of housing manager argued, perhaps optimistically, that

> so many families today are over-visited, by every sort of social worker, not always altogether free from a patronizing or inquisitive attitude. This is rightly resented. . . . [A] trained housing

manager, calling on her round of rent-collecting is at once in a business relationship with the housewife. She is the servant of the tenant as well as the landlord. After a time friendship is probably established, but there is no question of condescension or patronage.[34]

Labour women were encouraged by their female leadership to focus their activities upon issues of social policy and labor-market questions as they affected women and children. They gave them more prominence than did male members of the party. They were fully aware that every issue of state concern affected women and that too confined a focus could lead to the political ghettoization of women. They faced persistent criticism on these grounds and indeed for the very existence of separate women's sections of the party. WLL women responded by asserting that they emphasized women's disadvantages so that one day the organization need no longer exist because the disadvantages had been removed. However, under existing conditions, women had to stand up for their own needs since nothing suggested that men would do so. A women's organization within the party, they insisted, provided the necessary framework.

Why did some women chose to work in a mixed-sex political party rather than a single-sex interest group? Not all Labour women, of course, were feminist by any definition. Those who did desire change in the situation of women and in gender roles related these to some broader vision of social change. Generally they had concluded that changes could be gained in the foreseeable future only through political action. This could best be achieved through one of the major political parties of which Labour was the most sympathetic. They recognized that compromises would result but thought these inseparable from political activity; if constraints were built into this mode of action so too was some potential for achievement. Most of them also believed that just as they lived with men in a mixed-sex world, it also was necessary to work with men. They believed that it was more effective to convert and persuade rather than to struggle with men; to enter and change male institutions armed with female values rather than to assault them from without. They believed that a viable feminism must acknowledge the complementarity of male and female lives while using every effort to promote women's particular needs. A radical minority, including Dora Russell,[35] took a more confrontational line, but the majority, like most of the men in the party were pragmatic, reformist, and gradualist. They did not necessarily have high hopes of how far or fast the men could be pushed.

Dr. Ethel Bentham (a medical doctor, an early member of the London County Council and a founding member of the WLL) told the 1918 conference of Labour women, " . . . there would of course always be the woman's point of view . . . but . . . politics would in future have two eyes, see both sides of the road."[36] Another speaker said, "What we had to seek to do now was to make one peoples' party—a party of men and women using the different experience and knowledge of each for the common purpose of all."[37]

Labour women were persistently critical of those feminists who they believed were insensitive to the reality of the interdependence of most men's and women's lives. This accounts for at least some of their reservations about aspects of Eleanor Rathbone's proposals for family allowances. For example, Rathbone countenanced the payment of the allowances by employers in a package incorporating pay cuts for childless workers, at a time (the 1920s), when trade unionists in general were struggling against wage cuts in a period of serious recession. Labour women criticized such proposals for failing to relate questions concerning women and welfare to their wider consequences. It was hard for Labour women to believe that strengthening the hands of the employers against the unions in any respect could be in the long-term interest of women or men in the working class.[38]

At issue was a simple conflict between those giving primacy to gender or to class. Rather Labour women saw the two as indissociable. Strengthening the power of employers would harm the class, but the effects would be differentiated by gender. Also at issue was the character of gender roles and relationships that a specific social policy such as family allowances would shape. That social policy *did* shape such roles and relationships neither side doubted. Rathbone's vision of family allowances was rooted in an essentially adversarial view of the working-class family. Whereas she sought to strengthen wives against husbands,[39] the Labour women sought mechanisms supportive of the marital relationship.

The Labour Women and Marriage

Labour women expressed a particular conception of the current nature and desirable future of marriage. They recognized how insufficient income, even in families with a fully employed male, contributed to palpable tensions within the household.[40] They accused "middle-class feminists" of sharing the conviction of middle-class moralists of both sexes that the working-class male was characteristically drunken, selfish, and neglectful of his wife and children. Undoubtedly, some were. The irregular and brutalizing nature of some male occupations helped shape this role. Some women responded to the insecurity of life in a similar fashion. But the consensus emerging in a variety of comments and actions from the quarter-million Labour women was that most men, like most women, were or sought to be, responsible and caring spouses and parents, except when circumstances drove them to despair.[41] They believed that social policy should be designed to reinforce these aspirations. Their views were summed up in a letter from a Glasgow woman member (not herself very poor, she gave her husband's earnings as about sixty shillings per week):

> There are some men who spend too much on their own personal enjoyment and some who don't tell their wives what they earn. But they are a minority—just as the wives who shop wastefully are also a small minority. . . . Some questions put recently in the House of Commons suggested that it is usual for working class wives not to know how much their husbands earn. The Tories will use statements of that kind to argue that underfeeding is not caused by poverty but by men holding back their wages.[42]

Labour women insisted that the root of the problem lay not in male behavior per se, but rather in the impact of the organization of the economy on gender relations; in this sense also gender and class were indissociable. Marion Phillips feared the effects of "childhood pensions" (family allowances) on the behavior and perceptions of working-class fathers.

> The idea of a childhood pension, taking from the father all need to provide for his children, tended to increase the irresponsibility of fatherhood and to further the growing idea, so common now amongst middle class women that the father had practically no concern in parentage and the mother was the only who mattered.[43]

For similar reasons in 1911 the WLL held aloof from demands that maternity benefits, payable for the first time under the National Health Insurance Act (1911), should be payable directly to the wife only. This campaign was led by the WCG and marks a temporary point of divergence between these two organizations. The new and very small WLL may have judged it wiser not to differ from the male party leadership on this issue so soon. However this difference between the WLL and the WCG reflected differences of view on the subject among working-class women; and there were many views within the WLL. It should be remembered that there was, and remained throughout the period surveyed here, a very substantial overlap in membership between the WLL and the WCG. Their social composition was similar. Margaret Bondfield, for example, played a prominent role in the WCG campaign, while being a leading figure in the WLL.[44]

In principle the WLL favored an independent cash resource for wives, but pointed out that such payments in themselves would not prevent a brutal husband from keeping his wife short: he could simply withhold a larger sum from his wages and might even feel a resentful incentive to do so. The report of the executive to the 1914 annual conference explained:

> The practical result of the proposed amendment would not be at all what was supposed—the drunken, brutal husband would still be able to get the money if he chose and the wife would many a time find it of more advantage to ease her mind by paying rent or getting boots *even for her husband* so that he might go to work properly shod than in buying comforts for herself. . . . [W]e did not oppose payment to the mother, but we felt that if it raised difficulties and delays in administration, it was not worth so much as to be considered of vital importance.[45]

The reality of the dilemma should not be underestimated. Some Labour women genuinely feared that such proposals rested on too simple a view of the complex, endless struggle of poorer households for survival and on a failure to understand how fragile survival mechanisms and personal relationships could be easily upset by the unintended effects of even well-intentioned changes. Once the National Insurance Act was implemented Labour women, and all female members of the national insurance committees established to administer it, were urged to observe how it worked in practice and to report cases of men treating the maternity benefit as their own.[46]

More generally, the Labour women saw full employment at adequate wages, improved social services, the diminution of the housewife's toil, the creation of space for marital companionship, access to birth-control information and techniques, improved maternity care—and above all a socialist reconstruction of society—as the means to reduce the tensions which made some husbands brutal and some wives miserable.

They recognized that not all marriages could, or should, be sustained and pressed with equal vigor, and some success, for improved divorce, separation, maintenance, and custody laws to diminish the very considerable barriers to a woman's escape from a bad marriage and to living independently free from it. Beginning in 1910 the WCG led a campaign for divorce-law reform, this time with full support from the WLL. Once again Margaret Bondfield was its "tireless" leader.[47] The WCG gave radical and controversial evidence to the Royal Commission on Divorce of 1910–12, based on the views of its members, supporting equal grounds for divorce between men and women, extension of those grounds, cheaper divorce proceedings (free for poor women), and female magistrates and judges to hear them. Many of the recommendations were incorporated in the majority report. The ensuing controversy, followed by the war, delayed legislation. However in 1918 women were able to become magistrates and judges; in 1923 equal grounds for divorce were introduced; in 1937 the grounds were extended on the lines proposed by the WCG; and free legal aid was introduced by the Labour government in 1948. The WCG and the Labour women supported all of these actions. Even before 1914, women of these and other organizations took advantage of a concession negotiated by the National Council of Women allowing them to sit in pairs at the lawyers' table during marital cases: "We felt this would be a help to (the women) in a predominantly male atmosphere," said Hannah Mitchell, who sat thus for some years.[48]

The first Labour government, in 1924, was persuaded, very largely by the WLL, to introduce the Separation and Maintenance Bill, enabling a woman to claim maintenance while living under the same roof as her husband, so that she no longer had to make herself homeless to obtain maintenance. This concession and another bill granting females equal guardianship rights over children were lost when the short-lived, beleaguered minority government went out of office. However, following demands from women, they were revived and passed under a Conservative government in 1925. Wives were also allowed, at the magistrates' discretion, a half share of the household furnishings and the right to take over a tenancy.[49] The latter clauses were drafted by the Labour women, rejected by the House of Commons and reinstated by the House of Lords. The extent of reshaping of the marriage relationship by British law in the interwar years and the role of women in bringing it about is notable. While support for these changes emerged from women across the political spectrum, Labour women had long made these matters central concerns.

Labour women were particularly well positioned to influence political debate about women's issues in Britain in the interwar years. First, they represented an impressively diverse body of female citizens in geographic, social, and occupational terms; second, over several decades, they had forged a comprehensive normative vision of women in society that called for the creation of economic conditions that would enable women to decide for themselves their relationship to the home and workplace. Their ideology was pragmatically informed by a keen awareness of the actual day-to-day experiences of women's lives. As more civic space opened up to women in the interwar years and Labour supporters became politically more powerful as voters and policy makers, the Labour women increasingly brought their vision of women and the state to bear on elections and social-welfare policies and programs.

The British State and Social Welfare

In order to evaluate the outcome of this activity and assess the influence of the Labour women on the creation of policy and the practice of social welfare more broadly we should be clear about the contexts in which they were acting. They necessarily operated within established state structures and systems and traditions of social-welfare provision.

The characteristics and institutions of the British state obviously had a major role in guiding and limiting what they could reasonably propose or achieve. Any simple dichotomy which defines states as "strong" or "weak" in such terms as the size of a central bureaucracy is unhelpful in the British case. The state system which was constructed in the mid-nineteenth century on the foundation of older institutions and principles was "minimal" in the sense of possessing a small central bureaucracy, and in consciously limiting the areas of activity of central government. But this state was in no useful sense "weak" because those areas were carefully selected as keys to effective central control and the central state operated in a clearly theorized relationship with the broader spheres of activity of local government and voluntary institutions.

This conception of the state was most clearly worked out under the premiership of W. E. Gladstone, though it had earlier roots. Gladstone believed in a strong initiating executive, guiding a decisive and efficient central-state apparatus, firmly molding the framework within which an active citizenry could enjoy as much freedom as was compatible with social stability and economic success. This state was highly efficient but remarkably unobtrusive at levying taxes, at constructing legal, fiscal, and other institutions; at building trading relations with other countries in such a way as to facilitate the smooth working of the expanding economy; at policing and maintaining public order through decentralized mechanisms; at administering and keeping under military control a huge and growing empire; and at limiting another serious threat to stability, endemic and epidemic disease, through increasingly effective public-health measures.

This system of government was made possible at least in part because Britain was, by the standards of its day, still a relatively small, stable, prosperous, culturally and linguistically homogeneous society.[50] A succession of clear-sighted governments with limited but efficient bureaucratic resources ensured this system's success. Wherever possible, as with the financing and administration of policing or public health, a high level of discretion and initiative was delegated to local government within the framework of national law and supervised by the central authority. The minimal state was also premised upon the capacity of a vast network of voluntary organizations, in cooperation with elected local authorities (whose role expanded from the mid-nineteenth century), to superintend, finance, and initiate, within limits established by law, most education and welfare services.

The important role of voluntarism in nineteenth-century Britain was not the fortuitous corollary of the limited state but integral to the conceptualization of that state by its leaders. Voluntarism was perceived by them as a form of active participation by citizens in the activities of the state, a means whereby they justified their political and social rights through exercise of responsibilities toward their fellow citizens. That rights did carry with them recip- rocal responsibilities was central to hegemonic social and political thought at the time, including that of the Labour party. The nine- teenth- and early-twentieth-century British state worked hard to appear to disappear behind a barrier of buffer institutions, official and voluntary but over which it exerted careful supervision.

Economic difficulties, threats to the empire, the danger of inter- nal social rifts, and war forced the state into greater visibility from the end of the nineteenth century and especially from World War I onward. It retained however, certainly until World War II, a preference for delegation to local authorities and voluntary insti- tutions and for working, whenever possible, with institutions and individuals outside the formal bureaucracy, especially in the area of social welfare. Though the period especially from the election of the Liberal government of 1906 is seen, rightly, as marking the decisive movement of the state into social-welfare provision, this movement was gradual. Every piece of social-welfare legislation between 1906 and 1914 created a state-controlled administrative framework and a set of operating principles within which local government or voluntary organizations (indeed in most cases a combination of the two) carried out the administration and often provided most of the finance.

It was an approach capable of flexibly extending the capacities of the central state by establishing channels through which it could draw when necessary on the large fund of ideas and people, female and male, in the voluntary and local-government sectors.[51] It was a state system which gave primacy to politicians over bureaucrats and in which party had a strong role, not least in providing a channel between politicians and unofficial advisors.

By 1914 the leading characteristics of the British state were efficiency and flexibility. The sternest test of state capacities is war. These characteristics were an important reason why Britain defeated the apparently stronger German state in the First World War. The German state was hampered by the size and rigidity of its bureaucratic system from responding flexibly to the unforeseeable needs of the first "total" war.[52] The British bureaucracy expanded in wartime, partly through temporary recruitment of experienced people from business or the "knowledge-bearing professions," such as John Maynard Keynes and William Beveridge (who were to be more prominent still in the next war). The British state emerged from the war intact and strengthened while "the German state dissolved and competing interest groups grabbed what they could get."[53]

Bureaucracy became a more powerful autonomous force in Britain from around the time of World War I, though it continued to be modified by party and remained less monolithic and more flexible than those of other leading European states.[54]

Hence to understand the capacities of the British state for socio-economic intervention at any time before World War II it is not enough to examine only the institutions and personnel of the central state. It is essential also to understand its close and shifting relationship with local government and with the voluntary and private sectors. The importance of these sectors and their predominance in the administration of welfare encouraged and made possible the range and influence of women's voluntary organizations and women's influence in local government.[55] Their influence, for example, in the shaping of maternal- and child-welfare policy[56] was of a degree which certainly puts in question simple contrasts between a "maternalist" American and a "paternalist" British welfare system.

The actual character of and influences upon the shape of the emerging British welfare state are, of course, not simple to describe or analyze. Few have offered one-dimensional class or gender analyses. There can be no doubt that from the later nineteenth century on politicians were to some degree influenced by the assumed need to reassure new or potential voters, first working-class males and then females, of the benign intentions of the state, and to seek to incorporate them into the dominant political value system. Their capacity to do so was limited not only by the legacy of previous policy and institutions but by the relative weakness of pressure from below and the strength of opponents of public-welfare expenditure, including taxpayers. Another real constraint was the strength of liberal values and Liberal politics. Liberals could not, indeed did not wish to, prevent the implementation of state welfare but did oppose its falling entirely into the hands of the state and valued a society of voluntarily participating citizens. They continued to value this approach because it was functionally effective. Weight must be given to the roles of liberal intellectual reformers and also to those businessmen who recognized the capacity of welfare to enhance "national efficiency." A cross-class, cross-interest-group, and/or cross-gender coalition was needed for state-welfare measures of any kind to be introduced.

Nor, anywhere in Europe, can the growth of infant and maternal welfare in particular but also social, especially health, policies more generally be dissociated from the sense of demographic crisis which hung over most of the Continent from 1880s to World War II. Throughout Europe fear of the effects of the declining birthrate, high rates of infant mortality, and low standards of physical fitness within the mass of the population upon the capacity of nations to be economically productive and to fight wars in an increasingly competitive world directed the attention of an unusually wide range of political and social groups toward the question of the physical condition of the population and thence to the needs and condition of mothers and children. The outcomes were various in the different European countries. By no means did they take everywhere the form of crude "pronatalism" or of attaching the blame for these conditions to mothers. In Britain pronatalism as such was weak and attention rather focused upon reduction of the infant-mortality rate. Women's organizations—most prominently the WCG and WLL—sought with some success to direct this concern into the creation of institutions which would give support to mothers. They did not create the impetus which led to the expansion of maternal- and child-welfare provision in the early twentieth century; demographic factors intersecting with economic and military imperatives were primary. But they did influence the outcomes.[57]

To this must be added the independent influence of two world wars in expanding the institutional and fiscal capacities of the state and the expectations of citizens as to its role and effectiveness in socioeconomic matters. In Europe after 1945, governments including that led by Labour in Britain, also saw universal welfare measures as one means to promote social integration after the crises of the two wars and the interwar period, but the content of these measures could be influenced by interest groups such as the Labour women.[58]

The historiography of British welfare has long moved beyond unicausal explanations to a structured complexity. One thing that it makes clear is that both class and gender did some of the "work" of making the British welfare state, but neither can plausibly be claimed as the dominant influence.

The Influence and Achievement of the Labour Women

As described earlier, it was among Labour women that the demands of class and gender most obviously intersected. From World War I onward, as the Labour party became more powerful and women obtained more civil rights, they had more opportunity to seek to put their ideals into practice. They were active in both voluntary and official sectors of the welfare system administering existing provision and, within the framework just described, seeking to shape new developments. How influential were they? The WLL in 1913 established a mother-and-baby clinic in a poor part of West London. They believed that mothers needed and wanted advice and material help and that this should be provided by the state, ideally through democratically accountable local administrative structures in which women played significant roles. But until this could be effected, like other socialist groups they believed that voluntary effort was necessary, provided that it was done without condescension. They believed that, if sensitively provided, it could be as supportive as state action and perhaps more humane; and that it was also important to ensure that state services did not become excessively bureaucratized and unresponsive to need, by striving for maximum public accountability. These principles guided their actions.

During the First World War the WLL and the WCG (again with Margaret Bondfield prominent)[59] played leading roles in successfully pressing for significantly increased central-government funding of maternity and child-welfare services. They did not create this as a public issue. This owed more to the prewar and international demographic panic, exacerbated by fears of the effects of the loss of young male life in the war. But the women took advantage of the unusually high level of public interest in an issue of especial importance to women and they played a major role in shaping the policy proposals which resulted in ways designed to meet the needs of women. By 1918 Britain had remarkably improved services and a wide-ranging Maternity and Child Welfare Act had been passed. The Labour women put much of their energy in the interwar years into coaxing local authorities into putting the discretionary elements of this legislation into operation. By the 1930s the type and level of maternity and child-welfare provision was certainly comparable with that of the U.S.[60] Also during the war the WLL was active in successful campaigns for improved allowances and pensions for the dependents of servicemen, including the unmarried mothers of servicemen's children; for higher old-age pensions, better housing, and restrictions on soaring rents.[61] The policy areas to which they gave especial attention after the war included not only the changes in the marriage laws already discussed, but all aspects of child and maternal welfare, education, health, family allowances, birth control, housing, the poor law, unemployment, juvenile crime, women's pay and work conditions, school meals, and medical inspection. They campaigned vigorously and often effectively against attempts by Conservative governments to cut services during the depression and for such innovations as "mothers' pensions," including for unmarried mothers. They felt that they had achieved the first steps toward the latter when insurance pensions for widows and orphans were introduced by the Conservative government in 1925. Labour women had played an important part in bringing them about, with support from Labour men, and women and men in other parties. The brief Labour government of 1924 had planned a similar move but lost office too soon.[62] One hundred sixty-three thousand of the poorest women and 262,000 of their children benefited immediately, widows receiving ten shillings per week, children five shillings. In 1929 the Labour government extended the pension further to cover 725,000 widows and 340,000 children.

At various times in the 1920s WS members were deputed to investigate housing conditions, the implementation of rent controls, levels of malnutrition, and conditions in maternity hospitals. Their findings provided the substance of detailed reports which formed the basis of policy recommendations and which were repeatedly pressed upon the Labour-party leadership and upon whichever party was in office at the central or local levels. The only issue on which there was open conflict with male party members was that of making birth-control advice and techniques available to women through local health centers. Here the Labour men were more responsive to the vigorous propaganda and threats of the Catholic church than were the women. Though the vote at the male-dominated national party conference was close on occasion (1,656,000 to 1,620,000 in 1926), it did not become party policy despite intense effort by the women. The trade-union vote could be wielded against them however hard they had worked in the local parties.[63] Nevertheless, in 1930 the Labour government did allow local-authority clinics to give birth-control advice, in restricted circumstances.[64] Also Labour women made such advice available through voluntary clinics, often operated by the WCG.[65]

As a minority governing party in 1924 and 1929–31, Labour responded cautiously to the constant critical pressure of the women for improved services, levels of employment, and civil rights for women, as it did to similar pressures from men, for example, to help the unemployed. Indeed Labour's refusal to raise the level of unemployment benefits in 1931 created so much dissension in the party that it destroyed the government. Nevertheless, these governments were responsible for some real advances in social policy, notably in housing, despite the fact that on each occasion Labour did not command a majority of votes in Parliament and faced a highly unfavorable economic situation.

A handful of Labour women were elected to Parliament from 1924 onward and Margaret Bondfield became Britain's first female cabinet member as minister of labour in 1929. However, women remained most effective at the local-government level. Electorally they were notably successful in London. In 1934, 729 Labour borough councillors in London were elected of whom 150 were women. Fifteen Labour women were elected to the Bermondsey council, 15 also in Hackney, 16 in Southwark, 12 in Stepney, 8 in Poplar, all poor boroughs; by 1937 there were 21 women on the Labour benches of the London County Council.[66] Larger numbers were co-opted or appointed to statutory authorities as Labour increased its municipal power in the 1930s. It is highly probable that the influence of these women on public bodies was greater than their numbers, due to their enthusiasm and new ideas.

Labour women had developed a carefully considered set of ideological and political desiderata in the years before World War I. And, in the decades following the war, they were increasingly in positions to put their ideas into practice as elected officials and as vocal members of the Labour party. The varied influence and effectiveness of Labour women in realizing their goals—and the obstacles and limitations they faced—are best illustrated through three case studies.

Local Housing

The building and design of working-class housing, like maternity and child welfare, had been an important political issue throughout Europe from the time of World War I. In Britain there was a significant expansion of municipal house building in the 1920s and 1930s. As with maternal and child welfare, women did not create housing as a political issue but they made important contributions to this debate and influenced policy outcomes.

The WLL's wartime housing campaign appears to have played the decisive role in leading the government in 1917 to appoint a cross-party women's subcommittee to scrutinize houses built by the government for munitions workers and the designs recommended to municipalities.[67] Its criticisms were so scathing that they were omitted from the published report.[68] However in further reports the subcommittee made detailed positive recommendations about housing design and equipment "based on the results of extensive enquiries into the wishes and requirements of the working women. . . . [W]e can say with confidence that our recommendations embody only such improvements as are demanded by working women themselves."[69] For example, they demanded that windows should be so designed as not only to look attractive and to admit ventilation, but to exclude draughts and be easy to clean; that skirting boards should be "simple and rounded" rather than angled or heavily molded dust traps. Local authorities seem to have taken more heed of such proposals than was always admitted; certainly many of the recommendations were incorporated into the much-improved design of interwar housing. Some local authorities, for example, in Manchester, set up similar local committees, made up of representatives of local women's organizations, including Women's Sections of the Labour party, to scrutinize housing plans. Housing was a major preoccupation of active feminists, and other women, in the 1920s, but it was an especial concern of Labour women in view of the appalling condition of much working-class housing. Improved housing was an essential means to improve living standards; and working-class women believed that changes in the design and conditions of housing significantly improved their lives.[70]

Glasgow, for example, had the worst housing conditions in Britain. Before the war women played a leading role in campaigns to improve them, in which the WLL was especially prominent, cooperating with women from the WCG and the Women's Freedom League. They drew on diverse female support, including both Catholics and supporters of the Orange Order in this bitterly sectarian city. In 1914 the Glasgow WLL, with the local Independent Labour party (ILP), formed the Glasgow Women's Housing Association and led the great rent strikes of 1915.[71] They led to the first statutory rent controls, which have never since been wholly withdrawn.[72]

Women, Labour, and Welfare in Lancashire Cotton Towns

Nelson and Preston were predominantly working-class, single-industry towns of similar size. There were striking differences in their levels of expenditure on public and social services, as illustrated in table 1. There were similar differentials in all other areas of welfare expenditure.

Table 1
Approximate per capita net expenditure on maternity and child welfare services (women aged 15 to 44)[73]

	Nelson	*Preston*
1924–25	5s. 11d.	8d.
1935–36	8s. 2d.	5s. 6d.

In Nelson a municipal maternity and child-welfare clinic had been provided by 1916 following a women's campaign. In 1921 a municipal maternity hospital and antenatal clinic was built. By 1937 97.7 percent of births in the town were attended by a doctor. The council employed six municipal midwives who undertook confinement and postnatal care and home visits to children under five. Seventy-five percent of pregnant women received antenatal care compared with a national average of fifty percent. Its levels of postnatal care were exceptional. Generous milk and feeding schemes for expectant and nursing mothers were maintained through the interwar years despite the depression and despite central-government criticisms on grounds of cost.

The politics of the towns were also radically different. Nelson, from the First World War to 1927, had equal numbers of Conservative, Liberal, and Labour councillors. In 1927 Labour took control until the war and beyond. Throughout, Labour campaigned vigorously for, and while in office maintained, high levels and standards of housing, health, welfare, and education, including nursery schools; Nelson's superiority of public services predated Labour control, though it owed much to their strong presence there. Pressure from Labour women was an important reason for this. Nelson had been a center of prewar suffragism,[74] and socialism and women were dominant in the local ILP, which was highly influential in the Labour party, and also in the town's major trade union, the Weaver's Association. After obtaining the vote the exceptionally large numbers of female activists in Nelson largely removed their affiliation from single-sex organizations apparently believing that their objectives could best be achieved through the political parties, above all the Labour party. Its commitment to social reform appears to be the main reason for Labour's growing electoral success and pressure from women was an important reason for the growth of that commitment. High levels of public expenditure continued during the depression, from which Nelson suffered less severely than Preston, though still significantly.

In Preston, Labour was weak and working-class conservatism strong until the mid-1920s.[75] The success of Preston conservatism had a great deal to do with its commitment to social reform though Preston Conservatives delivered poorer services than Labour in Nelson; so, too, the emergence of the Labour party in Preston depended on its gradual adoption of a reform program promoted by women. Women in Preston, active in the prewar suffrage movement, found the Labour party unwelcoming after the war and formed their own Women's Citizens Association (WCA). Their arguments for women's rights in paid employment, opposition to the marriage bar for female council employees, demands for equal access for girls to technical and industrial education, their challenge to the gender division in the labor force as well as their concern for the needs of mothers and women in the home, aroused the antagonism of Labour-party men and they found more sympathy among the Conservatives. Members of the WCA stood in local elections as independent candidates on issues of education, municipal housing, child welfare, and so forth. Women voted for them or for Conservatives; they shifted to Labour when it took up a more advanced program.

A Women's Section was organized in Preston in 1923. By 1928 there were 635 members. The party seems to have attracted women not previously active in politics, most of them working-class. In 1926 the Preston Labour party had no policy on state-funded nursery schools, maternity and child welfare, education, public baths or washhouses, rents, or housing design. They opposed municipal house ownership, and preferred voluntary to socialized health care. Conferences and campaigns organized by the women led to public social services taking a prominent place in Labour's local electoral program. In 1929 Labour won both parliamentary seats in Preston and came close to controlling the town council. In 1930 the local party supported family allowances and did not object to the WS cooperating with the WCA. In the later 1920s the Labour women cooperated with the Women's Total Abstinence Union, the Women Liberals, and the Women's International League for Peace and Freedom in the Women's Peace Campaign. The level of female activism and cooperation across political, class, and issue lines in this provincial town is again striking.

Both female support for Labour and Labour's political success in Preston diminished during the 1930s. This appears to have been due above all to the failure of the Labour government of 1929–31 to support the unemployed; women textile workers were especially alienated by the discrimination against unemployed women even under a female minister of labour. Membership of the Women's Sections fell off. Labour nevertheless continued to support improved municipal health services, slum clearance, and municipal services in general. The women had a permanent impact on Labour policy in Preston, whose effects were only fully apparent after the war.[76]

To point up the importance of women's role: in the comparable town of Lancaster, Labour was weak and women's activism slight. Under Liberal control in the interwar years, its levels of social expenditure and social provision were notably lower than in Preston or Nelson.[77]

The level of women's activism was a major determinant of the levels of social-welfare expenditure in these towns and of the degree of Labour-party commitment to it. And Labour was most electorally successful when it promoted social-welfare policies. Whey were the women of Nelson especially active and successful? While women's levels of paid economic activity were comparably high in all three towns, gender relations differed significantly. Women workers in Nelson were among the highest paid in the country. They worked in the same occupations as men—predominantly cotton weaving—for comparable pay. This contrasted with a clear gender division of paid labor and of pay in Preston and the still more marked gender disparities in Lancaster (where the staple industry was linoleum not textile manufacture). The greater independence and equality of Nelson women in their political and work lives appears to have been paralleled in their domestic lives, though it cannot be claimed with certainty that their role in the labor market was the determining factor in all of these complex relationships.[78]

Women in New Industrial Towns

Cotton-textile towns cannot be taken as typical of interwar Britain. To provide some contrast, Coventry and Slough were midland centers of expansion of new industries in the interwar years, rapidly expanding recipients of largely working-class migration from the depressed areas. For most of this time Coventry was governed by a Tory-Liberal "shopocracy" which put economy and low rates before social reform.[79] By 1937 Coventry lagged behind comparable boroughs in almost every form of public expenditure.[80] Labour took control in 1937 on a program of planned expansion of social and public services. In the short time before the war Labour began the slow process of providing Coventry with an adequate infrastructure, prioritizing street improvements, house building, and rescuing the appallingly neglected education system. They took such policies further after the war.[81]

The Labour party grew steadily through the interwar years with very close links and much overlap of membership with the cooperative movement among men and women. A WLL branch was formed in 1910 and remained active through the interwar years and the WCG was very active. Before the war all that the local authority had done in the maternity and child-welfare area was to appoint three health visitors. From 1914 on the WCG and WLL devoted themselves, through public meetings, petitions and demonstrations, to pressing for it to take up government grants toward further services for mothers and children in association at various times with such local organizations as the Railwaywomen's Guild, women's trade-union organizations, the Women's Auxiliary of the Free Church Council, the Women's Suffrage Society, and the Coventry District Nursing Association (a charity providing free nursing care for the poor). Women of all classes were active in these organizations. The Coventry borough council refused to take up further government subsidies, though in 1917 they opened a single clinic, the last until 1948. In the face of such resistence, until Labour took control of Coventry, women's needs could only be met through voluntary action. The Labour women opened a voluntary clinic. A Labour women's committee consisting of the WLL, WCG, and women trade unionists in 1916 also established a maternity home and day nursery for mothers working in munitions factories. Members of Women's Sections and of the WCG were among the regular voluntary workers. They included a supervisor of cleaners in a car factory, who had personal experience of severe poverty, and a hospital laundry worker. This charitable effort was popular; volunteers were thought to be more sympathetic than local officials, as these working women indeed were. They weighed babies and sold milk and food at low prices.

> We used to sell Bemax, Marmite, Ovaltine and every food there was ... orange juice, vitamin pills, the lot. It was very big welfare. You can tell by the money we took, 'cause the food was cheap, very, very cheap. . . . If anyone said, "I've no money," I'd say, "Well get it." I'd lend them the money and they'd bring it back here. . . .

There would be tea and biscuits and Christmas treats. Oral evidence suggests that mothers appreciated and enjoyed their visits to these clinics. And the volunteers enjoyed the work.[82]

The Labour women of Coventry kept effective voluntary action alive and provided for women's needs when local authorities refused to act. They extended the limits of that action and helped set the agenda for the reforms which brought Labour to power and which Labour then implemented.

In other expanding towns women struggled against a similar reluctance of relatively prosperous and rapidly changing communities to finance public services. Another of these, Slough, was controlled by an essentially conservative Ratepayers Association dedicated to economy. Labour began to win council seats in the 1930s only when it followed the lead of the radical local ILP branch which had a high proportion of female members and a female schoolteacher as chair, Ruth Harrison. This grew in strength through focusing upon rents and other housing issues, and it jolted Labour when Ruth Harrison won a council seat in 1937 having deliberately sought female votes by proposing social reform. Thereafter Labour and the ILP worked together in Slough. Labour shifted from its previous reliance upon trade-union support to campaigning on such community issues as housing, health, and education services, gradually increasing its vote and reaping success on this basis after the war.[83]

In these towns, levels of paid employment for women and total household incomes were comparable with those in Nelson, but gender divisions in pay were greater. In the new industrial towns gender conflict over employment was acute due to attempts by employers to substitute cheaper female labor for male in the new, weakly unionized, industries (e.g., electrical engineering); hence the unwelcoming attitude of local unions and Labour-party branches to women.

These cases suggest that publicly funded social-welfare services were best where women were most politically active, regardless of the party in power, though high levels of services seem generally to have correlated with a significant Labour presence. Labour became increasingly committed to public social welfare in the interwar years, but was most likely to do so under pressure from women. Women voted for social-reform parties and Labour gained women's votes when it took up reform as did other parties. Everywhere there were signs of women's public activism on these issues which was channeled not only into political parties but also into other voluntary organizations and single-sex interest groups. What determined the receptiveness of local political structures to women will only become clearer when more local studies are completed.

The case studies give, above all, glimpses of quite ordinary women helping to shape public policies and their own and other women's lives. They suggest the variety of roles of Labour and other women in what is emerging as a rich variety of women's activism throughout interwar Britain. The activities of all of the groups to be found in the localities—most of them local branches of national organizations—require exploration before we can fully understand the complete extent of women's public activism and also the construction of the British welfare system through the period of the interwar years when it was emerging and malleable. The evidence also suggests considerable local variations in women's experience and influence and in the chronology of welfare developments.

Conclusion

This essay has sought to dispel notions that class was outstandingly salient in the making of the British welfare state and gender insignificant; that women were politically powerless before obtaining the national vote and exerted little political influence, and made little use of their civil rights thereafter. Nor does the British case, if we consider the period after 1920 when state welfare expanded most vigorously, support the view that "the power of women's social action movements was inversely related to the range and generosity of state welfare benefits for women and children."[84]

It does, however, support the view that while characteristics of the state "affected the extent and character of women's movements, it cannot explain their subsequent successes and failures."[85] Also it seeks to suggest, grounded in an analysis of the role of women in a major political party, that women in local government and voluntary organizations in Britain, sometimes but not always inspired by feminist goals, made a positive contribution to state formation, though one whose full extent cannot be assessed in the current state of research.

It also indicates that the influence of the Labour, and indeed of other, women on social politics has to be analyzed on a number of levels: local and central, short- and long-term, direct and indirect, and that the salience of each level varied from place to place. Labour was a much weaker, though growing, party in the interwar period than in the post-1945 Britain. This was a time in which ideas were formulated which could not always be put into immediate operation, but which helped shape postwar legislation. Women's ideas were sometimes rejected, or failed, as is the nature of politics. They were most effective when they could ally themselves with other forces, as is also normal in politics. That women's influence was more often local and their influence on central-government policy indirect indicates their weakness as well as their strength. Furthermore, though they promoted social welfare, it is legitimate to ask how far they promoted women. In giving women public voices, public offices, and new skilled jobs in welfare services they went some way, if less far than their ambitions. Above all, it is safe to say that the postwar British "welfare state" would not have looked the same without their work.

Notes

1. M. Charlot, "Women and Elections in Britain," in H. R. Penniman, ed., *Britain at the Polls, 1979: A Study of the General Election* (Washington and London, 1981), 244.

2. Christine Collette, *For Women and for Labour: The Women's Labour League, 1906–1918* (Manchester, 1989).

3. For some examples see S. S. Holton, *Feminism and Democracy: Women's Suffrage and Reform Politics in Britain, 1900–1918* (Cambridge, 1986), and Pat Jalland, *Women, Marriage and Politics, 1860–1914* (Oxford, Eng., 1986).

4. M. Pugh, *The Tories and the People, 1880–1935* (Oxford, Eng., 1985), 49; L. Walker, "Party Political Women: A Comparative Study of Liberal Women and the Primrose League, 1890–1914," in J. Rendall, ed., *Equal or Different: Women's Politics, 1800–1914* (Oxford, Eng., 1987), 165–91; and C. Hirschfield, "A Fractured Faith: Liberal Party Women and the Suffrage Issue in Britain, 1892–1914," *Gender and History* 2 (1990): 173–97.

5. B. Harrison, *Prudent Revolutionaries* (Oxford, Eng., 1987), 128.

6. Hirschfield, "A Fractured Faith," 174. The Scandinavian countries came closer to the British pattern in this respect. See Ida Blom, "Voluntary Motherhood, 1900–1930: Theories and Politics of a Norwegian Feminist, Katti Anker Moller," and A-L Seip and H. Ibsen, "Family Welfare, Which Policy? Norway's Road to Child Allowances"; both in Gisela Bock and Pat Thane, eds., *Maternity and Gender Policies: Women and the Rise of European Welfare States 1880s–1950s* (London, 1991).

7. Jalland, *Women*, 216.

8. Hirschfield, "A Fractured Faith," and M. Ostrogorski, *Democracy and the Organization of Political Parties*, vol. 1 (London, 1902), 531, 552–66.

9. It is important to be clear about the peculiar structure of the Labour party. It was, and is, possible to be a member of an "affiliated organization." The largest of these were/are trade unions. Members of such organizations were not necessarily active in the day-to-day running of local branches or in local politics, which are generally controlled by "individual members." Affiliated organizations do, however, have votes proportionate to the size of their membership in the selection of candidates and in party conference decisions.

10. Collette, *For Women*, 42, 60–61.

11. Harrison, *Prudent Revolutionaries*, 129–30.

12. Pat Thane, "The Women of the British Labour Party and Feminism, 1906–45," in H. L. Smith, ed., *British Feminism in the Twentieth Century* (Aldershot, Eng., 1990), 125. Report of the Annual Conference of Labour Women (hereafter AC), 1907, 1909.

13. Alastair Reid, "Intelligent Artisans and Aristocrats of Labour," in J. M. Winter, ed., *The Working Class in Modern British History*, Essays in Honour of Henry Pelling (Cambridge, 1983), 171–86.

14. The Guild was apparently similar in social composition to the WLL.

15. Pat Thane, "The Working Class and State 'Welfare' in Britain, 1880–1914," *Historical Journal* 27 (1984): 890.

16. J. Lawrence, "Party Politics and the People: Continuity and Change in the Political History of Wolverhampton, 1815–1914" (Ph.D. diss., Cambridge University, 1989).

17. Pat Thane, "Women and the Poor Law in Late Victorian England," *History Workshop* 6 (1978): 29–51.

18. *Labour Woman*, March 1911. For a similar argument using American evidence, see Carole Turbin, "Beyond Dichotomies: Interdependence in mid-Nineteenth Century Working Class Families in the United States," *Gender and History* 1 (1989): 293–308.

19. Thane, "Women of the British Labour Party," 125–26; AC 1912, 1936, 1927; and *Labour Woman*, April, June, and October 1926.

20. Collette, *For Labour*, passim.

21. See also, *Labour Woman*, November and December 1941; AC 1944 and 1947.

22. AC 1930 and 1945, though this was discussed on many other occasions at conferences and in *Labour Woman*. For further discussion of these and other ideas of the Labour women see Thane, "Women of the British Labour Party," and Thane, "Visions of Gender in the Making of the British Welfare State: The Case of Women in the British Labour Party and Social Policy, 1906–45," in Bock and Thane, *Maternity and Gender Policies*, 93–118.

23. *Labour Woman*, March 1922, among others.

24. *Labour Woman*, September 1928.

25. *Labour Woman*, June 1911.

26. *Labour Woman*, April 1920, July 1937.

27. See also *Labour Woman*, February 1918, September 1922 (quote).

28. The complicated and important story of women in English local government before 1914 has recently been admirably surveyed in Patricia Hollis, *Ladies Elect: Women in English Local Government, 1865–1914* (Oxford, 1987). Also see Rendall, *Equal or Different*.

29. Hollis, *Ladies Elect*, Appendix B.

30. *Labour Woman*, August 1920. Hannah Mitchell, *The Hard Way Up* (London, 1977), describes the experience of one of them, 225ff.

31. Hirschfield, "A Fractured Faith," 171.

32. AC 1970, 8.

33. *Labour Woman*, July 1925.

34. *Labour Woman*, September 1938.

35. Dora Russell's autobiographical account of this period should not be read uncritically; see Russell, *The Tamarisk Tree: My Quest for Liberty and Love* (London, 1975).

36. *Labour Woman*, November 1918.

37. Ibid. See also AC 1910, 1913, and 1943; *Labour Woman*, August 1928 and February 1945.

38. *Labour Woman*, May 1924.

39. E. Rathbone, *The Disinherited Family* (London, 1924), passim.

40. Ellen Ross, "Fierce Questions and Taunts: Married Life in Working Class London, 1870–1914," *Feminist Studies* 8 (1982); Pat Ayers and Jan Lambertz, "Marriage Relations, Money and Domestic Violence in Working Class Liverpool, 1919–1939," in Jane Lewis, ed., *Labour and Love* (Oxford, 1986); Elizabeth Roberts, *A Woman's Place* (Oxford, 1984), 110–12; and Andrew Davies, *Leisure, Gender and Poverty: Working Class Culture in Salford and Manchester, 1900–1939* (Eng., 1991).

41. Male Labour MPs expressed similar views and similar resentment of speeches by MPs of other parties which assumed that parental negligence was a male working-class norm and that where it occurred it was oral rather than material in origin. Pat Thane, "The Labour Party and State Welfare," in K. D. Brown, *The First Labour Party* (London, 1985), 183–216.

42. *Labour Woman*, May 1939.

43. *Labour Woman*, December 1913.

44. J. Gaffin and D. Thoms, *Caring and Sharing: A Centenary History of the Co-operative Women's Guild* (Manchester, 1983), 70–71.

45. AC 1914, 16.

46. *Labour Woman*, April 1913.

47. Gaffin and Thomas, *Caring and Sharing*, 174.

48. Mitchell, *The Hard Way Up*, 226.

49. *Labour Woman*, July 1924 and July 1925.

50. Despite steady immigration from Ireland and the limited localized Jewish immigration in the late nineteenth century, and the distinctive characteristics of Scotland, Wales, and England, Britain was more homogeneous than her European neighbors, with the exception of the much smaller Nordic states.

51. For a fuller development of this interpretation of the British state see Pat Thane, "Government and Society in England and Wales, 1750–1914," 1–62, and José Harris, "Society and the State in Twentieth Century Britain," 63–118, in F. M. L. Thompson, ed., *The Cambridge Social History of Britain, 1750–1950*, vol. 3 (Cambridge, 1990). See also the chapter entitled "Philanthropy" by F. K. Prochaska in the same volume, 311–56; H. C. G. Matthew, *Gladstone, 1809–1874* (Oxford, 1986); and John Brewer, *The Sinews of War* (London, 1989).

52. Jay Winter, "Some Paradoxes of the First World War," in Richard Wall and Jay Winter, *The Upheaval of War: Family, Work and Welfare in Europe, 1914–18*

(Cambridge, 1988), 9–42, and Gerald D. Feldman, *Army, Industry and Labor in Germany, 1914–18* (Princeton, N.J., 1966).

53. Winter, *The Upheaval of War*, 40.

54. R. Davidson and R. Lowe, "Bureaucracy and Innovation in British Welfare Policy, 1870–1945," in W. J. Mommsen, ed., *The Emergence of the Welfare State in Britain and Germany, 1850–1950* (London, 1981), 263–95.

55. See "Borderlands," Seth Koven's contribution to this volume.

56. Ibid. Thane, "Visions of Gender," surveys this in detail.

57. These issues are fully discussed and documented in Bock and Thane, *Maternity and Gender Policies*.

58. Peter Baldwin, *The Politics of Social Solidarity: Class Bases of the European Welfare State, 1875–1975* (New York, 1990).

59. Gaffin and Thoms, *Caring and Sharing*, 71–72.

60. Thane, "Visions of Gender" 104–7.

61. G. Thomas, "State Maintenance of Women during the First World War: The Case of Separation Allowances and Pensions," Ph.D. diss., University of Sussex, 1988; Susan Pedersen, "Social Policy and the Reconstruction of the Family in Britain and France, 1900–1945" (Ph.D. diss, Harvard University, 1989); and R. Harrison, "The War Emergency Workers National Committee, 1914–20," in A. Briggs and J. Saville, eds., *Essays in Labour History, 1886–1923* (London, 1971), 214–59.

62. *Labour Woman*, April 1923.

63. A. Leathard, *The Flight for Family Planning* (London, 1980), and R. Soloway, *Birth Control and the Population Question in England, 1877–1930* (Chapel Hill, N.C., 1982).

64. Leathard, *The Fight for Family Planning*, 30, 34, 40, 44–50; J. Lewis, *The Politics of Motherhood* (London, 1980), 212, n. 42; S. Rowbotham, *A New World for Women: Stella Browne—Socialist Feminist*, (London, 1977); and Thane, "Women of the British Labour Party," 136–37.

65. Oral evidence, Mrs. N. Branson.

66. *Labour Woman*, December 1934.

67. M. Swenarton, *Homes Fit for Heroes* (London, 1981), 91, based on detailed scrutiny of government sources.

68. Ibid., 91–92.

69. Ministry of Reconstruction Advisory Council, Women's Housing Sub-Committee, Final Report, Cd. 9232, 1919, 20.

70. Manchester Women's History Group, "Ideology in Bricks and Mortar—Women's Housing in Manchester between the Wars," *North West Labour History* 12 (1987): 24–48.

71. These were largest in Glasgow, but occurred also in other towns, with women always to the fore.

72. J. Melling, *Rent Strikes* (Edinburgh, 1983), and S. Damer, "State, Class and Housing: Glasgow, 1885–1919," in J. Melling, ed., *Housing, Social Policy and the State* (London, 1980), 91–101.

73. J. Mark-Lawson, "Occupational Segregation and Women's Politics," in Sylvia Walby, ed., *Gender Segregation at Work* (Milton Keynes, Eng., 1988), 160.

74. Jill Liddington and Jill Norris, *One Hand Tied behind Us: The Rise of the Women's Suffrage Movement* (London, 1978).

75. M. Savage, *The Dynamics of Working Class Politics: The Labour Movement in Preston, 1880–1940* (Cambridge, 1987).

76. Savage, *Dynamics*, 173–74, 181–82.

77. Mark-Lawson et al., "Local Politics," passim.

78. Mark-Lawson, "Occupational Segregation," and Mark-Lawson et al., "Local Politics," passim.

79. B. Lancaster and T. Mason, *Life and Labour in a Twentieth Century City: The Experience of Coventry* (Coventry, 1987), 342–66.

80. Ibid., 175.

81. N. Tiratsoo, *Reconstruction, Affluence and Labour Politics: Coventry, 1945–60* (London, 1990).

82. M. Lodge, "Women and Welfare: An Account of the Development of Infant Welfare Schemes in Coventry, 1900–1940, with Special Reference to the Work of the Coventry Women's Co-operative Guild," in Lancaster and Mason, *Life and Labour*, 81–97. Quotes on page 92.

93. M. Savage, *The Social Bases of Labour Politics in Britain, 1919–1939*, Department of Sociology, University of Surrey, Occasional Papers, no. 15, 1988.

84. Seth Koven and Sonya Michel, "Womanly Duties: Maternalist Politics and the Origins of Welfare States in France, Germany, Great Britain and the United States, 1880–1920," *American Historical Review* 95 (1990): 1079. The argument is more fully developed in Thane, "Visions of Gender."

85. Koven and Michel, "Womanly Duties," 1080.

11

A Revolution in the Family:
The Challenge and Contradictions of
Maternal Citizenship in Australia

Marilyn Lake

Australian women won the vote a year after the establishment of the nation-state in 1901, when six British colonies joined together in a federation to form the Commonwealth of Australia. It was the second country in the world, following New Zealand, to grant womanhood suffrage. From the beginning Australians generally entertained optimistic visions of the role of the state in securing the welfare and independence of its citizens.[1] The early political success of organized labor in Australia (the Australian Labor party (ALP) has just celebrated its centenary) promised a realization of this vision. The first federal Labor government came to office in 1904. A federal arbitration system, established in the same year, formally required that wage-fixation procedures accord priority to workers' needs rather than the employers' desire for profit—the Basic (family) Wage was institutionalized in the Harvester judgment in 1907 (a judgment that in defining the worker as male also formalized women's dependency).[2] In 1908 old-age and invalid pensions—paid out of general revenue—were established for men and women. In some states boarding-out schemes paid deserted or in other ways indigent mothers to keep their children. Australia acquired a reputation for "state experiments." Numerous visitors arrived from the Northern Hemisphere, from the United States, Britain, France, and Germany, to observe this "social laboratory."

Social policy was formulated in Australia in a context of self-conscious nation building. Developments in Australia were also, however, part of a broader international picture. As Seth Koven and Sonya Michel have recently written, "The decades before World War I were supercharged with nationalist agendas and anxieties concerning depopulation, degeneration and efficiency, as states vied for military and imperial pre-eminence."[3] These anxieties were especially acute in Australia, a new nation of just four million people and considered to be dangerously underpopulated. As a new nation, Australia was preoccupied with its future and possibilities of achieving "national greatness." As immigrants to a "newfound land" and the dispossessors of the original Aboriginal custodians, British Australians were anxious about the "future of the race" and their ability (and perhaps at an unconscious level, their right) to hold the continent. The long coastline and "vast empty spaces" heightened the young nation's sense of vulnerability. British Australians' proximity to the numerous peoples of Asia simply accentuated their sense of isolation and the insecurity of this outpost of empire.

The keystone of the national policy of defense and development, then, was a large increase in the white population. "The more young Australians we have," observed Labor Prime Minister Andrew Fisher, "the wealthier the country must be."[4] White women as mothers were to play a crucial part in the national population project: women's value to the nation lay precisely in their capacity to give birth and nurture, or in the words of the *Australian Medical Gazette,* "in the breeding of a stronger and sturdier race."[5]

In 1912 following concerted lobbying by Labor-party women, Labor Prime Minister Fisher introduced a Maternity Allowance of £5 (the equivalent of three to four weeks' wages for a woman factory worker) to be paid to mothers on the birth of a baby. Fisher's avowed intention was to alleviate the trials of childbirth. "Statistics show," he said, "that maternity is more dangerous than war."[6] The object was, he said, to "protect the present citizens of the Commonwealth and give to coming citizens a greater assurance that they will receive proper attention at the most critical period in their lives."[7] The Baby Bonus, as it came to be called, would be paid to unmarried mothers as well as married (a decision that caused heated, extensive, and revealing public debate), but not to "women who were Asiatics, Aboriginal natives of Australia, Papua or the islands of the Pacific" (a decision that went largely unremarked).[8]

The implications of the racial basis of national policy for all

Australian women were vast. Aboriginal women would be systematically deprived of their children as officials, operating under
state laws, removed half-caste children to institutions or white
homes, while at the same time motherhood was lauded as white
women's grandest vocation. The oppressions of national policy
would be compounded by feminist politics. Campaigns invoking
the concept of the "mother of the race" and utilizing the strategy
of maternal citizenship to promote white working-class women's
interests effectively, if unthinkingly, defined black women as ineligible, first for motherhood and as a corollary, for citizenship.

Opposition to the Maternity Allowance accused the prime minister of political corruption, of bribing the recently enfranchised
women voters: "the sudden desire to please the mothers of the
community must arise from something."[9] Conservatives deplored
the encouragement of dependence on the state, which they identified in such welfare measures, advocating instead the provision
of social security through the self-help model of social insurance,
recently exemplified in Britain in Lloyd George's 1911 Insurance
Act. The most strident criticism of the Maternity Allowance, however, focused on the extension of the payment to unmarried mothers, with opponents objecting in terms that anticipated later
objections to the more ambitious feminist proposal for motherhood endowment and that bear out Carole Pateman's argument
that the social contract of the democratic state rests on a sexual
contract.[10] Critics of the Maternity Allowance condemned the fact
that the extension of the payment (constituted by legislation as a
civil right) to the mothers of "illegitimate" children dissolved the
distinction between the "deserving" and "undeserving" and undermined the institution of marriage. The legislation substituted a
contract between mothers and the state for the rightful contract
between husband and wife. The extension of these new civil rights
to those who "have become mothers before they have become
wives" violated "the law of marriage, which the State exists to
safeguard." "Our national honour and well-being, our very existence is bound up with respect for the marriage bond."[11]

The main question, said the Reverend Professor D. S. Adam of
the University of Melbourne, when introducing a deputation to
the prime minister, was this:

> Assuming the state thinks it wise to give a maternity allowance
> in token of its appreciation and approval of the honourable

service rendered by a mother—and not as a dole—was it right to make no distinction between honourable mothers who became mothers under the sanctum of the law of marriage, approved by the state as the foundation of true national welfare and those who became mothers in a dishonourable way, and in a way the State did not and could not approve? They were specially concerned in maintaining the sanctity of marriage as an institution of supreme importance. (Hear! Hear!) They were concerned lest that institution be belittled through the Government's proposal.[12]

The mobilization of opposition forces had little effect. The legislation establishing the Maternity Allowance was passed by the federal Labor government to the loud acclaim of the Women's Organising Committee of the ALP which resolved on behalf of the "women workers of Victoria" to congratulate the prime minister for conferring "this instalment of the mother's maternal rights." Women of all classes rushed to avail themselves of the payment.[13]

Two years later, in 1914, the nation was at war and mothers were expected to deliver up their sons to do battle for Britain. Women were praised for their capacity for self-sacrifice—first sacrificing their "selfish" interests to perform the national duty of motherhood, then sacrificing their sons to the military authorities. At war their sons might make the "supreme sacrifice" but their collective death would bring forth immortal life, the birth of a nation.[14] The Australian participation in World War I, in particular the Landing at Gallipoli in 1915, acquired profound national mythological significance. The men's deeds, it was said, had made Australia a nation. In proving their manhood on a world stage the soldiers also proved Australia's nationhood. The day of the Landing—25 April 1915—became the de facto national day, a public holiday, commemorated ever after. Partly because of the mythic significance of their deeds and partly because the troops were all voluntary recruits—the defeat of two referenda on conscription in 1916 and 1917 meant that Australia alone of the combatant nations did not introduce conscription to fight the war—returned soldiers in Australia enjoyed a privileged status and incomparably rich rewards.[15] Their repatriation benefits, it was generally agreed, outmatched those of any other country. Their veterans' organization, the Returned Soldiers and Sailors Imperial League of Australia (soon abbreviated to the Returned

Servicemen's League (RSL), enjoyed more power. The war established the citizen soldier in Australia as the exemplary citizen.

In her study of the campaigns for family endowment in Britain
during and after the war, Susan Pedersen has suggested that the
allocation of separation allowances to the families of soldiers
provided a model for feminists seeking to establish the distinctive
claims of mothers and children.[16] Campaigners for child endowment in Australia also pointed to the precedent of wartime separation allowances. "The children of workers who did not go to the
war get just as hungry," said Jean Daley of the Women's Organising Committee of the Victorian branch of the ALP, "as do the
children of soldiers; so if endowment is good for the children of
soldiers, it is equally good and fair for the children of the rest of
the community."[17] But the war was important to postwar feminist
campaigns in Australia in another, more significant way. Military
service—as a form of citizenship—provided an important model
for feminists seeking to establish the economic independence of
women. The citizen soldier became a model for the citizen mother.

The war consolidated the idea of a sexually differentiated citizenship, but at the same time established the citizen soldier—the
male citizen—as the paradigmatic citizen. Women making claims
as citizens attempted to work within these contradictory terms.
The model of the citizen soldier allowed women to conceptualize
and argue for citizenship as a two-sided arrangement: citizens
owed a duty and responsibility to the state, but they in turn should
be cared for and their services economically rewarded. The model
of the citizen soldier allowed women to define the mother's primary contract as one with the state, not with her husband. It
promised women the possibility of disconnecting motherhood
from wifehood. So women activists began to campaign not just
for honor and recognition, but also for remuneration. The mother
of a family "has a status in her own home," explained Mary Perry,
the president of the Housewives' Association in New South Wales,
"but she has no status with the State; the State does not give her
any consideration for bearing a family. If a war happens, the State
does not hesitate to take her children; the children then belong to
the State and not to the mothers."[18] Women, in other words,
worked for the state and like soldiers, deserved "the consideration"
of payment. If money could be found to finance the destruction
of war, they argued, so it could be "to ensure a better and more
efficient life."[19] Ironically, as women campaigned for motherhood

endowment, for economic remuneration for their distinctive life-giving service to the state, they often did so by equating it with the death-dealing work of military service. The travail of the mother—the suffering, injury, and death—was said to equal that of the soldier.

Following the war activist women (Labor women and nonparty feminists) joined together in a campaign to win further "instalments" of women's "maternal rights." Enfranchised for almost two decades, Australian women sought the economic independence that would give substance to their political rights. Pride in their initial achievements (the vote, the Maternity Allowance, state-funded free clinics for mothers and babies, women's hospitals, old-age and invalid pensions, boarding-out allowances to deserted mothers) instilled confidence in future successes. "In no other part of the civilised world, as far as one can ascertain," commented Lilian Locke-Burns, president of the New South Wales Association of Women Workers in 1919, "is so much being done by the state in the way of providing for mothers and children as in the Australian Commonwealth."[20] She was particularly pleased that Australian provision took the form of direct grants from the state, because contribution-based insurance schemes discriminated against the wageless, especially women who could usually not afford the premiums. She elaborated:

> In Great Britain and some other countries which lay claim to some share in democratic reforms, the mothers are only protected (if protection it may be called) under some form of social insurance. In the American states also very little has been done so far in this direction beyond some attention to delinquent children, and the usual institutional efforts that we find in most countries which have evolved beyond the barbaric stage. Neither in England or America do we hear of any such humanitarian provision as the Australian Maternity Allowance.[21]

In the 1920s women embarked on a campaign to achieve the economic independence of women, single and married. They put forward a platform of three interdependent planks: equal pay, motherhood endowment, and childhood endowment. The last two were seen as distinctive, separate demands: childhood endowment to secure the welfare of all children and to remove the pretext for the men's family wage, and motherhood endowment as economic reward for women's work and to free women from a "humiliating dependence" on individual men and thus end their condition of "sex slavery." "Woman will be a sex slave," declared Nelle Rickie, delegate of the Theatrical Employees' Union to the Victorian Trades Hall Council, "until such time as the community and not the individual father and husband is responsible for the provision of the necessities of life for the rising generation—until such time as there is Childhood and Motherhood Endowment."[22] It was a program that addressed the differences between women as well as between women and men, a program that aimed to secure for women the economic rights that would give substance to their political rights, thus winning "full citizenship" for women.

Although the campaign was supported by women of different classes, its impetus and orientation came primarily from working-class women. "All over the world today," declared Henrietta Greville, first woman president of the Workers' Education Association, "the cry goes up for the Economic Independence of the Married Woman."[23] The choice of "independence" as a goal (rather than say, "equality") is significant in class terms. Labor women spoke to a socialist tradition that stressed the degradation of dependence for men, and hence, too, for women. "Today," wrote Muriel Heagney, leading union organizer and researcher, in 1923, "nothing exerts a more strangulating influence on trade union action and policy than the spirit of dependence that permeates the working class. The individual worker feels that he [*sic*] is dependent on the capitalist. The wife of the worker is dependent on her husband, the child on the parent and, in turn, the aged parent on the son or daughter. . . ."[24] Labor women's reading of socialist theory involved a particular orientation and interpretation conditioned and made possible by feminist discourse: sex slavery emulated wage slavery. Economic independence was the answer to both. There was a recognition that women's dependence made them vulnerable to sexual exploitation. "The economic dependence of women is responsible for the double standard of morality that now obtains," said Jean Daley, "and this attitude of men has been at the root of most women's troubles in the past and every mother should strive to make her daughter self-supporting." Women "who economically depended on men," she added, "moulded themselves to his desire." Women's need to win a man meant, moreover, that they concentrated on the "matter of sex attraction" to the exclusion of politics.[25] Single women who could not obtain an adequate wage, sufficient to allow them to live "decently," were of course vulnerable to exploitation, but it was the condition of working-class married women that really captured the imagination of these interwar working-class feminists.

Muriel Heagney referred to "the old belief that a nation's greatness may be measured by the status of its womanhood" in order to observe that "much remains to be done with regard to the working mother."[26] There was a sense that single women and unencumbered married women had won access to a relative independence through the labor market. Other, richer, women, enjoyed an independence made possible by inheritance or a husband's wealth. The relative independence of some women, however, simply highlighted the exploited and demeaning position of other women, especially the working-class mother, hence the emphasis on the "slavery of the married woman."[27]

The priority accorded to the "working mother" in these feminist campaigns attests to the success of working-class women in these years in developing a political strategy that transformed dominant national concerns about the "preservation of the race" into a program to advance the interests of working-class women. They drew on a discourse of motherhood to challenge the power of men in working-class politics and in the family, by opposing the dependent and demeaning category of "wife" with the alternative idea of the "mother citizen." To reiterate an earlier point, however, the strategy of fashioning a politics around the identity of "mother of the race" compounded the oppression of Aboriginal women and ultimately it rebounded on all women.

Working-class women also invoked the importance of the "mother of the race" to establish their equality of status with middle-and upper-class women, to challenge *their* perceived monopoly on "independence." Lilian Locke Burns looked forward to the day when there would be "a properly organised social system where the economic independence of women was fully recognised and assured." She anticipated a "stage of world evolution" when motherhood did not automatically entail dependence on the one hand or exhaustion on the other, when "One Woman One Job" was the order of the day. "Then indeed a mother will not be expected to combine half a dozen occupations to the serious detriment of herself and her children." Furthermore, "we have also to recognise that if a woman desires and chooses motherhood she should be as economically free, as little dependent upon others as the well paid woman who has climbed to the top of the ladder in the scholastic, commercial, literary or any other area of her own choosing."[28]

Working-class women entertained no illusions about the liberating character of paid work per se: decades before middle-class women experienced the costs of the "double day," these working mothers were all too familiar with the stress and strains resulting from a double or triple burden of paid and unpaid work. In evidence to the Royal Commission on Child Endowment in 1928, Lena Lynch, secretary of the Women's Central Organizing Committee, pointed out that in the working class, "the wages are always supplemented by the wife." Asked whether it was "a common occurrence for the mothers of working class families to go out to work," she replied,

> —Yes, it is a very common thing; that is, if there is no other assistance in the house, such as taking in a lodger, letting rooms, or the mother engaging in dressmaking. I find that they invariably do something else to assist in the family upkeep, such as charring, washing, working at pickle and jam factories, and so on.
> —Even when the husband is in work?
> —Yes.[29]

Working-class feminists believed that women without children could, indeed should, enter paid work. "The truly equal and happy marriage is often one in which both husband and wife are wage-earners," wrote Jean Daley. "When children come, however, they complicate the situation." At a time when breast-feeding was actively promoted as the best antidote for infant mortality and mothering was becoming an ever more demanding and "scientific" occupation, working-class feminists saw that the necessity to go "out to work" interfered with a woman's ability to mother. The work of mothering should not render a mother an inferior citizen, however. "Until mothering was regarded as national work and paid for as such," said Jean Daley, "some period of dependence is inevitable for the working class woman."[30] Motherhood endowment was thus considered an especially important policy for working-class women.

The proposal for motherhood endowment directly challenged

the institution of the family wage—the higher wage paid to all men on the assumption that they were breadwinners. Feminists wanted the portion due to the "family" paid directly to the intended beneficiaries, by the state. They wanted everyone to be paid as "individuals." The "individual" thus became an empowering concept for women struggling to shake off their conjugal identity. "Once we challenge the existing theoretical basis of wages," wrote Muriel Heagney, "and endeavour to introduce this new principle ["the right of every individual to an individual income"] we will be driven inevitably to reconstruct our whole policy on wages."[31] Feminists deployed the concept of maternal citizenship in a bid to achieve for mothers the status of independent individuals. The institution of the family wage "did not recognise women and children as individuals at all—they were just appendages to men," explained Lena Lynch of the New South Wales branch of the ALP, "endowment would recognise the women citizens and the child."[32]

Labor women had some success in having the goal of motherhood endowment written into the platform of the national trade-union congress and the Australian Labor party, but Labor-party men consistently interpreted motherhood endowment to mean child endowment and thus a policy to establish the independence of women was subsumed by a scheme to relieve child poverty. While some men thus paid lip service to the proposal for motherhood endowment, others actively condemned it as "of no benefit to the working classes" and as "unscientific."[33] Some attacked it as a threat to the single man's wage, while others saw the threat to men's power.

"As a mere man and a unionist," exclaimed one, John Newton,

> I wonder what is going to happen next. When the Movement foolishly allowed Mrs Nelle Rickie and a few misguided enthusiasts to put a "Motherhood Endowment" display in the last Eight Hours procession, they should have expected something like the present propaganda. For twelve months now there has been insistent propaganda for "women's freedom," the "economic independence of women" claptrap has been going on insistently and insidiously. The Trades Hall Council has foolishly adopted the sentiments of Mrs. Rickie and it seems inevitable that there will be change in the adjustment of wages. The family basis of the adjustment of wages must be maintained—a man must receive sufficient so that a wife need not go to work. The home

must be preserved. The married woman should not go to work, as she owes a duty to husband and children.[34]

The idea of "maternal citizenship" enabled feminists to reconceptualize women's duty, their "service," as one owing not to an individual master/husband, but to the abstract entity of the state.

In arguing for women's economic rights, feminists stressed that mothers, like soldiers, rendered distinctive services to the state *and* risked death and disability in the performance of their national duties. This theme and the insistence on the occupational hazards of women's work became ever more insistent as publicity regarding Australia's comparatively high and increasing maternal-mortality rate in the 1920s received more political attention. The national Royal Commission on Health concluded in 1926 that the high level of maternal mortality constituted a "grave national danger."[35] Since 1922 there had been a "steady and almost uninterrupted rise" in the death rate.[36] And, as in the case of soldiers, "the majority of mothers were lost in the prime of life."[37] But it was not just in the deaths that motherhood resembled military service; there was also the legacy of disability. Dame Janet Campbell, a visiting British "expert," made explicit reference to the casualties of motherhood in her report:

> For every woman who dies as a result of child-bearing many others are injured more or less seriously, more or less permanently. It is impossible to measure accurately this morbidity and the consequent amount of illness and suffering which women are called upon to endure. We can only guess at it from the records of gynaecological hospitals, though we know enough to be sure that in many ways this physical disability and the resulting loss of health and strength is an even more serious matter than the actual mortality.[38]

Whereas repatriation hospitals in the 1920s bore witness to the long-term cost of war, and medical records showed that about one third of returned soldiers drew invalid pensions, so hospital records also showed that "fifty percent of all mothers suffer from some weakening of bodily function following on child birth."[39]

As a result of the pressure of women's organizations and following the decision of the New South Wales Labor government to introduce a limited form of child endowment in 1927, a Royal

Commission was appointed to consider the desirability and feasibility of a national system of child and/or maternal endowment.[40]
Hundreds of women and men gave evidence. Prominent among
the witnesses was Muriel Heagney, one of two representatives at
the Royal Commission of the Victorian branch of the ALP. Heagney drew on classical mythology to stress the parallel between
the mother and the soldier. "Every mother," said Heagney, "like
Hercules in the quest of Alcestis, has been down into the Valley
of the Shadow and wrestled there with death in order to bring a
young life into the light of day." She continued: "Twenty-four
centuries ago, a mother, in the play Medea claimed that her lot
was harder even than a soldier's: 'They say that we women live a
sheltered life in the home while men go forth and fight with the
spear. They reason ill. For I would rather thrice confront an enemy
with my shield than once bring forth a child.' "[41] Heagney also
pointed to the vast sums spent on war and the repatriation of
soldiers—by 1926 estimated at £627,596,308; just a fraction of
the amount would pay for motherhood endowment, sufficient to
allow for the proper care and rehabilitation of mothers, to allow
them to emerge unscathed from their travail in the Valley of the
Shadow.

Heagney, like most feminists at this time, was a proponent of
individual incomes for all adults; hence their support for equal
pay, their demand for "the rate for the job" (and not the sex).
Women prevented from earning a wage by motherhood or other
nurturant labor should, they argued, be remunerated as separate
citizens. As Heagney told the Royal Commission: "the mother
would ultimately draw an income for her services as home-maker,
and not as a wife."[42] The dependent status of the wife was demeaning and oppressive. Citizenship demanded recognition of women
as independent individuals.

Irene Longman, president of the Queensland National Council
of Women, also put the case for the economic independence for
all women through recognition of maternal citizenship. The Royal
Commissioners' disbelief resulted in the following exchange:

> "Your theory is that the State should pay the wife for services
> rendered to the State?" "Yes, we say that her services to the
> state are as great as those of the men; and therefore, that those
> services should be paid for as an independent economic unit."
> "Women could live apart from their husbands? . . . That is an

alteration of the existing conditions." "Yes, absolutely. It is revolutionary, and that is what we wish."[43]

But it was mothers' positioning as wives to husbands in the democratic state and in working-class politics, the dependence of the social contract on the sexual contract, that defeated women's attempt to disconnect motherhood from wifehood.[44] The resistance to women's bid for economic independence highlighted the contradictions of "maternal citizenship" in a patriarchal state. The citizenship of men was predicated on the dependency and services of women. The Royal Commission put the proposal of an independent income for mothers to witness Ernest Barker, the general secretary of the Western Australia branch of the Labor party.

> —We hear a lot about the immense service they render to the nation and our obligation to recognise them. Do you consider that the wife should be included in any possible endowment scheme?
> —No, for the simple reason that the wife is necessary to keep the husband working; if she does not do so the man cannot keep on working.[45]

Men's citizenship rights included conjugal rights: the rights of husbands to the sexual and domestic services of a wife. In these exchanges women spoke of the "mother" and the "woman citizen"; men replied by referring to "the wife."

Labor men recognized that the logic of women's economic claim (that part of the family wage be redistributed to the intended recipients, to mothers and children) demanded acknowledgment that single men and men without children (estimated at some 60 percent of the male work force) were receiving the higher wage on "false pretences," as feminist Jessie Street put it.[46] The Royal Commission on childhood and motherhood endowment thus also became a site for the defense of men's rights, as working men closed ranks in support of the single man's right to the higher family wage. Labor men's solidarity on this point put Labor women into an impossible position, leading many to adopt the illogical policy of supporting both the family wage and family endowment. Others simply went with the men, rejecting any scheme of family endowment as not in the interests of the "working class."[47] After the establishment of the Communist party in 1920 the argument was put that mothers should be encouraged out of their homes into the paid work force, to hasten their acquisition of "the true proletarian outlook.[48] Accordingly, they looked forward to the establishment of state nurseries for the children of working mothers.

Men's defense of the higher family wage for single men was justified on many and varied grounds. In general they maintained that single men had greater needs than single women, because of their assumed right to and need for the services of women. Single men compared themselves with married men, not with single women. Single men needed a higher income, it was suggested by John Curtin, Royal Commissioner and future Labor prime minister, to pay for the services provided "gratuitously" to married men.[49]

One of the most original arguments for single men's rights to receive the higher family wage (also involving a novel conception of citizenship) was advanced by H. E. Boote, editor of the *Australian Worker*. Against the principle of the "standard of living," he posited the "standard of enjoyment." The single man needed the higher wage, said Boote, because he "has to help maintain the standard of enjoyment. . . . A civilisation that does not provide its members with reasonable opportunities for enjoyment, is, in my opinion, built on a false basis; therefore the single man who sets the standard of enjoyment in this country is rendering a valuable service to the state."[50] In a context that assumed the rewards due to citizenship, all became rivals in their claims of greater service to the state.

The Royal Commission declined to recommend the introduction of a federal system of child endowment. If it were adopted, they said, the most suitable unit for the family wage remained the husband and wife. They were completely opposed to "the idea of treating the wife as a separate economic unit on the payroll of the state." That idea involved "a claim that [it] is to the state that she is justified in looking for sustenance and reward while she is doing the state's work." If such an idea gained credence, "a very powerful solvent" would be introduced into "family life as we know it."[51] A minority report presented by John Curtin, the Labor representative, and Mildred Muscio, the president of the National Council of Women, recommended child endowment, but also drew the line at motherhood endowment. Motherhood endowment, they said, would replace the contract between husband and wife with a contract between the state and mothers "in their individual right . . . apart from the husband and father" and thus revolutionize the "organic unity" of the family.[52] Children might be recognized as individuals, but not women. Men's "independence" was made possible by women's dependence. Citizenship was constructed in terms of masculine attributes and privilege, while at the same time the meanings of masculinity and femininity were forged in the process of defining citizenship.

Labor women had some success in achieving the introduction of child endowment, paid directly to mothers. A minimal means-tested child endowment was introduced by the New South Wales state government in 1927 and a larger scheme by a Liberal federal government in 1941. It was extended, again by a Liberal government, in 1950.

Feminists working within and outside the Labor party attempted to win independence for women by casting mothers as citizens performing a service for the state; patriarchal political economy insisted on positioning mothers as wives, the dependents of men.[53] Maternal citizenship thus became a contradiction in terms. The campaigns for motherhood endowment also showed how difficult it was, contradictory even, to secure "women's independence" as part of "the great fight for the brotherhood of man."

The campaigns moreover rebounded on women. As the depression of the late 1920s and the 1930s intensified and unemployment reached alarming proportions—more than one third of the official work force out of work by 1932—the definition of women as mothers was used to justify attempts to exclude them altogether from the paid work force. Feminists jettisoned the politics of difference and rallied in defense of women's "right to work." The 1930s saw a renewed and single-minded campaign for equal pay and equal opportunity, espousing a discourse that cast women as identical to, and equal with, men. They sought emancipation in their capacity as workers, in the labor market, not as citizen mothers. "Women's right to work," wrote Muriel Heagney in her book *Are Women Taking Men's Jobs?* in 1935, "rests not on the number of her dependents, nor on the fact that she does or does not compete with men, but in the absolute right of a free human being, a taxpayer and a voter, to economic independence."[54] In 1937 Heagney was instrumental in establishing the Campaign of Action for Equal Pay. Women activists remade their political identity in terms of the apparently sex-neutral categories of "human being," "worker," "tax-payer," and "voter" (had "citizen" become a sexed category?). But within the confines of a patriarchal state, in which citizen and worker are defined in masculine terms, neither "sameness as" nor "difference from" men will produce a genuine democracy for women.[55] That will only arise with the effective reformulation of the meanings of citizen, worker, and mother.

Notes

1. Jill Roe, ed., *Social Policy in New South Wales: Some Perspectives* (Sydney, 1976); T. H. Kewley, *Social Security in Australia, 1900–1972* (Sydney, 1973); and Bettina Cass, "Redistribution to Children and to Mother: A History of Child Endowment and Family Allowances," in Cora V. Baldock and Bettina Cass, eds., *Women, Social Welfare, and the State* (Sydney, 1988).

2. Edna Ryan and Ann Conlon, *Gentle Invaders: Australian Women at Work* (Ringwood, Victoria, Austral., 1989), chap. 4.

3. Seth Koven and Sonya Michel, "Womanly Duties: Maternalist Politics and the Origins of Welfare States in France, Great Britain, Germany, and the United States, 1880–1920," *American Historical Review* 95 (1990): 1076–1108.

4. Andrew Fisher, quoted in *Commonwealth Parliamentary Debates* (*CPD*), House of Representatives, 21 August 1912, 3322.

5. Editorial, *Australian Medical Gazette*, 2 March 1912. On the imperial dimension of motherhood, see Anna Davin, "Imperialism and Motherhood," *History Workshop* 5 (1978): 9–65.

6. Andrew Fisher, quoted in *Argus* (Melbourne), 5 September 1912, 12.

7. Andrew Fisher, quoted in *CPD*, House of Representatives, 21 August 1912, 2478.

8. Of 52 letters to the editor concerning the Maternity Allowance published in two Melbourne newspapers, the *Age* and the *Argus*, only one objected to the "colour line"; see *Argus*, 19 October 1912, 8.

9. Debate over Maternity Allowance, quoted in *CPD*, House of Representatives, 21 August 1912, 2478.

10. Carole Pateman, *The Sexual Contract* (Oxford, Eng., 1988).

11. *Argus*: 29 August 1912, 6, and 13 September 1912, 9. "Our national honour . . . ," Rev. Professor D. S. Adam, quoted in *Argus*, 17 September 1912, 4.

12. Rev. Professor D. S. Adams, quoted in *Age* (Melbourne), 5 September 1914, 11.

13. Labor Women's resolution, quoted in *Age*, 6 September 1912, 8; *Argus*: 12 November 1912, 6, and 3 December 1912, 9.

14. For discussions of the relationship between masculinity and political "births," see Pateman, *Sexual Contract*, 35–36; Mary O'Brien, *The Politics of Reproduction* (Boston and London, 1981), 56; and Susan Jeffords, *The Remasculinization of America: Gender and the Vietnam War* (Bloomington, Ind., 1989), chap. 3.

15. Sol Encel, "The Study of Militarism in Australia," *Australia and New Zealand Journal of Sociology* 3,1 (1967); G. L. Kristianson, *The Politics of Patriotism: The Pressure Group Activities of the Returned Servicemen's League* (Sydney, 1966); Marilyn Lake, *The Limits of Hope: Soldier Settlement in Victoria, 1915–38* (Melbourne, 1987), 27–29, 195–97; Lake, "The Power of Anzac," in M. McKernan and M. Browne, eds., *Two Centuries of War and Peace* (Canberra, 1988); and Jill Rose, "Chivalry and Social Policy in the Antipodes," *Historical Studies* 22 (1987): 408–9.

16. Susan Pedersen, "Gender, Welfare and Citizenship in Britain during the Great War," *American Historical Review* 95 (1990): 983–1006.

17. Jean Daley, quoted in Royal Commission on Child Endowment or Family Allowances, *Commonwealth Parliamentary Papers* (*CPP*), 1929, Minutes of Evidence, 1197.

18. Mary Perry, quoted in ibid., 132.

19. Mary Perry, quoted in ibid., 922–23.

20. Lilian Locke-Burns, quoted in *Labor Call*, 26 June 1919.

21. Lilian Locke-Burns, quoted in Ibid.

22. Nelle Rickie, quoted in Ibid., 6 March 1924.

23. Henrietta Greville, quoted in Meredith Foley, "The Women's Movement in New South Wales and Victoria, 1918–38," (Ph.D. diss., University of Sydney, 1985), 252.

24. Muriel Heagney, in *Labor Call*, 1 February 1923.

25. Jean Daley, quoted in *Woman's Clarion:* February 1925, 5; December 1924, 7; and January 1925, 6.

26. Muriel Heagney, quoted in Royal Commission on Child Endowment, Minutes of Evidence, 1116.

27. Jean Daley, quoted in *Woman's Clarion*, February 1925, 5.

28. Lilian Locke-Burns, quoted in *Labor Call*, 19 June 1919.

29. Exchange between Lena Lynch and the Royal Commissioners, quoted in Royal Commission on Child Endowment, Minutes of Evidence, 922.

30. Jean Daley, quoted in *Woman's Clarion*, February 1925, 5.

31. Muriel Heagney, quoted in *Labor Call*, 1 February 1923, 9. On the promotion of "scientific mothering," see Philippa Mein Smith, "Mothers, Babies, and the Mothers and Babies Movement," paper presented to the American Historical Association, Pacific Coast Branch meeting, Kona Coast, Hawaii, 1991.

32. Lena Lynch, quoted in Royal Commission on Child Endowment, Minutes of Evidence, 923.

33. *Labor Call*, 26 April 1923, 1.

34. John Newton, quoted in Ibid., 28 February 1924, 4.

35. Royal Commission on Health, Report, *CPP* 1926–28, vol. 4, 32.

36. Dame Janet Campbell, "Report on Maternal and Child Welfare in Australia," *CPP* 1929–31, vol. 11, 4.

37. Royal Commission on Child Endowment, Minutes of Evidence, 1222.

38. Campbell, "Report," 6.

39. Lake, *Limits of Hope*, 60 and 262, and Dr. Marshall Allan, quoted in Royal Commission on Child Endowment, Minutes of Evidence, 1221.

40. See Beverly Kingston, *My Wife, My Daughter and Poor Mary Ann: Women and Work in Australia* (Melbourne, 1975), 10–12, for evidence of Labor women's role in winning child endowment in New South Wales.

41. Muriel Heagney, quoted in Royal Commission on Child Endowment, Minutes of Evidence, 1116.

42. Ibid., 1136.

43. Exchange between Irene Longman and the Royal Commissioners, quoted in ibid., 7–8.

44. See Pateman, *Sexual Contract*, esp. chap. 1.

45. Exchange between Ernest Barker and the Royal Commissioners, quoted in Royal Commission on Child Endowment, Minutes of Evidence, 348.

46. Jessie Street, quoted in ibid.

47. See, for example May Francis, "The Home and the Labor Movement," *Labor Call*, 23 July 1925.

48. Ibid., 9 July 1925, 5; see also debate between Nelle Rickie and Adela Pankhurst, ibid., 2 July 1925, 2.

49. John Curtin, quoted in Royal Commission on Child Endowment, Minutes of Evidence, 915.

50. H. E. Boote, quoted in Ibid., 152.

51. Ibid., Majority Report, *CPP* 1929, vol. 2, 1343–44.

52. Ibid., Minority Report, 1392.

53. Pateman argues that the modern civil order is not patriarchal but *fraternal; Sexual Contract*, 78.

54. Muriel Heagney, *Are Women Taking Men's Jobs?* (Melbourne, 1935), 12.

55. Anna Coote and Beatrix Campbell, *Sweet Freedom: The Struggle for Women's Liberation* (London, 1982); Marilyn Lake, "A Question of Time," in David McKnight, ed., *Moving Left: The Future of Socialism in Australia* (Sydney, Austral., 1986); Anne Phillips, *Hidden Hands: Women and Economic Policies* (London, 1983); and Carole Pateman, "The Patriarchal Welfare State," in Pateman, *The Disorder of Women* (Stanford, Calif., 1989), 203–4.

12

Feminist Strategies and Gendered Discourses in Welfare States: Married Women's Right to Work in the United States and Sweden

Barbara Hobson

A gender dimension has been conspicuously absent from models and paradigms of comparative welfare-state research, from T. H. Marshall's concept of social citizenship to the recent welfare-state policy regimes of Walter Korpi and Gösta Esping-Andersen.[1] The assumption in studies of welfare-state policy regimes is that class mobilization and class-political alliances appear as the most significant forces in the development of the institutional features of the Scandinavian welfare state—its universalism and the extension of social rights, even to women. Ironically, feminists who have cast the welfare state as patriarchal—reorganizing patriarchy from the family to the state, from dependent wife to the client or recipient of social-welfare services—have made similar assumptions about the marginal role of women's agency in the construction of the welfare state.[2] One finds ideological and structural analyses of the gendered distribution of power in welfare states: the divorce of reproduction from production;[3] the separation of the private sphere from the public;[4] the shift from the housewife contract to the equality contract.[5] Yet these conceptual frameworks do not tell us how these contracts were made and under what conditions, who acquiesced and who fought back.[6]

Recent historical and comparative studies of gender and the welfare state have begun to rediscover the importance of women's agency in the politics of social policy and the origins of welfare states.[7] Although these studies provide analytical tools for understanding the gendered origins of welfare states, they do not explore the period after the early reforms were introduced in different welfare states. What were the trajectories of maternalist and paternalist strands of the welfare state in the 1930s and beyond?[8] Most problematic is the Swedish case, where maternalist policies were forged into a base of universal citizenship rights and entitlements.[9]

In this essay I am offering a framework for incorporating the politics of gender into the development of welfare states during an early period of institutional building. By concentrating on a specific debate, married women's right to work, I consider how different gendered discourses around home and work shaped social policies in the American and Swedish welfare states during the 1930s. Married women's right to work provides an excellent case study for comparative analysis of the contested nature of social policy around gender-equality issues during this pivotal stage of welfare-state formation.[10]

Like the other authors in this volume, I take for granted that women activists have been able to influence public debates and social programs while at the same time I recognize that women inside and outside of policy making within all modern welfare states have had limited power resources and few channels to put issues on the public agenda.[11] Following this general premise, I assume that when gender-equality issues appear on the political agenda, they tend to challenge the boundaries of welfare-state policy-making structures, permeate the walls between the economic, domestic, and political spheres.[12] This element of contested policy arenas leads into my third premise: that, depending upon the area of policy making—the domestic (family issues), the economic (labor-market and workplace issues), or the political (citizenship and participatory rights)—those seeking to alter the gendered distribution of power in the welfare state have had to adopt different strategies in the face of shifting constraints and opportunities. That is, within welfare states the gendered distribution of power has varied across policy-making spheres—the domestic, economic, and political.

Recent scholarship has tended to focus on the bifurcation within modern welfare states between public and private; home and work; and male- and female-gendered channels of policy making.[13] I would argue, however, that the logical place to begin an analysis of gender and the welfare state is the point where a convergence exists in the status of women as citizens, workers, and mothers. Worker status emerged as the nucleus of citizenship within the modern welfare state. Therefore the discussion of married women's rights as workers at this critical juncture would have consequences and residual effects after the specific laws and proposals were forgotten.

The 1930s is a crucial decade for considering welfare-state formation in both the United States and Sweden; the Swedish Social Democratic party began its long tenure in 1933, and Roosevelt's New Deal took shape in this decade. Moreover, in both of these countries the issue of married women's right to work was hotly contested and became a major issue on the public agenda. As my comparative analysis shows, debates around married women's right to work were remarkably similar, yet the outcomes were radically different.

The question of married women's right to work became a major issue on the public agenda in Sweden and the United States during the economic crisis brought about by the depression.[14] In both societies, calls for policies that would remove married women from the labor market emerged at that time. However, married women represented only a fraction of the labor force in both countries (12 percent in the U.S. and 10 percent in Sweden).[15] Furthermore, Swedish and American hostility to married women working was not a new phenomenon but had been voiced for decades in union publications, government studies, and popular journals. In both countries opponents presented similar arguments: married women working demoralized the home; they took jobs away from employed husbands and single women; and they accepted lower wages than single earners and thus introduced unfair competition to male workers.[16]

In 1932 the U.S. passed a federal law (the Economy Act) prohibiting two spouses from being employed by the civil service. Although the specific provision was called the "married-persons clause," in almost all cases, wives were the parties discharged. The Economy Act led to a flood of discriminatory legislation from state and local governments seeking to bar married women from working. One member of the Association of Business and Professional Women claimed that it was open season "to wallop the ladies."[17] Teaching, more than any other profession that employed married women, faced an onslaught of firings and school-board policies against hiring married women. In 1938, a National Education Association Survey found that more than three-quarters of

192 city boards surveyed would not hire married women. Legal sanctions against women in the civil service inspired discrimination against women in other sectors of the economy. A 1939 National Industrial Board Study revealed that 84 percent of banks, 65 percent of insurance companies, and 65 percent of public utilities had restrictions against married women.[18] Though the Economy Act was repealed in 1937, hostility against the married woman worker remained strong in both the public and private sector. As late as 1939, a campaign to promote legislation barring married women from all types of employment was in full swing in several states and required a massive countercampaign for its defeat.[19]

Beginning in the mid-1920s, resolutions were introduced in the Riksdag, the Swedish parliament, to prevent married women from working in state jobs. It had only been a few years since women first gained the right to be employed as civil servants in the national government; now these employment opportunities were in jeopardy for married women. Severe economic depression in 1931 convinced many politicians that restrictions on married women were in order. In one heated parliamentary debate, Hamrin-Thorell gave his assessment of the problem: "Married women who understand their tasks in the home can never be unemployed—there are always socks to mend."[20] A range of proposals to limit married women's labor-force participation were under consideration by a government commission. Recommendations ranged from bans on married women's right to work to motions that took the form of "voluntary" inducements against married women working, such as early retirement pensions for women leaving the labor market after marriage. At the height of the economic crisis of 1934, at least nine motions were presented in the parliament demanding restrictions on married women's right to work. They resembled the American Economy Act in limiting public-sector employment to only one spouse. But the parliament turned down these proposals, and a commission formed to study the issues of married women's work in 1938 argued against any discriminatory legislation[21]

The Swedish case offers a dramatic counterpoint to the American one, since the disputes over married women working during the depression did not result in greater restrictions but actually brought women legal protection against discrimination. In 1939 parliament passed a law that prohibited employed persons from being fired on account of marriage, pregnancy, or childbearing if they had worked for more than two years in a job.

We might have expected different outcomes in these two cases if we considered earlier policy debates, the position of women in the welfare-state bureaucracy, and the strength of feminist movements in the past. A comparison of women's civil and legal rights in both countries reveals that Swedish women were laggards in obtaining basic citizen rights that American women had begun to take for granted by the 1910s and 1920s: property rights, access to public secondary schooling, and employment in the federal civil service. Not until 1920 did Swedish married women gain full civil status and the right to retain control over property and earnings.[22] Before 1927, Swedish women were not admitted to the gymnasia or *realskola* (public secondary schools); the only option for women who wanted an education beyond the seven years of primary schooling was a private female academy. Most relevant to this discussion of married women's right to work, Swedish women could not be employed in the national civil service until passage of the Competency Act in 1923. This permitted women to apply for jobs in the civil service, but, as noted above, by 1925, the year the law took effect, there were already motions in parliament to limit married women's right to government positions and appointments.

Swedish feminist groups existed in the nineteenth century, but they were disparate, small organizations divided by social group, urban and rural bases, and political affiliation.[23] Although in 1902 a coalition of women's groups united around suffrage, it was very much a single-issue campaign and part of the larger struggle for universal suffrage for women and men. Swedish women were enfranchised along with working-class men in 1919 and voted in the first election in 1921. By contrast, American women were organized in a broad spectrum of local groups and national organizations and networks that promoted a range of women's issues, including antiprostitution, temperance, education, divorce, and property rights as well as suffrage. At the onset of the depression in the early 1930s, Swedish women had neither the grass-roots organizations nor the influence on public policy that the Progressive Era American women's movement could boast.[24]

American women active in early settlement-house reform, philanthropy, and civic organizations, referred to in the current scholarly literature as "maternalists," helped to shape state policies aimed at women and children and then carved out a niche for themselves in emerging social-welfare institutions. Julia Lathrop became the first director of the U.S. Children's Bureau, founded in 1912, and women dominated the profession of social work. The U.S. Women's Bureau, under the leadership of Mary Anderson, and the National Consumers' League, with Florence Kelley at the helm, represented women's and children's interests in Progressive Era debates over social policy.[25]

In contrast to the place of American women, Swedish women played only marginal roles in the welfare bureaucracy that emerged during the first decades of the twentieth century.[26] In fact, none of the female members of the National Association of Social Work, the central organization of philanthropic societies, came to staff the powerful National Board of Health and Welfare, founded in 1913, or the Social Department in the Ministry of Social Affairs, founded in 1920. However, men from the same philanthropic organizations became the nucleus of the welfare bureaucracy.[27] Swedish women reformers who mobilized around child welfare lost ground when the state began to take more responsibility for the care of children. Pediatricians, who dominated the child-welfare boards, were the prime movers in constructing the child-welfare law of 1926 and, through their discourse, defined problems and solutions in medical terms.[28]

That Swedish women had a weak position in the social-welfare bureaucracy and lagged behind their American sisters in obtaining rights to property and public education makes the developments of the 1930s appear all the more surprising. The depression era was one of closure for feminists in many Western societies, and American women's groups found themselves fighting to protect the basic democratic right to employment. Yet Swedish feminists were able to initiate reforms, represent their claims in the welfare state, and even extend women's social citizenship. In analyzing the two cases, I consider the importance of alliances, particularly with trade unions, and state capacities (in this case the tactical advantage Swedish women had in dealing with the centralized policy-making structures of the Swedish welfare state). Perhaps most important, I focus on the discursive strategies feminists used in the public debate. Swedish feminists were able to link married women's right to work to concerns over declining population, low marriage rates, and the quality of life among Swedish families. Consequently, they were able to shift this issue from the political and economic spheres, where they were weakest, to the domestic sphere of policy making, where they had the greatest access and could use their power resources.

Alliances

Women's Organizations

Historians have alluded to the unity among American feminists groups in their attempts to combat discrimination against married women working.[29] Feminist groups that had fought bitterly over protective legislation and the equal-rights amendment a decade earlier, buried their differences temporarily. National associations of business and professional women, lawyers, social workers, the League of Women Voters, the Women's Bureau, the National Women's Party, and the Women's Trade Union League all publicly denounced the attacks on married women's right to work and became official sponsors of the bill to repeal the Economy Act.[30]

But American feminists in their public testimony and lobbying could not claim unilaterally that they were representing the women's point of view as was true in the Swedish case. For, at the same time, many rank-and-file single women in industry, business, and professional work expressed antagonism toward the married woman worker.[31] While not organized in a single group, they found a voice among conservative women's groups who claimed to speak for them. The most dramatic case was in Massachusetts where the Women's Political Club movement was nearly successful in getting legislation passed that would have removed all married women from the labor force. They mounted an intense propaganda campaign that played upon the bitter competition for jobs during the depression and pitted single women against married women.[32] Thus American women themselves were deeply divided on the issue.

Unlike their American sisters, Swedish women's groups appeared united in their opposition to restrictions against married women working. Even the most conservative of these groups, the National Homemakers Association (Husmödersförenigars Riksförbund), whose aims were to improve mothering, child rearing, and home economy, refused to support some of the least coercive measures to remove married women from the labor force. They rejected, for example, pensions or gratuities for women who retired from the labor market after marriage.

Women's groups which, a decade earlier, had viewed each other with suspicion, now cooperated across party and class lines.[33] Feminists within the state commissions appeared as if they were speaking for Swedish women in both their formal roles as investigators and as publicists. Activist and writer Britta Åkerman describes this new spirit: "During the 1930's something special happened to the world of women. Almost all women's organizations became involved in reform issues that they had not addressed previously."[34] Evidence of the chains of alliance among diverse women's groups can be seen in the "Call to Sweden's Women," a letter signed by twenty-five women's organizations and published in the key women's journals in 1936.[35] It called on women to become more politically active—to join a political party—any party.

Though they did not have a specific platform or agenda or present themselves as a voting bloc, women's groups formed alliances around a host of issues, such as paid vacations for housewives, decriminalizing contraceptives, increased political representation of women, support for single mothers without the stigma attached to other forms of public relief, and mothers' right to work. Throughout the 1920s, class and party alliances had inhibited coalitions among Swedish women's groups. However, they did not develop the same ideological fault line between equal-rights feminists and social feminists or maternalists that formed in the U.S. The core of Swedish feminism that emerged in this period was a multilayered social feminism.

Trade Unions

Swedish feminists found a powerful ally in the trade unions that opposed legislation restricting married womens' labor-force participation. Unions even came out against the nepotism motion to limit jobs to one spouse in public-sector employment. Alva Myrdal claimed that Swedish working-class men, whose wives had been compelled by economic necessity to work outside their own home for other households and to some extent in factories, obviously identified with the "family ideology" and family wage.

Yet in this instance, she claimed that trade unions and the Social Democratic party were motivated by their commitment to equal rights for women.

Social-democratic abstract principles notwithstanding, I would like to suggest two other reasons why unions did not join the chorus against married women working during the depression of the 1930s. First I would argue that Swedish workers did not feel the same competition from female workers. The industrial sector in Sweden was hard hit by the effects of economic depression,[36] and the 1930s was a period of conflict between organized labor and employers. Nevertheless, unions were strong enough in this era to protect themselves against any attempts by employers to cut costs by hiring women. Over half the industrial labor force was unionized and affiliated with the general trade-union organization (LO) in the 1930s. By the end of the decade (1938), the historic Saltsjöbaden agreement was signed between industrial unions and the Employers' Federation. At that meeting labor conceded its rights of ownership but in return secured the union's right to bargain collectively as well as the government's agreement to refrain from intervention.[37]

Swedish unions did not fear women's competition for jobs because the labor market was thoroughly sex-segregated and unions (fairly strong by the 1930s, and organized along industrial lines) had the power to define job categories and wage differentials. Not only were there different male and female job categories, but also male and female wage settings. The gendered wage differential was so institutionalized that in official reports on Swedish wages in the period there were three categories of workers: skilled male workers; unskilled male workers, and female workers.[38] In the report of the government's commission on Married Women's Work in 1938, economist expert Karin Kock concluded that it was impossible to evaluate women's competition for male jobs since one could not find jobs that men and women performed that were comparable. Describing the highly segregated labor market in Sweden, Kock found that in occupation by occupation, profession by profession, men were along one line and women another. Though training and upbringing were to some degree responsible for this segregation, the commission stated that the resistance of unions to changing the gendered division of jobs could not be discounted.[39]

One can also view the union position in support of married

women's right to work within the larger context of Swedish unions' jurisdictional claim on employer-employee collective bargaining: Swedish unions tended to oppose all legislative interference in worker-employer contracts, such as firing and hiring.[40] Unions also stated their opposition to government interference in the private financial life of the family.[41] To accept laws restricting married women working would have been to violate a core principle in Swedish unionism: no government regulations in work-life decisions.[42] In the hearings of the Commission on Married Women's Work, unions explicitly stated that any laws restricting married women workers might jeopardize the principle of seniority in dismissals.[43]

American feminists found few allies among unions in their defense of the married women worker. During public hearings on federal legislation, only the fledgling American Federation of Government Employees supported the feminist position, on the principle that merit should be the main criterion for job holding. The position of the American Federation of Labor with regard to the family wage was always unambiguous, but during the depression years it took on a highly aggressive tone.[44] In a 1934 article in the *American Federationist*, Weir Jepson suggested economic antidotes to "save the home," including the establishment of a "minimum unit of wage earning," as opposed to a minimum wage. He called for administrative acts that would require all employers to pay a wage-equalization tariff to the government equivalent to ninety percent of a married woman's wage.[45] Seniority principles, sacred to unionists, were often abandoned in the case of married women workers. Writing about her dismissal from the railway company to the president of the United States, worker Martha Hasting claimed that her union, without a vote of its members and in violation of its constitution, made a rule that married women should be relieved of their jobs. She took the matter up in several union courts, and even brought suit against the union in civil court, but the court ruled that the union could destroy rights they had created by collective bargaining.[46]

If we compare the impact of the unions in these two cases, American unions were vocal opponents of married women's right to work, while Swedish unions were passive supporters. LO, the largest and most powerful industrial workers' organization in Sweden in this period, was a champion of the family wage, yet it would not tolerate the same kinds of administrative intervention or legal precedents that restrictions on married women might have required. In fact, a motion at the LO congress in 1921 to ban married women from the labor force was voted down on the grounds that it would be too difficult to oversee.[47] The union leadership was unwilling to sacrifice union principles of seniority or risk government interference in the work-life issues which they perceived as the domain of unionism.

Policy-Making Structures

Feminists, in developing strategies against laws banning married women's work, had to confront different policy-making structures and institutional settings. In the United States, women's organizations had to mobilize against scores of local and state discriminatory laws and policy directives. Although the main union of state workers during the 1930s, the American Federation of Government Employees, actively supported the repeal of federal discrimination in the Economy Act, women's organizations were virtually alone in fighting countless state proposals.[48] Even as late as 1939, two years after the married-persons clause in the Economy Act was repealed, an epidemic of married-persons-clause restrictions broke out in twenty-six states. Only one, Louisiana, put through a total bar on married women's work, the result of a lame-duck governor's last ditch effort to win reelection. The Massachusetts Supreme Court struck down a bill that excluded all married women. But new legislation was always being introduced and campaigns mounted against it.[49]

The New Deal represented a quantum leap in the American welfare state. The federal government became a mediator and regulator of the market, and national programs of relief and social insurance were put into place. However, the ideology of the weak state and the institutional features of federalism could be used to block any reform.[50] In light of the expansive and extraordinary powers Roosevelt had in his first years of the New Deal, it is possible that he could have included a directive in his National Recovery Act codes against discrimination toward working wives. The National Recovery Act included all kinds of codes and interventions in economic life: bans on homework and child labor, minimum wage levels, and rights of unions to organize and bargain collectively. However he publicly claimed that he could do nothing to interfere with firings of married women on the state and local levels nor undercut the congressional initiatives in the Federal Economy Act. But privately, he expressed an unwillingness to become involved in this politically sensitive area.[51]

Swedish feminists, in their struggle to protect married women's work rights, had a tactical advantage over their American counterparts: the policy-making structures of the Swedish welfare state were centralized. Thus, instead of fighting hundreds of local battles with municipalities, activists could devote all their energies to one campaign at the national level, with the resulting policies covering all local employees of the state.

A crucial element in the struggle was the women's strategic position in one particular policy-making structure, the investigative commission. Existing for over 150 years, the *utredning*, or parliamentary commission of experts, is an institutional part of the Swedish system, the site of a vital stage of policy making that has become a prerequisite for formulating new proposals made to the Riksdag. The purpose of commissions is to gather the facts as well as build consensus around contested policies.[52]

During this period, several commissions on social questions in Sweden were in progress. A specific commission was formed to consider the issues surrounding married women's labor-market work. Four of the six members of the Commission on Married Women's Work were women. The head, Kerstin Hesslegren, had been a factory inspector and was also head of a Liberal-party women's organization. The expert investigator, Karin Kock, was one of the few women economists in the nation. The most influential woman in Social Democratic circles was Alva Myrdal, who was appointed secretary. Myrdal was the pulse of the commission, in touch with a whole set of policy arteries through her husband Gunnar, who was serving as an expert on a parallel commission on population policy. It is not surprising that the commission rejected all proposals to bar married women from the labor force in view of the fact that the majority of the persons chosen to be on the commission were women active in feminist causes.[53] But the more provocative question is how they were able to rechannel the public debate in order to promote legislation that prohibited discrimination against married women working.

Discursive Resources

Sweden

In the debates over married women's right to work, Swedish feminists had greater discursive resources than their American counterparts involved in the same struggle. By discursive resources, I mean two things: one, ways of formulating public debate that allow for linkages to other policy concerns and hegemonic ideologies; and two, policy arenas where groups can represent their claims and construct their own interpretations of the issues at stake and the policy measures needed.[54]

Where policy making is orchestrated by an inner circle of political groups, which has been the case in Sweden, women's claims can be made invisible.[55] Alternatively, a few women insiders can play a crucial role in shaping the public debates if they can link women's claims to a larger policy matrix. Women's political resources in Sweden were scattered among different political parties and by the 1930s what had been separate female trade unions had been absorbed into male trade unions in which women had no representation on either local or central committees. I am not suggesting that women's organizations did not have any political leverage, since party members, particularly Social Democrats, were courting women's votes during this period before they had secured a dominant position in Swedish politics. Rather, I do not see any evidence that suggests women's power resources appeared as a threat to political parties, that is, that they were wary of women voting as a bloc or interest group.[56] Nevertheless, in the debates concerning married women's right to work, Swedish feminists used their power resources in policy-forming bodies—though not strictly policy-making bodies. They became opinion builders and developed a highly strategic discourse that made possible measures that went beyond the original purpose of the Commission on Married Women's Work to consider the merits of laws restricting married women from employment.[57]

To understand feminists' strategies and their discursive resources within the Commission on Married Women's Work, it is useful to place the Swedish population debate in the larger European context. Throughout Europe during this period, there was anxiety over declining population, and policy measures were being enacted to increase the birthrate, particularly in France and Germany. However, in contrast to the narrow pronatalist approach in much of Europe, the thrust in Swedish population policy was toward a broader social-policy content. Although other European countries adopted coercive pronatalist policies, none of the recommendations of the Swedish Population Commission was punitive: contraceptive devices were not outlawed, instead they were legalized; marriage loans were not bound by the number of children or any children at all; and a maternity benefit for mothers was based on economic need rather than size of family.[58] A host of social reforms were finessed into the "social politic" of population decline in Sweden during the 1930s, when the country had one of the lowest birthrates in Europe.

The Myrdals' book on the population crisis in Sweden, *Kris i Befolkningsfrågan*, appeared in 1934 and had enormous influence in policy circles and the general public.[59] They analyzed the social and economic sources of Sweden's low birthrate and concluded that the solution lay in social reforms to improve living standards and redistribute resources, such as low-cost housing, marriage loans, and free maternal-health care. The overwhelmingly positive reception of the Myrdal book by conservatives and radicals alike laid the basis for extensive reform. Swedish Social Democrats were savvy enough to recognize the degree to which the Myrdals had given the working class an arsenal of arguments for social reform.[60] Gustav Moller, Social Democratic minister of social affairs in the 1930s, lay bare his motives: "I will not hesitate to frighten as many people from parties on the right, with the threat that our people will die out if this threat will get them to vote for social proposals I put forward. This is my simple view of population and is good enough for me."[61]

Alva Myrdal, perhaps the most visible and influential feminist actor in the political debates and policy-making bodies in this period, confessed to the strategic value of linking married women's right to work to the population question. Looking retrospectively at her role in shaping the debate within the commission on married women's work, Myrdal concluded that, had only arguments based on "emancipation ideals" been brought forward, women's position would have been weak. She admitted that some feminists were wary of this kind of strategy since past experiences had made them suspicious of the very term "population policy."[62] One suspicious voice was that of Elin Wägner, who characterized the population debate as a manly dialogue.[63] She spoke for a strand of feminism based on notions of women's culture and collective maternal identities that were embodied in the writings of her mentor, Ellen Key. Myrdal represented the different voice of a second generation of pragmatic feminists who believed that it was essential for women to be integrated into mainstream politics and channel the public debate in ways that promoted women's interests.[64]

In *Nation and Family,* Myrdal claimed that during this period a strong sentiment existed against married women working: "the opinions with regard to feminine questions and particularly the problems of wage-earning married women were thus especially sensitive to downward economic swings, unemployment and intensified competition in the labor market."[65] Moreover, at the same time that debates over married women working arose, a parallel concern over declining birthrates focused attention on married women as deficient propagators. According to Myrdal, in this potentially dangerous constellation, anything could have happened:

> The remarkable thing is that in this crucial moment the population argument was wrenched out of the hands of the antifeminists and instead used as a new formidable weapon for emancipation ideals. The old debate on married woman's right to work was turned into a fight for the working women's right to marry and have children. The change in public opinion was tremendous.[66]

Despite Alva Myrdal's claim that some women were anxious about linking women's social and economic rights to a policy discussion involving population decline, the commission hearings reveal that a wide spectrum of women's groups deployed that strategy. Feminists in their own journals made other arguments about women's democratic rights and women's contribution to the family economy.[67] But in their testimony they argued that restricting married women from working would have the unintended consequences of discouraging women from marrying and childbearing, or increasing the number of couples having children outside of wedlock.

Testimony in the commission presented both sides of the debate over women as reproducers and producers. On the one side, the Association of University Women maintained that to prohibit married women from working was to waste the educational investment the state made in them and to deny society their contribution. The association claimed that if restrictions were passed, the women most likely to follow careers were those who would not marry. Thus society would lose the reproductive capacities of women with the highest abilities, and these were the groups, according to the statistics in the commission report, who had the lowest birthrates.[68] On the other hand, the National Homemakers Association contended that working-class couples would be prevented from marrying when both incomes were needed for the family economy. Consequently, they argued that such legislation would increase the numbers of children born outside of wedlock.[69]

Examining the testimony of various women's groups during the commission hearings, one finds the constant refrain of fertility decline and illegitimacy. Defenders of married women's right to work invoked issues of professionalism and the economic rationality of utilizing women's educational investment, but always added a "lest we forget" clause about the threat to family and marriage that restrictions on married women's employment would produce. The Teachers Association, for example, argued that women differed in education and natural abilities and whereas some were suited for household work, others were not. By working outside the home, women created jobs for other women. But they also warned that prohibitions against married women in the labor market would lead to an increase in "free relationships" and "threaten marriage as a legal institution."[70] In the same vein, the Academic Women's Organization pointed to past experiences where private companies had applied similar restrictions. Such restrictions, they claimed, increased "so called free relationships," and created a weaker position for the social status of children.[71]

Although one can find anxiety, almost hysteria, over reported cases of couples not marrying because of restrictions against married women working in the hearings over the Economy Act in the U.S.,[72] the discussion of free relationships in the Swedish context had different social meanings and a different background. Nonmarital cohabitation was very common in rural areas, and in cities so widespread among the working classes in the nineteenth century that the term "Stockholm Marriage" really meant couples living together in nonmarital relationships.[73] In 1930 a comparatively low proportion of Swedish women were married: 47 percent, compared to 11 percent who were widowed or divorced and 42 percent who were unmarried. Thus the argument against creating more disincentives to marriage appealed to conservatives seeking to promote the traditional nuclear family and Social Democrats interested in improving living standards so couples could afford to marry.

By representing the question of married women's work as a domestic-policy issue (linked to marriage, fertility, and family stability), Alva Myrdal and other feminists employing this tactic were able to tap into ideological roots in the Scandinavian welfare state of the 1930s. Sweden's first Social Democratic prime minister, Per Albin Hansson, used the metaphor "People's Home" (*Folkhem*) to represent the universal reformist impulse of Swedish social democracy.[74] Absorbed into Social Democratic discourse, the image of the People's Home reflected a shift in party strategy toward building a mass political base, a promise that social democracy would create a home for all the people. Party regulars in the past did not address family or maternity policy—sickness insurance, unemployment, and pensions were the core issues—and Social Democratic women expressed frustration that the party did not consider women's issues to be "real politics."[75] Thus for women, the idea of a People's Home provided ideological space for a range of policy initiatives around everyday life and social reproduction: housing policies, maternal health and welfare, and fertility. Feminists using the population issue were able to link their concerns to a social-democratic discourse emerging in the 1930s that expanded the meaning of social politics. In so doing, they played to their strength within the Swedish welfare state— the domestic policy realm, where they had the greatest input and perceived legitimacy.

Given the creation of a commission to study married women's work with feminists in key positions as chairman and secretary, it is not surprising that Alva Myrdal believed that there were openings (policy channels) through which women could make claims within the emerging welfare state. True, the Commission on Married Women's Work did not make specific recommendations or suggest legislation.[76] But it set the terms of the debate, gathered masses of statistics, and co-opted all the arguments from the Right about the threat to home and family that married women workers posed. In effect, Hesslegren, Myrdal and the commissions on women's work paved the way for the policy initiatives that were formulated in the different commissions under the Royal Population Commission.

The proposals that came out of the various population subcommittees illustrate how a discourse that linked mothers and workers—the right of married working women to have children—was used for radical policy directives. The main recommendation of the commission was a law that prohibited all private and public employers from discriminating against women who were pregnant, married, or single mothers. But in addition the members proposed broad protections for working mothers:[77] one, that employees had the right to abstain from working for up to twelve weeks after childbearing and still retain their jobs; and two, perhaps the most significant initiative, that civil-service workers could have three months' paid maternal leave.[78]

Feminists boring into governmental policy-making bodies had been able to move a host of women's issues onto the social-welfare policy agenda. These were issues that had been put forward by women's organizations for many years, a wish list of maternity benefits and job protections. However, in the 1930s feminists were able to reach into the ideological ground of the People's Home and refashion the population question to support job protections for working mothers, maternal leave, and mothers' allowances. This was at the very time in most of Europe and North America when laws and union practices were locking into place the family wage and male-breadwinner ideology.

The United States

In the United States, those defending married women workers during the 1930s found a discursive terrain of "needs talk," a narrow channel with different interest groups trying to steer their needs ahead of others. A decade earlier, the National Women's party had launched a campaign for an equal rights amendment to the Constitution, charting a course for equal opportunity and constructing a discourse of women's economic rights. By contrast, maternalists in the 1920s were making rights-based arguments for entitlements such as mothers' pensions and maternal- and child-health care based on mothers' service to society.[79] However, during the depression years, even the Women's party was drawn into a vortex of arguments based on needs, modifying its stand from one of pure economic rights.[80] A discourse based on married women's need to help support their families, was, however, vulnerable during the depression. All sorts of unemployed workers portrayed themselves as the truly disadvantaged and needy, and pointed to married women as unfair competition.[81]

Women's advocacy groups and policy makers inside the Roosevelt administration assumed a defensive posture about the right of married women to hold jobs. The League of Women Voters openly attacked the discriminatory principle in the marriage bar, but at the same time argued that the laws did not take into account the economic status of the family or total family economy.[82] Eleanor Roosevelt frequently spoke out against the marriage bar, seeking to tie married women's employment to discourses of economic rationality and New Deal policy based on Keynesian economics— the principle that jobs created jobs. She asked if the married woman worker who is a poor housekeeper should go back to the home and fire her maid. The result, according to Mrs. Roosevelt, was to have a discontented wife and a maid out of work. But she always came back to the question of family needs. Criticizing the firing of women in public-sector jobs, she stated that civil-service jobs are often low-paying with the result that two incomes are needed to support a family. Furthermore, she added that many women have other family members to support, or children needing special care. In one magazine article she presented pages of statistics to demonstrate that the vast majority of women work in low-status, low-paying jobs, and therefore must be working out of need.[83]

Mary Anderson, as director of the Women's Bureau in the U.S. Department of Labor, was often called upon to respond to public denunciations of married women working. In their defense, Anderson frequently appealed to principles of economic rationality and efficiency. She claimed, for example, that firing married women with purchasing power would hinder economic recovery. But her main line of defense was that married women worked because their contribution to the family economy was essential, that often they had to support parents or other relatives.[84]

No matter how they framed their discourse around married women's economic needs, defenders of married women's work could not move the debate away from one that pitted worker against worker. The question of married women's rights as workers was lodged within the economic sphere of policy making, where women in the New Deal coalition seemed to be unable to argue for women's interests. Whereas in the earlier decade and in the 1910s, the Women's Bureau and Children's Bureau could make claims for special legislation and policy concerning working mothers and child labor, women in the New Deal bureaucracy were not able to find policy channels where they could represent the married woman worker.[85] They were unable to link her economic contribution to the policy debates and initiatives aimed at keeping families from poverty and dependence on welfare. Nor could they find a policy framework in which they could cast married women workers as producers and consumers helping to bring about economic recovery. Any support of married women's work appeared to challenge the family wage.[86]

At first glance, one might have expected that women in the New Deal would have had more influence in shaping the debates and policy around married women's right to work than they did. Frances Perkins, the first woman to hold a cabinet post, was secretary of labor. Molly Dewson, head of the women's division of the Democratic party noted that over a hundred women served in prominent positions in the New Deal.[87] But none were in Roosevelt's brain trust; his inner circle of economic advisors was exclusively male. Moreover, economic policy relating to wage codes, retraining, and public employment was channeled into departments where women had little voice. Consequently, despite intensive lobbying among women's groups inside and out of the New Deal bureaucracy, a gendered distribution of resources became the norm in the New Deal, discriminating against women in jobs, training, and employment categories covered by the minimum wage.[88]

More women had official policy-making roles in the Roosevelt administration than in the Swedish Social Democratic government. However, unlike Swedish feminists, they were unable to develop a discourse that could be linked to other hegemonic discourses during the New Deal era. Nor did they have the policy channels and power resources to make claims about women's economic rights or economic needs. Women policy makers and advocacy groups were caught in a losing ideological battle over what constitutes economic need. The old pin-money theory still held sway in the average American's view of the working wife.[89] It was also difficult to argue that women who worked to help pay mortgages, keep up a family's standard of living, or pay for college, should be considered as working out of economic necessity. As

Winifred Wandersee points out in her study of the depression era, married women wage earners were often from families not in dire straits; thus economic need was a relative category for most families.[90]

Only at the end of the decade were American feminists able to tie married women's right to work to the fight for democracy in the free world, an ideological discourse that resonated in American politics. They compared the married-persons' clause of the Economy Act with the back-to-the-home movement in fascist Italy and Germany.[91] In a similar vein, Congressman Emanuel Celler, the key sponsor of a bill to protect married women's right to work and to repeal the Economy Act, employed a gender-neutral human-rights argument. He maintained that if marriage is erected as a barrier to employment, then other qualifications that have no connection with fitness for a particular job, such as race, religion, nationality, are just one step away.[92]

Conclusion

In defending married women's right to work, American and Swedish feminists framed their strategies in response to the ability of oppositional groups to restrict certain areas of policy making around gender-equality issues. They faced different sets of political constellations, possibilities for alliances, and institutional and bureaucratic openings and closures. Swedish feminists were able to link married women's work rights to general societal concerns about population decline and nonmarital births. Had they framed the debate in terms of women's economic rights, trade unions might have seen this as a threat to the autonomy of worker-employer decision making. Moreover, feminists might have lost support among conservative women's groups, such as the National Homemakers Association. It is also possible that they would have alienated the rank and file in the Social Democratic party, who tended to have traditional views of women's role in the home and believed that the family wage should be the goal of the working-class family.[93]

Unlike their Swedish sisters, American feminists were unable to lodge their plea for married women's right to work either in the discourse and policy within the New Deal around solidarity and economic need or in Keynesian economic growth and consumer demand. American women's groups also met antagonists among conservative women's groups and the more conservative labor organizations, such as the Brotherhood of Railway and Steamship Clerks.[94] Trapped in a defense of married women's right to work based on economic need, American feminist groups had to vie with other interest groups pressing Roosevelt to intervene in their behalf by reducing unemployment and bolstering declining wages. Those defending married women's labor-market work found themselves marginalized in the policy-making spheres of economic recovery, such as job training, public-works jobs, and labor relations.[95] Moreover, they faced an onslaught of state and federal legislation against the married woman worker, and had to do battle on several fronts.

The Swedish case reveals how actors with limited political resources can use strategic discourses to extend citizenship rights even during periods where there is intense competition over needs.[96] Without a political party committed to gender equality or a large-scale grass-roots movement to push their agenda from without, Swedish feminists in policy-framing bodies were able to create a new policy constellation around women's roles as mothers and workers. Placed within the domestic sphere of policy making and linked to population issues, the debate on married women's right to work actually blurred the lines separating political, economic, and domestic spheres in public policy. The right to mother was cast as a citizen's right; the right to work as a mother's right.

Much attention has been paid to the population question in France,[97] and the ways in which French feminists in the early twentieth century used maternalist strategies to promote a range of women's issues, such as access to education, wages for housework, and the legal right to keep their earnings. However, French feminists' use of "Republican Motherhood" as a political strategy, which Karen Offen describes as subverting the sexual system from within, appears qualitatively different from the ways in which Swedish feminists deployed a strategic discourse around the population debate. The latter actually transformed a public discourse on population policy not merely to include women's contribution to the state as mothers, but to recast the meaning of motherhood and women's citizenship: it was linked to the right to work as a basic citizenship right in the Social Democratic policy regime. Feminists thus took a working normative definition of citizenship and broadened it to include the right of citizen workers to mother.[98] Another important difference between the two cases was the degree to which feminists could control policy outcomes. Whereas in France medical experts and republican politicians constructed the meanings and policy content connected with the population question, in Sweden, feminists were positioned at the central axis of policy making in this debate.[99]

In this comparative analysis of gendered discourses and women's strategies in two societies, I have tried to lay the groundwork for a more dynamic model of how social-policy channels evolve in different societal contexts. Instead of a two-channeled gendered model of welfare and work, which has been put forward to explain the development of the American welfare state,[100] I would suggest a more open-ended approach for comparative research that assumes that (1) social-policy configurations around work and home were constantly intermeshing and restructuring each other; (2) in the face of political constraints or opportunities, feminists were often shifting strategies and representations around work and home; and (3) women's power resources have varied across policy spheres in different historical periods and contexts.

More research is needed to unravel the impact of feminist political strategies on future policies in order to conceptualize how women's power resources and strategic discourses evolve in different welfare states. The Swedish case is a provocative one since it suggests that certain discourses may become embedded in particular policy spheres. In fact the very success of Swedish feminists in widening the scope of women's citizenship through appeals to motherhood and family within the domestic-policy realm may offer some insight into the paradox of Swedish gender equality alluded to by many feminist scholars.[101] On the one hand, Swedish feminists have been successful in obtaining a range of policies and services that enable women to combine employment with motherhood, and that weaken women's economic dependency on husbands. Yet these feminists have not been able to penetrate the gendered distribution of power in economic and political spheres of policy making.[102] Is it because women's issues have been embedded in the domestic-policy sphere that it has been difficult to employ different discursive strategies—strategies that address women's rights as citizen workers within the economic sphere of policy making? Is this why Swedish women have not been able to engender a wage-equity policy through comparable worth or affirmative action or to restructure full-time work as the six-hour day?

Notes

The research for this paper was supported by the Swedish Council for Social Research. I would like to thank Sonya Michel, Seth Koven, Nancy Fraser, Linda Gordon, Marika Lindholm, Ann Orloff, and Lynn Weiner for their careful readings and critical comments on this paper; not all of their excellent suggestions could be incorporated into this already complex argument, but many will appear in future studies. Also I am indebted to Diane Mitchell and Marika Lindholm for tracking down documents for me in the Swedish archives, and Randi Storch for her research in the U.S. Ruth Milkman was kind enough to share some of the materials she had collected on this debate in the U.S.

1. Ann Orloff, in "Gender and Social Citizenship in the Welfare State" (paper presented at the Mini-Conference on Gender, Citizenship, and Social Policy, Social Science History Conference, New Orleans, 1991), provides an over-view of various models of welfare-state research that have failed to incorporate a gender dimension, from Marshall's concept of citizenship through Richard Titmuss's construct of residual/institutional welfare states to Gösta Esping-Andersen's policy regimes of welfare states: liberal, corporatist/conservative, and social-democratic. Similar critiques can be found in Drude Dahlerup, "Confusing Concepts—Confusing Reality: A Theoretical Discussion of the Patriarchal State," in Ann Showstack Sassoon, ed., *Women and the Welfare State* (London, 1987); Helga Hernes, *Welfare State and Woman Power: Essays in State Feminism* (Oslo, 1987); Barbara Hobson, "Economic Dependency and Women's Citizenship," paper presented at the Mini-Conference on Gender, Citizenship, and Social Policy, Social Science History Association, New Orleans, 1991; and Birte Siim, "The Scandinavian Welfare States—Towards Sexual Equality or a New Kind of Male Domination?" *Acta Sociologica* 30 (1987): 255–70.

2. See, for example, Harriet Holter, ed., *Patriarchy in a Welfare Society* (Oslo, 1984); Hernes, *Welfare State and Woman Power;* Gillian Pascall, *Social Policy: A Feminist Analysis* (London, 1986); and Elizabeth Wilson, *Women and the Welfare State* (London, 1977).

3. Kerstin Abukhanfusa, *Piskan och Moroten: Om Könens tilldelning av skyldigheter och rättigheter* (Stockholm, 1987); Joan Acker, "A Contradictory Reality: Swedish Women and the Welfare State in the 1980's," paper presented at the Society for the Advancement of Scandinavian Studies, Eugene, Oregon, April 1988.

4. Zillah Eisenstein, *Capitalist Patriarchy and the Case for Socialist Feminism* (New York, 1979), and Carole Pateman, "The Patriarchal Welfare State," in Amy Gutman, ed., *Democracy and the Welfare State* (Princeton, N.J., 1988).

5. Yvonne Hirdman, *The Swedish Welfare State and the Gender System: A Theoretical and Empirical Sketch*, The Study of Power and Democracy, English

Series, Report. no. 7 (Uppsala, 1989), and Hirdman, *Att Lägga Livet Till Rätta, studier i svenskfolkhemspolitik* (Stockholm, 1990).

6. I do not include in this group Marxist capital-interest explanations that assume class and not gender structures are the driving mechanism for reproducing gender inequalities, i.e. those that assume that the state's role is to support capitalist strategies; examples include Mary McIntosh, "The State and the Oppression of Women," in Annette Kuhn and Ann Marie Volpe, eds., *Feminism and Materialism: Women and Modes of Production* (London, 1979); Frances Fox Piven, "Women and the State—Ideology, Power, and the Welfare State," in Naomi Gerstel and Harriet Gross, eds., *Families at Work* (Philadelphia, 1987); and Jennifer Schirmer, *The Limits of Reform: Women, Capital and Welfare* (Boston, 1982).

7. Jane Jenson, "Paradigms and Political Discourse: Protective Legislation in France and the United States before 1914," *Canadian Journal of Political Science* 22 (1989): 235–54; Seth Koven and Sonya Michel, "Womanly Duties: Maternalist Politics and the Origins of Welfare States, 1880–1920," *American Historical Review* 95 (1990): 1076–1108; and Johanna Brenner and Barbara Laslett, "Gender, Social Reproduction and Women's Political Self-Organization: Considering the U.S. Welfare State," *Gender and Society* 5 (1991): 311–33.

8. Theda Skocpol, *Protecting Soldiers and Mothers* (Cambridge, Mass., 1992). Skocpol contraposes maternalist and paternalist forms of welfare-state development. The U.S. is the paradigm maternalist welfare state, which was steered by female reform groups and men and women in public agencies established programs directed at women and their children. The paternalist welfare state is characteristic of most European welfare-state development: in these states, policies were administered by male bureaucrats and geared toward a male-breadwinner head of household. Women's entitlements were based upon their position as dependent wives. These paradigms, however, do not seem elastic enough to capture variations in women's power resources to define the policy content at different points in time and in different historical contexts. While there may be maternalist and paternalist strains in social-policy regimes, they are fluid categories and have articulated in different ways in welfare-state formation.

9. Diane Sainsbury, "Welfare Variations, Women's Equality: On Variations of the Welfare state and Their Implications for Women," paper presented at the ECPR Workshop, Equality Principles and Gender Politics, Paris, 10–15 April 1989.

10. Given the paucity of comparative research on how gendered concepts have been translated into policy, the possibility of constructing alternative models or regime types that are based upon the politics of gender awaits more empirical and theoretical studies.

11. Jenson, "Paradigms and Political Discourse"; Brenner and Laslett, "Gender, Social Reproduction"; Birte Siim, "The Scandinavian Welfare States."

12. Feminist political pressure may also disturb conventional alliances. This was the case in the U.S. with the Democratic-party stand on affirmative action and unions' opposition in the 1970s; see Cynthia Harrison, *On*

Account of Sex: The Politics of Women's Issues, 1945–1968 (Berkeley, Calif., 1988).

13. Barbara Nelson, "The Gender, Race and Class Origins of Early Welfare Policy and the Welfare State," in Patricia Gurin and Louise Tilly, eds., *Women in Twentieth-Century Politics* (New York, 1987); and Pateman, "Patriarchal Welfare State."

14. Per Silensam, *Arbetskraftsutbudets utveckling in Sverige, 1870–1965* (Uppsala, 1970), 83, estimates that 15 percent of Swedish workers were unemployed between 1931 and 1940. The American depression cut more deeply; in the "rock-bottom" years 1931–32, unemployment reached an all-time high of 25 percent. But after that period, the level was also about 15 percent; see Alan Dawley, *Struggles for Justice: Social Responsibility and the Liberal State* (Cambridge, Mass., 1991), 350. Nevertheless, the speed with which Swedish government policy moved the country out of depression depths by public spending is worth noting; see Herbert Tingsten, *The Swedish Social Democrats: Their Ideological Development*, trans. Greta Frankel and Patricia Howard-Rosen (Totowa, N.J., 1973), introduction.

15. In contrasting the Swedish and American response to the married woman worker, I suggest that rather than the depth of the economic crisis, the more relevant point in this comparative analysis is the perceived threat the women worker posed to male jobs and pay structures. In both countries the small percentage of married women in the labor force and the small percentage in the industrial sector reveals the symbolic aspect of the crusade against the married woman worker: she was perceived as a threat. Would employers begin to replace highly paid male workers with low-paid female workers during hard times (something American unions may have feared more than Swedish unions)? Would the increased participation of married women in the labor force undermine other political agendas, such as the campaign for a family-wage policy?

16. Betänkande angående gift kvinnas förvärsarbete, 1938 (hereafter Commission on Married Women's Work); Alice Kessler-Harris, "Gender Ideology in Historical Reconstruction: A Case Study from the 1930's," *Gender & History* 1 (1989): 31–49; and Lois Scharf, *To Work and to Wed: Female Employment, Feminism, and the Great Depression* (Greenwich, Conn., 1980), 75–80.

17. Scharf, *To Work and to Wed*, 51.

18. Nancy Cott, *The Grounding of Modern Feminism* (New Haven, 1987), 209–10; Winifred Wandersee, *Women's Work and Family Values, 1920–1940* (Cambridge, Mass., 1981).

19. Scharf, *To Work and to Wed*, ch. 3.

20. Quoted in Ruth Lindström et al., eds., *Kvinnors röst och rätt* (Stockholm, 1969), 135.

21. Commission on Married Women's Work.

22. The Swedish law actually went further in assuming gender equality than had American legal precedents. It gave both parents equal responsibility for the financial and emotional care of children. Describing legal conventions after suffrage, Cott, *Grounding of Modern Feminism*, 185–86, maintains that

American wives gained political independence, but lacked the clear right to economic independence. A husband, according to common-law traditions, still had the right to his wife's domestic labor and had the obligation to support her financially.

23. The Fredrika Bremer Society, the most explicit feminist organization, founded in 1885, was composed of urban upper-class women. Its goals were to improve educational and employment opportunities. Rural middle-class women tended to join conscious-raising groups called "the dozens" (*Toflt-erna*), while working-class women formed their own associations, beginning in 1892, in connection with the emerging Social Democratic party: see Richard J. Evans, *The Feminists: Women's Emancipation Movements in Europe, America and Australasia, 1840–1920* (London, 1977); Marika Lind-holm, "Swedish Feminism, 1845–1945: A Conservative Revolution," *Journal of Historical Sociology* 4 (1991): 121–42; and Christina Carlsson, *Kvinnosyn och Kvinnopolitik: En studie av svensk socialdemokrati, 1890–1910* (Lund, 1986).

24. For a thorough discussion of the importance of women's grass-roots organi-zations during this period, see Kathryn Kish Sklar, "The Historical Founda-tions of Women's Power in the Creation of the American Welfare State, 1890–1930," in this volume.

25. See the essays by Sklar, Molly Ladd-Taylor, and Alisa Klaus in this volume.

26. Ann-Sofie Ohlander, "The Invisible Child? The Struggle for a Social Demo-cratic Family," in Gisela Bock and Pat Thane, eds., *Maternity and Gender Policies* (London, 1991).

27. Sven E. Olsson, *Social Policy and Welfare State in Sweden* (Lund, 1990).

28. Ohlander, "Invisible Child."

29. Scharf, *To Work and to Wed*, chap. 3, and Cott, *Grounding*, 264–66.

30. U.S. House, Committee on the Civil Service, *To Amend Married Persons' Clause*, Hearings, 18, 19, 23, and 24 April 1935 (Washington, D.C., 1935).

31. One can find numerous examples of unemployed widows and single women who wrote letters to President Roosevelt excoriating the married woman worker for taking jobs away from single women in need of wages. Typical of such letters is one from a young woman laid off from her job at a box factory. She complains that three-fourths of the employees still working are married who do not have to work and makes the plea: "Hope that you will put through legislation that will forbid all married women from taking single girls' places"; U.S. Women's Bureau, RG 86, box 832, folder entitled "Married Women," National Archives, Washington, D.C. (hereafter cited as Women's Bureau records).

32. Scharf, *To Work and to Wed*, 78.

33. Britta Åkerman documents the fear on the part of Social Democratic women of the newly formed National Homemakers Association: they expressed anxiety that the middle class of the Homemakers Association would become the voice for all women; see Åkerman, ed., *Vi Kan, Vi Behoves! Kvinnorna Går Samman i Egna Foreningar* (Stockholm, 1983), 185. Alternatively, mid-

dle- and upper-class women's organizations tended to look down on their working-class sisters as uneducated and agitators of revolution and conflict; see Margareta Lindholm, *Talet om det Kvinnliga: Studier i feministkt tänkande in Sverige under 1930 talet,* University of Gothenburg, Department of Sociology Monograph Series 44 (Gothenburg, 1990), and *Morgonbris* [Swedish Social Democratic newspaper] (1931), 9.

34. Britta Åkerman, *Vi Kan,* 196. Many thousands of Swedish women joined organizations for the first time. The Social Democratic Women's Union, for example, increased its membership from 7,302 in 1930 to 26,882 in 1940 (Lindholm, *Talet om det Kvinnliga,* 88). The National Association of Housemothers' mailing list grew steadily from 10,000 in 1930 to over 23,550 by the end of the decade (Lindholm, *Talet om det Kvinnliga,* 99). This is almost twice the number of women who actively fought for suffrage; see Beata Losman, "Kvinnoorganisering och Kvinnororelser i Sverige" ["Women's Organizations and Women's Movements in Sweden"], in Gunhild Kyle, ed., *Handbook i Svensk Kvinnohistorie* [Handbook of Swedish Women's History] (Stockholm, 1987), 199. In 1937 the Fredrika Bremer Association had 37 local organizations with over 6,000 members (Åkerman, *Vi Kan,* 122), and by the end of the 1930s, the Swedish Women's Business Organization boasted 4,000 members (Lindholm, *Talet om det Kvinnliga,* 108).

35. It appeared in *Hertha* (organ of the Fredrika Bremer Society); *Morgonbris,* aimed at Social Democratic women; and *Arbetets Kvinnor,* the LO women's union paper.

36. Even as late as 1939, 10 percent of the industrial labor force was still unemployed; Ron Eyerman, "Rationalizing Intellectuals: Sweden in the 1930s and 1940s," *Theory and Society* 14 (1985): 777–808.

37. Walter Korpi, "Power, Politics, and Social Autonomy in the Development of Social Citizenship: Social Rights during Sickness in Eighteen OECD Countries since 1930," *American Sociological Review* 54 (1989): 309–28. American women constituted 25 percent of the labor force in 1930, but only 3 percent were unionized. Nancy Gabin, *Feminism in the Labor Movement: Women and the United Auto Workers, 1935–1975* (Ithaca, N.Y., 1990), 16. In 1930, 20.8 percent of the Swedish labor force was female; Swedish women constituted 14.6 percent of the LO.

38. Gosta Bagge, Erik Lundberg, and Ingvar Svennilson, *Wages in Sweden, 1860–1930,* pt. 2 (Stockholm, 1935); Annika Baude, *Arbete och Kon: En narstudie av segregerat industriarbete* (Stockholm, 1992); and Ulla Wikander, "Kvinnoarbete i mansamhället; et historiskt perspektiv på arbetsmarksnaden och underordning av kvinnor," Uppsala Papers in Economic History, Research Report no. 9 (Uppsala, 1985).

39. "Married Woman in the Labor Market: A Swedish Investigation," a report published in English from the Commission on Married Women's Work, box 29, Hesselgren Archive, 1938, Royal Library, Stockholm. According to Ruth Milkman, sex typing of jobs was also fairly well established in the U.S. in the early 1930s, and remained intact throughout the depression; Milkman, *Gender at Work: The Dynamics of Job Segregation by Sex during World War II* (Chicago, 1987). The most consistent differentiation by sex was by sector

(service vs. industrial jobs). However, in Sweden in the 1930s, the service sector was relatively underdeveloped compared to other Western industrial societies. Thus Karin Kock's conclusion was based on the fact that the sex segregation of the labor market was deeply embedded within the organization of work and hierarchies of skill, as well as the branches of industry (Baude, *Arbete och Kon,* and Wikander, "Kvinnoarbete i mansamhället").

40. In the 1970s unions invoked this principle in their opposition to gender-equality laws. Even after antidiscrimination laws were passed, union collective agreements continued to supersede in all cases.

41. The Metalworkers Union argued that to accept a law against married women working might have the consequence of unwanted investigations into the private family situations of workers (Commission on Married Women's Work).

42. One of the largest unions, the Metalworkers, even rejected the idea of government contributions to union unemployment insurance in the 1930s; see Bo Rothsten, "Marxism, Institutional Analysis and Working-Class Strength: The Swedish Case," *Politics and Society* 18 (1990); 317–45. (Swedish unemployment insurance was modeled on the Ghent system where unions control unemployment benefits but receive government moneys.)

43. Commission on Married Women's Work, 10.

44. Maurine Greenwald's research on the Seattle Labor Council, an organization of industrial unions in the 1920s, suggests that even leftist unions faced with strong opposition from working-class feminists held firm on the family wage and supported restrictions on married women's work; see Greenwald, "Working-Class Feminism and the Family Wage Ideal: The Seattle Debate on Married Women's Right to Work, 1914–1920," *Journal of American History* 76 (1989): 118–49.

45. Weir Jepson also recommended that employers should pay a 50-percent penalty for hiring single women and men; although the tariff would not apply to bachelors under twenty-five years of age; see Jepson, "Save the Home," *American Federationist* 40 (July–December 1933): 1368–72.

46. The union claimed that it would allow extenuating circumstances to be considered, but in Martha Hasting's case it ignored the fact that she was supporting an invalid sister and that her husband had part-time employment; Women's Bureau records, box 382, folder entitled "Married Women," 1929–1939, Hasting to Roosevelt, 1938.

47. Gunnar Qvist, *Statisik och politik: Landorganisationen och kvinnorna på arbetsmarknaden* (Stockholm, 1974).

48. Scharf, *To Work and to Wed,* chap. 3.

49. Ibid., 50–65.

50. Dawley, *Struggles for Justice,* chap. 10.

51. Scharf, *To Work and to Wed,* 49. Roosevelt, the ultimate pragmatist, in other cases placed the issues of race and gender inequality outside the New Deal program. Domestics and sharecroppers were excluded from minimum-wage and social-security protections to keep the South in his coalition.

52. Hugh Heclo, *Modern Social Politics in Britain and Sweden* (New Haven, 1974), 43, claims that the use of studies by experts extends back to the early civil service of the medieval period. Between 1855 and the 1970s, he estimated, there had been over 4,000 commissions established.

53. Since investigative commissions are used to build consensus, one rarely finds expressions of minority opinions.

54. Here I am using discursive resources along the same lines as Nancy Fraser does in her analysis of discursive politics; see Fraser, *Unruly Practices: Power, Discourse and Gender in Contemporary Social Theory* (Minneapolis, 1989). But I am expanding the notion of discursive resources by suggesting that, depending on the policy area, social actors have different resources for making claims on the state.

55. Maud Eduards, "Toward a Third Way: Women's Politics in Sweden," *Social Research* 58 (1991): 677–705, and Joyce Gelb, *Feminism and Politics: A Comparative Perspective* (Berkeley, Calif., 1989).

56. Skocpol, *Protecting Soldiers and Mothers*, suggests that male politicians fearing that American women would vote as a bloc gave women a certain clout in policy making during the 1920s.

57. These included protections against firing women because of marital status, pregnancy (whether married or not), and twelve weeks' leave for all employees and paid maternal leave for women employed as civil servants.

58. The exception was abortion policy. The commission rejected a proposal to allow abortions for social reasons (poverty) but they were permitted on grounds of a mother's health; see Ann Katrin Hatje, *Befolkningsfrågan och välfärden: Debatten om familjepolitik och nativitetsökning under 1930 och 1940 talen* (Stockholm, 1974). Recommendations of the Swedish population commission studies were not merely aimed at increasing the number of children but enhancing the quality of family life. Benefits did not necessarily favor large families or punish childless couples. See Ann-Sofie Kälvemark [Ohlander], *More Children of Better Quality: Aspects of Swedish Population Policy in the 1930s* (Uppsala, 1980).

59. Alva and Gunner Myrdal, *Kris i befolkningsfrågan* (Stockholm, 1934) became household names in Swedish society selling over 16,000 copies during the 1930s. This was more than the popular novels sold in the period; Hatje, *Befolkningsfrågan och välfärden*, 8.

60. There were dissenting voices among the clergy who insisted that the causes of birth decline were not economic as the Myrdals claimed but were moral, rooted in individualistic and selfish tendencies. When the Myrdal's book first appeared, some social democrats expressed concern over the ideological conservatism implicit in population issues, the bourgeois breeding or stud viewpoint. But the party organizers recognized the potential of population politics, that it could open the door for many redistributive policy reforms: see Allan Carlson, *The Swedish Experiment in Family Politics: The Myrdals and the Interwar Population Crisis* (New Brunswick, N.J., 1990), 112, 120–22.

61. Hatje, *Befolkningsfrågan och välfärden*, 31. Other rank and file in the Social Democratic party also saw the instrumental value of the population debate,

which according to one writer in *Arbetets Kvinnor*, gave the working class an arsenal of arguments to bring about demands for a better standard of living: *Arbetets Kvinnor* (1935): 22.

62. Alva Myrdal published a summary and analysis of the population question in English, *Nation and Family: The Swedish Experiment in Democratic Family and Population Policy* (London, 1945). It is difficult to assess what kinds of reservations women had about the strategic deployment of population issues for improving the situation of women and children during the 1930s. Ohlander, "Invisible Child," suggests that by the 1940s, there was skepticism among Social Democratic women. She alludes to a survey of the Social Democratic Women's Organization in 1941 (when a new population commission was established), in which a majority voiced concern that population views were inherently undemocratic.

63. See Margareta Lindholm, *Elin Wagner and Alva Myrdal: En dialog om kvinnorna and samhället* (Uddevella, 1992), 101.

64. Among feminist researchers, there is a diversity of opinion over whether Myrdal or Wägner was more representative of the women's movement or women in general: see Hirdman, "Swedish Welfare State"; Lindholm, *Talet om det Kvinnliga;* and Hatje, *Befolkningsfrågan och välfärden*. However, Myrdal's position of integration in mainstream politics appears to be the dominant one in feminist politics in postwar Sweden.

65. Myrdal, *Nation and Family*, 402.

66. Ibid., 403.

67. Swedish feminists' stand against protective labor legislation is illustrative. They were the only group, with the exception of the Finnish representatives, to protest the International Labor Organization protocols banning women in night work and certain industries. Swedes were active in an international organization called the Open Door. During the 1920s and early 1930s, their slogan was "The right to work is the right to live"; see *Hertha*, 12 January 1935, 12, and Otto Wangson, "Kvinnan och arbetet," *Tiden* (1935): 475.

68. One finds both in the Myrdals' discussion of the population issue and in the Population Commission public debates a eugenicist strain; see Hatje, *Befolkningsfrågan och välfärden*. Scholars disagree over the extent to which the Myrdals' book and population commission studies had a eugenicist cast. On the one side, Gunnar Broberg and Mattias Tydèn argue the Myrdals were indirectly responsible for sterilization practices; see *Oöskade i folkhemmet: Rashygine och sterilisering in Sverige* (Stockholm, 1990), 74–82. On the other side, Allan Carlsson takes the position that eugenic concerns were not in the forefront of the Swedish population debate, and for the Myrdals population questions were geared more toward social engineering than eugenetic engineering in housing, day-care subsidies, school lunches, and other redistributive measures; see *The Swedish Experiment*, chap. 3, "A Socialist Pronatalism."

69. Commission on Married Women's Work, 18.

70. Ibid.

71. Ibid.

72. U.S. House, Committee on the Civil Service, *To Amend.*

73. Jan Trost, "A Renewed Social Institution: Nonmarital Cohabitation," *Acta Sociologica* 21 (1978): 303–16, and Margareta Matovic, "The Stockholm Marriage: Extralegal Family Formation in Stockholm, 1860–1890," *Continuity and Change* 1 (1986): 385–414.

74. Hirdman, *Swedish Welfare State;* Tingsten, *Swedish Social Democrats;* and Lindholm, "Swedish Feminism."

75. Carlsson, *Kvinnosyn och Kvinnopolitik,* 23.

76. The Royal Population Commission was the central policy-making body in this period. From 1935, its founding, to 1938, the committee published eighteen reports created by numerous experts (55 men and 15 women) who sat on a variety of subcommittees. The Royal Population Commission made its recommendations on married women workers in a report based on the Hesselgren commission study on married women's work; see "Betänkande angående försvärbetande kvinnors rattsliga ställning vid äktenskap och barnsbörd" [Population Commission Report on Married Women's Rights], SOU befolknings commission (Stockholm 1938), 57.

77. Their definition of mothers' citizenship rights was broad enough to encompass job protections for single mothers as well. This was an important issue for Social Democratic women who, since the early twentieth century, had campaigned for policies that would create more independence for women bearing children out of wedlock and thus would result in removing the stigma from unwed mothers, state enforcement of paternity payments to single mothers, and state support (not relief) when fathers failed to support their offspring; see Ohlander, "Invisible Child."

78. Population Commission Report on Married Women, 13.

79. Ann Shola Orloff, "Gender in Early U.S. Social Policy," *Journal of Policy History* 3 (1991): 249–81, and Wendy Sarvasy, "Beyond the Difference versus Equality Policy Debate: Post-Suffrage Feminism, Citizenship, and the Quest for a Feminist Welfare State," *Signs* 17 (1992): 329–62.

80. Scharf, *To Work and to Wed,* chap. 6.

81. Kessler-Harris, "Gender Ideology."

82. U.S. House, Committee on the Civil Service, *To Amend,* 11–18.

83. "Should Married Women Work? A Californian Asks Mrs. Roosevelt to Explain Her Statement to the Democratic Digest," *Democratic Digest* (September 1939).

84. Mary Anderson, "Wives Are Also People," *Democratic Digest* (September 1939). The Women's Bureau conducted numerous investigations to show that married women were essential contributors to the family economy; they found that nine out of ten married women worked to support family members; Women's Bureau records, box 1280, folder 213.

85. In *Muller v. Oregon* (1908), Progressive reformers employed the rationale that low wages and dangerous working conditions jeopardized women's capacity for mothering and potential childbearing. *Adkins v. Children's Hospital* in the following decade made broader claims for state protection based

upon women's weak position in the labor market, which posed an indirect challenge to the family wage. See Sybil Lipschultz, "Social Feminism and Legal Discourse, 1908–1923," *Yale Journal of Law and Feminism* 2 (1989): 131–60; and Linda Gordon, "Social Insurance and Public Assistance: The Influence of Gender in Welfare Thought in the United States, 1890–1935," *American Historical Review* 97 (1992): 19–54.

86. Gordon, "Influence of Gender," argues convincingly that social feminists in the New Deal constructed Aid to Dependent Children as public assistance in order not to threaten the family wage. The notion of universal rights and entitlements became linked to a male-breadwinner status with the bifurcation of social insurance from social assistance. For a similar dilemma in Australia, see Marilyn Lake, "A Revolution in the Family," in this volume.

87. Susan Ware, *Partner and I: Molly Dewson, Feminism, and New Deal Politics* (New Haven, 1987), 190.

88. Brenner and Laslett, "Gender, Social Reproduction," and Scharf, *To Work and to Wed,* chaps. 6 and 7.

89. Lynn Y. Weiner, *From Working Girl to Working Mother: The Female Labor Force in the United States, 1820–1980* (Chapel Hill, N.C., 1985), 25–26, 108.

90. Wandersee, *Women's Work.*

91. See Ruth Shallcross, "Should Married Women Work?" Public Affairs Pamphlet no. 49 (Washington, D.C., 1940); and Victoria di Grazia, *How Fascism Ruled Women* (Berkeley, Calif., 1991).

92. U.S. House, Committee on the Civil Service, *To Amend,* 2. It is possible that concerns about war preparedness provided an impetus for removing obstacles against married women in the work force in both countries. Yet I find no evidence of this issue in the Swedish debate. Lindholm, *Talet om det Kvinnliga,* suggests that it might have had some influence, but does not offer any evidence and it does not appear in any of the investigations or debates.

93. Marika Lindholm, "The Good Home of the People: Ideology of the Folkhem and the Process of Political Consolidation in the Rise of the Swedish Welfare State," paper presented at the American Sociological Association Meetings, Pittsburgh, 1992; and Myrdal, *Nation and Family.*

94. Alice Kessler-Harris, *Out to Work: A History of Wage-Earning Women in the United States* (New York, 1982), 257.

95. Elizabeth Faue, " 'The Dynamo of Change': Gender and Solidarity in the American Labor Movement, 1935–1939," *Gender and History* 1 (1989): 192–212; Brenner and Laslett, "Gender, Social Reproduction"; and Susan Ware, *Beyond Suffrage: Women in the New Deal* (Cambridge, Mass., 1981), passim.

96. Korpi, "Power, Politics, and Social Autonomy," argues that working-class organizations, for example industrial unions, which are weak in terms of market resources, can use their political resources to obtain favorable outcomes—to extend social rights. Swedish feminist groups, although they had

many organizations with growing memberships, did not have the same numerical strength in any major party.

97. Jane Jenson, "Gender and Reproduction or Babies and the State," *Studies in Political Economy* 20 (1986): 9–46; Alisa Klaus, "Depopulation and Race Suicide: Maternalism and Pronatalist Ideologies in France and the United States," in this volume; and Karen Offen, "Depopulation, Nationalism, and Feminism in Fin-de-Siècle France," *American Historical Review* 89 (June 1984): 648–76.

98. Fraser's discussion of politicized and reinterpreted needs (for example how feminists renamed wife beating to wife battering) is illustrative of how transformative discourses can work in the politics of gender; see Fraser, *Unruly Practices*. Analyzing the politics of class, William H. Sewell, Jr., *Work and Revolution in France: The Language of Labor from the Old Regime to 1848* (Cambridge, 1980), and E. P. Thompson, *The Making of the English Working Class* (New York, 1963), provide examples of how working-class activists transformed existing vocabularies and created new idioms that changed people's ways of thinking and acting.

99. Klaus, "Depopulation and Race Suicide."

100. Nelson, "Gender, Race, and Class Origins."

101. Acker, "A Contradictory Reality"; Gelb, *Feminism and Politics;* and Mary Ruggie, *The State and Working Women: A Comparative Study of Britain and Sweden* (Princeton, N.J., 1984).

102. Though women occupy about a third of parliamentary seats in Sweden, they have not been included in the central policy-making committees and cabinet posts; see Hernes, *Welfare State and Woman Power,* for a discussion of the corporate structures of Scandinavian societies.

Index

Contributors

Eileen Boris, Associate Professor of History at Howard University, is a mother as well as the author of *Art and Labor: Ruskin, Morris and the Craftsman Ideal in America* (Temple University Press, 1986) and *Sweated Motherhood: The Politics of Industrial Homework in the United States* (Cambridge University Press, 1994). She has co-edited *Homework: Historical and Contemporary Perspectives on Paid Labor at Home* (University of Illinois Press, 1989) and *Major Problems in the History of American Workers* (D. C. Heath, 1991). Her new project, tentatively entitled *Desperate Equality: Race, Gender, and Federal Employment Policy from World War II to the Present*, will place the 1991 Civil Rights Act in historical context.

Barbara Hobson is Associate Professor of Social Policy and Director of Graduate Studies at the International Graduate School at Stockholm University. She is the author of *Uneasy Virtue: The Politics of Prostitution and the American Reform Tradition* (Basic Books, 1987; University of Chicago Press, 1990), and has published several articles on comparative research on gender and the welfare states, including "No Exit, No Voice: Women's Economic Dependency in the Family and Welfare States," *Acta Sociologica* (forthcoming), and "Women, Work, Family, and the State," in *Unresolved Dilemmas: Women, Work, and the Family in the United States, Europe, and the Former Soviet Union* (forthcoming). She is also editor of the forthcoming journal *Social Politics: International Studies in Gender, State, and Society*.

Alisa Klaus received her B.A. from Yale University and her Ph.D. from the University of Pennsylvania. She is author of *Every Child a Lion: The Origins of Maternal and Infant Health Policy in the United States and France, 1890–1920* (Cornell University Press, 1993). She teaches history at the University of California, Santa Cruz.

Seth Koven is Assistant Professor of European and Women's History at Villanova University where he teaches courses in British history and in cultural and gender studies. He is currently completing *The Spectacle of Philanthropy: The London Settlement House Movement and the Politics of Culture* (Routledge, forthcoming).

Molly Ladd-Taylor is Assistant Professor of U.S. History at Carleton College in Northfield, Minnesota. She is editor of *Raising a Baby the Government Way: Mothers' Letters to the Children's Bureau, 1915–1932*, (Rutgers University Press, 1986) and author of *Mother-Work: Women, Child Welfare and the State, 1890–1930*, forthcoming from the University of Illinois Press.

Marilyn Lake is a Reader in History and Director of Women's Studies at La Trobe University, Bundoora Victoria, Australia. She is the author of *The Limits of Hope: Soldier Settlement in Victoria, 1915–38* (Melbourne, 1987), as well as many pioneering articles on the history of Australian women and men. She is also co-author, with Marian Aveling, Patricia Grimshaw, and Ann McGarth, of a forthcoming history of Australia, *Man's Space, Woman's Place* (1993).

Sonya Michel teaches American women's, gender, and social-welfare history at the University of Illinois at Urbana-Champaign. She is a co-editor of *Behind the Lines: Gender and the Two World Wars* (Yale University Press, 1987) and has written on gender and popular culture as well as women and social welfare. Currently she is completing *Children's Interests/Mothers' Rights: A History of Child Care in the United States*, forthcoming from Yale.

Susan Pedersen is Associate Professor of History at Harvard University, where she teaches courses on British history, women's history, and twentieth-century politics. She is the author of *Family, Dependence and the Origins of the Welfare State: Britain and France, 1914–1945* (Cambridge, 1993), and the co-editor, with Peter Mandler, of *After the Victorians: Private Conscience and Public Duty in Modern Britain*, forthcoming from Routledge in 1994.

Jean H. Quataert is Professor of History and Vice-Chair for Graduate Studies at Binghamton University. She is the author of *Reluctant Feminists in German Social Democracy, 1885–1917* (Princeton, 1978) and, together with Marilyn J. Boxer, editor of *Connecting Spheres: Women in the Western World from 1500 to the Present* (New York, 1987). Currently, she is turning to a new research project on women and war.

Christoph Sachße is Professor of the History and Theory of Social Policy at the University of Kassel, Germany. Together with F. Tennstedt, he has published a three-volume history of social welfare in Germany. Other recent publications include *Mütterlichkeit als Beruf* (Frankfurt, 1986) and *Sicherheit und Freiheit. Zur Ethik des Wohlfahrtsstaates* (Frankfurt, 1990) (together with H. T. Engelhardt).

Kathryn Kish Sklar, Distinguished Professor of History at the State University of New York, Binghamton, is the author of "Hull House as a Community of Women Reformers in the 1890s," *Signs* (1985); "Why Did Most Politically Active Women Oppose the ERA in the 1920s?" in Joan Hoff-Wilson, ed., *Rights of Passage: The Past and Future of the ERA* (Indiana, 1986); and "Who Funded Hull House?" in Kathleen McCarthy, ed., *Lady Bountiful Revisited: Women, Philanthropy and Power* (Rutgers, 1990). She is also the editor of *The Autobiography of Florence Kelley: Notes of Sixty Years* (Charles Kerr, 1986), and co-editor of *The Social Survey Movement in Historical Perspective* (Cambridge, 1992). Her writings on protective labor legislation include " 'The Greater Part of the Petitioners are Female': The Reduction by Statute of Women's Working Hours in the Paid Labor Force, 1840–1917," in Gary Cross, ed., *The International History of the Shortening of the Workday* (Temple, 1988). Focusing on the antebellum era, she is the author of *Catharine Beecher: A Study in American Domesticity* (Yale, 1973); and " 'Women Who Speak for an Entire Nation': American and British Women Compared at the World Anti-Slavery Convention, London, 1840," in Jean Yellin and John Van Horne, eds., *An Untrodden Path: Anti-Slavery and Women's Political Culture* (Cornell, 1993). She is currently completing *Florence Kelley and Women's Political Culture: "Doing the Nation's Work, 1830–1930,"* forthcoming from Yale.

Pat Thane is Reader in Modern Social History at the University of London and teaches at Goldsmiths College, University of London. She has written a number of books and articles, mostly on the history of social welfare and of women in Britain, including *The Foundations of the Welfare State* (London, 1982), and co-edited *Maternity and Gender Policies: Women and the Rise of the European Welfare States, 1880s–1950s* (London, 1991).